The Laws of the Internet

Nabarro Nathanson
The Laws of the Internet

by

Clive Gringras LLB (Hons); M Juris (Oxon)

Competition
Peter Willis LLB (Eur) (Exon)
Diplôme D'Etudes De Droit Privé Français (Aix-Marseille)
Solicitor, Nabarro Nathanson

Banking
Susan Knüfer BA
Solicitor, Nabarro Nathanson

Taxation
Conrad McDonnell MA (Oxon)
Barrister of Lincoln's Inn

Securities and Financial Services
Christopher Luck LLB (Hons) (KCUL)
Partner, Nabarro Nathanson

Butterworths
London, Edinburgh, Dublin
1997

United Kingdom	Butterworths, a Division of Reed Elsevier (UK) Ltd, Halsbury House, 35 Chancery Lane, LONDON WC2A 1EL and 4 Hill Street, EDINBURGH EH2 3JZ
Australia	Butterworths, SYDNEY, MELBOURNE, BRISBANE, ADELAIDE, PERTH, CANBERRA and HOBART
Canada	Butterworths Canada Ltd, TORONTO and VANCOUVER
Ireland	Butterworth (Ireland) Ltd, DUBLIN
Malaysia	Malayan Law Journal Sdn Bhd, KUALA LUMPUR
New Zealand	Butterworths of New Zealand Ltd, WELLINGTON and AUCKLAND
Singapore	Reed Elsevier (Singapore) Pte Ltd, SINGAPORE
South Africa	Butterworths Publishers (Pty) Ltd, DURBAN
USA	Michie, CHARLOTTESVILLE, Virginia

A CIP Catalogue record for this book is available from the British Library.

ISBN 0 406 00249 5

Typeset by Doublestruck Limited, London
Printed and bound in Great Britain by Mackays of Chatham plc, Chatham, Kent

For Z.

'... That is the Law. How could there be a mistake in that?'
'I don't know this Law,' said K.
'All the worse for you,' replied the warder.

The Trial, Franz Kafka

Foreword

Judging by some of the stuff one reads – particularly from journalists – the Internet will throw laws, or many of them, into chaos. The suggestion seems to be the law cannot cope with the breakdown of national barriers, the cross-border implications of the interlinking of computers world-wide. The scenario painted is that the Internet will be a lawless dimension, with lawyers and clients having no idea what to do or how to control the activities of others. Clive Gringras is to be congratulated on not only debunking this myth but by doing so in a constructive (and readable) way. What he has done here is to consider, subject by subject, what rules the courts will develop and apply. As always what the law will do is develop appropriate rules by analogy. Contract, tort (including special variants of old torts, eg negligently allowing a virus to spread and new ways of defaming people), intellectual property (particularly trade marks and copyright), questions of jurisdiction, crime, data protection, and so on all have passed under his intelligent consideration. Of course there are, as yet, few actual cases on most points. So he has used his imagination to create problems and indicate how the law is likely to answer them. Because he understands the Internet and how it works well, his imaginary problems are realistic. Moreover he has up-to-date intelligence of case law from other countries (particularly the US) which supplement his fictional examples. Anyone with an Internet problem will find this book a first port of call – and in many cases may well find an answer, or a reasonable prediction of the answer. In one area where he obviously does not feel entirely at home, namely tax (who would blame him?), he has sought assistance from Conrad McDonnell of Gray's Inn Chambers.

There is something of a spate of books which carry the names of firms of solicitors. Many (but not all) are rather slight works, rushed out after some new piece of legislation and not telling you much that is not in the Act. This is far from such a work. Nabarro Nathanson are to be congratulated on allowing Mr Gringras to put in what must have been a vast amount of work.

Hon Sir Robin Jacob
January 1997

Preface

This book's title is carefully chosen. The book is a collection of the laws that apply to those who use the Internet. It does not attempt to present any overarching view of the Law of the Internet. It indulges in little of this prophecy. There is no single law that does or should apply to the Internet. The book is concerned only with the application of the *current* body of law to this new communications medium. Its pages present, in pragmatic form, the various laws that, directly or indirectly, impinge on the Internet; it provides reasoned answers to relevant questions. Often these answers are to questions not yet asked of English courts. For the moment, therefore, you, the reader, are the sole judge of their cogency.

Some say that, like a dog, one year for a human is like seven for the Internet. It has a substantial, and growing, presence in society. When I first used the Internet in August 1981 it consisted of only 213 computers connected together; conservative estimates suggest that there are now over sixteen million 'hosts', each acting like a single machine linked to the others. But the Internet is not merely growing. Every month it seems to pervade a new, unwired, area of culture and business. Legal issues and disputes involving the Internet will rapidly become more commonplace. For this reason this book does not apply the law to a 'snapshot' of the Internet but to the Internet as an evolving phenomenon. For similar reasons, those who rely on this book should not do so in isolation. Unlike any area of legal practice, it is not simply the laws of the Internet that are developing; its persona is too.

My five Internet-years writing this book have been greatly assisted by the solid support of Nabarro Nathanson. In particular, I wish to thank three of the firm's solicitors for their excellent contributions to the book: Chris Luck, Susan Knüfer and Peter Willis. I also wish to thank all members of the Intellectual Property department in London and Reading who provided their time and knowledge to review the book. In addition, thanks must go to Dan Levy for his painstaking library work, evident on each page.

I have also benefited from external help. Thanks to: Sir Robin Jacob for kindly writing the foreword; Conrad McDonnell of Gray's Inn Chambers for crafting the chapter on taxation; John Austen of New Scotland Yard; G C Borland of McGrigor Donald; Warren Burch of Microsoft, Seattle; John Browning of *Wired*; Rob Bradgate of the University of Sheffield; Adrian Briggs of St Edmund Hall College, Oxford; Simon Dawson of the Crown Prosecution Service, London; Stephen Dooley of Sidley & Austin, London; Richard Fentiman of Queen's College, Cambridge; Andrew Graham of Balliol College, Oxford; Rosemary Jay, of the Data Protection Registrar; Alistair Kelman of ILC/Telepathic, London; Mathew Mildenhall of Coopers & Lybrand, London; Paul Mitchell of Tory Tory Deslauriers & Binnington, Toronto; Yvonne Nobis, of the Bodleian Library,

Oxford; Edwin Peel of Keble College, Oxford; David Rickard of Boult Wade Tennant, London; Peter Sommer of the London School of Economics; Colin Tapper of Magdalen College, Oxford; Sir Guenter Treitel of All Souls College, Oxford; and John Woolds, of the Data Protection Registrar. The flaws in the book are mine; any qualities I share with these generous people.

For sharing the pain, I want to thank my publishers, friends, family, and Linzi.

Clive Gringras
Clive@Pobox.com
Ides of March 1997

About the author

Clive Gringras has programmed computers and used the Internet since 1981.

In 1990 he co-wrote the best-selling computer game 'Elite' for the Archimedes RISC PC. He earned an LLB with Honours with the University of Sheffield and the Magister Juris from St John's College, Oxford where he focused on the 'Licensing of software'.

He has advised New Scotland Yard on computer crime, is a UK correspondent for both the *European Intellectual Property Review* and *Computer and Telecommunications Law Review*, and has written articles and editorials for many legal and computer journals. He has also presented papers on Internet Law, including in New York at Internet World – Fall '96. *Wired* magazine wrote that he is 'a young man fast becoming one of the UK's leading authorities on Internet law'.

Contents

Table of statutes

References in the Table to *Statutes* are to Halsbury's *Statutes* of England (Fourth Edition) indicating the volume and page number at which the annotated text of the Act may be found.

Table of statutory instruments

Table of cases

Decisions of the European Court of Justice are listed below numerically. These decisions are also included in the preceding alphabetical list.

Chapter one

Introduction

The Lord came down to look at the city and tower that man had built, and the
Lord said: 'If, as one people with one language for all, this is how they have
begun to act, then nothing that they propose to do will be out of their reach.'
... That is why it was called Babel, because there the Lord confounded the
language of all the earth ...

Genesis 11:6-7

The Internet is a global network of computers all speaking the same language.
To understand the Internet, therefore, it is useful first to appreciate computers.
Computers are simple machines: they understand only the numbers zero and
one. The reason that computers are able to show colours on a screen, play
sounds and process data is that they are very accurate and quick translators.
With incredible speed they are able to convert a colourful picture into a long
stream of zeros and ones. And with the same speed they can convert a similar
stream of zeros and ones into a sound, or a document, or a program. Everything
passing into and out of a computer will, at some point, be reduced to binary:
two numbers, zero and one.

It is not difficult to connect two computers, say by a wire, and send a stream of
these binary numbers from one computer to the other. Each number one in the
stream is represented by an 'on' electrical pulse; each zero by an 'off' pulse. These
pulses last for a fraction of a second allowing the numbers describing a picture to
be transmitted in minutes. A difficulty arises in ensuring that the computer
receiving the stream translates the zeros and ones correctly. As a simple example,
the receiving computer may be ready to receive a binary description of a picture,
but is instead sent a binary translation of a document. The receiving computer will
attempt to translate the zeros and ones, actually a document, into a picture; there
will be confusion. It is evidently crucial that to connect computers successfully they
both must speak the same language. This 'digital Esperanto' is the key to the
Internet.

LANGUAGE AND NETWORKS

The many variations of this digital Esperanto are called 'protocols'. As long as the
sending and receiving computers are using the same protocols, they will be able to
share information, in a raw binary form, with absolute accuracy.

A 'network' is a group of computers connected together *using the same protocols*; they are using the same phrase book. Information stored on one computer on the network can be readily sent, or accessed, by any other computer on the network. In a company this allows one individual to access a file that has been created on somebody else's machine: a network or 'intranet'. The connection between these computers on a network is not always a simple copper wire. A fibre-optic cable is increasingly used as a link; it conveys information using pulses of light rather than electricity. These links between computers do not even have to be in the same building. Wide Area Networks, or WANs, can stretch across many miles. The key is to ensure that each of the computers connected to the network uses the same protocols. If they do, it will not matter greatly whether a stream of ones and zeros has come from across the corridor or from across town. The receiving computer will be able to translate them appropriately, no matter the length of their journey. The Internet builds on this technology.

INTERNETWORKING

In 1969 America's Department of Defense commissioned the construction of a super-network called ARPANET: the Advanced Research Projects Agency Network. This military network was intended to connect computers across the American continent, with one special feature. If one part of this great network was destroyed, the communications system would remain operative. The information passing through the system was required to detour around the damaged part and arrive at its destination by another route.

In 1972 the ARPANET was demonstrated. The network consisted of 40 computers connected by a web of links and lines. The detouring feature was accomplished by allowing a stream of binary information from one computer to pass through other computers on the network, rather than always having to flow directly from A to B. One example will illustrate this: three computers, A, B and C, are connected in a triangle. A can communicate directly with both B and C. Similarly, B has a line of communication with A and C. If A has to send information to B it has a direct route. But if this route is damaged, or blocked, it can send the information to C with an instruction to pass it on to B: A to B through C. On the larger scale, this allows every computer connected to a network to send information to any other computer on the network. The information simply has to be passed from one computer to another, gradually nearing its destination.

One further advance was made to secure the information being sent from A to B. Instead of sending the information as one long stream, the sending computer splits the data into discrete packets. Each packet, like an envelope, contains the information being sent and has an address of where it must arrive. The packet also has a number that denotes its place in the whole data stream. If any packets are lost, or blocked, they can be re-sent. When all the packets have arrived, the receiver assembles the chunks of digital data into the continuous data stream. This so-called 'packet-switched' network allows many computers to use the same communication lines and allows one data stream to travel by different routes to speed delivery over congested lines.

The demonstration of packet-switched networks and routing in 1972 was such a success that the InterNetworking Working Group was created. The Internet was born.

THE INTERNET

The forty or so computers on the seventies' ARPANET, each using the same protocols, were added to: by 1981, over two hundred computers were connected, from all around the world. At the last count over fifteen million computers were permanently connected, each one able to speak the same language as the others. This vast collection of computers is the Internet and it is the largest network of computers in the world.

The majority of the links and connections are permanent and allow digital streams to be sent back and forth extremely quickly. In addition, each computer connected to the Internet has a unique numeric address or Internet Protocol address. This means that a digital stream can be directed from any computer connected to the Internet to any other computer connected to the Internet, anywhere in the world. The impact of this is great when one appreciates that almost the whole of modern culture can now be reduced to a digital form. Digital information includes colour pictures, animations and movies, high-quality music and sound, text with typefaces and layout, even three-dimensional images.

The real power of today's Internet is that it is available to anyone with a computer and a telephone line. By connecting a piece of hardware called a modem to a personal computer a digital stream of ones and zeros can be converted into a series of audible staccato beeps. The modem can then send this noise down a normal telephone line to one of the computers already connected to the Internet. The two computers can then pass information between themselves, using a common protocol. Because the computer connected to the Internet can connect with any other computer on the Internet, the personal computer can now connect with any of the millions of computers on the Internet.

Like human languages, computer protocols work in both directions. They allow information to be easily sent from a home or office computer to any other computer on, or with access to, the Internet. What is more important is that it allows any computer to gain access to information from any other computer on the Internet: libraries are now literally at our fingertips; a shop simply needs to connect to the Internet to advertise to the world. One language allows a world of computers to share a world of information. The law, in contrast with this transnational system, operates within defined jurisdictional boundaries. The practical resolution of these opposites forms a common thread through each of the following chapters.

THE COST

Sharing a world of information sounds expensive, but it is not. To connect to the Internet, one needs only to connect to a computer already connected. The first cost is therefore the price of the telephone call to that connected computer. The user is not charged for the cost of sending or receiving information beyond that first computer unless a particularly quick or secure route is chosen. What is levied, however, is a price to connect to this computer. The firms controlling these first-port-of-call computers are Internet Access Providers. Their computers are called 'servers', as is any computer permanently connected to the Internet. The computers that pay for the local telephone calls, the users' computers, are called 'clients'.

Other companies provide more than purely a connection to the Internet through their server: they provide materials and services on their server. This has the advantage of being quicker to view and more focused on the needs of the users. These companies that provide both Internet access and other commercial services are Online Service Providers. Examples include Microsoft Network, Compuserve and America Online. All these companies provide more than simply an e-mail address and a ramp to the Internet: they commission, license and provide their own services tailored for their members. And they charge for these value-added services. Increasingly these companies form the targets for litigation. They are sued for the infringing copyright material that *other* people leave on their computers; they are prosecuted for facilitating the transmission of obscene images and movies; they are even sued for publishing defamatory statements. Each chapter raises the question of whether these piggies-in-the-middle, as well as the individual primarily responsible, can be liable. American case law is used for examples of these questions.

INTERNET FEATURES

Using several different protocols, the Internet has been able to provide various services to its connected computers. In the similar way that the word 'chat' has a different meaning in French from its meaning in English, so can two protocols used across the Internet allow servers to pass different information to clients. Different uses of protocols give the Internet its utility. What follows is a tour of the different features of the Internet. To appreciate the tour it may help to remember that the information being shunted around the network is still that digital stream of ones and zeros. The various features are produced by simply applying a different protocol to this stream before and after it is sent between computers. The method of conversing is largely the same; what changes is the language being used.

Server addresses

Every server permanently connected to the Internet has a unique identification number, or Internet Protocol address. To make it easier for humans to remember, these numbers have a unique literary equivalent called a domain name which is allocated by one of the Internet Registries. Ours is 'nabarro.com'; the 'com' suffix indicates that Nabarro Nathanson is a commercial organisation. Academic institutions use the suffix 'ac'. Often the suffix includes information over where the domain has been registered. For example, the University of Oxford has the domain, 'oxford.ac.uk'. Scuffles arise because there are a limited number of domain names and they are allocated on a first-come-first-served basis. The chapter on intellectual property therefore considers the legal implications of this.

E-mail

'E-mail' is short for electronic mail. The word 'mail' should be understood at its widest: the electronic mail system over the Internet can carry more than simple messages and letters. A picture, a sound, in fact anything which can be created and stored on a computer can be sent as electronic mail to any other computer connected to the Internet. First, the item is digitally packed into an appropriate parcel. Like physical items sent by the post, items require suitable packaging. The equivalent of a vase sent through the conventional post is a picture, or a sound or a movie sent over the Internet. These require a digital 'padded envelope' called Multipurpose Internet Mailing Extensions (MIME) or UUencoding. These are special ways of treating every eighth fragile one or zero that make up multimedia objects. Plain text, that is without formatting such as italics and underlining, does not need each eighth one or zero so does not need to be parcelled up in any special way: the standard Internet protocols are adequate to cope with this simple text. Most e-mail packages automatically choose the correct type of encoding to ensure that the object survives its electronic transmission to its recipient.

It is vital to realise that electronic mail *copies* the contents of the digital envelope; it does not actually *send* the material from the creator's machine. So, electronic mail, unlike its terrestrial equivalent, does not touch the original created by the sender; instead it provides an identical copy to each recipient. This has its advantages: copies are automatically retained of all out-going mail. It also has some disadvantages: malicious code which piggy-backs electronic messages may also be copied onto the recipient's computer. And, of course, in the eyes of copyright law, a copy is being made of a copyright work.

Once the text or multimedia object is appropriately encoded the sender simply needs to tack on an address for the e-mail. 'clive@pobox.com' is an example of an e-mail address. This may look complicated but this chapter has already introduced the back half of the address: the domain name. All e-mail addresses are in this format: username@domain. To receive electronic mail, one needs to have an agreement with the controller of the domain. Some domains, like nabarro.com, are controlled by employers and they provide e-mail addresses to their staff like direct telephone lines. Each member of staff will have their name, or other reference, before the '@'. Controllers of other domains, like Internet Service Providers, rent out user names on their domains and also provide access to the Internet or other services.

PSEUDO-ANONYMITY

Sending a postcard anonymously is easy: simply do not sign it. Sending an e-mail anonymously is more difficult: it is 'signed' by it being sent from you. The way that Internet users have attempted to remain anonymous is to send their e-mails via an 'anonymous remailer'. This is a computer on the Internet which runs a special program. This program strips any incoming e-mails of their headers: this removes the identification of from where the e-mail originated. The program then sends this stripped e-mail to the intended recipient purporting, say, to be from nobody@anonymous.com. If the anonymous remailer keeps a log of who is the actual author of a message, they may be ordered by a court to reveal who is the actual sender of the message. If the remailer automatically deletes a log, or never even kept one, of course no court order will restore the identification of the e-mail sender.

A stronger method of remaining anonymous is to send an e-mail via more than one anonymous remailer and to scramble or 'encrypt' all but the next e-mail in the chain. In this way, even if a court were to order a remailer to reveal the sender's identity they would only have access to the details of the remailer who sent them the message and to the next in the chain. To reveal the identity, therefore, all the remailers would have to co-operate with the court order and then all the remailers would have had to have maintained logs. This said, problems of identifying defendants over the Internet should not be exaggerated; it is far easier to send a truly anonymous postcard than a truly anonymous e-mail.

Bulletin boards

Digital bulletin boards are similar to their physical counterparts. Anyone with access to the board can pin up a message or question and any other person can leave a reply on the board. Also like a physical bulletin board, someone is ultimately responsible for it. Someone must remove old messages, perhaps even remove rude or defamatory messages. On the Internet that person is often called a Moderator or is simply the Service Provider which 'hosts' the bulletin board. This means that the Provider stores the messages on equipment under their control; what is a moot point is whether the messages left are also under their control. This will be considered throughout the book but particularly in relation to defamation and copyright.

When a message is posted onto a digital bulletin board what is technically occurring is that the person is sending an e-mail to the board. This is reproduced in a readable format for any user of the board to see. If a reader wishes to reply to the message they have a choice. They may either send an e-mail directly and privately to the person who left the message, or, they can send a reply that will be stored on the bulletin board itself. It will be listed just below the first message for all to see. This process of replying to a message can occur many times, thus creating a 'conversation thread'.

As explained earlier, an e-mail does not need to be a written note; it may be a digitised picture, a digitised sound recording or even a digital movie. These families of e-mails can also be left on bulletin boards not for people to reply to, but for people to download to view or hear. Obscene and indecent pictures and copyright infringement are rife on bulletin boards. The issue of whether the operator of the board may be liable for such illegal postings is a vital point that is addressed throughout this book.

FORUMS

Many Service Providers run bulletin boards only for access by their members. These are called 'forums'. Each forum has a title which indicates the sorts of conversation threads and files which can be found on the board. For example, Compuserve is a Service Provider that hosts a legal forum. Within the forum there are many different sections, some deal with family law, others with recent cases. Occasionally these forums are unmanned, or 'unmoderated'; anything posted on the board will remain for a certain time. It is more usual to find that forums have a moderator who vets and deletes offensive messages. This book tackles the vexed question of whether by doing this, the Service Provider becomes legally responsible for the messages left on the system.

USENET

Forums are accessible only by a Service Provider's members. 'Usenet', in contrast, is a collection of over 15,000 bulletin boards called newsgroups which can be accessed by any person with an Internet connection. Instead of one particular Service Provider being responsible for maintaining and storing the newsgroups, like for a forum, *all* the subscribing Service Providers store the conversation threads. Each Provider is responsible for posting messages from *its* members onto the relevant newsgroups but is able to display the messages posted by all the other members. Newly posted messages are 'flooded' through the Usenet system until all the Providers are able to display the newly posted message. In this way, all the Providers who allow Usenet access are able only to regulate the content of the messages left by their members.

The majority, necessarily, of the messages displayed or files uploaded are out of the control of the majority of the Providers. There will therefore be times when a Provider has had no way of knowing the content of a file or of a message. But there are some good clues; most of the newsgroups have amply descriptive titles. For example, if a Provider is worried about allowing its members access to a pornographic newsgroup it would be wise not to provide access to 'alt.erotica.male'. Some Providers have seen this selective hosting of newsgroups as one of the easiest methods of avoiding the majority of complaints. This rule of thumb has been endorsed by the police suggesting to the United Kingdom's Service Providers not to subscribe to certain newsgroups.

File transfer protocol

File Transfer Protocol, or 'ftp' for short, is what it purports to be: a language that allows files to be transferred from one computer to another. For ftp there are usually two significant computers: the ftp server and the client. The ftp server is simply a computer connected to the Internet that stores the files to be transferred. The client is the computer which receives the files stored, and transferred by, the server. To access an ftp site, unlike a web site, one usually is required to enter a password. This should not indicate that an ftp site is particularly secure: the majority of ftp sites are termed, 'anonymous ftp' meaning that anyone may gain access simply by using the word 'anonymous' or 'guest' as a password.

When a client has gained access to a site it is rather like seeing the contents of a computer's hard disk. There are directories or folders and within those directories there are files. Each of the files may be retrieved usually by double-clicking on the file name or icon. In addition to retrieving files though, rather like a bulletin board, it is possible to upload a file from one's computer to the ftp server. This lack of control over the content of a site can cause legal problems for the owner of the ftp site. If copyright materials are uploaded by an anonymous depositor the owner may be a secondary infringer of the copyright in the works. And because the primary defendant may be difficult to trace, the ftp site owner is an obvious alternative choice.

Telnet

Telnet is a way of allowing a user to gain full access to a remote computer via the Internet. Once a user has logged into such a computer they can easily run programs which are stored on the *remote* computer and view data also stored on that computer. It is as though the user is sitting at the keyboard of the remote computer rather than sitting thousands of miles away at the keyboard of another. For most users, Telnet has taken a back seat to the World Wide Web because it is text-based and requires the knowledge of some UNIX operating system commands. For hackers, in contrast, Telnet remains a useful tool. A hacker can cover his tracks by logging on to one computer and then, from that computer, logging on to another *from that computer*, and so on. This leapfrogging can make it very difficult for law enforcement officers to trace and find a hacker; it also makes it difficult to collect the necessary evidence to prove that the accused in court is the person who committed the crime.

World Wide Web

When most people refer to the 'Internet', they are really talking about a large aspect of it called the World Wide Web. It is about three years old. The World Wide Web, or the web, is the most user-friendly and hence most popular use for the Internet. But it is not the Internet and the Internet is not the World Wide Web. The web, like all the technologies described so far, is merely a common language that allows one computer to understand another when they communicate across telecommunications lines.

Accessing a computer on the web allows a user, or viewer, to do many things. Viewers can see colourful images and graphics, hear sounds and music, see animations and short movies. They can also interact with the accessed computer, or server, in such a way as to allow the viewer to download any material in digital form to his own computer. But these superficial aspects of the web do not explain where it got its name. This explanation reveals the most powerful aspect of the web and the source of the main legal issues involved in its use.

LINKS

Computers connected to the World Wide Web store their information in a special form; it is called Hypertext Markup Language, or HTML. This common language is primarily a language of layout and design. It allows the owner of a computer to format some information, say a table, and store it on their web site or 'home page'. Anyone who accesses that site will see the table as intended. The same goes for graphics and, thanks to some recent advancements, even animations. The web therefore offers, for the first time, an opportunity for the owner of a server computer to control *exactly* what is seen by a person accessing that computer. HTML also offers hypertext.

Hypertext is a way of designing a document with links to other documents. It is most easily understood with an example. Some of the footnotes in this book refer an interested reader to other materials, often a case. But if that interested reader wanted actually to read the referred case, they would have to go to their law library, pick the book from the shelf and turn to the appropriate page. A hypertext version of this book would work as follows. If a reader is interested in a footnote they would merely position an on-screen arrow over the footnote and depress a button on their mouse. The case would then appear on the screen replacing or neighbouring the page of the digitised book. So hypertext is a way of connecting one document to another by means of a link. Links on web pages are usually shown by the word denoting the link being underlined and coloured blue. Pictures can also serve as links.

The real power of a link on a web site can be understood when one appreciates that the link may be to a document held on *any* other computer *anywhere else* on the World Wide Web. So, the Internet version of this book could just as easily link a reader to an American case stored on a web server in the United States as to an English case stored on a web server at Butterworths in England. And having followed a link to another web page one can just as easily follow a link from *that* page to another page on the web. These vast numbers of links, criss-crossing between digital pages across the planet, warrant the title 'World Wide Web'.

BROWSERS

Like other aspects of the Internet, the web only works while all the computers that use it understand a common language. The web's main language is HTML. To allow a viewer's computer to interpret this language into a collection of text, pictures and sound, the computer must use a 'browser'. This is a program that not only shows the web page on the viewer's screen as was intended but it also helps the viewer navigate around the World Wide Web. All browsers have a core of common features. They all allow a user to visit a particular site on the web by typing in the site's address. All browsers also have a set of navigation buttons. These are vital if one is to get back to where one came from. In a sense, the browser lays down digital string through the maze of the web so allowing one to click the 'back' icon to the last turning. As a final aid to navigation, browsers will store a collection of the addresses of favourite pages or sites so that one can return to a favourite place without having to retrace one's steps.

NAVIGATION AIDS

Of course, having millions of pages of information at one's fingertips is useful only if it is easy to find the information needed. However well-stocked a library, there will be few visitors if the books are in an uncatalogued random order. Link lists and search engines bring order to the chaotic layout of the web.

Link lists are simply a collection of links under a particular topic. For example, a law firm may wish to advertise to its clients. To do this it could have a page on its web site which features a list of links to its clients' web pages. An academic may use a web site to collect a series of links to useful web sites for research purposes. Some web sites, such as Yahoo!, consist only of lists of links. Link lists bring to the Internet what the Dewey decimal system brings to our randomly stocked library.

Search engines are web sites that find every site on the web that mentions a particular term. Most search engines can trawl the web's 16 million documents for one word in a matter of seconds. For example, in ten seconds the Alta Vista search engine found over 30,000 instances of the word 'needle' on the web.

Sunrise features

The Internet is changing at a staggering rate. New companies are springing up on a daily basis; each claims to have the new 'killer application'. Lawyers who seek to advise in this area should try to keep abreast of these changes. While some new technologies are legally superficial, others may have a profound impact on what constitutes good advice in relation to the Internet. Three examples are provided below of the features that are on the sunrise of the Internet industry and which are here to stay.

EXECUTABLE CODE

At the beginning of 1996 most web pages were still and silent. Their graphics may have been colourful, but they were static; their presence was indicated at the most by a short 'beep'. This has now changed. The language used to construct web pages has been refined and it is now able to supply not only page layout details to viewer's computers, but also programs currently called applets or objects. These programs run automatically on a viewer's computer so long as the used browser understands the programming language.

The two most powerful and widespread program families are Java applets and ActiveX controls. They allow a web site to show and perform almost all the same functions as an entire computer. Web sites now can show animations; they frequently play music or sounds. Using a Common Gateway Interface in conjunction with these programs, sites can also now interact with their viewers. For example, a weather site may permit viewers to type in their town at which point an area on the screen will be filled with a live, animated satellite picture of the weather in that area. From a commercial perspective these applets and controls are big business; they are allowing web sites to take orders and look more like televisions and less like computers.

From a legal perspective this executable code is also important. Executable code interacts directly with a viewer's computer; this increases the risk that computer viruses, once thought to be rare on the World Wide Web, can be hosted, spread and contracted. But because executable code is usually run automatically, the first a viewer may know of a virus is its symptoms. For less malicious purposes, executable code allows viewers to instruct remote computers, over the World Wide Web, to perform certain tasks. One Java applet takes an order for a compact disc and then searches the web for the retailer selling it most cheaply. These second-generation 'digital robots' have opened up new fields of commerce. To protect them from being copied their creators must rely on strong intellectual property rights as technical copying of the program is far from difficult. For each transaction with the applet, a contract may have to be formed to secure the payment.

Executable code is changing the face of the World Wide Web. This book refers to its implications, but advisers should periodically check the accuracy of their advice to ensure it has not been out-paced by technology.

NETWORK COMPUTERS

Building on the use of executable code is the 'network computer', or NC. Instead of creating bigger and faster computers on the desktop, so the reasoning goes, put all the power in the server and allow a cut-down computer to draw on that power. The network computer would need the smallest of hard disk drives, its data could be stored on a remote server. It would also not need to store programs: these would be stored on remote servers and charged for use on an access-basis. An NC does not even need to be particularly quick; all the really tough calculations would be performed by its remote server and only the answers sent to the NC. Logistically the Network Computer is missing one feature: bandwidth.

Bandwidth should be thought of as the digital width of the pipe that lies between a web site or server and the client computer. At the moment, most people utilise a bandwidth of 28,800 baud; this means that every second the viewer's computer can receive a maximum of 28,800 on and off pulses. In comparison to this hose pipe, NCs will need the equivalent of a two-foot pipe. This may require the telephone companies to lay new cables to everyone's door who wants a network computer.

The legal implications of network computers are vast. Data protection legislation will need to ensure that personal data held is secure and is not being transferred or disclosed without permission. Users will also need to be assured both technically and contractually that their data, perhaps their life's work, is safe and will be accessible for 24 hours every day. At present, if one is unable to connect to the Internet one is only out of e-mail and Internet contact; with a Network Computer you may be out of contact with all your files and programs.

MOBILE TECHNOLOGY

Another sunrise technology is the use of mobile phones as ways of communicating with the Internet and World Wide Web. As the price of mobile phones falls, so will their use with computers rise. People using laptop computers are already able to use the World Wide Web as easily from a beach in Barbados as from an office in the city of London. Similarly, users of laptop computers are able to send and receive e-mails as easily from a plane crossing the Atlantic as from their home in Edinburgh.

For those lawyers who are concerned about where contracts are formed, and where works are published or viruses released, this mobile communication may become a hindrance. It is becoming naïve to assume that e-mails accepting a contract from an account ending, 'company.plc.uk' are actually sent from the United Kingdom.

THIS BOOK

This book tackles the legal issues arising from the Internet under the usual chapter headings for a law textbook. This does not mean that the book is for lawyers only. Where possible, the law is explained in plain English; it is hoped that someone from the Internet Industry will be able to use this book as a first port of call. To help both these clients and their advisers, the text is highlighted with over one hundred and fifty factual scenarios and their legal effect. For some basic questions, a glance at one of these may be all that is needed to appreciate the law on a point. This said, readers should always seek specific legal advice rather than rely entirely on the text and scenarios in this book.

The author appreciates that many legal readers of this book will be unfamiliar with its use of technical Internet terms. For this reason three policies have been adopted. First, the book includes a glossary co-written with a leading journalist in the field. This is written in a non-technical style rather than in the form of a dictionary definition. The second policy is never to assume technical knowledge;

whenever required, this book explains the technology either in the body of the text or in its glossary. The third policy adopted is never to use a technical term where a simplified one will suffice. It is more important that lawyers who advise about the Internet truly understand it rather than simply repeat the latest Internet jargon.

There are many excellent general texts on contract, tort, crime, and the topics of the other chapters of this book. This book is not intended to replace these works; the intention is that it will supplement them. This book, therefore, only refers to laws when it is apparent that the Internet raises unique issues about the legal area that may not be covered in existing general literature. Even when this book does examine unique and new issues, it considers them conservatively. It is this author's strong belief that most legal issues raised by the Internet can be resolved, at common law, from first principles.

Finally, a disclaimer. This book examines the English laws that apply to the Internet. The Internet is a transnational beast however. It will therefore often be prudent to consult the laws from other jurisdictions to check what they have to say on the same issue. Similarly it is hoped that this book will serve those from abroad who wish to know English law's approach to an Internet issue.

Chapter two

Contract

The customer pays his money and gets a ticket. He cannot refuse it. He cannot get his money back. He may protest to the machine, even swear at it. But it will remain unmoved. He is committed beyond recall. He was committed at the very moment when he put his money into the machine.

Lord Denning, *Thornton v Shoe Lane Parking*[1]

The law of contract creates binding obligations between those wishing to do business with each other. The Internet, built for and used as a means of communication, provides a new arena for agreements. This chapter will consider the English law of contract, so far as it relates to consumer contracts and business contracts on the Internet.

The Internet gives businesses access to a vast number of consumers. Current estimates are that there will be over 60 million private users of the Internet by the millennium. The first large-scale consumer and business use that was made of the World Wide Web was the erection of web sites for marketing and advertising purposes. These sites promoted companies and products. Initially, they did not offer the possibility of selling products and services. Sales took place in parallel through more traditional means of communication.

It is now apparent, particularly with enhanced security, that web sites offer international and cost-effective opportunities for selling goods and services to consumers. A web site is rapidly and easily accessible. It can include static or moving graphics, it can be interactive, it is easily updated and purchases can be made immediately. A web site can operate like a shop window and a web site can act as the cashier and till. Where appropriate, a web site can send digital products directly to the consumer.

These commercial benefits create new issues for contract law. This chapter considers the following:

1. What are the requirements for a binding contract to be made over the Internet?
2. How do you decide when a contract formed over the Internet is made?
3. How can digital forms of payment be used to bind agreements?
4. What type of contract should be used to provide digital information over the Internet?
5. Which country's courts will resolve the disputes arising out of an online contract?

1   [1971] 2 QB 163 at 169.

6.   Which country's law will apply to an Internet contract?
7.   What are the special rules that apply to contracts made with European consumers?

FORMATION OF CONTRACT

In the main this chapter does not consider the *terms* of a contract made over the Internet; the main concern is to analyse the *validity* of an Internet contract.[2] This is an important distinction. Under English law, an agreement becomes legally binding when four main factors are in place: offer, acceptance, consideration and intention to create legal relations. Along with these formal requirements, law and statute limits the content of a contract. For example, an Internet contract may be validly formed, but one of its terms may be ineffective under other rules. This section focuses on the formation of a contract, examining each of the four factors in turn, highlighting those features special to the Internet about which contractors and their advisers should be aware.

Offer

It is discussed below that an offer, met with suitable acceptance, can form a contract binding both parties. On the Internet, an owner of a web site may not want to contract with every party who gains access to a site. For example, the owner may want to contract with parties from the locale rather than from any country.[3] Owners of web sites should therefore ensure that the advertising aspect of the site is construed as an 'invitation to treat', not as an offer.

WEBVERTISEMENTS

Suppliers are beginning to use web sites to conduct business. Like a billboard it advertises products and services, but unlike a billboard a web site can also assist the supplier to complete the sale. In doing so, a web site can be designed to advertise the features of a product; it can even allow a viewer to examine the product in a restricted form.[4] After examining the product, or the advertising, a viewer may then select the part of the web site to enter a contract to acquire the product or services. The Internet in effect fuses the advertising and the shop. The law, in contrast, has distinguished between advertising and shop displays.[5] This unique commercial situation has legal ramifications.

2   Contractual terms that will be examined include choice of court and law clauses.
3   This is happening increasingly where a supplier wishes to create geographical price differentials.
4   Software can be downloaded from a web site in a 'crippled' form. For example, a word processor may be downloaded but may be prevented from printing or saving: it provides a 'test drive'. If the user is content with the product he may *then* re-access the web site to form a contract to receive the uncrippling key.
5   *Pharmaceutical Society of Great Britain v Boots Cash Chemists Ltd* [1952] 2 QB 795; cf *Carlill v Carbolic Smoke Ball Co* [1893] 1 QB 256.

SHOPS AND ADVERTS

Shop invitations

Old and much-considered authority has it that the display of goods and their prices in a shop window or on shop shelves are not offers to sell those goods; they are merely invitations to any customer to make an offer to make the purchase.[6] The mechanics are that a customer makes an offer to the retailer, which the retailer may choose to accept or reject. Web site owners should desire the same legal mechanics.

Advertisement offers

For the purposes of offers, the law distinguishes shop displays from certain advertisements. It is therefore essential that those who wish to contract over the Internet understand this difference. The law assesses advertisements in two categories: those which promote unilateral contracts and those promoting bilateral contracts. A unilateral contract is one in which money, generally, is offered to another party to perform some act without that person promising anything in return. A person accepting the offer does not need to communicate this fact to the offeror to complete the contract; he simply needs to do what is required of him.

---

1. **A web site that offers advertising space to vendors runs a promotion. Its site advertises, 'If you visit our pages three times this month and don't buy anything from our traders, we'll credit £10 to your bank account.' This site risks creating a unilateral contract which the entire Internet community may accept.**

A bilateral contract, in contrast, has both parties making a promise. Each offer is usually accepted by a communication of the other's promise.

WEB INVITATIONS

The owner of a web site has little reason to prefer a unilateral contract to a bilateral contract, and where possible should seek to be viewed by the courts as a shopkeeper. The main point to make is that the law looks not simply at the words used for a contract, but the objective intention behind them. This means that if a web site would induce a reasonable person into viewing statements on the pages as offers, so will a court. An owner of a web site therefore must err on the side of caution in creating a web invitation.

One method is for the owner of the web site to state that it will not be bound by any communication from a third party, but the site owner will inform that party if it accepts the communication. This creates two factors in favour of the site owner. First, it goes some way to preventing the reasonable person from thinking the owner has made an offer. The second point relates to the first: it provides evidence to a court that the site owner did not intend to make an offer. Simply using indicative words above a link such as 'make an offer' may not be enough.[7]

---

6   See *Warlow v Harrison* (1859) 1 E & E 309 and its more modern equivalent, *Pharmaceutical Society of Great Britain v Boots Cash Chemists Ltd* [1952] 2 QB 795.

7   Eg *Harvela Investments Ltd v Royal Trust Company of Canada (CI) Ltd* [1986] AC 207.

> **2. A watch company advertises its products on a web site and states its prices in dollars, despite its prices being higher to consumers outside America. To process an order, the consumer must provide certain information and then click the button labelled 'Submit'.** *Before* **the consumer submits this information a clear statement should be made that their information is to allow the site owner to decide whether to accept their offer. This acceptance will be communicated to them on clicking the 'Submit' button. This allows the site owner to check electronically the consumer's residence and reject the offers from non-US residents, directing them to a local supplier, perhaps.**

It is mentioned above that the courts view a shop's shelves as invitations to treat and not offers. A web site owner may therefore attempt to argue that the site is more like a shop's shelves than anything else, and that it should be viewed accordingly. While this analogy appears reasonably accurate, it may not withstand the strain of a court's detailed scrutiny.

A justification for not holding shops as making offers is to ensure that, if the shop's stock is depleted, a willing consumer cannot sue the shopkeeper for damages.[8] Where a web site is offering not physical but digital goods for 'sale'[9] it is difficult to assert that supplies can be exhausted. One of the features of digital products distributed over the Internet is that they are in infinite supply. It may therefore be that the primary justification for the rule that shops do not offer but invite to treat is based in part on a commercial factor that is absent from a digitally distributing web site.[10]

MISREPRESENTATIONS

The distinction between an invitation to treat and an offer is that an offer, met with acceptance, may form a contract. An invitation to treat does not serve as an offer: the courts construe that taking up the invitation is an offer. The distinction does not, however, entitle a web site to induce a consumer to enter a contract by using misleading statements. If a factual statement prior to a contract being formed is classified as misleading, the induced party may be entitled to claim damages, rescind the contract, or even both. If an individual is concerned that an invitation to treat or statement on a web site may constitute such a misrepresentation, he should take proper legal advice. It is worth noting that the established law and statute on misrepresentation are equally and fully applicable to a contract formed over the Internet as to one formed in other ways. Web site owners who simply use their sites as a 'billboard' for contracts that are formed in other ways must therefore consider that the content of their site may induce someone to enter a contract.[11] It makes no legal difference to the law of misrepresentation that the misrepresentation is on a web site but that the contract is not formed over the Internet.

---

8   See *Esso Petroleum v Customs and Excise Comrs* [1976] 1 WLR 1 at 11.
9   See *'Type of contract'*, at page 32.
10   Of course, a limited licence may have been imposed on the supplier restricting the number of digital products he can supply.
11   There may also be a misrepresentation by the viewer, say, as to the means of payment or the country of his residence.

TIMING AND LOCATION OF OFFERS

That an offer was made provides two useful pieces of information: when the offer was made and where it was made. When a court deems an offer is made is often vital. At any moment up to acceptance, an offer can be retracted. Where an offer was made has some relevance to the applicable law for a contract, in the absence of choice, and the relevant section of this chapter will consider this more fully.[12]

When is an offer made

It is often relevant for the purposes of a contract dispute to determine when an offer is made. A contract may only be formed by accepting an offer. However, any offer can be revoked before acceptance. Therefore the first question to answer is when was an offer made. The need for discussion arises because offers are often delayed in transmission and a court will have to decide whether a revocation of an offer will be deemed to take effect before an acceptance of that offer. In short, the court has a choice: offers may be deemed to be made at the time of sending or at the time of receipt.

Delayed offers

Adams v Lindsell[13] is old and approved authority as to when an offer is deemed to take effect. In the case wool was offered for sale by a letter sent to the plaintiffs. Because of a mistake made by the offerors the letter arrived two days late at which time it was promptly accepted. The court held that the contract was formed on acceptance, despite the offer being delayed. The court indicated, more than once, that its decision was partially founded on the reason for delay being the offeror's mistake. If the offeror had included a time-limit on the efficacy of the offer, however, a late acceptance would not have bound them.

Despite the technology e-mail can suffer from the same delays and problems as experienced by the defendants in *Adams v Lindsell*. People wrongly consider e-mail is a quick method of communication and compare it to a fax, or perhaps even a telephone.

Post, faxes and e-mails

An e-mail is more like a posted letter being delivered to a pigeon-hole ready for collection. E-mails are not instantaneous, unlike faxes and telephone calls. An e-mail message is sent to a Service Provider who, like the Royal Mail, attempts to deliver it as quickly and accurately as possible. But as with the Royal Mail, mistakes can occur and e-mails can arrive garbled, late or even not arrive at all. The similarities with the Royal Mail go further: the Royal Mail does not actually deliver post abroad; that is left to the local postal system of the foreign country. The Royal Mail delivers the mail to only the 'first stop' outside England. The same applies to e-mails: they are passed between many different carriers to arrive at their final destination.

---

12   See 'The Rome Convention', at page 46.
13   (1818) 1 B & Ald 681.

Unlike a telephone call and fax, some e-mails are delivered not to the recipient's desk, but to an electronic pigeon-hole for collection. This pigeon-hole is called an 'inbox'. Many users of e-mail must dial their Service Provider to check on the arrival of an e-mail; often users must collect their e-mail, it is not 'delivered' to them. This technical framework serves as a useful backdrop for the discussion which now follows on when an offer is deemed to have been made. It will also be useful when acceptances are considered later.[14]

E-mails can be misaddressed, delayed by any server or router on the way, and worse than ordinary mail, they may not be 'collected' for some time after delivery. This is a situation comparable to sending an offer to a pigeon-hole abroad. Many parties are involved in the transmission of the message and even on arrival, the recipient must act to retrieve it.

Before dealing with the legal resolution to this situation, a technical point must be made. Certain e-mail systems permit a 'read' and a 'receive' receipt to be automatically returned to a sender of an e-mail. The 'receive' receipt informs the sender that the e-mail has not been received by the individual, but by his Service Provider; if analogies are useful, the receipt informs when the mail arrives in the pigeon-hole. The 'read' receipt informs when the individual retrieves the e-mail from the Service Provider. Even there, like a letter in an unopened envelope, the e-mail may not be read for some time. It is therefore unwise to rely on these receipts for anything but evidence. Legally, the best practice is to make any offer by e-mail subject to a date on which the offer will lapse. Specifying this date in relative terms, for instance, five days after receipt, poses problems unless the offeror provides a definition of exactly what is 'receipt'. A simpler and more certain method is to specify an objective date and time.[15]

---

3. An e-mail offer is made to a person that is delayed by two days owing to the recipient's Internet Service Provider having a computer fault. Unlike *Adams v Lindsell* the delay was out of the control of the offeror; a court is likely to assume a time of offer at the time it should have arrived.

Acceptance

There is little special about the terms of an acceptance made over the Internet, as opposed to one made in any other way. The acceptance must unequivocally express assent to all the terms of the offer. Much has been written about what constitutes such an acceptance. It is useful here to draw out the special methods of accepting over the Internet.

It has been mentioned that an e-mail can have a 'read' and a 'receive' receipt.[16] Receiving one of these will not constitute an acceptance of an e-mailed offer. A receipt is not an acceptance of the *terms* of an offer. Even an e-mail sent in reply

14 See 'Timing of acceptances', at page 22.
15 If no mention is made of the life-span of the offer the courts will imply a lapse after a reasonable time. See *Chemco Leasing SpA v Rediffusion Ltd* [1987] 1 FTLR 201. To assess what is reasonable the courts will take into account many factors including the subject matter of the contract and the method of communicating the offer. Clearly with an e-mail offer, the expiration will be implied sooner than an offer made by post. See *Quenerduaine v Cole* (1883) 32 WR 185.
16 See 'Delayed offers', at page 17.

that states the recipient's intention to reply in due course will not be an acceptance.[17]

An acceptance needs only to assent to an offer; it does not, in general, need to be in writing, or by another means of communication. For this reason, where a web site is established to make or complete contracts, its owner should be aware of what conduct may bind him. This is of paramount importance. Contracts made over the World Wide Web are rarely completed by two humans: a web site operates automatically according to a set of instructions, called a script. In this respect, it is crucial that the owner of a web site understands how a contract can be completed because, generally, a web site operates without supervision. This section examines two scenarios that: where, as advised, a web site accepts an offer and second, where it makes one.

WEB SITE ACCEPTANCE

Having discussed when and how offers can be made it is now relevant to determine how and when acceptances are made. The general rule is that an acceptance must be communicated to the person making the offer. The person making this *offer* may waive the general rule and permit acceptance by conduct. This general rule is examined in respect of the Internet.

Communication of acceptance

The acknowledged rule is that acceptance of an offer must be communicated to the offeror.[18] In addition, as the Court of Appeal has stated:[19]

'We have all been brought up to believe it to be axiomatic that acceptance of an offer cannot be inferred from silence, save in the most exceptional circumstances ...'

The question is, what are the 'most exceptional circumstances' when it is appropriate for an acceptance to be silent? These exceptional circumstances stem from the reasons for the rule: to protect both offeror and offeree.

The rule protects the offeror from being bound by a contract without knowing that the offer is accepted. An exception to this may be, therefore, where the offeror expressly or impliedly waives the requirement of communication. For example, an offer to sell goods may be made by sending goods to an offeree who can accept the offer by using them.[20] Here there is not mere silence or inactivity; there is conduct indicating acceptance.

Conversely offerees are also protected by this rule. If they do not wish to accept an offer, it is undesirable that offerors can put them to the trouble of communicating a refusal.[1] Indeed, authority from an established precedent, *Felthouse v Bindley*,[2] indicates that the offeror can waive communication of

17   See *OTM Ltd v Hydranautics* [1981] 2 Lloyd's Rep 211.
18   [1974] 1 WLR 155 at 157.
19   *Allied Marine Transport Ltd v Vale do Rio Doce Navegacaao SA* [1985] 1 WLR 925 at 927.
20   *Weatherby v Banham* (1832) 5 C & P 228.
1   *Chitty on Contracts* Volume 1 at §2-047 (27th edn).
2   (1862) 11 CBNS 869.

acceptance, but not waive an unequivocal external manifestation of acceptance so as to bind the offeree.

That the above is good law is not doubted; its bearing on standard practice on the Internet is. For the most part it is suppliers who draft the offers being made over the Internet, particularly on the World Wide Web. In this situation it is difficult to see any unfairness in holding an acceptor, ie the supplier, bound despite making no contact to that effect: it would appear that the onus is on the owner of a web site to state categorically what will constitute acceptance. Contracting over the Internet may reverse the court's assumptions in *Felthouse v Bindley* because the offeree generally drafts the offer. If that party does not specify the method of acceptance, and also does not reply to a submitted offer it risks the serious possibility of being bound by numerous contracts without having made explicit approval. Even if a stipulation as to the method of acceptance is made in the e-mail or on the web site, if the offeree drafted these terms and accepts by another method, the offeree can be viewed as having waived that specified method. A court will look to whether the offeror has been prejudiced by the changed method of acceptance.[3]

Acceptance by conduct

The web site can accept an offer, 'on behalf' of its owner, by certain conduct. For example, a viewer can click a button on a web page to send a request for some software and the software may then begin to download to the viewer's computer. This positive action can be viewed as an acceptance of the offer made by the viewer without the owner (or offeree) having expressly assented to the offer itself.[4] But, our courts commonly apply an 'objective' test to interpret the actions of the offeree.[5] Conduct will therefore be regarded only as acceptance if the reasonable person would be induced into believing that the offeree has unequivocally accepted the offer.

Completing an order by downloading a file to the consumer is likely to be construed as acceptance by the reasonable person. Owners must therefore carefully construct their web sites. The owner must ensure that the web site is able to validate the terms of the offer from the viewer. Generally this is achieved by the web site having a contract page that the viewer is encouraged to submit, or offer, by clicking a link or button. On receiving this notification the web site will automatically start the downloading of the digital material to the viewer. But the automation of this acceptance places a burden on the site owner: he must ensure that the terms of the offer submitted are the terms of the offer expected. It is essential that a viewer cannot submit an offer with an adjustment to the terms, say lowering the price. This would be a counter-offer which may, unwittingly, be accepted by downloading the requested material to the viewer.

There is a technical method to achieve this certainty. The web page should clearly state the terms of the order. Included within these terms should be a clause to the effect that an acceptance will only be valid where an offer is received through the web site.[6] This, to some extent, prevents an adjusted offer being sent by e-mail and automatically accepted.

---

3   See generally *Robophone Facilities v Blank* [1966] 1 WLR 1428.
4   See *Brogden v Metropolitan Rly* (1877) 2 App Cas 666.
5   See Vorster [1987] 104 LQR 274.
6   See *Frank v Wright* (1937) OQPD 113 where acceptance was specified to be received in writing, but was not valid acceptance where made orally.

If a web site is not being used to receive orders, but orders are placed by e-mail instead, the acceptor must have an automatic check as to the contents of that e-mail. The use of a checksum is the most convenient method of checking this. Only if the checksum of the e-mailed order corresponds precisely with that of the expected order should the web site accept the order. Controllers of sites should pay much attention to their automatic checking programs: an error may result in the owner being bound to a contract that would have been unacceptable.

---

4. A web site provides the terms of an offer to download software from the site at a cost of £60. The site is structured so that the viewer must type the words, 'I Agree' in a box, at which point the web site accepts the offer by downloading to the viewer the requested software. One viewer types 'I Agree to paying £30'. Because the automatic checking program looks simply for the words 'I Agree', but not exclusively, the software is downloaded to the viewer in error. A contract may have been formed at the lower price.

Consumer acceptance

This chapter advises against web sites making offers. Nevertheless, for the sake of completeness, rather than recommendation, this section examines this method of contracting.[7] Many of the same legal considerations are applicable here as for when the web site accepts an offer.

ACCEPTANCE BY CONDUCT

It has been explained that conduct can constitute acceptance.[8] In the scenario where a web site makes an offer, it will be the conduct of the consumer, or viewer, which the courts will examine to check for acceptance. It is in the interests of the web site to ensure that the conduct by the consumer is therefore as unequivocal and unambiguous as possible.

---

5. A web page has a scrollable window headed 'Licence'. Below this window is a button labelled, 'download software'. A viewer clicks on this button to download the software and is later accused of breaching the licence provisions. The viewer may have an arguable case that his conduct was not in relation to the terms of the licence, but in relation simply to gaining access to the software. A more thoughtful page design may have removed this problem.

Conduct is regarded as acceptance only if the reasonable person would be induced into believing the offeree has accepted. This 'objective' test can create difficulties for the operator and designer of a web page. An increasing number of consumers using the World Wide Web for commerce will view it like a shop, only a 'virtual' one. They may therefore be surprised, and not aware, that to acquire a product they must not only provide payment but also consent to a licence. Their more

7   See 'Shop invitations', at page 15.
8   See 'Acceptance by conduct', at page 20.

usual tangible purchases involved simply paying in exchange for receiving the product. On this basis it is difficult to fathom how a court could objectively construe as acceptance the clicking of a button that denotes downloading the product rather than accepting the licence. Owners of web sites should therefore not shy from explaining that clicking a button will bind that person to obligations regarding the material that they will acquire. This provides the background for the final issue pertaining to the acceptance by the conduct of a consumer: ignorance of offer.

Ignorance of offer – lack of intention

It can be appreciated that without explicit statements, consumers could click on a button labelled 'download' without envisaging they may be entering an explicit, rather than implied, contract: consider the eagerness to acquire some new software or material and consider the typical ignorance that the acquisition is subject to an explicit licence. It is also possible to press the wrong button. In such a situation the courts may be reluctant to bind unwitting offerees simply because they have performed an action[9] that purportedly indicates acceptance. A further reason that the courts may not hold consumers bound by their action is that, in not knowing of the offer, the consumers have no intention to be legally bound by their actions.

The solution to these possible problems is for any web site that seeks to bind consumers to be explicit and avoid uncertainty. One method is to prevent the viewer being able to perform the conduct before they have scrolled, or paged through the entire contract. True, a consumer may simply click on a 'next page' link without actually reading the text of the contract; but, at least they then have a weaker argument that their conduct does not objectively indicate acceptance and that they were ignorant of the offer.

---

6. **The home page of a web site features only one line of legal text to avoid looking too ominous. It states, 'By proceeding you agree to be bound by our *terms*.' The word 'terms' is underlined on the site to indicate a link to the terms of the web site. This may not bind the viewer, but if it does, there is a likelihood that onerous exclusions of liability will not operate against the viewer. The web site owner should find other ways of ensuring that those onerous terms are definitely read by the viewer.**

Timing of acceptances

Because an offer may normally be revoked at any point until acceptance, it is obviously vital to appreciate when acceptance is deemed to have taken place over the Internet. One person makes an offer which is accepted immediately by another person. But if that offer is withdrawn before the acceptance is *received* there is a conflict. The possible solutions are that the contract was made when the acceptance was sent; or when, and if, it arrives at the recipient. As no cases have covered this point in the English courts it is necessary to extrapolate from the law relating to acceptance by post, telephone and telex.

---

9   Eg clicked on a link or icon.

When a viewer is online with a web site packets of digital information pass between the site and the client almost constantly. An acceptance by either party will generally be immediately received by the other. The more difficult questions of timing of acceptances are therefore seldom pertinent for web communication. For e-mails the issues are more complex.

This discussion is therefore in halves: the first considers acceptance by e-mail where it is reasoned that the 'postal rule' will usually apply; the second considers acceptance over a web site where it is submitted the more general rule will apply that the contract is formed when the acceptance is received.

ACCEPTING BY POST, TELEPHONE AND TELEX

Where acceptances are sent by post there is a generally applicable rule that the English courts have used to determine the deemed time of acceptance.[10] Acceptance takes place when the letter is posted. Where acceptances are made by an instantaneous form of communication, such as telephone or telex, another rule has been generally applied.[11] Acceptance is deemed to take place when the acceptance is communicated to the offeror.

It is a moot point whether these rules should be mechanically applied, or whether they are, as is more likely, a starting point to assess what is fair between the parties.[12] Certainly the courts have stated that the posting rules should not be applied where it would lead to 'manifest inconvenience or absurdity'.[13] And there are occasions where this is would be the case: it would be absurd for an acceptance to be deemed accepted at the time of posting if it is delayed in the post because the offeree wrongly addressed it. It is perhaps as much as can be hoped, therefore, that this chapter analyses, at the least, what would not be manifestly inconvenient or absurd for e-mail acceptances. It is essential that those who would seek to rely on the following section for e-mail acceptances are aware that it is simply guidance. Even after over 150 years of examination of the postal rule, there is no universally applicable rule; there are merely pointers for the parties and the court.

ACCEPTANCES BY E-MAIL

As mentioned earlier, e-mail is not quite like the post and it is certainly not like instantaneous communication by the telephone. It is sometimes slower than the post, and the arrival of the acceptance by e-mail is far more reliant on the recipient than the sender. It is not like a fax or telephone for two reasons. First, there is no direct line of communication between sender and receiver. Instead, the e-mail is broken into chunks and sent as a collection of packets, each with an address for the recipient. The arrival of an e-mail is therefore far more fragmented than a telephone call. The second, and central, difference between the two is that with a telephone call it is possible to check that the intended recipient has heard the acceptance. With e-mail this is near to impossible but is often quite necessary. E-mails are sent using protocols, precise languages, which allow one computer to

10   See *Adams v Lindsell* (1818) 1 B & Ald 681.
11   See *Entores Ltd v Miles Far East Corpn* [1955] 2 QB 327, and *Brinkibon Ltd v Stahag Stahl und Stahlwarenhandelgesellschaft mbH* [1983] 2 AC 34.
12   See Treitel G, *The Law of Contract* (Sweet & Maxwell, London, 1995), at page 26.
13   *Holwell Securities Ltd v Hughes* [1974] 1 WLR 155 at 161.

pass on information accurately to another. But sometimes these protocols are used incorrectly and an e-mail may arrive entirely garbled or missing a few important characters such as zeros and pound signs. This problem must be combined with the issue that an e-mail requires its recipient to collect it, rather like collecting mail from a pigeon-hole. It is therefore difficult, unlike a phone call, to check that the offeror has received the acceptance and to check that it is unequivocal.

Reasonableness of e-mail acceptance

Like the posting rules, the first issue to consider in relation to an acceptance is whether it is reasonable to use e-mail to accept. A rule of thumb applied in postal cases has been that if an offer is made by post, it is reasonable to accept by post. This, at first blush, appears applicable to e-mail; it may not be. Some e-mail users are permanently connected to their Service Provider: as soon as an e-mail arrives for them, they are notified and can immediately view the message. What is more common, however, is that a user's e-mail arrives to a server which the user must contact by modem to access any messages: the connection is not permanent. What may appear strange is that these users are not notified that an e-mail awaits them. They must simply login on the off-chance that an e-mail is ready for them. For these remote e-mail users, a period of days may elapse before they check their Service Provider for any e-mail. It may therefore be less reasonable that an important *acceptance* is e-mailed to one of these remote users, than for an *offer* to be sent from one of these users. That said, it is submitted that the senders have at least some responsibility to inform their recipients not to reply by e-mail if they collect their e-mail infrequently.

Priority over subsequent communications

Because an e-mail is not instantaneous, if it is reasonable to use e-mail to accept,[4] it is not absurd to deem the time of making the contract as the time of sending the e-mail where otherwise a later acceptance *sent* would act prejudicially. A later posting or e-mail should not 'beat' the earlier acceptance sent by e-mail. Of course, convenience and policy have a role to play in balancing the interests of the two competing offerees.[5] It would not be reasonable to prefer the earlier sent e-mail if it was addressed incorrectly, or was sent in full knowledge that the offeror's e-mail server had crashed.[6]

Accepted but not received

E-mails can be delayed in their transmission, sometimes through no fault of the offeree. Less often an e-mail will not be received at all. There are three possible reasons for this. First, the sender sends the acceptance to an incorrect e-mail address: it is extremely unlikely that a court will grant such carelessness with the benefit of the doubt; the e-mail will not be acceptance. A second reason that the e-mail may not be received is owing to a fault at some point in the transmission

---

4   See 'Reasonableness of e-mail acceptance', above.
5   *Brinkibon Ltd v Stahag Stahl und Stahlwarenhandelgesellschaft mbH* [1983] 2 AC 34 at 41.
6   See *Bal v Van Staden* [1902] TS 128 in which it was held unreasonable to insist that an acceptance be deemed accepted where the sender knew of postal delays.

process. Like a loss in the Royal Mail, a court must weigh the fairness to the offeree against the unfairness to the offeror, who may have already contracted with another party. Even so, it is still likely that the contract will have been formed at the time of sending the e-mail.[7] The third, and most common, reason that an e-mail acceptance will not be received is that its recipient does not retrieve it. This may be because the person no longer checks their e-mail inbox, or because the person sees who the message is from and deletes it without reading it. In both of these situations, the e-mail would constitute acceptance; an offeror's recklessness will not prevent the formation of a contract.

It follows from the above that an e-mail acceptance sent, but not yet received, cannot be 'beaten' by a later sent revocation of the offer. This rule is well established under rules of postal acceptance and there seems little justification to adjust it for acceptances and offers over the Internet.[8]

Inaccurate transmission

It has been mentioned that an e-mail may arrive missing, or including, certain characters and it may even be entirely illegible. But the legally significant point about a flawed e-mail is that its sender may never know. In this way e-mail differs to a large extent from a telephone acceptance, and to a smaller extent to a fax acceptance. During a telephone call one can check that an acceptance has been heard; fax machines will report an error if a fax cannot be sent with sufficient quality, or there is not paper at the receiver's end. In contrast, if an e-mail is garbled, it is impossible for the offeree to know before it is too late. For this reason, it would be both inconvenient and absurd for any other rule to apply other than making the offeror bound by a garbled e-mail. The offeror, having not specified an alternative method of acceptance, is not at liberty to presume it is a counter-offer.

This rule is not purely based on technical realities and policy; it is also based on evidential matters. As with a fax, the sender retains a copy of that which is sent. On the other hand, it is often possible, using digital translators, to unscramble the received e-mail to establish whether it was an unequivocal acceptance.[9]

Practical solution

The examination of when an acceptance is deemed to have been made is clearly applicable only where there is a dispute between the parties. It is useful for those who wish to trade and negotiate over the Internet to appreciate how to avoid these disputes. It is best for the offer to contain as much detail as possible about the acceptance which is sought. The offer should be explicit on how acceptance must be communicated, where it is to be received and when it must be in the place of receipt. Because e-mail relies on a third party's equipment, guaranteeing a time of

7   See *Household, etc Insurance Co Ltd v Grant* (1879) 4 Ex D 216.
8   Offerors over the Internet must not forget that to revoke an offer the withdrawal must actually reach the offeree. A reversal of the postal rule will not apply. See *Re London & Northern Bank* [1900] 1 Ch 220.
9   A binary document, say a word processing document, which is e-mailed as text, will be irreversibly scrambled. Other types of modification, however, such as a '£' becoming a '#', can be reversed to indicate to the court the true nature of the acceptance.

arrival of a message is impossible. An offeror may wish to stipulate a time-limit for acceptance.

---

7. An insurance firm establishes a web site and allows potential customers to submit details of their works of art for insurance. All valuations and contracts are formed over the Internet. The firm sends by e-mail to a customer an offer of insurance; the customer replies by e-mail but the reply is delayed because the customer has not paid his monthly fee to his Service Provider. While the reply is in 'transit' the painting the subject of insurance is stolen. The customer will not be able to benefit from the delay in the post, as the reason was attributable to his fault.

ACCEPTANCES OVER THE WORLD WIDE WEB

Unlike e-mail communications, on the World Wide Web the client and server are in simultaneous communication for most purposes. The communication between the two has the quality of a telephone conversation but between computers rather than humans. Either party will be immediately aware if the other party 'goes offline'. This is because when one party sends digital data to the other these data are sent together with a checksum which allows the receiving computer to check that the correct information has been received. A checksum is almost the equivalent of someone saying 'Okay?' after asking a question over the telephone; it is a way of checking that the silence is due to acquiescence rather than absence.

If the client loses contact with the server, the server will 'know' of this situation within seconds, its checksums and 'received data' will not arrive; if the server loses contact from the client very often a message will appear to the effect of 'server not responding'. In law this 'knowledge' of non-transmission makes a crucial difference. In *Entores Ltd v Miles Far East Corpn* Lord Denning considered for the first time when an acceptance sent by telex should be considered as making a contract.[20] It is instructive to follow closely Denning LJ's reasoning in this case: this will demonstrate that a web site acceptance greatly differs to an e-mail acceptance and should be treated like a telephone, or telex, acceptance.

First, Denning LJ considered the hypothetical case where one person, in the earshot of another, shouts an offer to the other person.[1] The person hears the offer and replies but his reply is drowned by noise from an aircraft flying overhead. Denning LJ was clear that there is no contract at the moment of the reply. The accepting person must wait until the noise has gone and repeat the acceptance so the other can hear it. Next, Lord Denning took the case of a contract attempted to be made over the telephone. An offer is made but in the middle of the reply of acceptance the line goes 'dead'. Denning LJ was again clear that there is no contract at this point because the acceptor will know that the conversation has abruptly been broken off. Finally, Lord Denning considered use of telex to form a contract. Again, if the line goes dead in the middle of the sentence of acceptance, the teleprinter motor will stop. If the line does not go dead, but, say, the ink dries up, the clerk at the receiving end will send back a message 'not receiving'. In all

---

20   [1955] 2 QB 327. Applied by the House of Lords in *Brinkibon Ltd v Stahag Stahl GmbH* [1983] 2 AC 34.
1   [1955] 2 QB 327 at 332.

Denning's examples the person sending the acceptance knows that it has not been received or has reason to know it.

Parallels with acceptance over a web site are now obvious: if a communication of acceptance is sent from or to a web site, it will become immediately obvious if a problem has occurred which blocks the communication. Like a telephone acceptance, a server will always 'know' whether a message has been received by its intended recipient; it is waiting for received data to signify that the message has been received. And like a telex acceptance, if a client sends a message to the server but there is some problem preventing transmission, the client will receive, not unlike the telex clerk's message, a 'server not responding' message. It is therefore submitted that communications over the World Wide Web differ from those by e-mail. The contract is complete when the acceptance is received by the offeror.

---

8. **A company which sells ties establishes a web site that allows viewers to select a pattern and length for a tie. After selecting the tie, the viewer is asked to click the 'I want to buy' icon. The company's web server then sends an automatic acceptance. The server is notified that this acceptance does not reach the viewer. No contract is formed because the non-delivery of the acceptance was known to the company before the viewer left its site. It should have retransmitted the acceptance.**

BATTLE OF THE FORMS

The rapidity of e-mail and automatic confirmations of receipt lend the Internet to contractual negotiations where previously faxes had been used. This may allow a 'battle of the forms' to commence. This is where two standard-form e-mail contracts are exchanged, each differing slightly to the other but claiming to govern the legal relationship entirely. The situation may be resolved by no contract being formed; there is no agreement. What can be more problematic is that a contract is formed on one party's terms when that was not expected. Except for the issues of location and timing already mentioned, there is little that the Internet will add to established methods of judging the result of a battle of the forms.[2]

Consideration

As an oversimplification, perhaps, it can be stated that the English law of contract distinguishes breakable promises from enforceable contracts.[3] Consideration given in return for a promise is the main ingredient that turns promises into contracts. Consideration has been variously defined as 'something of value in the eye of the law';[4] '[d]etriment to the promisee';[5] 'the price for which the promise is bought';[6] and there is much academic debate as to its exact ambit.

---

2   *BRS v Arthur V Crutchley Ltd* [1967] 2 All ER 785 and *Butler Machine Tool Co Ltd v Ex-Cell-O Corpn (England) Ltd* [1979] 1 WLR 401.
3   Although, a promise made in a deed may be enforceable. This is considered out of the scope of this chapter, but it may be noted that there appears little preventing a deed being made using electronic methods.
4   *Thomas v Thomas* (1842) 2 QB 851 at 859.
5   Holdsworth W, *History of English Law*, Volume 8, at page 11.
6   *Dunlop Pneumatic Tyre Co Ltd v Selfridge Ltd* [1915] AC 847 at 855.

English law has always recognised that mutual promises may be adequate consideration for each other, thus forming a contract. If a builder promises to repair a roof and the unfortunate home owner promises to pay on completion of the repair, a binding contract is formed. No services have been provided yet and no money has been given.[7]   Similarly, promises to pay over the Internet are enough to form the consideration to create a contract.

---

9. A music shop with a web site offers CDs for sale. A viewer selects a CD for £15 from the web site and types 'I Agree' in the requisite box together with a credit card number. The CD is shipped immediately at which point the shop discovers that the credit card number is fictitious. That the agreement has been completed over the Internet is of no legal consequence: the viewer's promise to provide the £15 will be 'valuable' (ie of value) consideration for the shop to enforce the contract.

It is only important for this chapter to assess whether the factual reality of contracting using the Internet affects the doctrine of consideration. For general statements, readers are advised to look to specialist texts. One contractual situation is particular to the Internet: the consideration needed to cement a web-wrap contract.[8] These are agreements at the 'front' of a web site which purport to bind their viewers to a contract should they proceed to view the rest of the site.

WEB-WRAP CONSIDERATION

It is now common that to enter a web site one must click a link labelled, 'I Agree to the terms above'. These terms are generally divided into two sections: the top section expresses the intellectual property rights that the site owner licenses to viewers; the bottom section attempts to exclude liability for any damage caused by the site. This section will not address the *terms* of these contracts, but merely whether there is consideration for the licence.

If a web-wrap contract is properly constructed it seems likely that there is consideration to form a binding contract with the viewer. What the programmer of the web site must attempt to create is a set of mutual promises that will form the consideration for the contract. One method of achieving this is to *actually prevent* a viewer who does not click the 'I Agree' link or icon from entering the site itself. Promising the viewer access to the site if the 'I Agree' link is selected then forms one of the promises to bind the contract. The other promise must come from the viewer. This, of course, is to promise to abide by the terms of licence. This prevention can then be classed as a promise to allow the viewer into the web site if he agrees to the terms on the screen.

Web site designers and legal advisers should work together to ensure that the contract is formed at the correct time. The contract will not work retroactively; if a web site owner is concerned to exclude liability for material on his home page a

---

7   If this was not the law, there could never be an action in contract for non-payment. The defendant would argue that, having not paid, no consideration has been provided, no contract therefore subsists.

8   The use of 'digital cash' in exchange for goods or services raises issues not of consideration but of performance of a contract. For this reason the legal issues involved with digital cash are examined under 'Performance' at page 30.

contract should appear *before* the home page. From a designer's perspective, foisting a legal document on a new viewer may not be appropriate.[9]

Intention

The fourth and final ingredient to create a binding contract is an intention to create legal relations. The reason that this is a factor in resolving a contractual issue over the Internet is that often only one human is involved. When a person makes an agreement with a web site, the site accepts or rejects the communication by the person according to a computer program being run at the time. A human is not sitting on the server side of the web site. This raises the issue of how the contract can be formed without this *direct* intention. It is not complicated, nor unique to the Internet, but is a factor which advisers should not overlook: bugs in these programs will not negative the owner's intention.

PROGRAMMED INTENTION

In *Thornton v Shoe Lane Parking*[10] Mr Thornton accepted a contract by driving a car into a car park. In that case, Lord Denning stated that the automatic reaction of the car park turning a light from red to green and thrusting a ticket was enough to create a contract.[11] All the ingredients were present. It is of no *legal* consequence that the contract was physically completed by a machine. The court looks objectively to whether a contract can be said to have been made: has the user been induced reasonably to believe that a contract was being made or offered? In comparison, it is of no legal consequence that a computer program completes the contract over the Internet; as shown above, many contracts are 'made' with machines. That a computer program is being relied upon, however, can be of commercial significance to its owner.

Usually web-wrap contracts and automated e-mail contracts use an express agreement. If, as a result of a bug in the contracting program, the viewer's offer is accepted in error, the court will presume that there was the requisite intention. The offeror has the heavy burden to prove that there was no intention to have a legal consequence.[12] The subjective opinion of, say, the owner of the web site is of little consequence to the court,[13] unless the viewer knew of the lack of intention.

---

10. For the payment of £10 a web site allows its viewers to download pictures of a certain quality. An additional payment of £2 allows viewers to download the pictures at a higher resolution, which are more appropriate for professional use in brochures and magazines. An error in the CGI script permits viewers to download any of the pictures for £10. The web site owner will be hard pressed to claim the extra £2: the viewers are unlikely to know of the mistake.

---

9   A contract in a frame and a simple home page can be an acceptable compromise.
10   [1971] 2 QB 163.
11   [1971] 2 QB 163 at 169.
12   *Edwards v Skyways Ltd* [1964] 1 WLR 349 at 355.
13   See *Smith v Hughes* (1871) LR 6 QB 597.

Owners of web sites who seek to use them for forming contracts should be aware that an error in their automated program may be of great financial consequence. These programs should be carefully checked and, where possible, the owner should seek to obtain an indemnity from the programmer against such loss or, if not, insurance.

PERFORMANCE: PAYMENT

Internet payment

It has been discussed that the Internet can be used to make an offer and accept that offer. What has not been explained is how the Internet can be used to pay for the goods or services that may be the subject of the offer.

The introduction to this book explains in detail that everything passing through the Internet consists of digital ones and zeros. What varies is the way that digital stream is translated into an item at the end of its journey. The same can be said for methods of payment: unless the payment is made outside the confines of the Internet, the payment must be converted into zeros and ones.[14] There are two problems with this that do not concern us, but which are mentioned for completeness. The first problem is associated with the way the Internet moves digital streams between computers: they do not move directly; they can pass through many different computers on their way to a destination. Passing money through unknown computers is clearly unsafe. The second problem is that if digital money consists of only ones and zeros in a long string, it may be easy to duplicate the money. Any computer could potentially become a forgery for digital bank notes.

The technical solutions to both these problems are being addressed by many companies across the world. There are two main camps both using sophisticated encryption methods to secure technically the payment. Visa and Mastercard have joined forces to allow credit card details to be sent over the Internet securely; other companies such as DigiCash issue what is, in effect, a digital traveller's cheque that can also be sent securely across the Internet.[15] To the banking industry, the Bank of England and banking lawyers this issue of cash is obviously both interesting and important. These issues are covered in the chapter on banking. For the seller, buyer and their lawyers these new 'forms' of payment do not have any dramatic impact on contract law.

CREDIT CARD NON-PAYMENT

That there is a contract must be distinguished from who should pay for the goods or services, and what happens if that payment does not arrive. With a charge or credit card, the customer, by presenting a valid card, or by issuing a valid set of numbers, honours his obligations under the contract. Of course, at this point, a

---

14   A contract could be made over the Internet and a cheque sent by conventional mail.
15   For an acceptable summary of the non-legal issues involved, see Lynch DC & Lundquist L, *Digital Money* (John Wiley & Sons, New York, 1996). Readers should note that Daniel Lynch is the Chairman of Cybercash Inc, one of the larger digital cash providers; the book provides a tinted view of digital cash and does not address the use of credit cards over the Internet.

further contract comes into existence between the card company and the user to pay to the card company the full sum under the vendor's contract. If the card company does not pay the vendor, *and the card was valid*, the vendor's right of action is against the card company, not the individual.[16] One justification for this is that if the vendor was entitled to pursue the customer for payment in cash, the customer would lose the benefit of the payment by credit and, often, the insurance over the goods.[17] This would therefore increase the burden on the customer.

The commercially safest way of trading over the Internet is for vendors to insist on receiving and then validating payment *before* providing their side of the bargain. Terms to this effect should be incorporated into any standard form contract for trading over the Internet.

DIGITAL CASH NON-PAYMENT

Digital cash has two species. The first, more primitive, is like a charge card. The issuing bank provides the payment to the vendor on presentation of appropriate authority. The sum is then withdrawn from the user's account and transferred to the vendor's. Over the Internet this appropriate authority will be no more than the card number and, perhaps, its expiry date. This species can be called 'third party digital cash'. The second species of digital money is close to actual cash and will be called 'pure digital cash'. A customer has an agreement with a digital cash provider who allows the customer to send encrypted messages which represent sums of money. Once a customer sends one of these encrypted messages to a vendor, it can then be subsequently used by the vendor without having to go to the issuing bank for exchange into cash. The only time when the message will be exchanged into more regular currency is when someone seeks to deposit it in their bank. This new form of payment is a fascinating use of technology and is considered from a banking perspective in the banking chapter. It does not, though, greatly strain existing legal principles of payment.

Third party digital cash

As with a credit card, it is likely that a court will find that the issuing company is liable for the payment, rather than the user.[18] This view is carefully stated as being 'likely'. Both vendor and user should consider that the Court of Appeal has concluded that, merely because a third party has agreed to make payment to a vendor does not *automatically* mean that the risk of non-payment is removed from the user.[19]

Pure digital cash

Paying by the second species of digital money can be thought of as sending cash for most legal purposes. If the encrypted sum is lost in the Internet, or perhaps intercepted, the intended receiver will, no doubt, claim that payment has not been

---

16   *Re Charge Card Services Ltd* [1988] 3 All ER 702.
17   See, for example, the Consumer Credit Act 1974, s 75 which makes the credit card company liable for the vendor's misrepresentations and breaches of contract.
18   See 'Credit card non-payment', at page 30.
19   *Re Charge Card Services Ltd* [1988] 3 All ER 702 at 707.

made. To some extent this is the *general* rule: sending a banknote in the post, which is lost, will not constitute payment.[20] However, this appears inequitable where the intended receiver expressly permits payment to be made by such a method. Indeed, there is followed authority that if the intended receiver impliedly, or as will be the situation over the Internet, expressly, authorises transmission of payment in a particular way, the sender is discharged of liability if he follows the guidelines of transmission.[1]

---

11. A web site offers two methods for its viewers to pay to gain access to its materials: by credit card and by digital cash. A viewer sends by e-mail the digital cash, accesses the materials, but the cash is never received. The viewer may not be liable to pay again. The site impliedly authorises its customers to pay using the Internet as the conduit: the owner may not be able to transfer this risk to its customers having so authorised them.

If a web site seeks to allow payment to be made using digital cash, in either species, it must face the reality that the sum may not arrive. It should therefore incorporate into its contracts a term stipulating that its performance under the contract will be honoured only after *receipt* of the digital cash. Customers, in anticipation of this, should be wary of sending uninsured digital cash over the Internet. If the contract is suitably worded and held enforceable, the customer may lose the money and not benefit from the contract.

TYPE OF CONTRACT

Many owners of web sites do not only make contracts over the Internet, but also try to perform them over the Internet. Software companies distribute software from web sites; information and picture libraries provide digital copies of their information. As compression techniques are improved, movies and music will be sent across the Internet for payment. The various intellectual property rights that may vest in these items are discussed in the chapter on intellectual property. What is important here is to examine what should be the nature of the contract with the receiver of the digital information. The answer is a licence, and certainly not a sale, but justification for this is provided below.[2] The first justification is to attempt to side-step the principle of exhaustion of rights; the second, peculiar to digitised material, is to grant a licence to the user of the material.

Exhaustion of rights

If digitised copyright goods are *sold*, rather than licensed, within the EC there is a risk that the exhaustion of rights principle will apply. This principle is broadly that

---

20   See *Luttges v Sherwood* (1895) 11 TLR 233.
1   *Norman v Ricketts* (1886) 3 TLR 182.
2   Of course a sale contract is appropriate where goods are sent by mail to the customer. This section focuses on only the transmission of digital material such as software and digitised copyright material.

once goods protected by intellectual property rights are sold in any member state with the consent of the owner, national intellectual property laws cannot be used to block the goods' entry into another member state. The Copyright, Designs and Patents Act 1988 states this explicitly at section 27(5). Section 27(3A), for good measure, applies that principle to computer software: a copy of a computer program which has previously been sold in any member state by or with consent of the copyright owner will not be classed as an infringing copying within section 27(3).

RETENTION OF TITLE

Partially as an attempt to avoid the application of this principle, many producers of digital material do not sell it; they license it. To avoid being viewed as selling the material many manufacturers include a 'shrink-wrap' licence which explicitly retains title in the goods being passed to the consumer and states words to the effect, often in emboldened capitals, 'This software is not sold to you; we are licensing it to you.'

Using is copying

The material downloaded over the Internet is likely to be given legal recognition and protection as a copyright work under the Copyright, Designs and Patents Act 1988. It is this intellectual property right that forms the significant basis for any transaction.

For digital material to be used, it must first be transferred into a computer's memory.[3] This transfer exactly reproduces in the memory of the computer the words and characters of the material sent from the server. The material on the server remains unchanged and intact; two copies of the material now exist. An obvious comparison is that when one views a painting, the painting remains on the canvas and there is no need to copy the work. A digital version of the same painting can only be viewed by being copied.

The Copyright, Designs and Patents Act 1988 grants certain rights to the owner of a copyright work. In particular, section 16(1)(a) states that the owner has the *exclusive* right to copy the work. Thus, without a licence from the owner, under section 16(2), copying the work can constitute infringement of the copyright in the work. Copying any copyright work is defined widely as reproducing the work as a whole, or any substantial part, in any material form. This includes storing the work in a medium by electronic means.[4]

The viewer of the actual painting, like the viewer of the digitised version, is able to enjoy viewing an artistic work which attracts copyright protection. However, the viewing of the canvas does not involve a reproduction of the work in a material form. It can be seen, therefore, that normal use of a painting does not copy the copyright work. Conversely, an accurate application of the Copyright, Designs and Patents Act 1988 suggests that normal usage of any downloaded material *will* be regarded as a copy of the copyright work. This is because the

---

3   This transfer is coined 'loading'. This should not be confused with 'running' a program when a computer carries out the instructions specified by a program that has *already* been loaded.
4   Copyright, Designs and Patents Act 1988, ss 17(2) and 16(3)(a).

digitised material is necessarily reproduced by downloading it from the server into the computer's memory.

IMPLIED LICENCE

The above analysis may appear to indicate that if the owner of a web site does not give an express licence to each viewer of the site, each viewer is an infringer. This is not the case: copying a copyright work is not infringement if there is a licence permitting that copying. In the situation of the Internet there is undoubtedly a licence for authorised viewers and downloaders of material to copy the work.

First, the law is likely to imply a licence into the actions of the web site owner for reasons of business necessity. Second, a court could apply the so-called 'rule of non-derogation from grant' to prevent the publisher, having supplied the material, then alleging infringement.[5] Third, but specifically for computer programs, the Directive on the Legal Protection of Computer Programs at Article 5.1 specifies that the 'lawful acquirer' of a computer program shall not require authorisation by the copyright owner to run a computer program *in the absence of specific contractual provisions*.[6]

EXPRESS LICENCE

For programs, therefore, the Copyright, Designs and Patents Act 1988 expressly provides that a user has a right to copy the program into memory for its use. Viewers of graphics and sound, conversely, must rely on implications by the common law to legitimise their activities. And for programs, graphics and sound alike, the supplier of those materials may have to accept a court's wide understanding of what type of licence is implied. For example, an owner of a web site which sports a clever Java applet may only wish that program to be copied when the site is accessed; he may not wish that the applet is included on viewers' own web sites. Similarly, a designer of a graphic image used as a backdrop for a web site frame may not want its viewers to copy the image on to their own publications. To expressly prevent these unwanted uses, owners of copyright material used on the Internet are advised to use on-screen licences that leave no uses of the material to doubt or disagreement.

In providing a licence over the copyright material some publishers go further to attempt to exclude liability for certain damage caused by the material. The efficacy of these exclusion clauses is examined in the chapter on tort, but one point is worth noting here. The English courts will not uphold every exclusion clause. This is particularly true where the clause excludes liability to a consumer.

The conclusion from this section is simple: publishers should include express licences over their digital work to avoid exhaustion of rights and disagreements over acceptable use of the work.

---

5   See *British Leyland v Armstrong* [1986] RPC 279.
6   See the Copyright, Designs and Patents Act 1988, ss 50A, 50B, 50C, inserted by the Copyright (Computer Programs) Regulations 1992, SI 1992/3233, reg 8.

JURISDICTION

Every contract may form the basis of a dispute. Because the Internet allows an owner of a web site to form contracts with consumers from anywhere on the planet it is convenient for that owner to know where he can rightfully sue and be sued. The question over where a contract should be litigated is a question of private international law, or the conflict of laws.

The Civil Jurisdiction and Judgments Act 1982 incorporates the Brussels Convention on Jurisdiction and the Enforcement of Judgments in Civil and Commercial Matters.[7] This is the appropriate starting place for any contract formed over the Internet with a European element. First, one must assess whether the Convention applies or whether it 'transfers' jurisdiction to the English common law.

Jurisdiction of Conventions

CIVIL OR COMMERCIAL MATTER

Most contracts made over the Internet will fall within Article 1, that is, the resulting dispute is a civil or commercial matter. Before deciding that the Convention applies, litigants are advised to consider specialist texts and cases from the European Court which highlight the broad scope of Article 1.

DOMICILE OF DEFENDANT

Subject to Articles outside the scope of this chapter,[8] the fundamental issue is where the defendant is domiciled. Article 2 establishes that persons domiciled in a state party to the Conventions, a contracting state, can be sued in the courts of that state, sometimes with the plaintiff having a choice of another forum. Articles 52 and 53 direct the English courts to consider the domicile of the defendant with reference to the Civil Jurisdiction and Judgments Act 1982, sections 41 and 42 respectively. Even for contracts made over the Internet, jurisdiction hinges on 'domicile', an essentially static concept which is mostly unrelated to the complex factors such as where a server is based.

For Convention purposes, a defendant can be domiciled in two types of state: a contracting state or a non-contracting state. If the defendant is domiciled within a contracting state, the Convention rules apply; if outside, the common law rules will apply. These two outcomes are decided with reference to the Civil Jurisdiction and Judgments Act 1982.

---

7   For the purposes of this section the relevant articles of the Lugano Convention remain identical to those in the Brussels (1979 OJ C 59), Greek Accession (1989 OJ C 298), and San Sebastián (1990 OJ C 189/35) Conventions. Readers are nevertheless advised to check on which Convention they are relying to provide advice.
8   The articles which are excluded from discussion are: Article 54, supervening Conventions; Articles 21 and 22, *lis alibi pendens*; Article 16, exclusive jurisdiction; Articles 7-12A, insurance *contract* provisions.

Individual's domicile

United Kingdom domicile

An individual is domiciled within the United Kingdom only if he is resident in the United Kingdom and the nature and circumstances of his residence indicate that he has a substantial connection with the United Kingdom.[9] It is presumed, unless proved otherwise, that being resident for the last three months will constitute the requisite substantial connection.[10] The ownership, control or access to a web site anywhere in the world is wholly irrelevant for the purposes of jurisdiction over an individual under the Conventions. If an individual is a United Kingdom resident nothing will be gained for jurisdiction purposes by locating a web server 'offshore'.

Convention state domicile

If an individual is not domiciled in the United Kingdom for the purposes of the Conventions, one must decide whether the individual is domiciled within another contracting state. If he is not, the Convention will not apply to the dispute; questions of jurisdiction are resolved at common law.

An individual is domiciled in a state other than the United Kingdom if that other state would view him as domiciled in that state. Therefore, to determine whether a defendant in an Internet contract dispute is domiciled within a contracting state that person's domicile must be assessed from *that* state's legal perspective. Failing this, the Civil Jurisdiction and Judgments Act 1982, section 41(7) establishes the test to determine whether a defendant is domiciled outside contracting states.

Non-contracting state domicile

An individual is domiciled outside all the contracting states if none of those states would deem him to be domiciled within their jurisdiction and if a further two-part test is satisfied. First, the individual must be resident in the non-contracting state, and second, the nature and circumstances of his residence indicate that he has a substantial connection with that state.[11] One is not required to consult the non-contracting state's law on domicile.

---

12. **An English programmer who lives in England licenses his programs from an American web server. Another programmer, also from England, transfers his digital cash payment for the software but does not receive a working copy of the software so litigates. Without a jurisdiction clause in the contract, the English courts will have jurisdiction over the dispute as the defendant is domiciled in England. The location of the server is of no relevance for jurisdiction over the programmer in the English courts.**

---

9   Civil Jurisdiction and Judgments Act 1982, s 41(2).
10   Civil Jurisdiction and Judgments Act 1982, s 41(6).
11   Civil Jurisdiction and Judgments Act 1982, s 41(7).

If the result of the domicile tests is that an individual defendant is domiciled within a contracting state, the Conventions will apply to any other questions of jurisdiction. If the result is that the defendant is domiciled outside the contracting states, the English common law rules on jurisdiction will apply.[12] These are described after the Convention rules.[13]

Corporation's or association's domicile

A corporation or association has its domicile in the state where it has its seat.[14]

United Kingdom domicile

A corporation or association is domiciled within the United Kingdom only if it was incorporated or formed under a law of a part of the United Kingdom, *and* its registered office or other official address is in the United Kingdom.[15] Alternatively, a corporation or association can be considered as having a United Kingdom seat if it exercises its central management and control in the United Kingdom.[16] Again, the ownership, control or access to a web site anywhere in the world is mostly irrelevant for the purposes of jurisdiction under the Conventions. A corporation which is, in effect, based in the United Kingdom will not be able to avoid the jurisdiction of the English courts simply by using an offshore server.

Convention state domicile

If a corporation or association is not domiciled in the United Kingdom for the purposes of the Conventions, one must decide whether it is domiciled within another contracting state. If it is not, the Convention will not apply to the dispute; questions of jurisdiction are decided with recourse to the common law. A corporation is domiciled in a state other than the United Kingdom if it satisfies two tests: one under English law, the other under non-English law.

First, the English courts must be satisfied that the corporation or association has its seat in a contracting state. As under Civil Jurisdiction and Judgments Act 1982, section 42(3), the corporation or association must be incorporated or formed under the law of that state and have its registered office or some other official address there.[17] Alternatively, a corporation or association will be deemed as seated in another contracting state if its central management and control is exercised in that state.[18]

The second test that must also be affirmatively answered, is that the courts of the contracting state must agree that the corporation or association has its seat there. Both tests must be satisfied for the defendant corporation or association to be judged as having a domicile within a contracting state. If either test is not

---

12 Article 4.
13 See 'Common law jurisdiction over contracts', at page 40.
14 Article 53.
15 Civil Jurisdiction and Judgments Act 1982, s 42(3)(a).
16 Civil Jurisdiction and Judgments Act 1982, s 42(3)(b).
17 Civil Jurisdiction and Judgments Act 1982, s 43(6)(a).
18 Civil Jurisdiction and Judgments Act 1982, s 43(6)(b).

satisfied, the common law rules on jurisdiction will apply;[19] these are discussed after the Convention rules.

---

13. A health-food company is incorporated and operates from England. It sells health-foods across the world. Its server is physically based in New Zealand and the domain name has a suffix indicating a New Zealand firm. A French supplier of health-food enters into a contract, over the Internet, for a large shipment of dried mushrooms. The contract does not have a jurisdiction clause. The mushrooms do not arrive and the health-food company claims it is not at fault. The French supplier tries to sue the company in the English courts. The use of an off-shore server will have no bearing on the court's jurisdiction over the company. The English courts will have jurisdiction over the company at least for the reason that it would consider the company having its seat within England.

Non-contracting state domicile

If both of the previous tests fail to establish the defendant as domiciled in the United Kingdom or another contracting state, the common law rules on jurisdiction will apply.

Convention jurisdiction over contract

Having decided that the Convention applies, unless the contract is classed as a consumer contract or unless the contract has a jurisdiction clause, the defendant may only be sued in his domicile.[20] Europe-based owners of web sites who are concerned about being sued outside their home state should be concerned only if their contracts are with consumers. As will be discussed, for consumers, the general rule is reversed and consumers can sue and can only be sued in *their* home state.[1] As the majority of users of the Internet are consumers but the majority of web site owners are suppliers or professionals, this reversal will frequently occur. Those who own web sites, therefore, may find themselves having to litigate and be sued away from home unless they can persuade a court that the nature of the dispute does not concern a 'consumer contract'.

Consumer contracts

At first glance it may appear there is a straightforward answer to the question of which is the correct forum for a dispute over a contract made with a consumer. The Brussels Convention contains rules to protect consumers in relation to consumer contracts, from being sued, or having to sue, otherwise than in the

19   Article 4.
20   Article 2.
 1   Articles 13 and 14.

member state of their domicile.[2] This would appear to settle the issue: those who trade over the Internet risk only being able to sue European consumers in Europe, and may face litigation in Europe.

Looking more closely at the Convention though, there is an argument that it is incorrect always to apply these exclusive rules. Many contracts made over the Internet are not for the supply of physical goods or even services; they are licences in which it is stated expressly that no sale is taking place.[3] In contrast, under the Convention, a 'consumer contract' includes only contracts for the sale of goods or the supply of services.[4] So, although the viewer or downloader of digital material is a 'consumer' in the wide sense of this word, on a strict view the contract in dispute may not be a 'consumer contract' for the Convention.[5]

General provisions of jurisdiction

If this analysis is correct so that an on-screen or web-wrap licence over digital material is not a 'consumer contract', a court's jurisdiction over licence disputes will be assessed under the general jurisdiction rules of the Brussels Convention as already examined. This removes the protection for the consumer in respect of the litigating forum and jurisdiction clauses.[6]

If a web site owner seeks to sue a consumer domiciled in England, the litigation will take place in England. This is similar to the situation with a consumer contract. Differences occur if the consumer wants to sue the web site owner, for

---

2   The Brussels Convention, Articles 13 and 14, in conjunction with the Civil Jurisdiction and Judgments Act 1982, s 44.
3   This said, classification of a contract as a contract for the sale of goods or supply of services, as opposed to a licence, should be determined by examining the terms of the contract, 'the substance of the contract'. See *Robinson v Graves* [1935] 1 KB 579 at 587. A web-wrap licence passes to the consumer only *rights* over the digital material, never *title* to it; the licence is therefore *not* a contract for the sale of goods. A supply of services generating a product, such as a fur coat, generally is with reference to 'bespoke tailoring' of a product for one or some individuals. In contrast, one would not expect that the purchase of clothes from Marks & Spencer is governed by a contract for the supply of services merely because a 'service' has created the garments; Mark & Spencer's 'service' creates a product which is then *sold*. Similarly, the creation of a web site is not performed for any specific individual, it is simply the necessary procedure to create the digital material then *to license*. This analysis accords with the admitted obiter dictum of Sir Iain Glidewell in *St Alban's City and District Council v International Computers Ltd* [1996] 4 All ER 481. Sir Iain stated, at 493, that 'the program is not "goods" within the statutory definition [of the Sale of Goods Act 1979]. Thus a transfer of the program [where it was transferred on to the computer by a third party] does not, in my view, constitute a transfer of goods.' Over the Internet, similarly, goods do not pass between server and browser, so it seems to be true at law to state that there is no contract for a sale of goods.
4   The Brussels Convention, Article 13(1).
5   This is unless a court adopts an extreme teleological approach to the legal nature of the web-wrap or on-screen licence. Under the Civil Jurisdiction and Judgments Act 1982, ss 3(3) and 3B(2) the court may interpret a term with reference to the Jenard, Schlosser, 1982, or 1989 reports (see Schlosser Report [1979] OJ C 59/117 at para 153). For example, see *Shearson Lehman Hutton Inc v Treuhandgesellschaft für Vermgensverwaltung und Beteiligungen mbH* [1993] IL Pr 199 at 220[13], '[Some terms] must be interpreted independently, having regard primarily to the general scheme and the objectives of the Convention. *This must apply particularly to the term "consumer"* ... ' Emphasis added. Cf restrictive interpretation in *New Hampshire v Strabag Bau* [1992] 1 Lloyd's Rep 361 at 367, col 1-369 col 1.
6   The Brussels Convention, Article 15.

example for a *declaration*[7] that an exclusion term in the contract is invalid and not binding. In this situation, if the owner is not domiciled[8] in the United Kingdom, the consumer will have to brave the courts of another state.

JURISDICTION CLAUSES

In practice, most on-screen licences specify that the courts of one state have exclusive jurisdiction. As one of the parties is domiciled in a contracting state, if the term refers to the court of a contracting state then that court has jurisdiction.[9] This applies only for those contracts not considered by a court to be a 'consumer contract'; even a jurisdiction clause cannot derogate from the protection afforded to consumers.

---

14. A UK consumer downloads some software from a French web site after selecting an icon labelled 'I Agree' at the bottom of a set of terms and conditions. The contract makes clear that no goods are being sent to the consumer and that, anyway, no title passes to the consumer; the consumer is gaining only a licence to use the software. The final clause of the contract, in capitals, is 'By clicking "I Agree", you submit to the French courts to resolve any dispute arising under or related to this licence.' The consumer at a later date seeks to sue in an English court the owner of the web site for breach of contract as the software is defective. The French web site owner may have some success in preventing the English courts from accepting jurisdiction because the contract was a licence of software not a contract for a sale of goods or supply of services. As a result the jurisdiction clause may apply despite the contract being with a consumer.

Common law jurisdiction over contracts

If the defendant to an Internet contract is not domiciled within a contracting state,[10] the court must apply its domestic laws to determine jurisdiction.[11] Two main methods will be considered below: service by presence in England as of right, and service abroad with leave. The first of these methods is considered in detail in the chapter on tort[12] and readers are advised to consider this before reading this section on service abroad with leave.

7   RSC Ord 15, r 16. Despite the legal issue, it is accepted that it is unusual for a consumer to seek a declaration; more usually a consumer would wait to be sued and then plead as defence and counter-claim the invalidity of the contract. However, a declaration would be necessary to allow the consumer to avoid a web-wrap licence's broad exclusions of liability and rely on narrower common law and statutory exclusions. See Zamir J & Woolf J, *The Declaratory Judgment* (Sweet & Maxwell, London, 1993, 2nd edn).
8   The Brussels Convention, Article 53(1) provides that the 'seat' of a company is its domicile. The term 'seat' includes companies that have a registered address or *other official address* in the UK. So, non-domestic publishers with sales divisions in the UK may be considered as being domiciled in the UK.
9   The Brussels Convention, Article 17(1).
10   See 'Domicile of defendant', at page 35.
11   Article 4.
12   See pages 117 to 120.

SERVICE OUT

There are two separate and distinct aspects to serving out of the jurisdiction.[13] The first aspect is jurisdiction: does the plaintiff's claim fall within one of the heads of RSC Ord 11, r 1(1). This test does not need to be satisfied to any high degree of proof: a good arguable case that the claim is covered by the one of the heads is sufficient.[14] The second aspect, which will not be covered here in great detail, is one of discretion: no leave to serve out will be granted unless it is sufficiently shown that the case is a proper one for service out of the jurisdiction. This is specified by RSC Ord 11, r 4(2).

Jurisdiction under a contract head

The most common head that will apply in certain cases for contracts entered over the Internet is RSC Ord 11, r 1(1)(d). This is where:[15]

> 'the claim is brought to enforce, rescind, dissolve, annul or otherwise affect a contract, or to recover damages or obtain other relief in respect of the breach of a contract ...'

This subsection then goes on to describe a number of contracts which will fall for consideration under this rule. These include: a contract which is by its terms, or implication, governed by English law;[16] a contract with a term to the effect that the High Court shall have jurisdiction to hear and determine any action in respect of the contract; a claim brought in respect of a breach committed within the jurisdiction; a contract made by or through an agent trading or residing within the jurisdiction on behalf of a principal trading or residing outside of the jurisdiction. For the purposes of Internet contracts, however, the most contentious head is where the contract was made within the jurisdiction.

Where a contract is made

The earlier part of this chapter focuses on *when* a contract is deemed to have been made when formed by e-mail or over the World Wide Web. It is now appropriate to consider *where* such a contract is formed. The implications of where a contract is formed are great. For example, if contracts made over the web are made at the place of the server it will be simple for an organisation always to ensure that their contracts are formed outside Europe, or any other jurisdiction they wish to avoid. A server can be physically located anywhere in the world despite its owner and clients being elsewhere. Conversely, if a contract is deemed to be formed wherever a consumer is situated at the time of making a contract the owner of a web site may find himself making contracts throughout the world.

There is no case law on this area although by analogy it is submitted that contracts made using e-mail will be viewed as being made where the acceptance

---

13 See *Seaconsar v Bank Merkazi Jomhouri Islami Iran* [1993] 4 All ER 456.
14 See *Attock v Romanian Bank for Foreign Trade* [1989] 1 All ER 1189.
15 Of course, RSC Ord 11, r 1(1)(a) or (b) may be more appropriate in some circumstances.
16 This question would probably be settled by recourse to the Rome Convention, see 'Choice of law', at page 45.

e-mail is sent, and contracts made over the World Wide Web will be viewed as being made where the client is.

E-mail contracts

It has been suggested that an e-mailed acceptance is very like a posted acceptance in the eyes of the law: it can go astray and it depends on the actions of a third party for proper delivery without the sender necessarily knowing of its arrival.[17] In such circumstances this chapter has suggested that the exception should apply to the general rule of 'communication of acceptance': the so-called 'postal rule' should apply deeming the time of making the contract the time of its posting, not its receipt. It follows that the contract is completed when the letter is posted, or for our purposes, when the e-mail is sent.

The 'postal rule' also applies if an acceptance is not simply delayed in the post but if the acceptance never reaches the offeror.[18] It must therefore be true that the contract is also made at that *place* of posting; if this were not the case, a letter which becomes lost in the post may be deemed to form a contract at a place where it was *meant to arrive* at a time before it *could have arrived* and, in fact, at a place where it *never arrives*. To avoid such fictions, the rule applied by the English courts has been that 'acceptance is complete as soon as the letter is put into the letter box, *and that is the place where the contract is made*'.[19]

For a contract made using e-mail, it is submitted that the place where the contract is made is the place from where the acceptor sent the e-mail; it is not from where the server which sends the e-mail is located. Just as a postal contract is made from the place at which the acceptor no longer has control over the letter, ie the letter box, so the place where an e-mail contract is made is at the acceptor's computer.

---

15. An American, who uses a German Internet Service Provider, sends an e-mail to an English property developer. The e-mail contains a certain offer to buy the individual's holiday home in Florida. The English property developer firmly accepted the offer by sending an e-mail from his London offices. Technically, this e-mail acceptance is sent from London, to a French server and then on to the American's inbox located in Germany. The American reads the e-mail using a laptop computer and a mobile phone while in Mexico. If the contract is deemed to be formed when the English e-mail was sent, it will be formed at the place where it was sent: London.

Web site contracts

Contracts made over the World Wide Web, as previously examined, differ considerably from e-mail contracts.[20] On the assumption made earlier that the general rule applies, and that there is no binding contract until notice of

---

17   See 'Acceptances by e-mail', at page 23.
18   See *Household, etc, Insurance v Grant* (1879) 4 Ex D 216.
19   *Entores Ltd v Miles Far East Corpn* [1955] 2 QB 327 at 332, per Denning LJ. Emphasis added. See also *Benaim v Debono* [1924] AC 514.
20   See 'Acceptances over the World Wide Web', at page 26.

acceptance is received by the offeror, the contract is made at the place where the offeror receives notification of the acceptance; where the offeror is.[1]

> **16. A bookseller based in Chicago establishes a web site within a digital mall which is based in New York. The mall uses a standardised online order form which ensures users make offers which are then accepted, if appropriate, by the individual stores. A teacher in England orders two books by American authors and the web site responds with an acceptance notice that the books would be delivered to the teacher's address. This contract is made in England because the notification of acceptance, to the teacher, is received in England.**

The conclusion that a web site make contracts wherever its customers are, assuming the web site accepts, accords with the case law and also accords with the business reality of the World Wide Web. The web, more than any other medium, allows vendors from around the world to sell easily to English consumers. For a vendor, it is akin to having an agent in every town in the world who can visit every customer at home. A user only needs to make a local 'phone call to and receive acceptances from foreign vendors at home. The contracts being formed have every indication that they are being made in England.

The reason for discussing where a contract is made, it will be recalled, was to determine whether an English consumer could serve a writ out of England in respect of a contract to a foreign web site owner. However, even if a dispute falls within one of the heads of RSC Ord 11, r 1(1) a court has discretion whether to permit the service out.

Discretion under service out

It is not sufficient simply to satisfy a court of a good arguable case under one of the heads of RSC Ord 11, r 1(1). The claim must also be a proper case for service out under RSC Ord 11, r 4(2). The discretion to serve out includes as a main factor, an assessment, perhaps not overtly, of whether England is the *forum conveniens*, the most suitable forum in which to hear the dispute. This will be considered briefly in the following section on staying actions.[2] This discretionary factor should not be overlooked by legal advisers: for a contract made over the Internet it may be difficult to persuade a court to serve out. If the defendant, in contrast, is domiciled in Europe, the court has far less discretion over jurisdiction.[3]

---

1   See *Entores v Miles Far East Corpn* [1955] 2 QB 327 at 336 per Parker LJ; also *Brinkibon Ltd v Stahag Stahl GmbH* [1983] 2 AC 34 at 41 and 43 respectively, per Lord Wilberforce and Lord Fraser.
2   The court's assessment is the same, although for service out, the plaintiff must ask the court to exercise discretion; for staying service as of right, the defendant must persuade the court to stay the action.
3   See the Court of Appeal's interpretation of the Civil Jurisdiction and Judgments Act 1982, s 49 in *Re Harrods (Buenos Aires) Ltd* [1991] 4 All ER 334.

STAYING ACTIONS

It is always open to a putative defendant to apply to stay the common law jurisdiction of the English courts by pleading that it is not the most suitable forum in which to resolve the dispute. Whether a court stays an action is decided with recourse to the principle of *forum non conveniens*. This principle is impressively explained and stated in the House of Lords' decision in *Spiliada Maritime Corpn v Cansulex Ltd*.[4] A full discussion of this case is beyond the scope of this chapter, but an appreciation of its *implications* is worthwhile. Until courts approach Internet disputes with the familiarity and understanding that they approach, say the telephone and telex, litigators must be prepared to argue that despite the transnational nature of the Internet, some forums are more suitable than others.

Lord Goff provided the leading judgment given in *Spiliada*. He set out a number of guidelines[5] that may guide a court as to whether England is a suitable and appropriate forum: the court must, in effect, balance the suitability of England against that of another forum. This forum must be clearly and distinctly more appropriate: one 'with which the action [has] the most real and substantial connection'.[6] Once this clearly and distinctly more appropriate forum has been found the court will stay the action unless the plaintiff can prove that he clearly will not be able to obtain justice there.

This discretion, unlikely to be disturbed on appeal,[7] may be of paramount importance in an Internet dispute. In contrast to most other means of communication, the Internet can make it appear that a defendant has little connection with any country. A server may be in a country far away from the defendant's domicile. Worse than this, a defendant may be using a mall situated on the other side of the world. The contract and possibly digital product that is the root of the dispute may have passed through as many as one hundred countries. Worse still, it is a question of technical semantics to resolve whether the digital product moved from the server to the plaintiff or whether the plaintiff 'collected' the digital product from the server.

These issues, and many more like them, may be used to cloud the answer to which is the *forum conveniens* for the dispute. The pivotal question before the courts should be: which is the suitable forum in the interests of all the parties and the ends of justice?

The answering of this question involves examining the mechanics of hearing the dispute as well as its geographical basis. In illustration, often it is important to know where the relevant evidence is held and where the relevant witnesses live.[8] For many Internet disputes, however, such factors may not be weighty enough to disturb the jurisdiction of the court. Computer files will often be the main evidence and often the consumer in England will be the sole human witness to the contract itself. So, for an Internet dispute, the jurisdiction of the English court may be less easily upset. As a further illustration, the issue of convenience, often a factor for the court, may be less convincing when all of the actual evidence is in a digital format. Such evidence can be sent to England, over the Internet, cheaply, quickly and accurately. Again, the actual nature of the Internet may lead to the conclusion that little is lost by hearing the dispute in England.

---

4   [1986] 3 All ER 843.
5   The necessary details of these guidelines can be found in specialist texts.
6   *The Abidin Daver* [1984] 1 All ER 470, at 478 per Lord Keith.
7   [1986] 3 All ER 843 at 846–847 per Lord Templeman.
8   See [1986] 3 All ER 843 at 855.

The court must consider all the relevant factors, such as where the defendant and plaintiff are and which law will apply to this dispute. It is discussed in the next section that, without a choice of law clause, English law will generally apply to contracts made over the web with English consumers. Even with a choice of law clause, protection for English consumers will apply in addition to the stated law. And Lord Goff in *Spiliada* notes that the law of the dispute will often be a relevant factor.[9] What can be concluded from all this is that presence of the Internet in a contract dispute will never create the situation where no court is appropriate to hear the case.

CHOICE OF LAW

The Organisation for Economic Co-operation and Development has stated, perhaps a little pessimistically, the problems of examining the choice of law over the Internet.[10]

'[T]he question of choice of law ... is particularly difficult in the case of international computer networks where, because of dispersed location and rapid movement of data, and geographically dispersed processing activities, several connecting factors could occur in a complex manner involving elements of legal novelty.'

The following section is included because the Internet makes the questions of choice of laws more *prevalent*. As the use of the Internet expands, more commerce will be conducted using it; more contracts will be formed between consumers and suppliers in different jurisdictions.[11] It is essential that the law which applies to a contract is established *before* applying the reasoning in this chapter. This chapter describes nothing wider than the application of English law to a contract. That the conflict of laws is more relevant to transactions over the Internet should not suggest that the Internet demands any legal novelties in this area. After all, the principles in the conflict of laws exist for the very reason that multi-jurisdictional contracts can be made.

---

9   With reference to *Crédit Chimique v James Scott Engineering Group Ltd* 1982 SLT 131. In this Scottish case, Lord Jauncy goes further and asks that a court look not simply at the fact that foreign law will be applied, but to look deeper at the *nature* of the foreign law. It may be that it is trivial for an English court to turn its mind to the foreign law, but it also may be that the law is so alien that the most appropriate court to consider the legal issues is a court which regularly deals with them.

10 Organisation for Economic Co-operation and Development, Explanatory Memorandum, *Guidelines on the Protection of Privacy and Transborder Flows of Personal Data*, 13, 36 (1980).

11 It is, of course, correct to state that the telephone, telex and fax also allow transnational contracts to be made. The significant difference between the Internet and these other means of communication is that there are no temporal, financial or logistical problems with contacting a web site abroad. The site is permanently switched on, time differences are not a relevant factor; the cost is that of a local phone call, there is no increase in marginal cost, unlike fax, telex and telephone; and the new generation of web sites can translate their content and instructions into the home language of the person contracting. These factors will increase the popularity of the Internet as a method for consumers to contract.

The Rome Convention

Where the litigation over a dispute takes place in England, and its substance is a contractual obligation made over the Internet, the Rome Convention[12] will generally apply.[13] This section is concerned mainly with those contracts where one party contracts using a web site.

For the purposes of the Rome Convention, and therefore English law, there are two possible types of contract that can be made over the Internet: one in which the law that will govern the contract is agreed, and one in which it is not. These two possibilities will be dealt with, but it is worthwhile noting here that there is little justification for not including an applicable law in a contract. It provides more certainty, and some insurance policies will protect only contracts governed by English law.

EXPRESS CHOICE OF LAW

The first issue to understand is that although an Internet contract may contain an agreed choice of law, other laws may be applicable in addition. It will be seen below that certain mandatory laws of England will be applied despite choice, and that consumers benefit from certain other protections.

It is significant that no special words are required to choose a law for a contract. The Convention states that a choice can be express, or demonstrated with reasonable certainty by the terms of the contract or the circumstances of the case.[14] Both parties should be aware therefore that an express choice may be deemed to have been made even where a contract does not express 'The Law governing this contract will be the laws of England'. Where an Internet contract does express the choice in such unambiguous terms, that law will apply to the contract. A supplier can choose a law to evade the application of less favourable rules, but in certain circumstances that chosen law will be modified by English mandatory laws and consumer protective measures.[15]

Demonstration of choice

The Giuliano and Lagarde report[16] provides some guidance of what is a demonstration with reasonable certainty that a contract is governed by a

---

12   The Rome Convention is incorporated into the Contracts (Applicable Law) Act 1990. References to articles within the Convention can be located in the Schedules to the domestic statute. The Convention can be interpreted by recourse to the Giuliano and Lagarde report (OJ 1980, C282/10), see the Contracts (Applicable Law) Act 1990, s 3(3)(a).

13   The justification for this bold statement is that the Convention applies to contracts made after 1 April 1991 (Article 17). In view of the youth of the Internet it is presumed that contracts made using it were made after this date. Attention is drawn to Article 1(2) which lists the exceptions of its application. These include, among others, contractual obligations relating to wills and succession (Article 1(2)(b)), obligations arising under negotiable instruments to the extent that the obligations arise out of their negotiable character (Article 1(2)(c)), questions governed by the law of companies such as creation, legal capacity, and personal liability of officers and members (Article 1(2)(e)), questions as to whether an agent is able to bind a principal (Article 1(2)(f)). To give definitive advice, therefore, advisers should consult a specialist text such as Dicey & Morris, *The Conflict of Laws* (Sweet & Maxwell, London, 1994, 12th edn).

14   Article 3(1).

15   See 'Modifications to express or demonstrated law', at page 47.

16   See fn 12, above.

particular law.[17] Where a standard form is used, such as Lloyd's policy of marine insurance, it can be taken that a choice of English law has been made. However, this does not suggest that a standard form of a lesser known company can suffice as a reasonably certain demonstration. This is especially the case when contracting over the Internet where it is possible, for example, unknowingly, to enter a contract to buy an American piece of software but from a French distributor. In this scenario there will not be sufficient certainty to demonstrate any choice of law for the contract.

Other indicators within the terms of the contract may demonstrate this certainty. For example, references to the courts of England, and English statutes, say the Copyright, Designs and Patents Act 1988 and the Consumer Credit Act 1974, may leave a court in no doubt that English law was always intended to apply despite the lack of its expression.

---

17. A web-wrap contract expresses that the jurisdiction of California shall apply for all disputes but that this will not exclude the application of any consumer protection laws applicable in the consumer's place of residence. No express choice of law is made. This confusion over jurisdiction and choice of law, and the lack of other indicators will be unlikely to demonstrate the reasonable certainty required that a particular law was deliberately chosen.

Modifications to express or demonstrated law

Mandatory rules

Even though an Internet contract may expressly state that the law of France should apply, if all the other relevant factors to the situation at the time of choice are connected with one country only, the mandatory rules of that country will remain applicable.[18] A mandatory rule is one that cannot be derogated from by contract.[19] Examples from English law include the Employment Protection (Consolidation) Act 1978, section 158(5), and the Sex Discrimination Act 1975, sections 6 and 10(1). The most relevant example for contracting over the Internet is the Unfair Contract Terms Act 1977, section 27(2).[20] This particular Act is discussed below.

A mandatory law will apply in the limited circumstances that *all* relevant factors are connected with *one* country. This is a high burden and one which will be difficult to satisfy where the parties reside in different countries. In such a situation, clearly not all the relevant factors are connected with solely one country. And where downloading, or shipment, occurs from a country other than that of the purchaser's residence the mandatory rules will be unlikely to operate.

One more point must be made about mandatory rules. The mandatory rules that may apply need not be those from England. The first test is to establish a country with which all the elements of the situation are connected. This country

---

17   OJ 1980, C282/10 at C282/17.
18   Rome Convention, Article 3(3).
19   To establish that a law is mandatory is a matter for interpretation of, generally, the relevant statute.
20   The Unfair Contract Terms Act 1977, s 27(2)(a) states that the Act will apply also if a term in a contract appears to have been included 'wholly or mainly' to avoid the operation of the Act.

may be somewhere other than England. And if the second aspect of the test is satisfied, that the laws are mandatory, the English court must apply them in addition to the chosen or demonstrated law of the contract.

---

18. A web site, based in England and controlled by an English company, uses the same contract for all those who wish to download its software. The contract specifies that the law of New York will apply. If an American contracts with the web site and is then sued in England, it is unlikely that English mandatory rules will apply. In contrast, if an English consumer contracts with the site, it may appear that all the relevant elements relate to England so that the mandatory rules will apply.

This difference in application depending on who makes a contract with a web site can pose certain difficulties: the main one is that, if the same contract is used for all jurisdictions, its effect will differ for different consumers. Web owners should be conscious that using one standard form contract, and allowing a person from any jurisdiction to complete that contract, may result in an unforeseen situation. Where possible a web site should use a contract that is, at the least, predictable for each of the possible locations from where a consumer may contract. Some web site owners have a home page where their viewers must select their residence from a list before a contract is presented for their acceptance.

Application of UCTA

Where a court deems that the mandatory laws of England do apply to a contract it is necessary to check whether UCTA applies. The Act will apply to certain contracts governed by *non-English* law, where either or both

> 'the [choice of law] term appears to the court ... to have been imposed wholly or mainly for the purpose of enabling a party imposing it to evade the operation of this Act; or
> in the making of the contract one of the parties dealt as consumer, and he was then habitually resident in the United Kingdom, and the essential steps necessary for the making of the contract were taken there, whether by him or by others on his behalf.'

It is important to realise that the operation of this does not strike down the choice of foreign law; it merely makes the operation of that law subject to the effect of UCTA.

Despite the above, not all the protection that UCTA provides to consumers and businesses will be applicable to certain contracts made over the Internet. This is because, if the contract is an 'international supply contract', UCTA's rules on 'excluding or restricting' liability[1] will not apply.

An international supply contract has three features.[2] First, it must be either a contract for the sale of goods or one under or in pursuance of which the possession or ownership of goods passes. Second, it must be made between parties whose places of business or residences are in territories of different states. The third feature is that there must be an international aspect to the contract: the

---

1   Unfair Contract Terms Act 1977, s 26(1).
2   Unfair Contract Terms Act 1977, s 26(3) and (4).

goods must be carried from one territory to another; or, the acts constituting offer and acceptance must have been done in different states; or, the contract must provide for the goods to be delivered to a place other than where these acts are done.

So, although an English court may decide that UCTA applies to regulate a foreign contract, a foreign seller of goods who forms contracts over the Internet will not be bound by UCTA's restraints on exclusion of liability clauses. Applying the same reasoning, the operation of UCTA *can* prevent a foreign supplier of services from unreasonably excluding liability.

> **19. An American wine seller sets up a web site with its standard form contract expressing no jurisdiction clause but an express choice that the law of New York shall apply to any disputes. A UK consumer is made ill by the wine delivered and understands that under the Unfair Contract Terms Act 1977 the supplier's contract could not exclude its liability. This is a mandatory law but it will not apply to prevent this exclusion of liability because the contract is for the international supply of goods.**

This contrast between the application of the Act to goods and services may be crucial to the supply of digital information over the Internet. It has been mentioned that the supply of software over the Internet is likely not to be classified as a sale of goods, indeed no title passes and there is no physical possession.[3] Certainly, if the obiter dictum of Sir Iain Glidewell is followed,[4] supplies of software made over the Internet will not be international supply contracts for the purposes of UCTA. As a result these contracts *will* be subject to UCTA's rules on the exclusions and restrictions of liability.

> **20. Two American software suppliers set up web sites to provide software to English consumers. Both suppliers utilise an on-screen contract which excludes all liability and choose the contract to be governed by 'the Laws of the State of New York to the extent that all non-American consumer protection provisions will be inapplicable.' One supplier provides the software by shipping it on a CD-ROM to the English consumer. UCTA will not operate to restrict the application of the exclusion clause because this is an international supply contract. The other supplier decides to download the software to consumers using the Internet. UCTA will operate to restrict the application of the exclusion clause because the contract is not an international supply contract as no goods are passed.**

Consumer contracts

Far more common than the application of a mandatory rule to a contract is the application of a particular mandatory rule, consumer protection laws. Article 5(2)

---

3   See fn 3, at page 39.
4   See *St Alban's City and District Council v International Computers Ltd* [1996] 4 All ER 481 at 492–494.

expresses that in certain circumstances a choice of law made by the parties shall not deprive the consumer of the protection afforded by the mandatory rules from the law of his country of habitual residence. Previously it has been said that this provision will have very limited effect because English consumers generally buy from English suppliers under contracts governed by English law.[5] This certainly was the case even for goods manufactured abroad. The Internet may alter this though; it is now feasible and attractive for manufacturers from abroad to contract directly with their consumers, missing out the domestic supplier. It is now relevant for these manufacturers to appreciate the effect of Article 5. It will affect their decision whether to sell over the Internet and what legal advice they should take.[6]

Before considering these circumstances, which are usually satisfied over the World Wide Web, one must address what is a consumer contract. For the same reasons as described under jurisdiction, the courts may not consider a licence over copyright material to be a consumer contract. On the basis that such a licence *is* classified as a consumer contract, parties contracting over the Internet should appreciate the conditions that must prevail for the consumer protection to apply.

Web sites and consumers

Article 5(2) specifies that there are three ways in which the mandatory consumer protective laws will apply to a contract where a choice of law has been made or demonstrated appropriately. One of these ways directly concerns a contract made over the Internet:

> 'if in that country the conclusion of the contract was preceded by a specific invitation addressed to him or by advertising, and he had taken in that country all the steps necessary on his part for the conclusion of the contract ...'

This chapter has explained that a court may view a web site as a form of advertising. This is very likely where the web site does not even attempt to block viewers from specified countries, either technically or by consent. It has also been explained that, clicking a download button, or simply agreeing to a contract, will be sufficient to show that the consumer has taken all the necessary steps[7] in the country of his habitual residence.[8] This provision will therefore often act to introduce consumer protective laws into a contract that a web site owner never envisaged.

---

5   See Collier JG, *Conflict of Laws* (Cambridge University Press, Cambridge, 1994), at page 195.
6   It may not be enough simply to seek the advice of a domestic lawyer; to understand fully the possible effect of a web contract, legal advice should be solicited from other jurisdictions where potential contracting parties may reside.
7   This careful drafting avoids the older problem of deciding where a contract was concluded. All that must be determined is where the consumer carried out all the steps necessary *on his part* to complete the contact. It will therefore make no difference whether the web site is so constructed as to accept offers or make them. The relevant country will be identical.
8   NB the Rome Convention, Article 5(2) refers to the country of habitual residence; the Brussels Convention, Article 13(3)(a) refers to the state of a consumer's *domicile*. These can differ.

> **21.** **A web site sells 'self-help' manuals. The web site allows any consumer to fill in his details, including address and payment details. The contract chooses Swiss law. On clicking a button labelled 'Let me help myself' (an acceptance button), the manuals are sent to the consumer by mail. By fulfilling each order without checking the habitual residence of the consumer, the web site may be leaving itself open to litigation or unexpected defences. It may be that the site should refuse to contract with consumers from certain jurisdictions.**

Avoiding certain consumers

Avoiding the effects of this provision is difficult both technically and legally because it remains impossible to 'block' all access to a web site from one particular jurisdiction. The web site owner must make a decision: is he happy to contract with a consumer from every country in the world? If there is a jurisdiction that the owner seeks to avoid there are two methods to employ. First, a technical one. Ensure that the web pages that precede the contract stress that the site is not intended for those consumers from the unwanted jurisdiction. This may be effective. The Giuliano and Lagarde report advises that[9]

> '[i]f ... the German replies to an advertisement in American publications, even if they are sold in Germany, the [Article 5(2)] rule does not apply unless the advertisement appeared in special editions of the publication intended for European countries.'

The second method is to ensure, as is suggested, that the contract is not accepted by the consumer, but rather offered; the web site should accept.[10] With this mechanism in place it becomes easy to ask consumers to complete details of where they are habitually resident. The site can reject the offers from the unwanted jurisdiction. It can be seen that if the web site made offers, even with conditional drafting as to habitual residence, it could be in breach of contract by refusing to supply to certain locations.

ABSENCE OF CHOICE

Although it has been advised that a contract should always have a statement as to the law that will apply, there will be situations where a contract has no such statement. To cover these situations, rather than endorse them, the following section considers how a court will establish the applicable law. As above for an express choice, the section later goes on to address the radical difference made by contracting with a consumer without an express choice of law.

Without a choice under Article 3, the general rule is that the applicable law shall be that of the country with which the contract is most closely connected.[11] There is a presumption, however, which is of direct relevance to web site contracts. Article 4(2) makes the presumption that the contract is most closely connected with the

---

9   OJ 1980, C282/10 at C282/24.
10   See 'Web site acceptance', at page 19.
11   Rome Convention, Article 4(1).

country in which the person is located who effects the characteristic performance. The following section breaks down this Article into two discrete elements: characteristic performance and location.

Characteristic performance

For a unilateral contract made over the Internet, the performance which is characteristic will always be straightforward. For a bilateral contract, as is recommended for the Internet, the answer may be more involved.[12] The Giuliano and Lagarde report illustrates the complexity over what is performance in a bilateral contract.[13]

> 'It is the performance for which the payment is due, ie depending on the type of contract, the delivery of goods, the granting of the right to make use of an item of property, the provision of a service ... which usually constitutes the centre of gravity and the socio-economic function of the contractual transaction.'

Where a viewer enters a web site to download material or order its supply, the web site owner will be the person effecting the characteristic performance. Providing money or digital cash is not, as seen, characteristic performance.[14] So it can be said with some conviction that a web site owner will usually be the contracting party making the characteristic performance.

Location

Once the characteristic performance of the contract is established, Article 4(2) provides a separate test to determine the law that will apply to that Internet contract. It is vital not to make the wrong assumption that having determined the characteristic performance of a contract one has also found the law that will apply. The correct approach is to assess *which party* makes the characteristic performance and then to determine which law reflects this transaction. There are two possibilities: first, the contract has been entered into in the course of that party's trade or profession; second, the contract has been entered into otherwise.

Course of trade or profession

It is likely that those parties who own a web site to make contracts will be considered to be acting within their trade or profession. In this situation, Article 4(2) states that the law that shall apply is that of the country where the principal place of business is situated, *with a proviso*. If the terms of the contract specify that

---

12   Article 4(5) explains that if the characteristic performance cannot be determined (not that where it is effected cannot be determined) the presumptions of Articles 2, 3 and 4 will not apply and the court may choose the country with which the contract as a whole is more closely connected as the basis for the applicable law.

13   OJ 1980, C282/10 at C282/20.

14   More involved transactions such as a contract for the provision of digital cash can result in strange results with this reasoning. It would appear that the bank's location determines the law of the contract rather than the location of the account.

the performance is to be effected through a different place of business, the law of that place shall apply.

> **22. A Paris clothes designer sets up a web site in Paris and allows retailers to place their orders over the World Wide Web. There is no choice of law made on the online order form. The clothes being shipped will constitute the characteristic performance of the contract. The designer effects this performance, so the law of the principal place of business, France, will apply to the contract. If the contract *specifies* that the clothes shall be shipped from a German warehouse, the law of Germany shall apply being a place of business other than the principal one.**

Web site's place of business

Contracts made over the Internet grant freedoms to both parties: neither needs to be located in the same country as the web site that takes and completes an order. It is possible that an order to acquire a digitised picture is made from England, and that the order is placed with a German company, trading out of Germany, but that the server which digitally effects the performance is located in the USA. It would be equally easy if the server is located in Vietnam, or anywhere else in the world with a telephone network. The obvious question is therefore, does a server that can effect performance constitute a place of business? It is submitted, in the absence of any direct authority, that a server per se cannot constitute a place of business. This conclusion is drawn from a number of factors.

The wording of Article 4(2) indicates that effecting the characteristic performance through a place does not necessarily constitute a place of business. This can be reasoned from the wording of the Article that performance must be effected through a place of *business* other than the principal place of business. It does not merely state that performance through another *place* will trump the principal place of business.[15]

The Giuliano and Lagarde report complements this point. It states that:[16]

> '[t]he law appropriate to the characteristic performance defines the connecting factor of the contract from the inside, and not from the outside by elements unrelated to the essence of the obligation such as the nationality of the contracting parties or the place where the contract was concluded.'

This interpretation suggests that it is naïve to look solely at where a server is plugged in. What the Convention requires is to look to the reality of the transaction; the characteristic performance must be linked to 'the social and economic environment of which it will form a part'.[17] Indeed, the Giuliano and Lagarde report endorses this holistic approach by later stating: '[t]he place where the act was done becomes unimportant. ... Seeking the place of performance or the different places of performance and classifying them becomes superfluous.'[18] A

---

15   It is admitted that such a literal analysis of a European Convention is, perhaps, inappropriate, and that a more purposive approach should be used. This follows.
16   OJ 1980, C282/10 at C282/20.
17   OJ 1980, C282/10 at C282/20.
18   OJ 1980, C282/10 at C282/21.

company needs to do far more than simply connect a server abroad to have established a place of business there.

What and where is a place of business is a vexed question for the purposes of choice of law and there are differing definitions concerning taxation and the service of proceedings. But there is little doubt that the policy considerations when establishing jurisdiction over a defendant differ from those to establish from where performance was effected. It is inappropriate and an over-simplification of the relevant factors to attempt to utilise a court's views on 'place of business' from one area of the law, say jurisdiction, to another, choice of law.

---

23. An Italian publisher charges viewers to read its newspaper which it uploads daily on to its two web sites, one in Italy and one based in New York for speed purposes. Its contract with viewers has no choice of law clause, but does stipulate that, when demand is high, the American server may supply the information. When a viewer accesses the newspaper, and unbeknown to him, receives this information through the American server, the law of the contract will not be that of New York. The server simply based in New York is an insufficient link to constitute a place of business. The law that will apply is that of the place of the principal place of business: Italy.

Outside trade or profession

Where a party is not acting within his trade or profession but uses a web site to make a contract, a slightly different, but more certain, rule applies. In this situation, Article 4(2) states that the law that shall apply is that of the country where, for an individual, he habitually resides at the time. For a corporate or unincorporated entity, the law that applies is that of the place of its central administration.

The commercial reaction to this academic debate is short: where possible specify a law for any contract made over the Internet. There is some truth in the statement that not providing a choice of law gives slightly more opportunity for argument at an interlocutory stage as to which law will apply to a contract. This opportunity comes at the cost of distinctive uncertainty.

Modifications to applicable law

Consumer contracts

What constitutes a consumer contract under Article 5(2) has already been addressed in some detail.[19] It was found that a contract made over the World Wide Web with a consumer will generally benefit from the protection afforded under the Convention.[20] Where the contract does not provide a choice of law, the effect of the transaction being a consumer contract is far more critical.

If no choice of law is made and Article 5(2) is applicable, Article 5(3) specifies that the law which governs the contract is that of the consumer's habitual

---

19   See 'Consumer contracts', at page 49.
20   See 'Web sites and consumers', at page 50.

residence.[1] This is in stark contrast to where a consumer contract does include a choice of law. In that situation, Article 5(2) does not deprive the consumer of the protection afforded by the mandatory rules from his habitual residence.

> **24. A web site sells 'self-help' manuals. The web site allows any consumer to fill in his details, including address and payment details. On clicking a button labelled, 'Let me help myself' (an acceptance button), the manuals are sent to the consumer by mail. By fulfilling each order without checking the habitual residence of the consumer, the web site will be forming contracts under many different laws all around the world. Its contracts may be unenforceable, or worse, they may be illegal. To avoid leaving itself open to these risks it must include a choice of law *and* refuse to contract with consumers from certain jurisdictions.**

There is an elementary solution to the problem that any law could apply to a contract if any consumer is allowed to contract: choose a law for the contract. Then, to ameliorate the effect from the consumer's mandatory rules, apply the technical and legal precautions already described to 'block' certain jurisdictions.[2]

CONSUMER CONTRACTS

The World Wide Web is growing as a marketplace for consumers. This chapter has explained that it is unwise to begin selling consumer products and services over the Internet without respecting their special legal considerations. This section briefly examines one new piece of legislation that will *directly* impact upon Internet transactions with consumers.[3]

EC Directive on distance consumer contracts

On 17 February 1997 the European Parliament and Council adopted Directive 97/7/EC on the protection of consumers in respect of distance contracts.[4] This important Directive certainly does[5] affect the practice of those who use the Internet to sell goods and services to European consumers.[6] The two main issues are: what is a distance contract, and, what is the Directive's effect.

---

1 Subject to the two exceptions that the rule does not apply to a contract of carriage or a contract where the services are to be supplied to the consumer exclusively in a country other than that in which he has his habitual residence. See the Rome Convention, Article 5(4).
2 See 'Avoiding certain consumers', at page 51.
3 General consumer protective measures include: the Unfair Contract Terms Directive 1993 (93/13/EEC); the Unfair Contract Terms Act 1977; the Consumer Protection Act 1987; and the Consumer Credit Act 1974. Specialist advice and texts apply equally to Internet contracts with consumers as any other.
4 Until reported in OJ, see Council common position at OJ C288/1.
5 Choice of law clauses will not be effective in ousting the consumer's rights. See Article 12.
6 This Directive has a similar cumulative effect as some of the United States federal laws and regulations. See Federal Trade Commission 16 CFR 310, 16 CFR 435 and Federal Communication Commission Restrictions on Telephone Solicitations, 47 CFR 64.1200. Also Federal Trade Commission Mail or Telephone Merchandise Order Rule.

DISTANCE CONSUMER CONTRACT

Communication at a distance

Communication at a distance will, almost certainly, include any contracts made using e-mail or web sites. The Directive broadly defines this communication as any means which, without simultaneous *physical* presence of the supplier and consumer, may be used for the purposes of concluding a contract between them.[7] As an indication of this term, Annex I provides e-mail as one of the possible examples. Web sites will also certainly fall within the definition. The Directive will cover the types of Internet contract envisaged by this chapter.

Contracts with consumers

For the purposes of the Directive, a consumer is widely defined as being any natural person acting for purposes outside his trade, business or profession.[8] The Directive applies to any contract concerning goods or services between a supplier and a consumer under an organised distance sales or service-provision scheme. The key point is that the supplier must make exclusive use of one or more means of communication at a distance up to and including the point of contracting.[9]

EFFECT OF DISTANCE CONSUMER CONTRACT DIRECTIVE

Disclosure

Every distance contract with a consumer must include the name and, if appropriate, address of the supplier, the main characteristics of the goods or services, the price including taxes, arrangements for payment and delivery or performance, the period for which the offer is open and the right of withdrawal.[10] Suppliers must include details of payment within these disclosures. Those suppliers who use web sites automatically to contract with consumers must therefore be prepared to alter the information on their pages.

These disclosures must be provided to the consumer not later than the time of delivery (for goods) unless the information is delivered before closing in writing or on another durable medium.[11] It is submitted that this will not include e-mail. Recital 13 warns against 'ephemeral' information not received 'on a permanent medium'.

Right of withdrawal

Every consumer party to a distance contract has seven working days to withdraw from it at will. No penalty can be levied and a full refund is due to the consumer.

---

7   Article 2(4).
8   Article 2(2). It should be noted that, in contrast to the consumer protective measures in the Rome and Brussels Conventions, the consumer must be a natural person.
9   Article 2(1).
10   Article 4.
11   Article 5(1).

The only costs payable are direct return charges, which will not be applicable for any goods digitally delivered.

The effect of this right is lessened for most supplies delivered conventionally for which contracts are made over the Internet because of an exception at Article 6. This exception ensures that the 'cooling-off' period will not apply to *unsealed* audio or video recordings, records or computer software and CD-ROMs. As a result it would appear that most digitally supplied goods will be excluded from the consumer's right of withdrawal. Where a supplier digitally seals its software, for instance where a consumer needs a digital key to use the software, and this can be proved not used, the exception may apply. In contrast, a disk containing the software that remains sealed will certainly benefit its consumer with a right to withdraw within seven working days.

This difference between shipping a sealed disk and downloading a digital version of the program on the disk may prove an incentive for suppliers to shift more of their distribution from physical channels to electronic ones.

Shipment

Unless it is agreed otherwise, shipment of goods must occur, not necessarily arrive, within 30 days. If it does not, the consumer must be informed of his right to obtain a refund within 30 days.[12] Suppliers may have to link their order and shipping databases to ensure that the 30-day trigger is not reached without having informed the customer of his right to refund.

12   Article 7.

Chapter three
Tort

> *[T]he difficulty and inconvenience of requiring operators to analyse either the message or the senders from either a factual or legal standpoint is manifest. The indispensability of the telegraph, on the other hand, is as unchallenged as the realisation that speed is the essence of its worth.*
>
> William M Martin, 1940[1]

The open nature of the Internet allows its users to connect both intentionally and unintentionally with more people than ever before. A web site created by an individual can be seen by all other Internet users. A message sent to a bulletin board can be read across the planet, almost simultaneously, by millions. Unfortunately, this global communication has its disadvantages. A computer file harbouring a computer virus can, in a matter of hours, spread across continents, damaging data and programs without reprieve.

The law of tort demands that, in certain circumstances, we are answerable for our actions and our inactions. Whether there is a contract between two individuals or not, the courts have the authority to make someone provide compensation for damage caused. Put simply, English law demands that users of the Internet operate with responsibility towards others.

This chapter considers these responsibilities in relation to three particular types of damage that can occur over the Internet. The opening section on negligence looks to the liability of those who, even accidentally, exacerbate the spread of a computer virus by particular conduct. The second section considers the possibility that if a person relies to their detriment on information provided by another over the World Wide Web, the provider of the information may, occasionally, be liable for the loss. The final tort that is examined from the perspective of the Internet is defamation. The openness of the Internet brings benefits to those who wish to publish information, but sometimes the courts will deem them responsible for the damaging words of another.

This chapter examines the following issues.

1. How may someone be liable for the damage caused from accidentally spreading a computer virus?
2. From a legal perspective, what type of damage occurs when digital data is altered?

---

1 'Telegraphs and Telephones – Qualified Privilege of Telegraph Company to Transmit Defamatory Message Where Sender Is Not Privileged', 2 Wash & Lee L Rev 141 at 147 (1940).

3. Might not using an anti-viral program, or not backing-up important data, be viewed by the courts as contributory negligence?
4. When may information published over the web be the basis of litigation over a negligent misstatement?
5. Can contracts and disclaimers prevent victims of these torts having a right of action?
6. What are the risks of Internet Service Providers being sued for defamation under the new Defamation Act 1996?
7. Which country's courts have the jurisdiction to adjudicate on these cases?
8. Which one law will apply to resolve such a dispute?

NEGLIGENCE

Although malicious code spreads through the Internet and infects computers, it is humans who help this code to proliferate. Viruses circulate because people using the Internet upload and download the *hosts* that house damaging code. Most of the people who spread this code do so unknowingly. But there are occasions, particularly where an internal network becomes infected, that further spread can be halted by stopping all digital communication with the Internet. This section considers what are the responsibilities for users of the Internet when they are aware, or should be aware, of infection. This is of fundamental importance to system operators of internal networks and to designers of web sites.

To examine negligence, this chapter focuses on its constituent parts: duty of care; breach of duty; type of damage; causation of damage. A defendant will only be liable in negligence where he breached his duty to the plaintiff resulting in a recoverable form of damage.

Duty of care

The Internet, more than any other medium, permits one person to affect almost every other person connected to it. Viruses can spread widely: it is possible for one person to make a fundamental difference to this spread. One only needs to alert potential victims of a virus where these people are one's legal 'neighbours', however.

An appropriate starting point to determine who is your neighbour on the Internet is the two-part test expressed by Lord Wilberforce:[2]

> 'First one has to ask whether, as between the alleged wrongdoer and the person who has suffered damage there is a sufficient relationship of proximity or neighbourhood such that, in the reasonable contemplation of the former, carelessness on his part may be likely to cause damage to the latter, in which case a prima facie duty of care arises. Secondly, if the first question is answered affirmatively, it is necessary to consider whether there are any considerations which ought to negative, or to reduce or limit the scope of the duty or the class of

Anns v London Borough of Merton [1977] 2 All ER 492 at 498.

person to whom it is owed or the damages to which a breach of it may
give rise.'

The first aspect of this test is therefore whether someone has a sufficient
relationship of proximity.

RELATIONSHIP OF PROXIMITY: VIRUSES

The law is less ready to impose a duty of care where damage to property results
from a failure to act, rather than by action of the defendant. In other words, the
law does not generally impose a duty to save a potential victim, but only a duty
not to harm that person.[3] Of course, it is semantically possible for an infected
plaintiff, and the court, to frame a system operator's activities as actions, rather
than failures to act. A train-driver was liable for *failing* to shut off steam, so
allowing his train to run into a dead-end.[4] The court described the driver's conduct
in the active terms of negligently managing the train to allow it to 'come into
contact with the dead-end'.[5]

I. A web site controller is aware that one of the Java applets on its home
page is capable of deleting data held on a particular type of browsing
computer. The site controller takes no precautions and then receives a
writ alleging damage as a result of his negligence. It is unlikely that a
defence that he was not negligent, having performed no action, would
succeed.

The courts have previously considered the duty that arises when storing biological
viruses. Widgery J had little doubt that a defendant had a duty to those owners of
cattle which would be affected by the spread of a virus.[6]

'In the present case, the defendants' duty to take care to avoid the
escape of the virus was due to the foreseeable fact that the virus might
infect cattle in the neighbourhood and cause them to die. The duty of
care is accordingly owed to the owners of cattle in the neighbourhood
...'

There appears little to suggest that, when a person is aware of a *computer* virus in
his control, the operator may not owe a duty to potential victims; the Foot and
Mouth Disease Research Institute owed a duty to all the farmers whose cattle were
killed.

Like their biological counterparts, computer viruses will infect not only the
direct recipients but also subsequent ones; this is well known. It may therefore be
alleged that the controller of an infected system is in a sufficiently proximate

3   Lord Diplock illustrates this by claiming that in the parable of the good Samaritan, there
     would be no liability under English civil law for the conduct of the Levite and the priest who
     passed by the other side, 'an omission which was likely to have as its reasonable and probable
     consequence damage to the health of the victim of the thieves'. *Home Office v Dorset Yacht Co
     Ltd* [1970] 2 All ER 294 at 326. This stated, this section takes a slightly less forgiving view of
     the liability which may fix to a system operator. In short, it is assumed that a 'pure omissions'
     argument will not save an operator from all liability.
4   *Kelly v Metropolitan Rly Co* [1895] 1 QB 944.
5   [1895] 1 QB 944 at 947 per Rigby LJ.
6   *Weller and Co v Foot and Mouth Disease Research Institute* [1965] 3 All ER 560 at 570.

relationship with the owner of *any* equipment which becomes infected by the virus emanating from his system. It is submitted that this is too wide. A system operator, like all tortious defendants, has a duty to a plaintiff not simply if the damage is foreseeable, but also where the whole concept of relationship demands it.[7] It is therefore impossible to speak generically of a 'system operator's duty to victims'; the law requires that the 'whole relationship' be taken into account.

Whole relationship

In an attempt to describe some of the relevant factors which may be present in this relationship, this section divides the duties of a defendant in respect of damage from e-mail, forum and ftp sites, and web sites.

Malicious code is as virulent when on a forum or web site as on any other computer. This can have the catastrophic result that infection can spread exponentially through the Internet. An e-mail with attached virus could be sent from one person to another. This person, unaware of the infection could then create another e-mail, to which the virus could re-attach, and send this e-mail to a group of individuals. Every one of these individuals may now be infected and be infectious. It is this replication and spread that leads to two types of damage: primary and secondary. By primary damage this book envisages damage which results from direct contact with an infected computer.[8] Secondary damage is any damage that is 'one removed' from the primary damage.

The greatest threat for a defendant is not in respect of the limited number of primary infections, but in respect of the unlimited numbers of secondary infections.

Primary damage

E-mail infection

It was previously thought that an e-mail could not spread malicious code; this is no longer the case. A person who is sent an e-mail from an infected system is owed a duty by the sender if that sender knew the e-mail was infected. The situation becomes more complex where the sender is aware that the recipient has an anti-viral program that should cull the virus. Here, if the recipient's computer becomes damaged, one must ask whether the recipient is contributorily negligent.

The practical solution is obviously to test each outgoing e-mail for viruses. If infection is suspected but the e-mail must nevertheless be sent, operators should include a suitable warning as the subject heading. This will not negate the duty to the recipient, but it may provide a defence of *volenti non fit injuria* – voluntary assumption of responsibility – if the person goes on to open the e-mail and is then infected.[9]

In the workplace, many people other than the system operator send e-mails. If an internal network is infected, the system operator should block all e-mails from leaving the system until the suspected malicious code is treated. If it is technically

---

7   See the 'widening' of Lord Wilberforce's first test by the Privy Council in *Yuen Kun Yeu v A-G of Hong Kong* [1987] 2 All ER 705.
8   It is appreciated that this contact is not *direct* but that, in fact, the digital material is broken into packets and shunted between many computers before reaching their intended recipient.
9   See 'Consent' at page 79.

difficult to block e-mails leaving, the system operator has a duty to external recipients to inform the employees not to send potentially infected material. As will be discussed below, viruses are often spread because system operators do not act quickly enough to prevent other users of the system from infecting others.

Forums and ftp sites

The controller of an ftp site or a forum has two serious problems. First, both a forum and an ftp site can allow other people to upload material to the site. This increases, dramatically, the risk from virus infection. It seems unlikely at law that a controller of one of these sites will be able to rely solely on a disclaimer to avoid liability.[10] This is because the law tends to impose a duty to act to prevent harm where the defendant is in control of both the plaintiff and the injuring third party.[11] For the controller of an ftp site or a forum, the controller has nominal control over the person who left the virus and control over those who become infected with it.

The second legal problem for the controller of an ftp site or a forum is that there will be a large number of people who experience primary damage. That is, many people will be directly infected by malicious code on a site, in contrast to an e-mail where probably only one person suffers primary damage.

Technical solutions obviously include ensuring that no files can be uploaded before passing through the site's anti-viral program first. This will probably be sufficient to extinguish the controller's duty to his visitors, although it would be legally safer if a contractual disclaimer is also provided.[12] Additionally it may be evidentially useful for the controller to maintain a log of which person leaves which file. If a claim is brought against the controller, it may be crucial that the plaintiff can add, as co-defendant, the person who deposited the virus initially.

Web sites

The potential for sites to become infected is growing now that executable code is becoming commonplace on web pages and that many sites are distributing software through the web. Controllers of these sites, therefore, need to be cautious about the risks of distributing malicious code through their pages. Like controllers of ftp sites and forums, controllers of web sites risk directly infecting a large number of people. Unlike ftp sites and forums, a web site controller has absolute power over the site: other people cannot easily leave malicious code on the site to infect others. It is difficult to 'write' to a web site without permission from the controller.

A web site should therefore operate a strict regime of checking all the material on the site and where possible attempt to disclaim, to some extent, liability for infecting viewers.

---

10   See 'Contracts and disclaimers' at page 87.
11   *Ellis v Home Office* [1953] 2 All ER 149. See also *Cowden v Bear Country Inc* 382 F Supp 1321 (DSD 1974) in which it was held an operator of an animal park had to exercise a high responsibility to prevent damage to the zoo's visitors. Some may say that there is a higher duty where a site's visitors access it not to view viruses but to download safe code.
12   See 'Contracts and disclaimers' at page 87.

2. A software programmer distributes software from her web site and is careful to include a disclaimer of liability on the licence downloaded with each item of software. Unless the programmer is sure that no damaging code can be distributed simply by viewing her site, say by executable code, a disclaimer should also be also placed on the web site.

It is an obvious and important point that any disclaimer of damage from the site must be shown on the home page and throughout the site. If the disclaimer is buried at the 'back' of web pages there is a risk that the viewer's computer becomes infected before liability is disclaimed. In this situation, the disclaimer will not operate as a contractual defence as notice is provided too late, and it will not be successful as evidence of *volenti* for similar reasons.[13]

Secondary damage

The duty to prevent damage for secondary infections will be less onerous than over primary infections. This is because the law tends to avoid opening up the 'floodgates' to too many similar claims. Also the courts will only impose a duty where that is fair, just and reasonable. It is true that the infectious character of viruses is well known. It may therefore be difficult for a defendant to state that he did not reasonably contemplate his carelessness would damage secondary victims. It is the nature of viruses that they spread; it is not improbable and is not unreasonably foreseeable that a victim will be infected far removed from the source of the infection.[14] By Lord Wilberforce's test it may appear trivial for a victim of secondary damage to allege successfully that the system operator owed a duty of care. But, as mentioned, a duty is wider than mere foreseeability.[15]

'As Lord Wilberforce himself observed in *McLoughlin v O'Brian* [1982] 2 All ER 298 at 303, [1983] 1 AC 410 at 420, it is clear that foreseeability does not of itself, and automatically, lead to a duty of care ... Foreseeability of harm is a necessary ingredient of such a relationship, but it is not the only one. Otherwise there would be liability in negligence on the part of one who sees another about to walk over a cliff with his head in the air, and forbears to shout a warning.'

This statement makes it clear that a plaintiff, having suffered secondary digital damage, will have to show more than simply that the system operator knew this would be possible. Each plaintiff will have to prove a close and direct relationship with the system operator. The court should impose the duty only where it is 'fair, just and reasonable'.[16] This will depend greatly on the facts before the court, the balance of powers of the parties, and the potential to open the floodgates to similar claims. In the main, few claims from secondarily-damaged defendants will be successful.

---

13 See *Thornton v Shoe Lane Parking Ltd* [1971] 1 All ER 686.
14 Cf, the catalogue of unlikely events in, say, *Palsgraf v Long Island Railroad* 162 NE 99 (1928).
15 *Yuen Kun Yeu v A-G of Hong Kong* [1987] 2 All ER 705 at 710 per Lord Keith.
16 See *White v Jones* [1993] 3 All ER 481 at 502.

> **3. A famous brewery provides on its web site a free novelty program which mimics its television advertisement. Viewers are free to download this software; unbeknown to the brewery the program is infected with a virus. The program is very popular, so, to ease the strain on its web server, the brewery encourages owners of the program to copy it for their friends rather than direct them to the web site.**
>
> **Some time after the promotion finishes, a virus infection breaks out on those computers which have the program. The brewery may owe a duty to those who downloaded the program from the web site, and to those people who were directed to copy the program. Those plaintiffs who became infected from the spread of the virus, rather than the program in which it incubated, are unlikely to be owed a duty: they do not have a sufficiently direct relationship with the brewery.**

Standard of care

At this point it is useful to recap: negligence is where a defendant owes a duty of care and then breaches that duty causing damage as a result. Victims must prove that the defendant breached his duty; they must prove on the balance of probabilities that, say, a system operator was negligent in allowing a virus to be spread.[17]

REASONABLE MAN

To assess negligence the courts compare the actions and inactions of the defendant with those of a reasonable man 'guided upon those considerations which ordinarily regulate the conduct of human affairs'.[18] In the situation of a system operator, the court may take into account industry practice and the rapidly advancing sophistication of computer viruses.

Industry practice

Professional negligence cases can teach a system operator something about his obligations. The most important point is that the courts will construe the level of duty by reference to industry practice. This is not to say that a court will simply assume that the latest notice of advice from the Computer Emergency Response Team[19] should be followed to avoid acting negligently.[20] The court may, however, draw an inference of negligence and reverse the burden of proof forcing the system

---

17 Sometimes the evidential burden on the plaintiff can be lessened by the court accepting an allegation of *res ipsa loquitur*.

18 *Blyth v Birmingham Waterworks Co* (1856) 11 Ex Ch 781 at 784 per Alderson B.

19 The Computer Emergency Response Team, CERT, is an American, publicly-funded establishment that tracks Internet security issues.

20 In *Thompson v Smiths Shiprepairers (North Shields) Ltd* [1984] 1 All ER 881, Mustill J held that an employer was not in breach of his duty when advice was contained in the *Lancet*; breach occurred 12 years later when the government released an advisory note.

operator, in effect, to argue against the industry.[1] In the converse situation if a system operator does keep up to date with industry practice and current anti-viral programs, the victim will have a burden that is 'heavy'.[2] System operators should not have reliance solely on official industry statements; they should also aspire to reach the generally understood standards of Internet security.[3]

Proportional precautions

The law does try to inject some proportionality into the standard that it expects from defendants. System operators will be judged not purely on the extent of risk but balanced with the difficulty of taking precautions to avoid that risk. Lord Denning put this succinctly:[4]

'[T]his is an obligation which keeps pace with the times. As the danger increases, so must the precautions increase.'

The risk of a virus spreading is great. It is undoubtedly foreseeable[5] that if a virus is sent to a person connected to the Internet without an appropriate anti-viral program, that virus will infect the user's computer. From this point on, it is also foreseeable that further infection could occur. Whether the virus is damaging to any considerable extent is obviously something that will vary with the species. The more dangerous a virus, the greater obligation to take adequate precautions to prevent its spread.

The precautions that a system operator should take are unlikely to be expensive, but, as the aphorism prescribes, they must keep pace with the times.[6] System operators must ensure that the seriousness of virus control is understood by all users of a network. They should maintain equipment audits to check that the users of the network are not connecting modems; these would permit viruses to enter the system without passing an anti-viral program. The main precaution, of course, is to keep installed the latest anti-viral program while watching the industry press for any other security issues.

1   Of course, occasionally the industry practice itself is below the standard required by the law. See *Edward Wong Finance Co Ltd v Johnson Stokes & Master* [1984] AC 296.
2   *Morris v West Hartlepool Steam Navigation Co Ltd* [1956] 1 All ER 385 at 402 per Lord Cohen.
3   In *Aiken v Stewart Wrightson Members' Agency Ltd* [1995] 3 All ER 449 at 480, Potter J relied on the 'common ground' that in the USA there was an escalation of asbestosis claims which would therefore increase the risk that the level of claims against Lloyd's would rise. Similarly, even without any industry guideline, it is 'common ground' that the move towards using executable code on web pages will escalate the amount of malicious code which can be transmitted. A system operator who seeks to avoid negligence actions should not wait for a reported instance from CERT before employing precautions.
4   *Lloyds Bank Ltd v Railway Executive* [1952] 1 All ER 1248 at 1253.
5   There will be occasions where a system operator may view the spread of a virus as a slim possibility. For example, the better anti-viral programs are regularly updated to cope with the newer strains. There will be a chance that even the latest update will allow a new virus through its vetting procedures. It is unlikely that, without other factors, a court will be persuaded that this lag means that a system operator has not reached the required standard of care.
6   In *Tutton v AD Walter Ltd* [1985] 3 All ER 757 a landowner sprayed a chemical on his yellow rape field which killed a neighbouring beekeeper's bees. The court held that the precautions he could have taken would have prevented the bees from dying and cost little. Similarly, a recent anti-viral program at the firewall of a network will prevent most malicious code leaving or entering: prevention at little cost.

> **4. An owner of an old Apple computer traces the source of a viral-infection to an e-mail that was forwarded to him by a friend in an accountancy firm. It is discovered that this virus was present on all the computers in the firm as well. The reason that no symptoms were present on the firm's computers was that they are IBM compatible computers, not Apples, and the virus was specific to the latter. The system operator will owe a duty of care to the owner of the infected computer, but it is unlikely that he breached this duty. It is a slim possibility that cross-infection can occur and one which has an expensive precaution: buy every other system together with its anti-viral programs merely to prevent this unlikely occurrence.**

Damage

If it is proved that a defendant has breached a duty of care, the plaintiff must then prove that this breach caused the complained-of damage. The law of negligence does not impose a burden on people to keep their duties to others; it imposes a duty not to *harm* others. In a virus-damage case, the plaintiff may have an additional burden: English law does not permit the recovery of damages for pure economic loss. There is an argument, explored below, that damage to data may be pure economic loss.

When malicious code infects a system it is often said that the code has 'damaged' the computer. For the purposes of litigation, a plaintiff must be more precise. It is very rare for code to damage the physical aspects of a computer. Simply because a computer or program may stop working does not mean that there has been any damage to the physical aspects of the machine, like the keyboard, the screen, the chips and the storage systems. What will more probably have occurred is that the so-called 'hardware' is *prevented* from working properly.

A plaintiff infected by a virus spread over the Internet may seek to claim for the cost of 'repairing' his computer.[7] In addition, plaintiffs who rely on their computers for commerce will also seek to claim their wider losses such as loss of business and loss of profit. The relevant issue here is that the law will not permit the recovery of damages for pure economic loss. Recovery is permitted only where this economic loss is dependent on the negligently caused damage to property. Accordingly, it is initially necessary to establish that altering the orientation of magnetic particles, how programs and data are stored, is damage to property. Then, the question can be addressed as to what will constitute economic loss dependent on that damage.

DAMAGE TO DIGITAL MEDIA

The operating system of a computer is a complex program that digitally binds together the various aspects of a computer. For instance, it ensures that the central processing unit responds appropriately for each key pressed on the keyboard. It also allows the central processing unit to store data on the screen, the memory or on a storage device. Application programs, such as word processors and drawing

---

7   Technically, this should read 'cost of *cleaning of malicious code and the reinstallation of software*'.

packages run 'on top' of an operating system: they rely on the operating system to run; the operating system relies on the hardware. Data files are the raw information that are used, or shown through an application program. A word processing document or a list of client names would be classed as data files.

When any of these programs or data are 'damaged' the question arises as to exactly what has occurred. It will be recalled that computers work with and store only ones and zeros. Programs and data are stored as magnetic representations of zeros and ones either in memory or on a device, usually a disk.[8] To damage a program or data, therefore, is not to cause any physical damage in the way in which it is normally considered: all that is occurring is that the magnetic particles are being altered. The memory or disk remains operative in a physical sense, what it was *storing* has been altered.

This discussion on the technology suggests that a virus causes no property damage. It is more accurate to state that virus damage causes no physical damage: property is a wide term and encompasses more than 'that which can be touched'.

In two cases the criminal courts[9] decided, for the purposes of the Criminal Damage Act 1971, that altering magnetic media can be classed as damage to property.[10] The Court of Appeal, based on previous authorities,[11] read widely the concept of damage.[12]

> 'Where ... the interference with the disc amounts to an impairment of the value or usefulness of the disc to the owner, then the necessary damage is established.'

Applying the reasoning that an impairment of the value or usefulness of a disk will constitute damage, it is clear that part of a damages claim could justifiably be for the price of the program or software which the disk held.[13]

---

5. An accountancy firm distributes free tax-assessment software from its web site. An individual retrieves this software, which works well, only to discover that it had harboured a virus that crashed his word processing application program which he had installed from CD-ROM. The firm admits its negligence but disputes that its damages should include the cost of a new word processing application. The firm is correct: there is no recoverable damage to the word processing application; it can be easily reinstalled restoring the individual to the same position as he was in before the infection. The only new piece of software that the individual can claim for in his damages is an anti-viral program to clean his disk drive.

---

8   CD-ROMs use a method of storing these ones and zeros optically, but, it is submitted, very few of these units allow the media to be re-used. The programs or data stored on them are generally impossible to alter or corrupt *electronically*.
9   It is accepted that one cannot simply transpose the judgment on a point of law in a criminal case to answer a point of law in a civil dispute. However, here the transposition is not of the *ratio*, rather merely the judicial reasoning: it is persuasive not authoritative.
10 By s 1(1) of the Criminal Damage Act 1971: 'A person who without lawful excuse ... damages any property ... intending to ... damage any such property ... shall be guilty of an offence'; by s 10(1): '... "property" means property of a tangible nature'. This chapter does not suggest that tortious damage to property is restricted to tangible property.
11 *Cox v Riley* (1986) 83 Cr App Rep 54; *Morphitis v Salmon* [1990] Crim LR 48.
12 *Nicholas Alan Whiteley* (1991) 93 Cr App Rep 25 at 29 per Lord Lane CJ. Lord Lane distinguished between tangible property being damaged and the damage itself being tangible.
13 See fn 14.

ECONOMIC LOSS

It has been seen that a plaintiff would be justified in claiming damages for the cost of repair, or if the program must be replaced by a new version, the cost of that.[14] What is questionable is the additional economic damages that the plaintiff can claim. For example, a plaintiff whose business is the quick design and production of leaflets may well lose trade as a result of his operating system being infected by a virus. But, speaking strictly, the virus has damaged the operating system and not the additional programs that the plaintiff uses for the design and printing. Whether the plaintiff can claim for this loss of business is partly a question of causation, but it is also one of economic loss.

In *Spartan Steel & Alloys Ltd v Martin & Co (Contractors) Ltd*[15] the plaintiffs manufactured stainless steel alloys. The power for this was supplied by cable from a nearby electricity station. The defendants damaged this cable stopping power to the factory for 14½ hours. They admitted their negligence, but appealed to the Court of Appeal on the sum of damages awarded by the judge at first instance. Three damages claims had been awarded: £368 for the value of the steel melt which was actually damaged in the furnace as a result of the drop in power; £400 for the profit which should have been made on this melt; and, contentiously, £1,767 for the profit which they would have made on four melts that they were unable to process.

Lord Denning was clearly unimpressed by the plaintiffs but he was able to decide the case on policy[16] rather than merely personality.[17] He stated that:[18]

'it is better to disallow economic loss altogether, at any rate when it stands alone, independent of any physical damage.'

So the relevant question, policy aside, is when are the damages claimed by a plaintiff for infection by damaging code 'dependent' on physical damage? Applying Lord Denning's analysis above it would appear that the loss of business profit while an operating system is being repaired or replaced is irrecoverable, either as being too remote, or as pure economic loss. What would be recoverable is any work that is *at the time of infection* damaged by the virus.

---

14   It is unlikely that a new operating system would have to be purchased: it is usual that a user of an operating system will have a legal backup copy for just this sort of occurrence; alternatively, the supplier of an operating system will often provide a free additional copy where it can be shown that the original is no longer able to be used. See the Copyright, Designs and Patents Act 1988, s 50A(1).

15   [1972] 3 All ER 557.

16   'At the bottom I think the question of recovering economic loss is one of policy. Whenever the courts draw a line to mark out the bounds of *duty*, they do it as a matter of policy so as to limit the responsibility of the defendant. Whenever the courts set bounds to the *damages* recoverable – saying that they are, or are not, too remote – they do it as a matter of policy so as to limit the liability of the defendant.' Per Lord Denning [1972] 3 All ER 557 at 561.

17   '[T]he cutting of the supply of electricity ... is a hazard which we all run ... When the supply is cut off, [most people] do not go running round to their solicitor. They do not try to find out whether it was anyone's fault. They just put up with it. They try to make up the economic loss by doing more work the next day. This is healthy attitude which the law should encourage.' Per Lord Denning [1972] 3 All ER 557 at 564.

18   [1972] 3 All ER 557 at 564.

> **6. A data warehouse performs processing operations on behalf of poll researchers for general elections. It is imperative that this processing is not delayed, as such a delay would make the results inaccurate. The larger polls can take many hours to process. During the processing of one such poll the entire system crashed, as a result of a virus spread from a negligently operated Internet Service Provider. The warehouse will be able to claim damages in respect of the poll being processed, but probably not for the profit from the polls which it is unable to process during the disinfection. These damages will be pure economic loss.**

Data damage

It has been mentioned that damage to programs is often cheap to repair.[19] Any damage caused to data may be expensive, with large consequential losses. For a business, damage to data may be catastrophic: orders may be unable to be fulfilled; research and development may have to be repeated; business may be lost through customers' qualms as to the security of the system. It will be recalled that economic loss not anchored to and resulting from physical harm to property is not recoverable.

If it is accepted that data being corrupted is damage to property it becomes easy to see that the economic loss, such as profits from the use of that data, will be recoverable. But it is vital to appreciate that this is the key to recovery: a plaintiff must hang any claim for economic loss on the corruption of the data being damage to property. Of course, a plaintiff must also be careful not to value the data twice: the 'value' of the data and business profits lost as a result of its damage can overlap in certain circumstances. It is this problem of calculation of which Lord Denning was wary:[20]

> 'It would be well-nigh impossible to check the claims. If there was economic loss on one day, did the applicant do his best to mitigate it by working harder next day?'

Ongoing damage

A program or data that is damaged by a malicious code will suffer repeated damage unless it is stopped by an anti-viral program which digitally cleans the infected computer. At law, without suitable settlement after initial damage, a plaintiff can bring numerous actions for each repeated damage caused by the defendant's negligence.[1] This, in theory, would suggest that a plaintiff infected by a virus spread through the negligence of another could bring a new claim each time the computer is prevented from working properly as a result of the ongoing infection. In practice, a plaintiff who became infected by a virus but attempted to continue working with that computer without cleaning it first would not have mitigated his damages, and probably would have made a voluntary assumption of risk so denying a cause of action.

19 See fn 14.
20 [1972] 3 All ER 557 at 564.
 1 See *Hudson v Nicholson* (1839) 5 M & W 437.

Causation of damage

The final aspect to recovering for damage caused by the defendant's breach of duty is that the defendant caused the recoverable damage. A plaintiff whose software or data is damaged by malicious code must show that the defendant's negligent conduct was responsible for the loss. To show this the plaintiff must satisfy two tests: one factual and the other legal. The application of these tests to a virus victim does not greatly differ to any other type of claim. There are, however, a few issues that are specific to the Internet.

FACTUAL TEST: CAUSATION

The first test is factual: did the defendant actually cause the damage? This is particularly relevant for the Internet because there is a chance that a person infected by a virus from one site is already infected by the same virus from another location.[2]

Absolute nature of viruses

Viruses are rife on the Internet and, like viruses of a biological variety, a strain cannot be eliminated completely without destroying every last active virus and carrier. Unlike biological viruses, a computer virus can cause as much damage with one infection of a computer as with one hundred infections on the same computer. Having one copy of a virus on a computer at the time of a subsequent infection by the same virus may not alter the potential damage of that first virus. Also unlike biological viruses, a computer virus will generally act absolutely: if it is programmed to delete certain files on a certain date, those files will be deleted on that unfortunate date. No more files will be deleted by there being an additional copy of the virus infecting the system.[3] There is no increase of risk of damage, or damage, by there being two infections. These statements make a significant difference to the way that a defendant will approach the question of causation.

Previous infection: same code

One legal approach to whether the defendant factually caused the damage is to structure a question using the 'but-for' test. This is often employed by the courts. For example, but for the system operator's negligence would the user have suffered damage to data? Where the plaintiff can prove that the code which caused the damage was downloaded from a site under the control of the system operator the test will apply and the court will be able to decide that the operator actually

---

2   This common occurrence on the Internet is a practical example of the three-house fire problem. This is where a house sandwiched between two others is burnt by a fire that has been started by the two separate negligent owners of each of the neighbouring houses. In the problem, each negligent owner may claim that but for their actions the middle house would still have burnt down.

3   It is admitted that there is possibility that malicious code could 'multitask', that is, run more than one copy at one time. In this situation it is technically possible that two copies of the virus will cause the same damage but more quickly than one copy of the virus. Much depends on the multitasking of the operating system and the nature of the malicious code.

caused the damage. It is common for a plaintiff to be infected more than once. A plaintiff may allege that but for the defendant's negligence her data would not have been damaged. The defendant could counter this by showing that the plaintiff was already infected from an unrelated site.[4]

Because most viruses do not become more damaging in numbers and act absolutely, a defendant may simply be able to allege that because of a prior infection the plaintiff was destined to be damaged *anyway*. The negligence by the defendant may have allowed the virus to spread but, unless proved, it did not cause the damage. Such an approach has been successful in *Barnett v Chelsea & Kensington Hospital Management Committee* in which a patient was admitted to hospital with arsenic poisoning.[5] The doctor was negligent in taking so long to see the patient, but, the court stated that even without this negligence, the patient had no reasonable prospect of living.

Although the courts should assess causation in fact as an issue divorced from duty there is inevitably some blurring of the two issues. This is why it may be considered unsafe to draw a principle from a medical negligence case to apply it to a computer virus infection. If anything though, the court in a medical negligence case, where the defendant has assumed responsibility and personal injury is in issue, would allow more generous causation than for a system operator who has assumed no such responsibility. It is, therefore, perhaps even less unlikely that a court would deem a system operator caused the damage where the plaintiff's computer was already infected.

---

7. A web site system operator is sued for negligence in allowing an animation file to be infected with a virus which damages a viewer's browser on the first of the month. During the discovery stage of the litigation the defendant is able to see that the viewer's computer had already been infected by this virus five times previously. While the web site operator may well have owed a duty of care to check his site for viruses, the breach of that duty did not cause the damage; the plaintiff's software would have been damaged with, or without, the negligence.

Previous infection: different code

A plaintiff who has browsed the Internet considerably may be infected by more than one family of virus. In such a situation the defendant may wish to allege that the plaintiff's software and data was going to be damaged in some way anyway, so, as above, the defendant is not liable. The problem with such a pleading is that with the help of expert evidence it should be easy to show which virus caused the damage. If it was not the virus contracted from the defendant's site, the defendant has not caused that damage and is not liable. If the virus was contracted from the defendant's site it is not relevant to the issue of causation that this is only one of the plaintiff's infections.

4   It may be possible using 'time-stamps' on infected code to assess exactly which virus caused
    which damage. Cf in *Cook v Lewis* [1952] 1 DLR 1, two hunters negligently shot through some
    trees. As a result of *one* of those shots, the plaintiff is hit by a bullet. The court, unable to
    prove absolutely which hunter was responsible for the wounding shot must decide whether the
    plaintiff can recover, and if so, whether from both or just one.
5   [1968] 1 All ER 1068.

One final scenario is where evidence is adduced that the plaintiff was already infected with viruses which all caused roughly the same type of damage but it cannot be proved which virus caused the actual damage. There are two House of Lords authorities on which a plaintiff may rely to prove causation; both cases indicate the difficulties in proving causation.

Material increase of risk

The boiled-down rule from *McGhee v National Coal Board* is that if a defendant is proved to have materially increased the risk of a plaintiff being damaged, the burden of proof moves to the defendant.[6] The defendant must then prove on the balance of probabilities that the negligence did not cause the damage claimed. A superficial interpretation of this rule may indicate that the plaintiff needs only to prove that the presence of the 'defendant's' virus could have caused infection to reverse the burden of proof. But, any reading of the case must be far narrower than this: a plaintiff must adduce that the defendant's negligence materially increased the risk of suffering *that* damage. It is not enough to show that the plaintiff simply increased the risk of data damage per se.

---

8. **A new word processor that integrates with the Internet becomes the target of many virus writers. Three particularly vicious viruses attach to the program and scramble or delete any documents at the point of saving them. A firm's internal network, with a 'safe' connection to its main supplier, becomes infected with one variety of the virus. They sue their supplier in negligence at which point it is discovered that the plaintiff's internal network is also infected with the other two strains also. Because of poor retention of the evidence the plaintiff is unable to show that the infection from the defendant is the actual cause of the damage complained of. But the plaintiff does adduce that the defendant's negligence added to their risk of damage. They have not proved in fact that the defendant's negligence increased the risk of damage from the offending code.**

Multiple possible causes

In *Wilsher v Essex Area Health Authority*[7] the House of Lords was faced with the case of a blind premature baby whose blindness could have been caused by a junior doctor's negligent insertion of a catheter into a vein rather than an artery. The problem of causation was that premature babies may be blind for four other reasons. The Lords judged that for the defendant to be liable the plaintiff would have to prove that the defendant's negligence was the most likely of all the reasons.

By cautious analogy it can be seen that if a plaintiff has a computer so riddled with infectious code that it cannot be said with certainty which code caused the damage, the plaintiff must prove that the 'defendant's' code was most likely to have caused the damage.

---

6   *McGhee v National Coal Board* [1972] 3 All ER 1008.
7   [1986] 3 All ER 801.

> **9. An unfortunate software programmer downloads the latest version of a programming tool from a supplier only to realise that, on running the program, her File Allocation Table (FAT) on her hard disk is corrupted. The FAT cannot be repaired and prevents the programmer retrieving any of her data. She sues the supplier who discovers that her hard disk was old and would have been prone to corruption at some point in the future. The court must take expert evidence as to the probability not merely of 'natural' corruption, but of corruption of the FAT. If this is less likely to have caused the corruption at that point in time than the presence of the virus, the court must deem that the supplier is the factual cause of the damage.**

LEGAL TEST: REMOTENESS

After satisfying a court that a system operator's negligence actually caused the damage, the plaintiff has in addition to prove that the damage was not too remote. Remoteness is a judicial limit to liability that is used by the courts to prevent a defendant being liable for 'all the consequences [of an act of negligence] however foreseeable and however grave'.[8] With malicious code damage it allows the liability of the defendant to be reduced by the actions of third parties or the plaintiff and condition of the plaintiff's equipment. This should be welcome news for operators whose systems are connected to the Internet. It may be perfectly possible that a system operator's negligence caused *at fact* damage to thousands of computers through cross-infections; remoteness, however, will reduce the liability.

There are two types of situation that may require proper regard to the rules on remoteness. The first is secondary damage, that is damage caused by subsequent infections of the virus after infecting the plaintiff's equipment. The second type of damage is where the plaintiff not only claims damages in respect of the damaged data but also of some apparently related event. As more computers that perform important tasks are connected to the Internet, more viruses will cause far-reaching effects. Many hospital computers are now connected to the Internet; financial institutions are often connected; Parliament is connected. Every system operator should be concerned to appreciate what the law will see as damage too remote.

This area of law is constantly in flux but a rough guide to a court's approach can be provided by summarising the approach taken in one particular case.[9] The facts are unimportant for our purposes. Woolf J asked the pivotal question:[10]

> 'Are the damages that the plaintiff has to pay to his victims so remote that, although they are the consequence of the accident, they are not recoverable at law?'

To answer this question one general statement of remoteness was made together with three 'glosses'.

---

8   *Overseas Tankship (UK) Ltd v Morts Dock and Engineering Co Ltd, The Wagon Mound (No 1)* [1961] 1 All ER 404 at 413 per Viscount Simonds.
9   *Meah v McCreamer (No 2)* [1986] 1 All ER 943.
10 [1986] 1 All ER 943 at 945.

General statement: Wagon Mound

The general statement of the law on remoteness is drawn from the case, *Wagon Mound*.[11] In that case the defendants allowed oil to pour from their ship onto the plaintiff's dockyard. The plaintiff's manager was assured by a manager of an oil depot that there was no reason to stop welding work; oil on the sea is not inflammable. The welding recommenced and some sparks fell onto some floating debris which in turn ignited the oil. The plaintiff's dockyard was burnt.

Viscount Simonds was convinced, as the courts have been since, that,[12]

> 'a man must be considered to be responsible for the probable consequences of his act. To demand more of him is too harsh a rule, to demand less is to ignore that civilised order requires the observance of a minimum standard of behaviour.'

So, the plaintiff in a digital damage case must show that it was reasonably foreseeable that the negligence by the system operator would lead to the damage. Where the plaintiff claims only for damage to the actual data or program it will be difficult for the defendant to rebut this claim with a statement that it was not reasonably foreseeable. For example, it is well known that if any binary files are sent over the Internet they can be hosts for malicious code. Not to screen for this malicious code before sending, or allowing the retrieval of this code, has the reasonably foreseeable consequence of damaging data or programs. The more difficult questions are addressed below, such as whether a system operator is responsible for events *resulting* from the data damage, and for secondary infections.

Glosses on remoteness

Cases following *Wagon Mound* have modified its effect on remoteness. Woolf J applied *Wagon Mound* together with these modifications; this section will do the same.

1. Thin skulls

In *Dulieu v White*[13] Kennedy J formulated the rule of English negligence law that a defendant takes his victim as he finds him:[14]

> 'it is no answer [to a negligence claim] that he would have suffered less injury, or no injury at all, if he had not had an unusually thin skull or an unusually weak heart.'

---

11   *Overseas Tankship (UK) Ltd v Morts Dock and Engineering Co Ltd, The Wagon Mound (No 1)* [1961] 1 All ER 404.
12   [1961] 1 All ER 404 at 413.
13   [1901] 2 KB 669.
14   [1901] 2 KB 669 at 679.

In *Smith v Leech Brain*[15] the court was asked to discount this rule in the light of *Wagon Mound*; if a plaintiff suffers from a rare condition the defendant should not be liable in relation to this condition as it is not reasonably foreseeable. The court was unconvinced by the defendant's argument and ruled that the thin-skull rule applied along with the *Wagon Mound* test.

The most relevant question for the damage caused by viruses is whether the thin-skull rule applies to property, not merely to the physical and mental condition of a plaintiff. If a victim's computer had an anti-viral program installed which would have eliminated the virus, but for some reason this program was not functioning properly, is the plaintiff able to rely on a rule akin to the thin-skull rule? This is an important question because it may be reasonably unforeseeable that an installed anti-viral program is not working which would mean that the damage is too remote to recover. But, if the thin-skull rule applies to property, this option will not be open to the defendant who must accept the plaintiff's faulty program as he finds it.

In the House of Lords case, *The Edison*,[16] Lord Wright stated that the thin-skull rule was concerned only with actual physical damage.[17] This would indicate that the thin-skull rule may not apply to the state in which a plaintiff leaves a computer. However, *The Edison*, although not overruled, has been heavily distinguished and will be unlikely to be followed.[18] It may therefore be said, with some conviction, that a fault or vulnerability of the plaintiff's computer to infection will not make the damage suffered too remote. A plaintiff may be able to rely on the thin-skull rule: this does not, as will be discussed, prevent the defendant alleging contributory negligence for the plaintiff not having a working anti-viral program.[19]

2. Type not kind of damage

The second gloss on the *Wagon Mound* test distinguishes between the need for the type of damage to be foreseeable rather than the need to foresee the precise extent and manner of infliction. Lord Denning puts this as follows.[20]

> 'It is not necessary that the precise concatenation of circumstances should be envisaged. If the consequence was one which was within the general range which any reasonable person might foresee (and was not of an entirely different kind which no one would anticipate) then it is within the rule that a person who has been guilty of negligence is liable for the consequences.'

Damage to programs and data, the very *modus operandi* of malicious code, will always seem to be reasonably foreseeable. What will entertain the courts is whether *resulting* damage from this data damage will be foreseeable.

---

15   [1961] 3 All ER 1159.
16   *Liesbosch, Dredger v Edison SS* [1933] All ER Rep 144, *sub nom The Edison.*
17   [1933] All ER Rep 144 at 159. See also *Bailey v Derby Corpn* [1965] 1 All ER 443 at 445 per Lord Denning.
18   In particular see the Court of Appeal's ingenious distinguishing of the case in *Dodd Properties (Kent) Ltd v Canterbury City Council* [1980] 1 All ER 928.
19   See 'Contributory negligence' at page 77.
20   *Stewart v West African Terminals Ltd* [1964] 2 Lloyd's Rep 371 at 375.

3. Intervening acts

The final gloss, and one that may come into play when a plaintiff suffers secondary damage, is a general principle. The chain from breach of duty to damage can be broken by an intervening act by another person including the plaintiff. In a malicious code situation the main intervening act will be in relation to secondary damage: that is, it is the action of the first *victim* which allows the spread of the virus to a second victim.

The first point to make is that any intervening act by a third party in the chain of causation must reduce the probability that the plaintiff was responsible *in fact* for the damage suffered. Each new entrant into the chain of actions which finally result in the damage will decrease a judge's conviction that the defendant was liable for the harm. But under remoteness the court is posing a different question: are the actions of others so significant as to exonerate the defendant?

This area is one of substantial academic debate.[1] There are also cases that indicate a retreat from *Wagon Mound*[2] or a realignment of its terms.[3] Here, it will be assumed that *Wagon Mound* and its glosses will apply to the question of third party intervention. A relevant question is therefore whether the interventions or their consequences were reasonably foreseeable by a person such as the defendant at the time of the accident. For damage occurring from secondary infection the answer is clear: it is foreseeable that a victim of a computer virus infection will pass the infection on to another *whilst their computer has not developed any symptoms*.

---

10. An Internet Service Provider admits negligence in allowing a virus to spread to its member's computers. One member refuses the ex gratia settlement offered by the Provider and sues for the damage done not simply to the connected computer but to the entire Intranet of which this computer forms a part. One aspect of the damages claim is for the emotional distress suffered by the Head of the IT Department. On remoteness the Provider has two main arguments: first, it was unforeseeable that an entire Intranet would be connected to an Internet computer without any firewall in place; second, it was unforeseeable that the virus would result in the emotional distress of the Head of IT. The first argument will probably fail as the Provider must take the company as found. This will not, however, preclude a defence of contributory negligence. On the second argument, it is possible that a court would view the damage to data and physical property as within the type of foreseeable damage. The court would be less likely to view the emotional distress to the Head of IT as within the same type.

Defences

There are two main defences to a negligence action for malicious code damage. The first, and one that will most commonly be invoked, is contributory negligence.

---

1   See Howarth, 'My Brother's Keeper? Liability for the acts of third parties' (1994) 14 Legal Studies 88.
2   *Lamb v Camden London Borough Council* [1981] 2 All ER 408.
3   *Home Office v Dorset Yacht Co Ltd* [1970] 2 All ER 294.

This is where the defendant admits that he caused to an extent the damage but that the plaintiff also caused some of the damage himself. An analogy may be able to be drawn from an Internet user not having an anti-viral program and a car driver not wearing a seat belt. Not having a backup of important data may also be an issue of contributory negligence, although it is admitted that this blurs somewhat with mitigation of damages and remoteness issues. The second defence is that of consent or *volenti non fit injuria*. Not only has this defence lost much of the court's support, but also it is likely to be ineffective in a virus scenario.

CONTRIBUTORY NEGLIGENCE

The Law Reform (Contributory Negligence) Act 1945 provides the partial[4] defence of contributory negligence. The scope of the defence is clear from section 1(1):

> 'Where any person suffers damage as a result partly of his own fault and partly of the fault of any other person or persons, a claim in respect of that damage shall not be defeated by the reason of the fault of the person suffering the damage, but the damages recoverable in respect thereof shall be reduced to such an extent as the court thinks just and equitable having regard to the claimant's share in the responsibility for the damage.'

Anti-viral programs

Anti-viral programs are fortunately more effective than medical anti-viral treatments: they work absolutely either preventing an infection or allowing an infection to take place. If a plaintiff had used an anti-viral program that covered the damaging strain, no damage would have occurred. The presence of an anti-viral program would have prevented the litigation being brought, the 'victim' may not even have known that his computer had been the object of an attack. Without an appropriate anti-viral program the computer will be infected; there are no proportions of damage. Similarly there are road traffic accidents where the victim's damage could have been completely prevented by the victim wearing a seat belt. Before moving to the law's treatment of this, it should be understood that a direct comparison between data damage and personal injury is inappropriate. Clearly, whether the policy is stated or underlies a court's decision, a plaintiff with severe personal injuries will be looked upon more favourably than a computer user with corrupted data. This said, the comparison does reveal that a negligent defendant will not be able to avoid all damages merely by casting the aspersion that the plaintiff should have used an anti-viral program.

In *Froom v Butcher*,[5] Lord Denning's analysis was given unanimous approval by the other members of the Court of Appeal. He said,[6]

> 'the cause of the accident is one thing. The cause of the damage is another. The *accident* is caused by bad driving. The *damage* is caused

---

4   See the Court of Appeal's decision in *Pitts v Hunt* [1990] 3 All ER 344.
5   [1975] 3 All ER 520.
6   [1975] 3 All ER 520 at 525.

in part by the bad driving of the defendant, and in part by the failure
of the plaintiff to wear a seat belt.'

This drawn distinction between accident and damage allowed Lord Denning to
ensure that,[7]

'[i]t should not lie in [the defendant's] mouth to say: "You ought to
have been wearing a seat belt."'

This has parallels with negligence resulting in data damage. It too consists of an
accident that would not have resulted in damage if the plaintiff had taken
precautions. And it is submitted that, in these cases it is even less reasonable for
the defendant to call for the plaintiff to have used an anti-viral program. In 1975
seat belts were fitted as standard on most cars and the Highway Code encouraged
their use. Anti-viral programs are not installed as standard on Internet-connected
computers and advisory statements are not included with each modem or
computer.[8]

Lord Denning said of those plaintiffs who would not have been damaged at all,
had they worn a seat belt:[9]

'Whenever there is an accident, the negligent driver must bear by far
the greater share of responsibility. It was his negligence which caused
the accident. It was also a prime cause of the whole of the damage ...
[Sometimes] the evidence will show that the failure made all the
difference. The damage would have been prevented altogether if a seat
belt had been worn. In such cases I would suggest that the damages
should be reduced by 25 per cent.'

This reasoning is logically and equally applicable to the infection of a user's
computer. The plaintiff is in no way to blame for the accident itself.[10] While it may
be wise to use an anti-viral program, not to do so does not eliminate the
defendant's duty not to cause an accident through negligence. The aspect of Lord
Denning's judgment that cannot be so readily extrapolated is the level of 25 per
cent as the appropriate reduction in damages.

At the time of *Froom v Butcher* it was well known that one should wear a seat
belt and the government encouraged it.[11] In a later endorsement of *Froom v
Butcher* the Court of Appeal applied Lord Denning's guidelines to the situation
other than an accident involving a seat belt. In this case, a moped rider failed to
secure his crash helmet.[12] But it was a breach of the Motor Cycles (Protective
Helmets) Regulations 1980 to ride a moped without securely fastened protective
headgear. So the Court of Appeal's agreement with the guidelines was in relation
to a similar obligation to protect oneself.

---

7   [1975] 3 All ER 520 at 525.
8   'Everyone is free to [use] it or not, as he pleases ... Free in the sense that everyone is free to run
     his head against a brick wall, if he pleases. He can do it if he likes without being punished by
     the law. But it is not a sensible thing to do.' [1975] 3 All ER 520 at 525 per Lord Denning.
9   [1975] 3 All ER 520 at 528.
10   This is in the generalised scenario. Clearly a user who chooses to download some sample
     viruses will be unable to suggest that the defendant is wholly or even partially responsible.
11   Between 1972 and 1974 the government had spent £2½ million on advertising to encourage
     people to wear seat belts.
12   *Capps v Miller* [1989] 2 All ER 333.

The use of anti-viral programs by users is not at a similar level of awareness to wearing a seat belt or crash helmet. It is therefore submitted that a court should take this into account and apply Lord Denning's reasoning but reduce the upper boundary of 25 per cent to allow for the lower level of awareness.

II. A corporation's network is infected by a virus and it claims over a million pounds in damages from its law firm which allowed the virus to pass through their 'safe' connection. The law firm is both shocked at the claim and at the fact that the infected corporation does not use a virus checker which would have prevented all the damage. The firm is advised to focus their attention on proving that they had no duty of care as it is unforeseeable that a commercial organisation would have no anti-viral program. This is because it is unlikely that even a successful defence of contributory negligence would reduce the damages by more than 50%.

Data backups

Where the damage caused by malicious code is purely loss of data there is a factual, and possibly legal, argument that if the plaintiff had backed up the data far less damage would have occurred.[13] A legal basis for this argument could be based on contributory negligence, but it has less force than an argument that the victim should have used an anti-viral program. As to other arguments, the defendant could allege that the victim may have mitigated his damages by making a backup *before* the damage. It is submitted that such a claim is better pleaded as a remoteness issue: mitigation is usually a post facto issue.

CONSENT

It may be alleged by an operator of a web site, forum or ftp site that, by a plaintiff choosing to use the site, he consented to the risk of virus damage. To plead such a defence is to rely on consent or *volenti non fit injuria*. Although a consent defence remains appropriate for intentional torts such as assault, particularly in sport, there is now some doubt as to the extent of the defence for negligence.[14]

Whether or not the defence applies to negligence, what is certain is that if it does, a high degree of complicity is required by the plaintiff. Asquith J compared the degree of consent needed for a defence of *volenti* to 'inter-meddling with an unexploded bomb or walking on the edge of an unfenced cliff'.[15] For example, the Court of Appeal judged that a plaintiff who watched a pilot drink the equivalent of 17 whiskies would have his claim for negligent flying defeated by the defence of

---

13 Some damage would have occurred owing to the time taken to restore the data from the backup and the loss of data which may be unrecoverable and was created after the last backup.
14 See *Morris v Murray* [1990] 3 All ER 801 at 806 in which Fox LJ distinguishes between the dicta of Diplock LJ in *Wooldridge v Sumner* [1962] 2 All ER 978 at 988 and Asquith J's test in *Dann v Hamilton* [1939] 1 All ER 59 at 63.
15 [1939] 1 All ER 59 at 64. Applied by the Court of Appeal in *Morris v Murray* [1990] 3 All ER 801.

volenti.[16] Fox LJ stated, 'Flying is intrinsically dangerous and flying with a drunken pilot is great folly.'[17]

---

12. A ftp site acts as a depository of supposedly neutralised virus code. A plaintiff downloads one of the latest viruses with a view to writing an anti-viral program as an antidote. The code was not actually neutralised and the plaintiff's computer becomes infected forcing him to lose one day's working time. On poor advice he sues. Putting aside the inherent difficulties of establishing negligence, a court will probably allow the full defence of *volenti*: dealing with virus code is tantamount to dealing with unexploded bombs.

As for contributory negligence, it is difficult to extrapolate from a personal injury defence to one for data damage. If lessons can be learnt, clearly any defendant, who by negligence has caused data damage, will have a struggle to convince a court that the plaintiff was entering a dangerous area.

Why negligence?

This section has dealt exclusively with using the law of negligence to claim for damage from a viral infection. For the sake of completeness, this final part of the section considers why a claim for occupier's liability, strict liability or nuisance is inappropriate.

To understand the Internet, metaphors are often employed. A presence on the Internet is called a web *site*. Collections of web sites are now called *malls*. People using the Internet are said to *browse* it. Even the 'information superhighway' implies a tangible presence like a set of roads, the web sites being like shops and billboards along the way. Such comparisons are useful to conceptualise the Internet, but they may not be reliable for legal analysis.

When one's data is harmed by a computer virus caught from browsing a company's web site, nothing physical occurs. The site is no more than a collection of digital information, browsing is simply the transferral of information in the form of ones and zeros from one computer's memory to another's. Damage occurs, not because of faulty wiring or fire but because of inappropriate vetting of the digital information stored on the accessed computer. Laws, both statutory and common, that relate to occupier's liability, product liability and nuisance are inappropriate to apply.

OCCUPIERS' LIABILITY

The Occupiers' Liability Acts 1957 and 1984 replace common law rules on occupiers' liability with a statutory equivalent. A web site controller is liable only as an occupier of premises, which is any fixed or movable structure.[18] A web site may be notional premises but the reality is that a person who browses a web site has no physical presence there. The Act will not apply between web site controllers and those who gain access to them.

---

16   *Morris v Murray* [1990] 3 All ER 801.
17   [1990] 3 All ER 801 at 809.
18   Occupiers' Liability Act 1957, s 1(3).

PRODUCT LIABILITY

The Consumer Protection Act 1987 provides that almost anyone connected with the sale of a defective product may be liable for harm caused by the product.[19] The Act is unlikely to be applicable to digital materials transmitted over the Internet, but it will still apply to physical products conventionally sent. This is because the Act applies to defective products, and does not explicitly include information: incorrect information on a web site is unlikely to be classed as a product, and even defective software, unless incorporated into a machine,[20] is arguably not a product. In addition, there is a defence for new technologies which may be applicable to exclude liability where the state of knowledge at the time was not such that a producer of the products might have been expected to discover the defect.[1] Arguably, using the latest anti-viral program is enough to be able to rely on this defence.

NUISANCE

Comparisons seem reasonable between a reservoir owner allowing water to damage another's property and a web site owner allowing code to damage another's property. However, in *Rylands v Fletcher*, in which the reservoir owner was liable for damage done owing to the escape of water, the House of Lords was careful to stress the ruling applied only to escapes from land.[2] This was affirmed by the House of Lords in *Cambridge Water Co Ltd v Eastern Counties Leather plc*[3] in which Lord Goff considered an earlier case[4] stating:[5]

'there can be no liability under the rule except in circumstances where the injury has been caused by an escape from land under the control of the defendant.'

It seems, therefore, that the ruling in *Rylands v Fletcher* is narrowly focused on escapes from land, and often to other land. It seems unreasonable that the courts will stretch its application to the Internet, particularly as the Law Commission has expressed misgivings about any generalised test for 'especially dangerous' activities.[6]

NEGLIGENT MISSTATEMENT

The Internet allows wide, unfocused dissemination of information, and also a concentrated, targeted distribution. For commerce this is special. The web site that

19   Consumer Protection Act 1987, s 2.
20   Consumer Protection Act 1987, s 3(2).
1   Consumer Protection Act 1987, s 4(1)(e).
2   (1868) LR 3 HL 330; affg *Fletcher v Rylands* (1866) LR 1 Ex 265.
3   [1994] 1 All ER 53.
4   *Read v J Lyons & Co Ltd* [1946] 2 All ER 471.
5   [1994] 1 All ER 53 at 76.
6   *Civil Liability for Dangerous Things and Activities* (Law Com no 32) 1970 in paragraphs 14–16. Lord Goff stated, 'If the Law Commission is unwilling to consider statutory reform on this basis, it must follow that judges should if anything be even more reluctant to proceed down that path.' [1994] 1 All ER 53 at 76.

acts as a brochure for a mortgage adviser can also act as the conduit for quotes to be given to a customer. A stockbroker can host a web page that lists the current prices of stocks, allows customers to buy shares and provides, at an additional cost, tips on which shares to buy.

This ability easily to provide information, advice, and help to any person, anywhere in the world has huge commercial potential. But this potential should be balanced with the law on negligent misstatements. In appropriate circumstances, a web site controller or e-mailer may be found liable for the damage resulting from the information he provides. This section considers the scope of this doctrine in relation to the Internet.

Hedley Byrne v Heller

Much has been written on negligent misstatements and this will not be repeated here. What this section undertakes to do is to assess the stylised test for negligent misstatement considering the Internet. This section will only discuss the law where the peculiarities of the Internet affect the application of the test.

The ruling on negligent misstatements can be derived from *Hedley Bryne & Co Ltd v Heller & Partners Ltd*,[7] but Lord Oliver in a later case summarises the position well.[8] He suggests that there are four factors that indicate a necessary relationship exists between the maker of the statement and the recipient who acts in reliance on the advice.

1.   The advice is required for a purpose, whether particularly specified or generally described, which is made known, either actually or inferentially, to the adviser at the time when the advice is given.
2.   The adviser knows, either actually or inferentially, that his advice will be communicated to the advisee, either specifically or as a member of an ascertainable class, in order that it should be used by the advisee for that purpose.
3.   It is known, either actually or inferentially, that the advice so communicated is likely to be acted on by the advisee for that purpose without further independent inquiry.
4.   The advisee acts upon the advice to his detriment.

IDENTITY

There is a famous cartoon that depicts one dog, sitting at a computer, talking to another dog sitting on the floor. The dog at the computer is saying, 'On the Internet, nobody knows you're a dog.' There is some truth in this. Without the use of encryption authentication, the Internet makes it difficult to establish who (or what) has sent an e-mail and similarly who controls a web site. There are already many cases where even the domain name, the unique address for every server on the Internet, has been used by an impostor. This difficulty of identification does have legal ramifications.

---

7   [1963] 2 All ER 575.
8   In *Caparo Industries plc v Dickman* [1990] 1 All ER 568 at 589.

The rules on negligent misstatement do not apply between all individuals. It has been said that the ruling applies only to those who are possessed of some special skill or expertise.[9] But this is not limited to particular categories of persons or situations. The dictum has been followed[10] which states,[11]

> 'when an enquirer consults a businessman in the course of his business and makes it plain to him that he is seeking considered advice and intends to act on it in a particular way, any reasonable businessman would realise that, if he chooses to give advice without any warning or qualification, he is putting himself under a moral obligation to take some care ... [T]he principles established by the *Hedley Byrne* case ... translate his moral obligation into a legal obligation.'

This wider statement suggests that the courts will not allow an adviser to discount his duty by stating that he was not actually qualified to provide such advice. If a web site or an e-mail gives the impression, without limitation or disclaimer, that advice or information is *considered* advice, a plaintiff may rely on that to establish a duty. It will be remembered that the plaintiff needs only to show that the defendant could have *inferred* that the advice was to be relied upon.

---

13. An individual establishes a home page with the domain name 'www.mpg.com'. This web site, which is titled 'Official Petroleum Institute', lists a number of supposed methods of increasing the fuel consumption of a car. Poor proofreading allowed one piece of advice not to specify that the method applies only to unleaded vehicles. A plaintiff with a damaged engine sues. The defendant will not benefit from proving to the court that he was not qualified to provide the advice. The court will assess how the web site appeared to the plaintiff.

REASONABLE RELIANCE ON THE INTERNET

The courts need to establish that the reliance made by the plaintiff was reasonable. There are two aspects to this. First, is it reasonable to rely on the Internet *at all* for particular advice? Lord Denning interpreted the term 'considered advice' as excluding informal situations such as casual conversation in the street; or in a railway carriage; or an impromptu opinion given offhand; or 'off the cuff' on the telephone.[12] There are analogies over the Internet.

Internet Relay Chat

Internet Relay Chat is a method by which two or more users connected to the Internet can type messages to each other, these messages appearing as they are typed. It is like a telephone conversation using text not voice. This would appear to accord with the kinds of casual circumstances that Lord Denning envisaged. Other means of communication over the Internet are harder to pigeon-hole.

9   See [1963] 2 All ER at 594, per Lord Morris.
10   *Esso Petroleum Co Ltd v Mardon* [1975] 1 All ER 203 at 219.
11   *Mutual Life & Citizens Assurance Co Ltd v Evatt* [1971] 1 All ER 150 at 163.
12   *Howard Marine & Dredging Co Ltd v A Ogden & Sons (Excavations) Ltd* [1978] 2 All ER 1134 at 1141.

> **14.** A tenant who worried about being evicted from her flat logs on to Internet Relay Chat with an individual who purports to know her rights in this situation. He informs her that she can change the locks of the flat if she is worried about her landlady entering. The adviser's e-mail address is rogerg@aol.com. The tenant changes the locks and is given notice for having breached her contract. The tenant is unlikely to have a right of action against rogerg@aol.com; it will be difficult to show that the advice was 'considered' and that it was reasonable to rely on it in the circumstances.

Forums and Usenet

Certain Internet Service Providers, web sites and bulletin boards or forums allow members to 'deposit' questions for all other members to read. These members are then free to reply by leaving another message, and so on. The collective group of questions and answers is called a conversation thread.

Some may consider that these conversation threads are as casual as Internet Relay Chat but this may not be the case. First, any forum or group on the Usenet has a name. A name such as the Cancer Forum or alt.advice.cancer gives a far stronger impression that the material being discussed and advised upon is serious and in no way casual. The courts should take account of these surrounding circumstances. The second factor that distinguishes a forum from the informal situation is that the advice provided, unlike Internet Relay Chat, does not have to be given immediately. Users of forums are free to read questions, research and then provide an answer in due course. It does not need to be 'off the cuff' at all. Some messages remain unanswered for numbers of days. This may influence a court into thinking that the advice was considered.

> **15.** An individual logs in to a forum called **AIDSAdvice**. He is worried that he may have contracted **HIV** the previous night and seeks advice on how to assure himself that he hasn't. He leaves an appropriate question on the forum and checks for a reply the next day. As he wanted, his question had been replied to and the reply advises him to carry on as normal for the next three months as it takes this long for the virus to incubate; he will place no one at risk during this 'window'. On checking the source of the reply, the personal details revealed a doctor's name and surgery. These circumstances should influence a court into thinking that the advice was not off the cuff, despite potentially being lethally incorrect.

World Wide Web

The name 'home page' for a portion of a web site is quite an accurate description. The electronic documents stored on the World Wide Web are like pieces of paper. The authority of the information written on paper depends not on the fact that paper is used, but rather on the printing and the general impression given by the information. Similarly, a web site may contain official and considered advice from professional sources or it may be no more than a collection of ramblings from an individual. This spectrum of information from a high quality to no quality at all often presents a problem for users of the World Wide Web. If a site has a relevant domain name and looks official, is it reasonable to rely on the advice it provides? This is a question that can only be answered with the fullest understanding of the surrounding circumstances. Nevertheless, that the information was provided over the World Wide Web, without more, is inconclusive that it was reasonable to rely on the advice. Unlike Lord Denning's conversations in the street, the World Wide Web hosts a plethora of information; those who supply this information should be cautious of providing this information without appropriate warnings.

REASONABLE RELIANCE ON INFORMATION

The Internet, like any means of communication, can carry information of any quality; therefore, the medium itself is not conclusive of whether it was reasonable to rely on that advice. As for any negligent misstatement, the courts should look to whether *in the actual circumstances* it was reasonable for the plaintiff to rely on the advice. This issue depends on the facts but some issues specific to the Internet can be mentioned.

Those who publish on the web may believe that no liability will attach to them if the words on their home page are not advisory but are merely informative or are stated as opinions. Certainly, one could arrive at such a belief by taking a superficial glance at Lord Denning's speech in *Candler v Crane Christmas & Co*:[13]

> '[A] scientist or expert ... is not liable to his readers for careless
> statements in his published works. He publishes his work simply to
> give information, and not with any transaction in mind.'

However, this aspect of Lord Denning's much approved dissenting judgment does not classify what types of *words* are actionable, but rather, what types of *transactions*. It is perfectly possible for a scientist's published statement on the World Wide Web to be relied upon, with his knowledge, and to be the basis of a negligent misstatement suit. Lord Denning was attempting to provide an indication of to *whom* an adviser owes a duty, not over what he may owe a duty. Indeed, the court in a later case indicated that the operation of negligent misstatement is not restricted to a statement of fact or opinion, or even advice. It also applies where a notice should have been given but is not. The key is to establish whether a duty exists; if it does, it does not matter 'whether the breach takes the form of malfeasance or nonfeasance'.[14]

Tailored web sites

To create such a duty over the web, at first, appears difficult. The web seems to be no more than a collection of documents aimed at nobody in particular and of such a generic nature as to prevent a duty arising. But this is changing. As commerce begins to embrace the Internet, there are moves towards tailored web sites and material focused on potential clients. Advancements in hardware and software now allow sites to change the information that they provide for different viewers. Many sites already exist where, say, an investor inputs their stock portfolio and

---

13   [1951] 1 All ER 426 at 435.
14   *Midland Bank Trust Co Ltd v Hett, Stubbs and Kemp* [1978] 3 All ER 571 at 595.

the site not only allows the investor to trade in stocks but also advises the investor of stocks to add to balance the portfolio. It is likely that a duty to provide non-negligent advice will arise in this situation. As the software improves more customised sites will be created and so more individuals will be owed duties by the controllers of those sites.

Finding or requesting

Advice provided from a tailored web site raises a further issue that the courts have previously managed to avoid. In *Caparo Industries plc v Dickman* the plaintiff was considering making a takeover bid for a company.[15] To assess a good price it consulted the company accounts, prepared by auditors. Relying on the accounts, the plaintiff made its bid that was accepted, only to discover that the accounts were misleading. The plaintiff sued the defendant auditors but lost in the House of Lords. One justification for the Lords taking this restrictive view of negligent misstatement was that the defendant should not be liable for information which the plaintiff, in effect, finds rather than requests.

When a user of the Internet requires to view information that is stored on a web site, is this person 'finding' the document or are they requesting it from the controller? Certainly, where the site has no entry terms it may be analogous to picking up some company accounts from the foyer of a company: hardly the proximity required by the House of Lords. But where the viewer is required to enter some details as to who he is, where he heard about the information and why he requires it,[16] the situation approaches one where the defendant will be unable to deny the necessary inferential knowledge.

> 16. Sites on the World Wide Web often host a collection of commonly asked questions and answers on a particular subject; they are called, Frequently Asked Questions, or FAQ as an acronym. A web site with the URL, 'www.authors.co.uk', hosts an extensive FAQ on how authors can get their work published. It also contains a number of questions and incorrect answers on how to protect a work. If an author relies on these to her detriment, it will be difficult for the controller of the site to avoid having a duty to the author.

The Internet is an open source of information and material: if companies and individuals wish to avoid creating a duty with third parties they have two choices. First, they do not have to use the Internet. This sounds obvious although recently there has been a deluge of all types of material posted onto the Internet. Like any means of communication, the Internet is inappropriate for certain types of information. A more conservative attitude to the Internet will eradicate most of the glaring problems with negligent misstatements. The second choice is to publish the information but with a suitable contract and disclaimers. This is covered in the following section.

15   [1990] 1 All ER 568.
16   These type of questions are often asked, no doubt generally for marketing rather than legal reasons.

CONTRACTS AND DISCLAIMERS

The early phase of publishing on the Internet was simply a way of putting paper products, such as brochures and leaflets, in a digital form. The Internet is maturing: companies are using what is special about the World Wide Web to advertise and sell their products and services. Controllers of web sites are using more executable code on their sites to show animations and play sounds and music. They are also allowing a site to be tailored by the viewer to suit them. These changes, and the move away from having an 'order' to view web pages, is altering the conception that a web site is like a book. It may have many 'front covers' but individuals are no longer bound to view the pages in any particular order. Indeed, most web sites allow an individual to jump straight to any one of the pages of a site, rather than passing through the home page.[17] The introduction of frames that can be scrolled separately also adds to this fluidity. This creates a problem for legal advisers: to be effective, exclusions of liability are generally required before damage can occur; they should be the first text seen, but this hardly embraces the more modern vogues in web site design.

This section examines the exclusions required to reduce or exclude liability for digital damage.

Contractual exclusions

DIGITAL DAMAGE

The safest way of excluding damage from malicious code is to incorporate appropriate terms in a contract, rather than to rely simply on an exclusion notice. Details of how best to form a contract with a viewer of a web site are described in the chapter on contract.

A site should attempt to exclude any warranty as to the quality of any software downloaded on request or automatically by executable code and exclude its fitness for purpose.[18] In addition a disclaimer should be clear that the web site controller is not liable for any damage caused by the software or code attaching to the software; this covers viruses and worms. The drafting for such a disclaimer must be carefully worded and should refer to indirect and consequential losses as well as specifically excluding damages from loss of data, profit revenue and contracts of business. It is all too easy purely to draft general sweeping exclusions that have the advantage of being concise, but have the distinct disadvantage of being ineffective.

If a viewer is permitted to download an executable file he should be warned *before* he can download the code that, although the code has been checked, he is at risk from digital damage and its consequences unless he first checks the code himself for viruses.

---

17   This is particularly influenced by search engines that will locate any given text in a web site and permit the user to move straight to that page.
18   It is a moot point whether the Sale and Supply of Goods Act 1994 would include software as goods, or whether, in strict legal terms what is occurring is that the owner of the web site is making a licence with a viewer *over* goods. Sir Iain Glidewell in *St Alban's City and District Council v International Computers Ltd* [1996] 4 All ER 481 at 493 states that, 'the program is not "goods" within the statutory definition [of the Sale of Goods Act 1979]. Thus a transfer of the program [where it was transferred onto the computer by a third party] does not, in my view, constitute a transfer of goods'. See fn 3 at page 39.

NEGLIGENT MISSTATEMENT

To disclaim responsibility for damages from a misstatement, a term or notice should state that the web site or forum posting does not indicate any assumption of responsibility to the viewer or reader. The term or notice should ideally then address each element of the four-part test derived by Lord Oliver.[19] It should be stated that the wording and graphics on the site or posting are not provided for any specific or generally described purpose. To try to stop a third party seeing and relying on the advice[20] a notice or terms should insist that third parties are alerted to the same conditions. The last main disclaimer is that because the advice is not provided for any particular purpose it is assumed that no reliance will be made on the site or forum without having first taken specialised professional advice. Although strictly of no legal effect, for the avoidance of doubt, some sites and forums include a statement that the provider of information will not be liable for any loss caused as a result of doing or refraining from doing anything as a result of the wording, links or graphics.

NEGLIGENT LINKS

Often a site on the World Wide Web will feature links to other sites that may be of interest to its viewers; such is the nature of the web. In response to concerns that these links may increase liability, certain web site owners are using notices to viewers that on them leaving a web site the owners are not responsible for content outside their web site. To some extent, such a practice addresses a risk that is almost non-existent.

There are two situations where such a notice is used: first, where the linked site is a 'subsidiary' of the main site, often called a 'mall'; second, where the linked site is not associated with the first. Clearly, for the first situation, if the site is within the overall control of the web site owner, say where a set of web sites are collected together under the same domain, the controller will have some responsibility to viewers of the other sites. In the second situation, however, it is difficult to see how a duty would arise from providing a link to another's site.

The right of action against the first web site owner who provides the link will most reasonably be based on negligent misstatement.[1] The plaintiff will have to claim that by relying on the advice to follow that link the plaintiff suffered damage (probably as a result of further relying on advice on that linked page). Putting aside the rather stretched notion of causation that the court would have to accept, the fundamental question must be answered: was there a duty to the viewer concerning the link?

The four rules stated by Lord Oliver must apply. First, the links would have to be rather specifically referred to for a particular purpose. Advice required for a purpose known by the web site controller would not be satisfied by listing some links under the heading 'Other sites of interest'.[2] The site would have to use a

19   See '*Hedley Byrne v Heller*' at page 82.
20   It is very common on forums for statements to be copied from one forum, or section, to another.
1   It is admitted that a case of negligent construction of a web site could be brought, but it would appear easier for a plaintiff to satisfy the court as to the four rules of a negligent misstatement than to prove that a duty existed and that the web site designer fell below the standard reasonably expected of a web site designer!
2   In the same vein, the footnotes in this book referring to other sources do not amount to a statement as to the reliability of the information contained in those sources.

special heading like, 'Sites to consult for advice on swollen ankles'. The site owner would also have to know, either actually or inferentially, that as a result of the heading and the link that the viewer would not only follow the link but would take advice from the linked page without independent inquiry. It is submitted that it would be difficult for a plaintiff to convince a court that his reliance on the *link* could constitute reasonable reliance on the *information* contained in the linked site. In addition, there is the question of causation. It should be remembered that the advice is to follow the link; once at the linked page, the viewer will further have to act to be damaged. The courts will more readily break the chain of causation when the resulting damage depended on the plaintiff taking yet more negligent advice.

In short, although it is prudent to use markers such as 'You are now leaving our site' followed by a group of disclaimers as to the information on linked sites, it is submitted that it addresses a slim risk. A cleaner approach is merely to use a heading for the linked sites, 'Other sites of interest'. This simple statement distances the web site owner from the other content and is general enough not to form considered advice.

Effectiveness of exclusions

There are two factors that may limit the effectiveness of an exclusion or notice: incorporation and legal enforceability. The first is a factor which will have greatest impact on the World Wide Web.

INCORPORATION OF EXCLUSION

Unless an exclusion is within the terms of a contract, it must be incorporated to have binding contractual effect. On the World Wide Web such notices often are produced just before a viewer decides to download some executable code: 'If you proceed you agree that the file you are downloading may contain viruses and other damaging code which may damage your data and programs.' The controller of a web site does not need to show a court that a viewer understood such a notice, or even that it was read; the controller must, however, show that he took reasonable steps to bring it to the plaintiff's notice. This does not require having the actual wording of the exclusion shown but its wording should be made available by a simple link.

> **17. A viewer uses a search engine to search for the web sites that are supplying a free game. The search engine lists one particular page on a web site. The viewer downloads the software advertised on the web site's page by clicking a button labelled 'Download'. He sees no disclaimer because the web site has only one link to its disclaimer notices and this is on the home page that was bypassed by the search engine. The site will be unable to rely on the disclaimer as they did not take reasonable steps to alert each person who downloads software of the disclaimer.**

Owners of web sites must be careful not to assume that every viewer will read the pages on the site in a particular order. The very essence of the World Wide Web is that it is constructed with hypertext. That is, a viewer is free to browse around a site or many sites in *any* order. The terms may need to be incorporated repeatedly throughout the site with a simple link called 'disclaimer'. Alternatively a site can be designed with frames that allow certain text or graphics to remain on every page of the site.

Those who advise web site designers should be conscious that drafting a contract or disclaimer may not be enough: they should ideally also have an input into exactly where on the web site the disclaimer and links are placed. What is certain is that if the notice is intended to be incorporated into the web contract to exclude negligence, the viewer must have been able to view the notice or disclaimer before the web contract is made.[3]

---

18.   A software manufacturer decides to distribute its software utilities from its web site. Before each utility is downloaded a notice is shown which excludes liability for negligently caused damage. After downloading some software from the site, a viewer's computer begins to slow down. It is discovered that some executable code that was on the web site is retarding the computer. The notices provided before downloading the software will be inoperative: first, they relate to the web site's software not the downloaded software; second, the poorly written executable code will have been downloaded to the viewer's computer before he had a chance to view the notice.

LIMITATIONS ON EXCLUSIONS

It is vital to pay due regard to the Unfair Contract Terms Act 1977 and successors and the Unfair Terms in Consumer Contracts Regulations 1994.

The Unfair Contract Terms Act 1977

Despite the title of the Act, the Unfair Contract Terms Act 1977 applies to simple notices which are not incorporated into a contract in addition to contractual terms. In the main, this Act makes ineffective the exemption clauses in contracts in relation to a 'business liability',[4] and with a person 'dealing as a consumer'.[5] However, as the World Wide Web contains many amateur sites that are not operated in the course of a business it is worthwhile checking whether the Unfair Contract Terms Act 1977 will apply. A term that seeks to exclude liability for damage resulting from negligence will operate only where it is reasonable.[6]

It has been discussed that a term of a contract must be properly incorporated to be effective. A simple notice, in contrast, can be made at any point about the information being provided. The safest option, however, is to disclaim responsibility *before* a viewer has a chance to rely on any advice.

---

3   See *Olley v Marlborough Court* [1949] 1 All ER 127, approved by the Court of Appeal in *Hollier v Rambler Motors (AMC) Ltd* [1972] 1 All ER 399 at 407.
4   Unfair Contract Terms Act 1977, s 1(3).
5   Unfair Contract Terms Act 1977, s 12(1)(a) and (b).
6   Unfair Contract Terms Act 1977, s 2(2). For guidance on what is reasonable, consult the Unfair Contract Terms Act 1977, s 11. This includes where the provider of information attempts to construct a notice as stating he has no duty at all. Section 13 prevents the exclusion or restriction of the duty itself unless it is reasonable.

For a web site, a viewer should be confronted with a page or frame of disclaimers or at the least a prominent notice that the viewer should follow the link to the disclaimers page of the site.[7] For the Unfair Contract Terms Act 1977, what is relevant is not the precise wording of a disclaimer but more its reasonableness regarding all the circumstances.[8] An adviser can no longer simply draft a form of wording and allow the client to place the words on the site or forum. The adviser should check that the format and construction of the site or forum makes it reasonably clear to all viewers that the controller is disclaiming responsibility. Position on a site may be as legally relevant as wording.

Unfair Terms in Consumer Contracts Regulations 1994

The Regulations[9] strike at a more limited set of exclusions than those under the Unfair Contract Terms Act 1977. First, the Regulations apply only to contracts and only those contractual terms that have not been individually negotiated.[10] This will cover most contracts made over the World Wide Web. The second requirement is that the contract must be between a consumer and a supplier of goods or services.[11] The contract does not need to be for the supply of goods or services so it seems probable that the Regulations will apply to a licence over software. If applicable, the Regulations will exclude any term that is 'unfair'.[12] There is very little peculiar about the Internet which means that certain terms will be more or less fair. This said, terms must be incorporated before contracting with the consumer. The Regulations provide a term may be regarded as unfair if it has the object or effect of 'irrevocably binding the consumer to terms with which he had no opportunity of becoming acquainted with before the conclusion of the contract'.[13] This may occur on the Internet where terms are flashed up on a consumer's screen without him actually having an opportunity to review or even repudiate their content.

DEFAMATION + SOS

Out of the dearth of cases involving the Internet, a high proportion concern defamation. Part of the reason for this is that the Internet affords the man on the street with a unique opportunity to have his thoughts, often off the cuff, published instantaneously throughout the world. The main legal issue in this section does not, however, concern the primary defamer; nothing is special about the law as it relates to a person defaming over the Internet. What is legally special is that to 'publish' on the Internet, one generally must submit the material in an electronic form to a third party; it is this third party that, in effect, publishes the material. The key legal question in this section is therefore when will liability fix also to these

7   See 'Incorporation of exclusion' at page 89.
8   This general approach was affirmed by the Court of Appeal in *Smith v Eric S Bush* [1988] QB 743.
9   SI 1994/3159.
10   See Unfair Terms in Consumer Contracts Regulations 1994, reg 3(3).
11   See Unfair Terms in Consumer Contracts Regulations 1994, reg 2(1). Unlike the Unfair Contract Terms Act 1977, a consumer must be a natural person.
12   For detailed advice, readers should consult specialist texts.
13   Unfair Terms in Consumer Contracts Regulations 1994, Sch 3, para 1(i).

Internet Service Providers. Related to this is the liability of controllers of mirror sites, web sites, forums, and Usenet hosts.

Before September 1996, the answers to these questions were the subject of much speculation based on old English common law and stretched analogies from abroad. The Defamation Act 1996 now provides for when a third party Internet 'publisher' will have no liability and when the party will have to rely on one of the limited defences. Unfortunately, the application of the Act is not free from doubt. This section will provide the safest, and perhaps overly cautious, interpretation for Service Providers and their equivalents.

This section will also address the practicalities of a case where the defamatory statement has been made across the Internet. These practicalities include how damages are to be assessed and the considerations in the collection of digital evidence to defend an action.

Before considering these legal issues, it is useful to appreciate the technical aspects of the Internet that may impinge on any defamatory statement made over it. First, defamation over the Internet necessarily involves a third party, usually a Provider. Related to this is the issue that it is problematic to locate the person whose defamatory remark is published. A final issue is that defamatory remarks made over the Internet *may* be extremely widely published.

Technicalities

THIRD PARTY

Sending information over the Internet cannot be done single-handedly. In contrast to a poster that can be drawn and pinned to a wall without third party help, to publish on the Internet necessarily involves others. Forums that hold written conversation threads and web sites that show material are stored in a digital form on a server computer. The same is true for electronic mail: it is not generally sent directly to the recipient's computer; it is sent to a 'digital pigeon-hole' from which the recipient downloads new messages. This reliance on a third party to publish the material has a significant impact on the analysis of a defamation action. In defamation, it is not only the writer of the statement who may be liable, but also those who are involved in its publication and distribution.

IDENTITY OF FIRST DEFENDANT

The legal significance of this third party dovetails with the commercial reality of an Internet defamation action. Often it will be difficult to discover the identity of the person who typed the defamatory statement. It is trivial to use a pseudonym when an e-mail is sent to a person or a conversation thread. Worse still, it is possible to 'blind' an electronic message making it impossible to tell even the source of the statement. This is achieved by sending an e-mail to what is called an 'anonymous remailer' which is a computer program that automatically strips any message of any identifiers.[14] This difficulty of identification makes it inviting to litigate with the third party who actually distributed the message; this legal individual will be necessarily identifiable as the statement will be stored on the individual's

14   See fn 3 at page 107.

equipment. There is also some sense in proceeding with what is cynically called, 'deep-pocket litigation'; the commercial organisations such as Prodigy and Compuserve who may host the defamatory statement are in a more obvious position to meet the damages and costs flowing from litigation.

EXTENT OF PUBLICATION

The court, generally judge and jury, assesses the damages for a plaintiff on the basis of many factors. One clearly significant factor is the extent of the distribution of a defamatory statement. For a statement published on the Internet, this distribution has the potential to be global and numerous. The technical and legal difficulties of estimating the extent of distribution may be a stumbling block for any plaintiff.

The Defamation Act 1996

The Act does not alter what constitutes a defamatory statement; it addresses who should be liable for this defamatory statement and it introduces new procedures for claims.[15] For the sake of completeness, however, the following is a short summary of what constitutes a defamatory statement;[16] the issue of third party liability will then be tackled.[17]

DEFAMATORY STATEMENTS

Material is defamatory if it tends to 'lower the plaintiff in the estimation of right-thinking people generally', or if the material causes people to 'shun or avoid' the plaintiff or, more narrowly, hold the plaintiff up to 'ridicule, hatred or contempt'.[18] These tests are not entirely objective; part of the court's deliberations will be directed to the feelings of the people who actually read the statement.

Similar interests

On Internet forums and newsgroups the individuals involved often have similar interests and an understanding of the frivolity of the messages posted. This may be

15 Of particular relevance to Internet defamation are the new procedures of: *Offer to make amends* (ss 2–4); reduction of limitation period to one year from the date on which the cause of action accrued (ss 5–6); and *Summary disposal of claim* (ss 8–11).

16 There are two kinds of defamation: libel and slander. The importance of this distinction is that in a limited class of slander cases the plaintiff must prove 'special damage'; in libel the plaintiff does not need to prove any loss to succeed. It has generally been thought that slander is where the defamation is spoken whereas in libel it is written. Although it is a little more complex than that, it nevertheless appears that with the exception of Internet telephony, any defamatory material on the Internet will be a libel.

17 Specialist texts should be consulted in relation to what exactly can constitute a defamatory statement. The information provided here is the general position with application to some Internet specific issues.

18 Respectively: *Sim v Stretch* [1936] 2 All ER 1237 at 1240; *Youssoupoff v Metro-Goldwyn-Mayer Pictures Ltd* (1934) 50 TLR 581 at 587; *Thorley v Lord Kerry* (1812) 4 Taunt 355 at 364.

a factor that a court should take into account. Internet forums and newsgroups[19] with names such as 'sci.anthropology' are made up from like-minded people who have an interest in common. This interest forms the title to the forum. Interested parties can view the messages that have been posted on the forum and reply to any message that they choose. Each reply is appended to the existing written conversations and so the thread expands.

The nature of the replies vary with each forum, rather as conversations may vary in different pubs across the country. In some forums, like 'comp.legal', comments are generally directed to the subject matter and are quite academic and deferent. In other forums such as 'alt.erotica.male' the comments are far more personal, and to an outsider, far more insulting and rude. For example, in one of the sexually-orientated newsgroups it is not be unusual to read about a person being called a homosexual.[20] This should not suggest that in some newsgroups and forums some statements can never be defamatory. What it does indicate is that a defendant should be prepared to emphasise the readership of a forum. Merely because anyone connected to the Internet *could* have read the posting, does not indicate this has occurred.[1]

Types of defamatory material

It is not unique to the Internet that a person can be defamed by more than simply words. A defamatory statement means 'words, pictures, visual images, gestures or any other method of signifying meaning'.[2] Under this definition, it is possible that a computer-manipulated image posted on the Internet that shows a person performing a degrading act may be considered as defamatory. It is this wide scope of what is defamatory that makes it so difficult to operate automatic screening of potentially defamatory material.

THIRD PARTY LIABILITY

The cause of action in libel arises on publication rather than the writing of the defamatory material. The crucial questions for those who provide and store material on the Internet are therefore, can they be liable and, if so, what defences are available to them.

The Act attempts to provide an answer to these questions in section 1. First, the third party Provider must not be the author, editor or publisher of the material. Only if they are not considered to be one of these persons may they then rely on the defence.

19   Generally, the word 'forum' refers to a collection of written conversations that are hosted by a commercial online service provider; a written conversation group with the nomenclature xxx.yyy is generally called a 'newsgroup' and is hosted on a non-commercial basis on the Usenet system; they are therefore less prone to editing.

20   In 1992 a well-known Australian actor sued the general circulation magazine, *The Face*, over its statement that the actor was homosexual. Drake J told the jury that it was 'very debatable' whether being called a homosexual does lower an actor's reputation: *Guardian*, 9 April 1992.

1   Cf, *Rindos v Hardwick*, unreported, WA S Ct, AGIS-NO: 94/3397 (Vol 40:2). In this case the plaintiff was an academic who was defamed on the Usenet newsgroup 'sci.anthropology'. This case is relevant because the judge did not appear to analyse the nature of the forum and the extent to which the other academics who accessed it would have lowered their estimation of the plaintiff.

2   Defamation Act 1996, s 17(1).

Not authors, editors or publishers

The Act defines these individuals along with providing presumptions. The logical way to tackle this Act is therefore to check first whether a third party's activities fall within one of the presumptions listed below. If they do, they may then seek to rely on the defence. If they do not fall squarely within the presumption, they will have to prove that their activities are not those of an author, editor or the publisher as defined. If they do not fall within these definitions, ie they are not an author, editor or publisher, they may seek to rely on the defence.

Presumptions

The relevant presumptions for the Internet are that a person shall not be considered the author, editor or the publisher of a statement if he is only involved:[3]

> '(c) in processing, making copies of, distributing or selling any electronic medium in or on which the statement is recorded, or in operating or providing any equipment, system or service by means of which the statement is retrieved, copied, distributed or made available in electronic form;
>
> ...
>
> (e) as the operator or provider of access to a communications system by means of which the statement is transmitted, or made available, by a person over whom he has no effective control.'

The key to interpreting these sections is that the party must 'only' be involved in these activities. If a third party does no more than that described in section 1(3)(c) or 1(3)(e) they may be able to rely on the defences described below. To illustrate the scope of these presumptions, this chapter applies them to the following issues: sending and forwarding e-mails; hosting a web site; hosting a mirror site; designing web sites; providing access to newsgroups; and providing forums.

Sending and forwarding e-mails

One safe example of an activity that falls within section 1(3)(c) is the facilities of a Provider to send and forward e-mails. When an e-mail is sent to another individual, or a group of individuals, there are two third parties who are additionally often involved. The first is the defendant's Service Provider. The e-mail is sent out onto the Internet from this Provider's server computers. There will also be a second third party, the Provider or Providers to which the defamatory e-mail is sent. These Providers will pass on the e-mail to their respective intended recipients.

The Providers to the defendant and recipients will not be viewed as editors or publishers under the presumption. They will only have provided a service by means of which the defamatory e-mail statement is distributed (for the defendant) and retrieved (for the recipients).[4] Each of the controllers of the intermediary computers on the Internet that automatically shunted the e-mail nearer and nearer

3   Defamation Act 1996, s 1(3)(c), (e).
4   Ie Defamation Act 1996, s 1(3)(c).

its destination will also fall within the presumption that they are not an editor or publisher. A server linked to the Internet has packets of zeros and ones 'passing through' every second. These packets originated as messages and data created and sent by other servers over which they have no control. What is more, the nature of the Internet is such that it may be impossible even to know who was the original sender of a message.[5]

Hosting a web site

Another safe example of an activity falling squarely within one of the presumptions is where a Provider rents out space on a web server to individuals to use as home pages. For example, many of the Internet Service Providers, on subscription, will provide a person with a web site address at which he can leave material to be viewed by others. Again, such a provider has no hand in the actual content of the site and would be viewed as providing a service by means of which the material on the defamatory web site is made available.[6] The Provider would be able to rely on the defences, as would the Provider used by the viewer of the web site.[7]

Hosting a mirror site

A server that stores a web site or ftp site must be able to cope with all the requests, sometimes simultaneously, from viewer's computers. Occasionally the most popular sites become so inundated with digital requests that they begin to slow. To solve this problem, a controller of a web site will set up or rent space on a mirror site. As the name suggests, this site is an identical copy of the original site; it simply allows another route into the web site so reducing the strain on the original. The controller of the mirror site appears not to be presumed to be an author, editor or publisher as he is only providing equipment by means of which the statement is retrieved, copied, distributed or made available in electronic form.[8] He would be able to rely on the defences.

Designing web sites

The above examples should not be taken to indicate that all those involved in the web will not be viewed as authors, editors or publishers. There are many companies who design web sites for other individuals, companies and advertising firms. These designers are involved in more than *only* making the statement available in an electronic form and have effective control over their contractor. Indeed, often these companies will amend text and include graphics to best represent the client's activities on the web site. It is rare that a client will approach such a designer with the code ready to be used for the web site. For web site

---

5   There is also the technical argument that the e-mail is not even published by these intermediaries. Any e-mail is broken into packets which are in a human unreadable form, and some of the packets will not pass through the same computer. It would be a momentous task to prove that one of the intermediary computers actually transmitted all of the packets in relation to one particular e-mail, all in order.
6   Defamation Act 1996, s 1(3)(c).
7   Defamation Act 1996, s 1(3)(e).
8   Defamation Act 1996, s 1(3)(c).

designers, therefore, it is important that they acquire an indemnity from their client over any defamation actions.

Providing access to newsgroups

Newsgroups exist on the Usenet network of computers. Like forums, they are collections of written conversations and files that are left for everyone to reply to or purely retrieve. Many of these forums have fairly specialised and often sexual subject matters; these run a great risk of holding defamatory material. To access these newsgroups, a viewer will generally have only to access his Provider's servers. This is because Service Providers store copies of the newsgroups on their local machines. Because of this, they may re-publish defamatory material so they should be careful to fall within one of the presumptions.

There is, however, a problem with attempting to persuade a court that, in relation to the newsgroups, the Provider is *only* providing a service by means of which a statement is copied or made available in an electronic form. This problem occurs because a Provider will rarely carry all the many thousands of newsgroups; they are selective. For example, many providers avoid the overtly pornographic groups. In doing so, it could be alleged that the Provider is doing more than *only* electronically distributing the material: they are censoring, for whatever reasons, certain of the newsgroups. In doing this, it is arguable that they are acting as an editor. That is they are assuming responsibility for the decision to publish a statement.[9]

It is submitted that this reasoning relies on an excessively constrained view of the presumptions. The decision to exclude certain newsgroups *without having seen their content* should not be translated into having editorial responsibility for the content of the *others*: the Provider is still *only* making the copies of the newsgroups available in an electronic form.[10] Merely because there was certain material that the Provider chose not to make available should not indicate that the Provider has assumed some responsibility over the distributed newsgroups. It is when a Provider begins to edit the actual text of the individual statements *within* a newsgroup that the Provider approaches the position of editor.

Providing forums

Many Internet Service Providers provide forums for their members. These are collections of written conversations and files that can be accessed by any member of the forum. The Providers of these forums face the greatest problem of liability. Rather than simply allowing anyone to post up anything on a forum, the Providers will often moderate the text and messages before or soon after they are posted. They do this, presumably, to protect the other members of the forum from vulgarities and irrelevancies. Of course, in doing this, just like a newspaper editor edits a reader's letter, they are, in effect, acting as an editor. The Provider is no longer *only* making the copies of the statements available in an electronic form; the Provider is editing the statement.

This would appear to indicate that the prudent Provider who attempts to screen out defamatory comments may not be able to benefit from the defence. In

---

9   From the definition of an 'editor' in the Defamation Act 1996, s 1(2).
10   The nature of the 'flooding algorithm' through which the newsgroups are distributed amongst Providers also gives the Provider little effective control over material.

contrast, the Provider who turns a blind eye to defamatory comments and does not edit the messages will be able to rely on the defence.[11] There are two justifications for this seemingly counter-intuitive conclusion.

Stratton v Prodigy

The first is a commercial justification that is provided by the court in an Internet defamation case from America: *Stratton Oakmont Inc v Prodigy Services Co.*[12] Prodigy is a large Online Service Provider; one of its services was a bulletin board called 'Money Talk'. An unknown individual posted a defamatory remark that the plaintiff company was guilty of fraud. The plaintiff sought partial summary judgment against Prodigy on two issues, namely: whether Prodigy may be considered 'publisher' of the statements;[13] and whether the Board Leader for the bulletin board on which the statements were posted was Prodigy's 'agent' for the purpose of the claims.

Prodigy is a prudent Online Service Provider; it prides itself on exercising editorial control over the content of messages posted on its computer bulletin boards, differentiating itself from its competition and expressly likening itself to a newspaper. In the case, Prodigy is quoted as stating:

> 'We make no apology for pursuing a value system that reflects the culture of the millions of American families we aspire to serve. Certainly no responsible newspaper does less when it carries the type of advertising it publishes, the letters it prints, the degree of nudity and unsupported gossip its editors tolerate.'

It is precisely this editing, both manual and automatic, that the court reasoned brought the defendant within the realms of a publisher, or more widely, made the defendant responsible for the content. The court stated that,

> '... Prodigy is clearly making decisions as to content ... and such decisions constitute editorial control ... . That such control is not complete and is enforced both as early as the notes arrive and as late as a complaint is made, does not minimize or eviscerate the simple fact that Prodigy has uniquely arrogated to itself the role of determining what is proper for its members to post and read on its bulletin boards ... Prodigy is a publisher rather than a distributor.'

11   An example of this is provided by the American case, *Cubby Inc v Compuserve Inc* 776 F Supp 135 (SDNY 1991). Compuserve carried a forum, 'Rumorville', that was managed by a company unrelated to Compuserve. A defamatory statement was published on this forum and Compuserve was sued. The court compared Compuserve to an 'electronic, for-profit library' (at 140) and stated that summary judgment should be given in favour of Compuserve. This was primarily because the plaintiffs did not set forth any specific facts showing a genuine issue of Compuserve knowing or having reason to know of the forum's contents. (Cf Defamation Act 1996, s 1(1)(b) and (c).) Although this judgment and Compuserve's arguments were heavily steeped in the First Amendment, the case can be used to illustrate that the more distance a Provider puts between itself and the forum, the more likely it will be able to rely on the defence. Conversely, this imposes a burden on the plaintiff to *adduce* evidence that the Provider, by making this distance, was not taking reasonable care and should have known the risk of defamation. A forum name like 'Rumorville' must surely place the Provider on notice. See fn 7 at page 102.

12   NYS 2d Index No 31063/94, 1995 WL 323710.

13   In the case Prodigy were seeking to prove themselves as 'distributors' and thus able to rely on a defence of innocent dissemination.

So the court was content to rule that, despite Prodigy's aim to protect its members, it should be liable when this protection fails. To the proposition that this decision will simply force Providers not to edit postings, so avoiding liability, the court drew on a 'market forces' argument.

> 'For the record, the fear that this court's finding of publisher status for Prodigy will compel all computer networks to abdicate control of their bulletin boards, incorrectly presumes that the market will refuse to compensate a network for its increased control and the resulting increased exposure ... . Presumably Prodigy's decision to regulate the content of its bulletin boards was in part influenced by its desire to attract a market it perceived to exist consisting of users seeking a "family-oriented" computer service. This decision simply required that to the extent computer networks provide such services, they must also accept the concomitant legal consequences.'

Looking strictly at law, the *Prodigy* case provides little authority for an English court. Under English law the Defamation Act 1996 is quite clear that editorial decisions, like those made by Prodigy, will bring the Provider into the realms of an editor or publisher. This is particularly true where, like certain Providers, members are charged an extra rate to access certain 'moderated' forums. In this situation, the Provider appears to be within the definition of a 'publisher' under the Act.[14]

> '"publisher" means a commercial publisher, that is, a person whose business is issuing material to the public, or a section of the public, who issues material containing the statement in the course of that business.'

What the case does illustrate is one *justification* for a court imposing a ruling that a prudent Provider should be liable whereas a reckless Provider has an opportunity to rely on a defence. This justification is that individuals will pay for quality and editing; too much of the Internet is of very dubious quality. This increase in income gained by being able to charge more to a discerning member has a concomitant legal risk.

There is a second explanation for the seemingly unjust rule that 'the prudent Provider is punished'. This is described below.

Strength of defences

In much of the discussion about the Defamation Act 1996 there seems to be an assumption that if a Provider is reckless as to content, the Provider has an easy task to plead a defence. This is not so. As will be considered below, a Provider who turns a blind eye to defamatory material will have difficulties in meeting the test of reasonable care. But there is also a commercial advantage in being a prudent Provider: you are sued less often and will have lower insurance premiums. A prudent Provider screening as much content as is feasible will eliminate many potential defamation actions. In contrast, a reckless Provider may find itself defending many law suits having to hope that they will be able to satisfy the defences. These two situations will obviously affect the level of insurance premiums payable by the two types of Provider.

---

14   Defamation Act 1996, s 1(2).

This lengthy discussion on the liability for providing forums indicates that what at first appears as counter-productive legislation is explicable, even if not palatable, to those in the online industry.

Analogies

It is mentioned earlier[15] that even if a defendant does not fall within one of the presumptions,[16] they may still be able to prove to the court that they are not an author, editor, or publisher. This is necessary, as to rely on the defence one must not be author, editor or publisher.[17] Not falling within one of the presumptions does not necessarily mean that one *is* an author, editor or publisher. This remains open to argument by analogy with the presumptions and then with the definitions.

The following is an example of one possible analogy. There is a move on the Internet to feature not simply sounds and static pictures but also moving pictures and 'live' sounds. In illustration, there are over one hundred radio stations that broadcast their shows over the Internet by feeding to their server a live audio stream of their shows in a digitised format. Providers may worry that, by allowing their members to access this server, the Provider may be repeating a defamatory statement.[18] If they are seen as the publisher of this statement, they may be considered liable for the damage resulting from their transmission. By analogy, however, the Provider, as opposed to the controller of the station's server, will not be a publisher. Section 1(3)(b) creates the presumption that a defendant is not a publisher if involved only in processing, making copies of, distributing, exhibiting or selling a film or sound recording. Section 1(3)(d) creates the additional presumption that a defendant is not a publisher if involved only as the broadcaster of a live programme in circumstances in which he has no effective control over the maker of the statement.

These two presumptions should provide a court with an analogy that the Provider of live radio over the Internet is not a publisher for the purposes of defamation. The live radio is, technically, a sound recording. The method of sending the radio broadcast is as a collection of digital recordings of sounds from which the viewer's computer reproduces sounds.[19] Should a court feel that the transmission by the Provider is not a copy of a sound recording, as such, they may be more persuaded that the Provider is akin to a broadcaster of a live programme. This conclusion should be equally applicable to a Provider who permits access to live video or recorded video.

---

19. CDAccess is a company based in America that provides customers with a special program that allows them to download portions of music compact discs to evaluate. These portions are freely available over the Internet from the record company's web sites. A UK Internet Access Provider is sued for publishing defamatory material that was contained on the one of the downloaded portions. The Provider should be able to bring itself within an analogous situation to the presumptions in the Act; the defence will be available to the Provider through not being a publisher.

---

15   See 'Not authors, editors or publishers', at page 95.
16   Defamation Act 1996, s 1(3)(a)-(e).
17   Defamation Act 1996, s 1(1)(a).
18   The same worry of course may apply to live pictures.
19   Defamation Act 1996, s 1(3)(b) referring to the Copyright, Designs and Patents Act 1988, s 5(1)(a).

Definitions

If a third party has been unable to convince a court that it falls within one of the presumptions or an analogous situation, it has one last chance of pleading that, in the alternative, it is not an author, editor or publisher within the definitions of the Act.[20]

> '"author" means the originator of the statement, but does not include a person who did not intend that his statement be published at all;
> "editor" means a person having editorial or equivalent responsibility for the content of the statement or the decision to publish it; and
> "publisher" means a commercial publisher, that is, a person whose business is issuing material to the public, or a section of the public, who issues material containing the statement in the course of that business.'

It is clear from the definition of 'publisher' that the Act does not contemplate a person being a publisher where publishing is merely *incidental* to their business.[1] For example, many firms have internal networks or intranets on which various pieces of information are posted. Should defamatory material be posted on this internal network, by an employee, the employer is unlikely to be viewed as a publisher for the purposes of the Act. Their business is not the issuing of material to the public and they are not a commercial publisher; their business does not depend on the issuance of material on the intranet.

---

20. An employee posts a defamatory message about another employee on her firm's Intranet bulletin board. The defamed employee sues both the employee and the employer. Clearly the employee who typed the message is an author under the Act. The employer pleads that as they do not publish commercially, they are not a publisher. While this may be true, if they vet or censor any of the postings on the board they will be considered as the editor of the defamatory material. In such a case they will be unable to rely on the defence.

Defence

The Defamation Act 1996, section 1(1) introduces a statutory defence for a person who is not an author, editor or publisher of a defamatory statement.[2] This defence is, along with the common law defences of truth or justification, fair comment and consent. The common law defence of privilege is altered by the Act.[3]

---

20 Defamation Act 1996, s 1(2).
1   It should be noted that, although the words 'publication' and 'publish' retain their common law meanings, the word 'publisher' is specially defined for the purposes of section 1: Defamation Act 1996, s 17(1).
2   'It is intended to provide a modern equivalent of the common law defence of innocent dissemination, recognising that there may be circumstances in which the unwitting contributor to the process of publication may have had no idea of the defamatory nature of the material he has handled or processed.' The Lord Chancellor (promoter of the Bill) Vol 571, No 72, HL Official Report, col 211, 2 April 1996.
3   Defamation Act 1996, ss 14 and 15.

The section 1(1) defence requires two hurdles to be cleared by the defendant. First, he must show that he took reasonable care in relation to the statement's publication. In addition, he must show that he did not know, and had no reason to believe, that what he did caused or contributed to the publication of a defamatory statement.

To determine what is reasonable and what should be known, the Act provides three considerations to which the court *shall* have regard. The first consideration is the extent of the responsibility for the content of the statement or decision to publish.[4] This provides little guidance for a Service Provider. The second and third considerations are more helpful. Regard shall be had to the nature or circumstances of the publication and the previous conduct or character of the author, editor or publisher.[5]

These last two considerations indicate that to take reasonable care one must first judge the care which is required in a given scenario. It will not be reasonable care simply to re-publish an entire Usenet newsgroup that has a reputation for being scurrilous and defamatory. It is no defence for the Provider to state that it did not know that a particular *posting* was defamatory. This is because the court is required to judge that the Provider did not know *and had no reason to believe* that the material would be defamatory.[6] Service Providers are advised not to turn a blind eye to the nature of the material that they publish. If a forum or newsgroup is known to carry postings of dubious veracity, a Provider *is* taking a risk to publish its material without vetting.

The prospect of vetting the contents of a newsgroup or forum raises two problems: one commercial, the other legal. The commercial problem is simply put: how can a Provider feasibly vet the thousands of postings that are posted up on newsgroups each day? The answer is also simple: the Provider cannot; it would be impossible. The important question is whether the Provider is required to vet every posting. The Act does not impose an absolute requirement that all postings are vetted; it is more rational than that: *reasonable* care must be taken.

This does not mean vetting every posting, but it also does not mean blindly re-publishing dubious newsgroups and entertaining the postings made by known defamers. During the passage of the Bill through the House of Commons, Mr Streeter explained,[7]

'We must put distributors, printers, wholesalers and retailers on notice that they should have regard to the nature of a publication if they seek to rely on that defence.'

A commercial balance must be struck. Providers may choose to vet one hour of postings on a particular forum every day. Providers may also choose to allow members to alert them, by priority e-mail, of a defamatory comment.

---

4   Defamation Act 1996, s 1(5)(a).
5   Defamation Act 1996, ss 1(5)(b) and (c).
6   Defamation Act 1996, s 1(1)(c).
7   Parliamentary Secretary, Lord Chancellor's Department (promoter of the Bill), 280 HC Official Report (6th Series) col 119, 24 June 1996. This is added as an indication of the intention of Parliament; it is not mentioned as a statement upon which a court could rely under the strict criteria laid down in *Pepper (Inspector of Taxes) v Hart* [1993] 1 All ER 42 and *Melluish (Inspector of Taxes) v BMI (No 3) Ltd* [1995] 4 All ER 453. Although perhaps prejudicial to Internet Providers, it is this author's submission that the Bill does not meet the criteria of being ambiguous or obscure or its literal meaning leading to an absurdity.

The legal problem that has been raised about vetting material is that it produces a circular argument. This goes as follows. To take reasonable care a Provider must occasionally edit some material. By editing some material the Provider cannot now be *only* involved with one of the five presumptive activities. This conclusion strips the presumption from the Provider that it is not an author, editor or publisher.

This legal problem is not as confusing as it appears. As this section has shown, a Provider can rely on a presumption that it is not an author, editor or publisher, but failing that, the Provider is not *necessarily* an author, editor or publisher. The Provider remains able to plead that it does not fall within the definitions of author, editor or publisher. So, by editing material the Provider is not prevented from relying on the defence, it is simply prevented from relying on the *presumption*. The court remains able to hear evidence that the Provider is not a publisher or editor under the definitions. And if convinced, the court can still allow the Provider to rely on the defence of reasonable care.

Of course, the ramifications of this analysis are that the Defamation Act 1996 has impaled many Internet Service Providers on the horns of a dilemma. If they turn a blind eye to all content, they may be able to rely on the presumption that they are not a publisher. They will, however, be unlikely to convince a court that by doing nothing they took all reasonable care. Conversely, if they are prudent and edit out potentially defamatory material, they will not be able to rely on the presumption as they are now only involved in non-editorial activities. They will be left with convincing a court that they are not a publisher, which under the Act, as a person whose business is issuing material to the public, they probably are.

In this 'lose-lose' predicament an Internet Service Provider should be aware of four practical issues. First, if the Provider does edit its content, it will be sued less frequently as it will re-publish defamatory statements less often. Ignoring content will increasingly lead one to a position of being unable to ignore litigation. The second issue is that insurance is available to Internet Service Providers, but premiums will be significantly lower if the Provider takes some editorial responsibility. The third issue is one of identification. If a Provider ensures that each of its members provides a full name and address before entering a forum, it makes it more likely that a plaintiff may consider suing only the author of the statement. In *Prodigy* the offending posting was made by an unknown person.[8] The final issue is one of legal procedure. A court will often pay attention to whether the parties have 'clean hands'. In this respect, a court will not look favourably on a Provider who has deliberately avoided reading material to allow a technical plea of one of the presumptions.

Evidence

It is critical that Internet Service Providers appreciate the burden they are under, evidentially, to prove that they fall within the defence. It is the Provider, rather than the plaintiff, who must prove that it is not an author, editor or publisher. It is also the Provider that must meet the two tests to prove the defence.[9] It is therefore sensible for a Service Provider to maintain complete records of all its automatic or

---

8   This advice is applicable only to *internal* forums. Clearly, if a Provider re-publishes a Usenet newsgroup, many of the postings will be made from outside the control of the Provider.
9   This is in contrast, say, to secondary infringement under the Copyright, Designs and Patents Act 1988, s 23.

manual dealings with third party material. In particular, a Service Provider should be able to provide a court with evidence to satisfy the three issues to which the court will have regard to judge the level of care and knowledge of the Provider.[10] It is also worthwhile noting that the term 'reasonable care' introduces a relative test: Providers may find it useful to adduce expert evidence as to the reasonableness of their care in relation to industry practice.

Damages

Extent of publication

The damages for defamation are based on a number of factors, although the extent of publication is very relevant: 'a libel published to millions has a greater potential to cause damage than a libel published to a handful of people.'[11] This statement leads some to presume that the damages for an Internet libel will be huge because so many people have access to it. This is false. That the Internet has potentially millions of people accessing *it* bears no relationship to the number of people accessing *the defamatory piece*. The jury should not be allowed to infer that the extent of publication must be great because the material is available over the Internet. What the plaintiff should adduce is the *actual* extent of the publication of the defamatory piece. On the Internet, it is far easier to estimate how many people actually viewed a particular *piece* than it is to prove how many people had access to a newspaper.[12] Figures should be able to be provided with quite a high degree of accuracy.

> **21. An Internet Service Provider defames an individual on a much used forum called, 'GossipsVille'. Liability is not in issue. The individual claims that GossipsVille is the most popular forum on the Internet and hosts over 500,000 readers every day. Counsel for the Provider should attempt to provide evidence of the exact number of individuals who actually read the statement. It is very likely this will be significantly less than the 500,000 average so acting to reduce the award.**

Reductions and recommendations

The general level of defamation damages is lowering. Since the Courts and Legal Services Act 1990 the Court of Appeal has been able to reduce the damages on appeal.[13] The most spectacular example was when the singer, Elton John, saw his

---

10   Defamation Act 1996, s 1(1)(b) and (c) and s 1(5)(a), (b) and (c).
11   *John v MGN Ltd* [1996] 2 All ER 35 at 48.
12   It can be said, in contrast with this, that it is difficult to tell the number of times a particular piece was copied and redistributed to other servers. This, it is submitted, is as far as one could go: it is *difficult*. It is not *impossible* and it is the plaintiff's burden to adduce the best evidence of circulation.
13   Courts and Legal Services Act 1990, s 8. In addition, the introduction of RSC Ord 59, r 11(4).

£350,000 damages reduced by the Court of Appeal to £75,000.[14] Clearly, for Mr John, this was a significant reduction. What is of greater significance to *all* plaintiffs is what the Court of Appeal said about future defamation cases. The first, almost revolutionary, point of law made was,[15]

> '[t]he time has in our view come when judges, and counsel, should be free to draw the attention of juries to these comparisons [between the awards for personal injury and awards for injury to reputation].'

The court called it 'offensive to public opinion' that the damages for injury to reputation may be greater than if the plaintiff had been rendered a 'helpless cripple or an insensate vegetable'.[16] To guide the jury from such offensive awards the court also added that the judge should be free to give indications to the jury as to the realistic bracket for the damages.[17]

This judgment may have a chilling effect on plaintiffs who seek to gain vast damages from Providers. In negotiation of settlement, defendants should be aware that awards in the hundreds of thousands of pounds will become increasingly rare.

Strategy

The area of defamation is problematic for Service Providers because the law appears to place them under a huge burden. This section describes a strategy that may be of assistance in reducing their exposure to risk.

WITHDRAW QUICKLY

Internet Service Providers should have a quick response policy for dealing with defamation allegations. They have the advantage over the paper publishers that they can withdraw the statement from circulation in a matter of seconds. This reduces their damages liability and can also increase the chance of settling the matter more quickly.

GRIEVANCE CHANNEL

The Provider must have a channel available to receive complaints. If a postal address is the only point of communication provided, the statement may have

---

14   *John v MGN Ltd* [1996] 2 All ER 35. To avoid misleading the reader, the majority of the reduction is accounted for by the court's substitution of £50,000 for the awarded £275,000 for exemplary damages. This was justified by the statement of the law that exemplary damages are awarded where the publisher had no genuine belief in the truth of what he published, suspected that the words were untrue, yet deliberately refrained from taking the obvious steps to turn 'suspicion into certainty' (at 57–58). For Internet defamation, an exemplary damages award will only be appropriate where the Provider is not considered the author, editor or publisher of the statement. In these cases, the Provider would have had no real opportunity to read, let alone consider and investigate, the statements. The ruling on exemplary damages, therefore, will be applicable only where the Internet Service Provider is unable to field a defence because of being an author, editor or publisher.

15   [1996] 2 All ER 35 at 54 per Sir Thomas Bingham MR delivering judgment for the court.

16   [1996] 2 All ER 35 at 54.

17   [1996] 2 All ER 35 at 55.

been published hundreds of thousands of times before the Provider is made aware. A special e-mail address should be employed. Complainants should be requested to send a digital copy of the allegedly defamatory statement to the special e-mail address for consideration.

Offer to make amends

The quicker the Provider makes a decision over the allegation, the better. If the Provider decides that it is liable and that the statement was defamatory, the best course of action is to make an offer of amends.[18] This is introduced with the new Act.[19] This offer may be sent by e-mail and should be expressed as an offer to make amends under section 2 of the Defamation Act 1996 and state whether it is qualified.[20] If it is, the defamatory meaning conceived by the Provider should be expressed. The offer must consist of a suitable correction of the statement complained of and a sufficient apology to the complainant. These may be published in a reasonable and practicable manner in the circumstances: the correction in the forum on the web site, and, an apology sent directly by e-mail. In addition, the offeror should pay to the aggrieved party such compensation, if there is any, and such costs as are agreed.[1] If the offer is accepted, the complainant may not bring or continue with the relevant defamation proceedings.[2]

Indemnity and identity

Two further strategies relate to the relationship between the Provider and the author of the alleged defamatory statement. There will be times where the defamatory material is authored by a person who has no relationship with the Provider. This is generally the case with Providers who host Usenet newsgroups: any person may have access to the groups from any Provider in the world. There will be other times where the Provider already has a contract with the author of the statement. It may be that the author is renting space on the Provider's server for a web site, or that the author is a member of a particular forum hosted by the Provider.

In these contractual situations it is advisable to include a term in the contract that the member will indemnify the Provider against costs and damages as a result of any defamatory statement made by the author, published by the Provider. Of course, the problem with such a term is that it is worthless if the indemnifier is a man-of-straw. It may, however, provide some financial support in the wake of an action.

The second strategy is for the Provider to maintain records of the actual identity of a member. This can be used if there is litigation to provide, on request of the

18   This must be made before serving any defence to the defamation proceedings: Defamation Act 1996, s 2(5).
19   Defamation Act 1996, s 2.
20   Defamation Act 1996, s 2(3).
1   Defamation Act 1996, s 2(4). This may also be decided by a court on the same basis as defamation damages and costs (s 3(5) and (6)). The incentive is that the cost of the proceedings in time and money will be far less than for a full-blown defamation trial.
2   Defamation Act 1996, s 3(2).

plaintiff, the identity of the actual author of the statement.[3] Although there is a likelihood that a plaintiff will prefer to pursue a wealthy Provider than an individual, the plaintiff will have no choice unless the Provider can supply the identity of the first defendant. For example, in the *Prodigy* case, Prodigy was unable to identify the individual who made the defamatory remark. This duty to provide litigants with the details of a member should be alerted to each member. They should be reassured that their details will be only provided in the light of a bona fide dispute.[4]

JURISDICTION

The Internet allows digital material to be downloaded or seen simultaneously by individuals in every country in the world. If a person is damaged or aggrieved by the material, his claim will not necessarily fit neatly into a purely English legal dispute. The international growth of the Internet and its disregard for borders will probably introduce a number of non-English legal factors into the person's claim. More than any other means of communication, the Internet will produce truly transnational disputes. Users of the Internet and their advisers must therefore be fully conversant with the English court's rules on jurisdiction and choice of law. A deep understanding of private international law combined with the Internet's global dissemination can arm a litigator with additional causes of action and defence. It is crucial that advisers pay due regard to the conflict of laws that may be present in an Internet dispute *before* wading into an assessment of the substantive law.

This first section deals with jurisdiction: the English court's authority to judge a dispute.[5]

The Conventions

The Civil Jurisdiction and Judgments Act 1982 incorporates the Brussels Convention on Jurisdiction and the Enforcement of Judgments in Civil and

---

3   The House of Lords in *Norwich Pharmacal Co v Customs and Excise Comrs* [1973] 2 All ER 943 provided that where a person had facilitated or become mixed up in the wrongdoing by another, that person is under an enforceable duty to disclose to a party harmed by the wrongdoing the identity of the wrongdoer in order to enable the party to sue the wrongdoer. This statement of the rights of a plaintiff accords with the situation in which most Providers will find themselves. They have facilitated the tort of defamation by publishing the statement and so can be forced to provide to the complainant the identity of the author of the statement.
4   Providers should be careful not to provide personal details without first consulting their data protection registration and their terms of confidentiality with each member.
5   It should be noted that this section focuses on a stylised analysis of the Conventions: no attention is paid to the effect of *lis alibi pendens* (related actions) under Articles 21 and 22 or the power of the English court to stay a Convention case as indicated by the Court of Appeal's interpretation of the Civil Jurisdiction and Judgments Act 1982, s 49 in *Re Harrods (Buenos Aires) Ltd* [1991] 4 All ER 334. This should not detract from their vital importance: the opportunity to forum shop still exists under the Conventions and advisers must not consider this section as the final word on any conflict of law issue in an Internet dispute. Specialist texts should be consulted for issues that are not specific to the Internet.

Commercial Matters.[6] This is the appropriate starting place for any tort committed over the Internet. First, one must assess whether the Convention applies or whether it 'transfers' jurisdiction to the English common law. As a rough rule of thumb, if the defendant to a tortious claim is not domiciled within a signatory state, the common law will apply. It is perhaps safer, though, to take a robust and principled approach.

JURISDICTION OF CONVENTIONS

Civil or commercial matter

Most torts committed over the Internet will fall within Article 1, that is, the resulting dispute is a civil or commercial matter. Four specific examples of matters that are not civil or commercial are stated in Article 1:

> '1. the status or legal capacity of natural persons, rights in property arising out of a matrimonial relationship, wills and succession;
> 2. bankruptcy, proceedings relating to the winding-up of insolvent companies or other legal persons, judicial arrangements, compositions and analogous proceedings;
> 3. social security;
> 4. arbitration.'

Before concluding that a tort committed over the Internet is within the framework of the Conventions, litigants are directed to specialist texts and, in particular, to the European Court's cases which highlight the broad scope of Article 1.

Domicile of defendant

Subject to Articles outside the scope of this chapter,[7] the fundamental issue is where is the defendant domiciled. Article 2 establishes that persons domiciled in a contracting state can be sued in the courts of that state, sometimes with the plaintiff having a choice of another forum. Articles 52 and 53 direct the English courts to consider the domicile of the defendant with reference to the Civil Jurisdiction and Judgments Act 1982, sections 41 and 42 respectively. For an Internet issue it is useful to appreciate that the jurisdiction hinges on 'domicile', an essentially static concept which is mostly unrelated to the complex factors such as where is a server based.

For Convention purposes, a defendant can be domiciled in two types of state: a contracting state or a non-contracting state. If the defendant is domiciled within a

6   For the purposes of this section the relevant articles of the Lugano Convention remain identical to those in the Brussels (1979 OJ C 59), Greek Accession (1989 OJ C 298), and San Sebastián (1990 OJ C 189/35) Conventions. Readers are nevertheless advised to check on which Convention they are relying to provide advice.

7   These Articles are excluded from the discussion for two reasons. First, the excluded provisions, in the main, will be irrelevant for 'Internet torts' such as those described in this chapter. Second, and what is more important, a comprehensive discussion is best suited to a specialist text on the subject. The articles which are excluded from discussion are: Article 54, supervening Conventions; Articles 21 and 22, *lis alibi pendens*; Article 16, exclusive jurisdiction; Articles 7–12A, insurance contract provisions; Articles 13–15, consumer contract provisions; Articles 17, 18, agreements or submission to choice of court.

contracting state, the Convention rules apply; if outside, the common law rules will apply. These two outcomes are decided with reference to the Civil Jurisdiction and Judgments Act 1982.

Individual's domicile

United Kingdom domicile

An individual is domiciled within the United Kingdom only if he is resident in the United Kingdom and the nature and circumstances of his residence indicate that he has a substantial connection with the United Kingdom.[8] It is presumed, unless proved otherwise, that being resident for the last three months will constitute the requisite substantial connection.[9] The ownership, control or access to a web site anywhere in the world is wholly irrelevant for the purposes of jurisdiction over an individual under the Conventions. An individual will gain little legal benefit by locating a web server 'offshore' if he remains a United Kingdom resident.

Convention state domicile

If an individual is not domiciled in the United Kingdom for the purposes of the Conventions, one must decide whether he is domiciled within another contracting state. If he is not, the Convention will not apply to the dispute; jurisdiction is 'handed over' to the common law. An individual is domiciled in a state *other* than the United Kingdom if by that state's equivalent of Civil Jurisdiction and Judgments Act 1982, section 41 he is so domiciled in that state. In short, to determine whether a defendant in an Internet tort dispute is domiciled within a contracting state one is required to assess that person's domicile from *that* state's legal perspective. Failing this, the Civil Jurisdiction and Judgments Act 1982, section 41(7) establishes the test to determine whether a defendant is domiciled outside contracting states.

Non-contracting state domicile

An individual is domiciled outside all the contracting states if none of those states would deem him to be domiciled within their jurisdiction and if a further two-part test is satisfied. First, the individual must be resident in the non-contracting state, and second, the nature and circumstances of his residence indicate that he has a substantial connection with that state.[10] One is not required to consult the non-contracting state's law on domicile.

---

22. An English academic who teaches in an English University defames a Dutch academic by posting a message to a forum. This forum is stored on a server in America and the Dutch academic has a substantial reputation only in Holland. The English courts will have jurisdiction over the dispute as the defendant is domiciled in England. The location of the server and the reputation are of little relevance for jurisdiction over the academic in the English courts.

---

8   Civil Jurisdiction and Judgments Act 1982, s 41(2).
9   Civil Jurisdiction and Judgments Act 1982, s 41(6).
10 Civil Jurisdiction and Judgments Act 1982, s 41(7).

If the result of the domicile tests is that an individual defendant is domiciled within a contracting state, the Conventions will apply to any other questions of jurisdiction. If the result is that the defendant is domiciled outside the contracting states, the English common law rules on jurisdiction will apply.[11] These are described after the Convention rules.[12]

Corporation's or association's domicile

A corporation or association has its domicile in the state where it has its seat.[13]

United Kingdom domicile

A corporation or association is domiciled within the United Kingdom only if it was incorporated or formed under a law of a part of the United Kingdom, *and* its registered office or other official address is in the United Kingdom.[14] Alternatively, a corporation or association can be considered as having a United Kingdom seat if it exercises its central management and control in the United Kingdom.[15] Again, the ownership, control or access to a web site anywhere in the world is mostly irrelevant for the purposes of jurisdiction under the Conventions. A corporation which is, in effect, based in the United Kingdom will not be able to avoid the jurisdiction of the English courts by situating its server abroad.

Convention state domicile

If a corporation or association is not domiciled in the United Kingdom for the purposes of the Conventions, one must decide whether it is domiciled within another contracting state. If they are not, the Convention will not apply to the dispute; jurisdiction is 'handed over' to the common law. A corporation is domiciled in a state *other* than the United Kingdom if it satisfies two tests: one under English law, the other under non-English law.

First, the English courts must be satisfied that the corporation or association has its seat in a contracting state. As under Civil Jurisdiction and Judgments Act 1982, section 42(3), the corporation or association must be incorporated or formed under the law of that state and have its registered office or some other official address there.[16] Alternatively, a corporation or association will be deemed as seated in another contracting state if its central management and control is exercised in that state.[17]

The second test, that must also be affirmatively answered, is that the courts of the contracting state must agree that the corporation or association has its seat there. Both tests must be satisfied for the defendant corporation or association to be judged as having a domicile within a contracting state. If either test is not satisfied, the common law rules on jurisdiction will apply;[18] these are discussed after the Convention rules.

---

11   Article 4.
12   See 'Common law jurisdiction over torts', at page 117.
13   Article 53.
14   Civil Jurisdiction and Judgments Act 1982, s 42(3)(a).
15   Civil Jurisdiction and Judgments Act 1982, s 42(3)(b).
16   Civil Jurisdiction and Judgments Act 1982, s 43(6)(a).
17   Civil Jurisdiction and Judgments Act 1982, s 43(6)(b).
18   Article 4.

> **23. An estate agent company is incorporated and operates from France. It provides advice to wealthy Australians who are considering buying property in the South of France. Its server is physically based in Perth and the domain address has the suffix 'co.au' which indicates an Australian firm. An Australian arrives at a newly bought property to discover that the company's advice was negligent. Now having a base in France, the Australian decides that it will be cheaper to conduct the litigation from France. He will be able to do this as long as the French courts consider that the company has its seat within France.[19]**

Non-contracting state domicile

If both of the previous tests fail to establish the defendant as domiciled in the United Kingdom and another contracting state, the common law rules on jurisdiction will apply.

CONVENTION JURISDICTION OVER TORTS

Having established that the defendant to an action is domiciled in a contracting state it can be said with certainty that the Convention rules on jurisdiction apply. For matters relating to tort there are rules that *supplement* the main rule under Article 2, that the defendant can be sued in the courts of his domicile. The tort rules provide a plaintiff with additional jurisdictions in which the defendant can be rightly sued. For example, a German individual may have defamed an English individual by posting a message on a Spanish Provider's bulletin board. Without more than the Article 2 rule, the English plaintiff would have to sue in either Spain or Germany: a practice that may be expensive and complicated. The rules under the Convention broaden the jurisdiction for tortious claims and specify:[20]

> 'A person domiciled in a contracting state may, in another contracting state, be sued: ... in matters relating to tort, delict or quasi-delict, in the courts for the place where the harmful event occurred.'

What is a tort?

The heading above, 'What is a tort?' may surprise those who are unfamiliar with the Conventions. The reason it is included is that the terms 'tort, delict or quasi-delict' in Article 5(3) must be given an autonomous Community meaning; one cannot simply check whether the dispute would be included in an English textbook on torts. The European Court puts this:[1]

> '[T]he term 'matters relating to tort, delict or quasi-delict' within the meaning of Article 5(3) of the Convention must be regarded as an independent concept covering all actions which seek to establish the

---

19 Aside from the issues of Article 16(1) exclusive jurisdiction and a possible *Re Harrods* stay.
20 Article 5(3).
1 *Kalfelis v Schroder, Munchmayer* [1988] ECR 5565 at 5585 [18].

liability of a defendant and which are not related to a 'contract' within the meaning of Article 5(1).'

This approach has most recently been endorsed by the Court of Appeal in *Kleinwort Benson Ltd v Glasgow City Council*.[2] For the purposes of this section, therefore, Article 5(3) will apply in relation to digital damage, defamation and negligent advice.[3]

Location of harmful events

A defendant domiciled in a contracting state who commits a tort may be sued in the court of the defendant's domicile *or* in the court where the harmful event occurred under Article 5(3). Having examined above what constitutes a tort, it is now crucial to consider where a tort occurs.

The first European case to deal with this concerned a plaintiff who carried on the business of nursery gardening in the Netherlands and used water to irrigate the seed beds mainly from the Rhine.[4] The defendant mined in France and was alleged to have increased the salt content in the irrigating water by discharging from Alsace large quantities of residuary salts into the Rhine. On a reference from the national court the European Court held that the phrase 'the place where the harmful event occurred' could refer to *two* jurisdictions.[5]

> '[T]he plaintiff has an option to commence proceedings either at the place where the damage occurred or the place of the event giving rise to it.'

For an Internet tort, particularly one made over the web, this ruling has a significant effect. Defendants who are domiciled in a contracting state may face claims from any jurisdiction which is signatory to the Conventions. This is because it is technically very difficult to prevent a server from being accessed from a particular place in the world. In illustration, malicious code on a web site or ftp site can infect any person accessing that from anywhere in the world; negligent misstatements made on a web site or forum may be relied upon by any person anywhere in the world; and defamatory statements on a web site or forum may be read by any person anywhere in the world.

The commercial effects of this are substantial. Companies and individuals domiciled in a contracting state who use the Internet to provide information, services or products risk being sued in any jurisdiction party to the Conventions. Some more specific points are made below.

2   [1996] 2 All ER 257.
3   It is useful to note that Rix J correctly states in *Trade Indemnity v Försäkrings AB Njord* [1995] 1 All ER 796 at 820 that an action for misrepresentation or non-disclosures in making a contract is not covered by Article 5(1) which relates to contracts. One is therefore bound by *Kalfelis* (see fn 1 on page 111) to conclude that Article 5(3) will apply to misrepresentations. A misrepresentation made on a web site may be therefore sued upon not only in the defendant's domicile but also in any state in which the plaintiff acted upon the representation on the web pages; an exclusive jurisdiction clause in the contract will, for this claim, be to no avail.
4   *Handelskwekerij G J Bier BV v Mines de Potasse d'Alsace SA* [1978] QB 708.
5   [1976] ECR 1735 at 1745-1747 [19].

Digital damage

There are striking similarities between allowing a computer virus into the Internet and allowing pollutants into a water supply. Both cross borders. Both originate from a fixed source yet can spread in many directions, affecting many plaintiffs. In one way computer viruses have more impact because they have a longer life owing to their perfect replication. These comparisons make it probable that a court will follow the European Court's ruling in *Bier*. Under Article 2 the plaintiff will be permitted to sue the defendant in a court of the defendant's place of domicile. In addition, by Article 5(3), the plaintiff can sue the defendant in the place of digital damage, probably the plaintiff's 'home' and also in the court of the place of the source of the virus. The plaintiff therefore has three options; the option to sue at home will generally be the most favourable.

---

24. A Spanish architect sent some unsolicited plans to an English property agent. The plans contained a computer virus which corrupted some entries on the agent's database. Were the agent to sue the architect for damage caused by negligence, the agent would have the jurisdiction of the English courts because the damage occurred there.

Secondary damage

It has been discussed that viruses and other malicious code will damage not only those directly in contact with the contaminated computer, but also those in contact with an already infected computer. This is coined 'secondary damage'. Such 'ricochet' damage has been criticised as a basis for ousting the right that any defendant has to be sued in the courts of his domicile.

In *Dumez France v Hessische Landesbank (Helaba)*[6] two French parent companies sued in France two German banks. The claim was for compensation for damage arising out of the winding up of their two German subsidiaries. The subsidiaries, it was claimed, had to be wound up because the German banks had withdrawn credit facilities to one of the subsidiary's customers. The European Court was asked whether the 'place where the harmful event occurred'[7] can be interpreted as including damage claimed by a plaintiff that is the consequence of harm suffered by other persons who were direct victims.[8] An affirmative answer would have allowed the French companies to sue the German banks in France, as that place is where they claimed the harmful event occurred.

The court accepted the approach made by the Advocate General that a victim 'by ricochet' cannot bring an action in the courts of the place of that damage. The court is looking not for where damage is suffered, but rather where it occurs. As seems to be obvious, this ruling may often be applicable for digital damage by viral infection. For economic loss that may occur as a result of viral damage or negligent misstatement, the application is more difficult.

---

6   [1990] ECR 49.
7   See [1976] ECR 1735.
8   [1996] All ER (EC) 84 at 94[8].

> **25. A company based in Holland, through the negligence of a supplier also based in Holland, becomes infected by a logic bomb which damages important data. Before the logic bomb is triggered, the infected company sent an infected file to a customer in England. The customer's computer was damaged and there was no indication that the Dutch company was negligent in sending the file. The English customer's action must be solely against the Dutch supplier but the jurisdiction of the English courts will be not be supported by Article 5(3). The English customer's damage was the consequence of harm suffered by direct victims.**

Negligent misstatement

An individual or company domiciled in a contracting state providing negligent advice on a web site risks being sued in a court within any contracting state. This is because application of the judgment in *Bier* establishes that a plaintiff can sue the defendant in a state of his domicile, or, where the server was situated, or where the damage occurs. The damage will usually occur where the plaintiff accesses the negligent advice.

> **26. A luxury boat mortgage company is incorporated and operates from Italy. It provides mortgages and advice to wealthy Italian-Americans who are considering buying a boat moored in Italy. The company rents web space on a server that happens to be based in Ireland; its domain name 'moorings.com' clearly gives little indication of its base. An American mortgages a boat through the site that turns out to be far from sea-worthy and sinks off the coast of Spain. The Spanish courts will not have jurisdiction over the tort; the damage from the negligent advice occurred in Italy where the mortgage report was relied upon; that the actual damage was suffered in Spain is not relevant for Article 5(3).**

Often negligent advice results in economic loss as one of the heads of damage. Apart from the domestic question of whether such loss is recoverable, there is the issue of where economic loss occurs. If a plaintiff's bank account is in England but the plaintiff accesses and relies upon information on a web site from Germany, will the English courts have jurisdiction purely because the bank account was situated there?

A similar question was answered by the European Court in *Marinari v Lloyds Bank plc (Zubaidi Trading Co intervening)*.[9] Mr Marinari, domiciled in Italy, sued Lloyds Bank plc, whose registered office is in England. His claim was that he had deposited promissory notes with a value of $750m with a Manchester branch of the bank. The bank staff suspected that the notes were bogus, kept them and advised the police who arrested Mr Marinari. He sued in Italy for compensation for the payment of the notes, damage to reputation and loss of contracts. Lloyds Bank objected to the jurisdiction of the Italian courts arguing that the damage occurred in England.

The court derived from *Mines de Potasse d'Alsace* and *Bier* that the choice generally afforded to a tort plaintiff could provide a significant connecting factor

9   [1996] All ER (EC) 84.

from the point of view of jurisdiction. But, the choice must not be extended, so negating the general principle in Article 2, to encompass any place where the adverse consequences of an event that has already caused actual damage has occurred.[10] In short, it affirmed that one must look for where damage occurs, not where it is suffered.

Whatever the flaws in the court's solution, it does have the quality of certainty for torts committed over the Internet. By focusing on the tangible and fixed aspects of damage the court is able to ensure that the court with jurisdiction is appropriate to determine the legal dispute. The court was particularly wary of the fluidity of damaged assets and therefore the possibilities of 'entirely inappropriate' courts having to take the relevant evidence. It is submitted that this is correct. Although the Internet does allow intellectual property, advice and funds to be moved and accessed from any jurisdiction in the world, it is not necessarily in the interests of justice that any court in Europe could govern the relevant dispute. The rules on jurisdiction attempt to delineate which cases are appropriate to be heard and decided by which courts; it is naïve to suggest because the Internet has no technical boundaries to the flow of digital material that the law should drop its boundaries also.

> **27. A Russian entrepreneur owned a number of shares in an English company, held by an English Bank. From Russia he logged into a French investor's web page, and on the basis of information there, sold the shares in the English company. The information was provided negligently. Under the Conventions, the Russian will be able to sue only in France under Article 2: the damage occurred in Russia, which is not a contracting state, and where the damage was suffered is irrelevant under Article 5(3).**

Defamation

The Internet and associated technologies allow the whole world to have access to information about one individual; it is now possible to have a truly global reputation. For the same technical reasons it is possible for a defamatory statement to be read from anywhere in the world; it is possible to defame someone on a global scale. These two conclusions present the law with an issue as to a court's jurisdiction over defamation. If a celebrity is defamed on a worldwide forum, which court is appropriate to hear the dispute between the plaintiff and defendant?[11] The definitive answer is provided by the European Court in *Shevill v Presse Alliance SA*.[12]

Presse Alliance SA, a French Company, published its daily newspaper with an article that mentioned the plaintiff's name in relation to a drug trafficking network that was raided by the drugs squad. The plaintiff was in England at the time of the raid, having only been in France for three months. 237,000 copies of the

---

10   [1996] All ER (EC) 84 at 95 [10-15].
11   In the light of the Defamation Act 1996, it is not assumed that the defendant is necessarily an individual and may be the Internet Service Provider of the forum itself. If the Internet Service Provider is not domiciled within a contracting state it may still be brought within the regime of the Defamation Act 1996 where the actual defamer is domiciled in England. In this situation the plaintiff would be relying on Article 6(1) of the Conventions.
12   [1995] All ER (EC) 289.

newspaper containing the defamatory article were sold in France; 230 were sold in England. The plaintiff asserted that the English courts had jurisdiction over the dispute by virtue of Article 5(3); the defendants objected eventually appealing to the House of Lords. The Lords then referred seven preliminary questions to the European Court of the Convention.

The important answer provided by the court was that the plaintiff in a defamation action may sue in the courts of the defendant's domicile, under Article 2, and under Article 5(3) may sue in the courts of the place from where the libel was issued and circulated. These courts, although often the same, have jurisdiction to hear the action for damages for *all* the harm caused by the unlawful act. Alternatively, the plaintiff may sue in the courts of any contracting state in which the defamatory publication was distributed and in which the victim claims to have suffered injury to reputation. These courts have jurisdiction only to rule on the injury caused to the victim's reputation in that state.

Again, this answer takes due account of justice to the parties: the courts best suited to consider damages must include those which are territorially the best placed to assess the libel committed in the state and determine the corresponding level of damages. That the plaintiff has the option of suing once for all the damages in the court of the defendant's domicile accords with the basic rule of the Convention: 'defendants should be sued at home'.

Of course for the Internet such a decision has a great impact. Without expensive and complex technology, a web site or a forum will be available throughout the world. A victim defamed on one of these globally accessible sites needs only to find a very limited number of 'hits' from a particular contracting state to be able to litigate there.[13] In most cases of Internet defamation the plaintiff will be able to sue in the courts of their domicile; a scenario that was to be avoided under the Convention. It is a scenario, however, which makes legal sense. There are advantages and disadvantages with every form of communication. The Internet's advantages include that there is little increase in marginal cost to distribute information throughout the world. If it is useful information, the *global* reputation of the provider will increase; if it is defamatory information, the *global* reputation of the victim will decrease. That this is somehow, 'unfair' or 'prejudices the Internet', does not take into account that one cannot expect to reap the rewards from global distribution without bearing its risks.

---

28. A United Kingdom resident soap star is defamed on a French bulletin board by an Australian co-actor who had since left the programme. The bulletin board operator included the Australian's comments in a highlighted section of the bulletin board called 'Celebrity Clangers'. The victim can sue the French bulletin board in England as long as it can be proved that the board was accessed from England. This will be sufficient to establish that damage occurred in England giving the English courts jurisdiction under Article 5(3).

---

13   In *Shevill* less than 0.1% of the distribution was in England. There presumably must be some *de minimis* amount although the court did not appear to take notice that less than a thousandth of the distribution occurred in England. This said, the amount of distribution in absolute terms may reduce the possible damages which may be awarded.

COMMON LAW JURISDICTION OVER TORTS

If the defendant to an Internet tort is not domiciled within a contracting state,[14] the court must apply its domestic laws to determine jurisdiction.[15] Two main methods will be considered below: service by presence in England as of right, and service abroad with leave.

Presence

If a defendant is in England at the time of being served with a writ, the courts have jurisdiction. The defendant may ask the court for a stay, but the court will have jurisdiction over the defendant as of right: it is under the court's *discretion* to grant a stay.

Presence of individuals

For an individual to be present, he needs to be physically within England at the exact time of service. It does not matter that he is purely passing through England on his way elsewhere.[16] There is no doubt that the nature of presence must be physical; logging on to a computer based in England or accessing a web site server in England will not, without more, be sufficient to constitute presence. It is for this reason that with most torts committed over the Internet by individuals from abroad, plaintiffs will have to serve out with leave.

Presence of companies

The Companies Act 1985 determines whether, for the purpose of service, a company is 'present' within England. If a company has its registered office in England, it is present in England; service can be effected at its registered office.[17] If it is incorporated abroad but has an established place of business in England, the company should have filed details of the name and address of an English resident; service can be effected through that person.[18] Finally, if the company incorporated abroad has an established place of business in England but has not provided the registrar of companies with details of an English resident,[19]

> 'a document may be served on the company by leaving it at, or sending it by post to, any place of business established by the company in Great Britain.'

Overseas defendants in Internet tort actions will often have no more than a server or even less, space rented on a server, within the jurisdiction. This raises two crucial questions: can a server ever constitute an established place of business? The

14 See 'Domicile of defendant', at page 108.
15 Article 4.
16 See *Colt Industries v Sarlie (No 2)* [1966] 3 All ER 85.
17 Companies Act 1985, s 725(1).
18 Companies Act 1985, s 691(b)(ii).
19 Companies Act 1985, s 695(2).

second relates to the first: can one serve a writ on, what is in essence, material stored in a digital form?

Established place of business

It is submitted that whether a server, and nothing more, may constitute an established place of business, is a question whose answer depends on the facts at hand. Certain businesses operating on the World Wide Web have nothing more than a server to conduct commerce: they advertise, take orders and deliver goods and services using the server and little else. The issue therefore turns on whether material on a digital storage medium may constitute a place of business, rather than whether a computer can operate as a place of business; it clearly can.

In *Re Oriel Ltd*[20] the Court of Appeal relied on an old Scottish case[1] to construe the words 'established place of business'.[2] In this Scottish case, the court was considering whether a Canadian company was established in Great Britain through its presence of a number of agents who forwarded the responses to advertisements. The Lord President Dunedin described the expression 'establishes a place of business' as connoting that the company must have 'what I may call a local habitation of its own' at or from which it carries on business.[3] Lord Justice Oliver, speaking for the other members of the Court of Appeal in *Re Oriel Ltd*, added to this Scottish dictum. He said that the relevant phrase also connotes a 'degree of permanence or recognisability as being a location of the company's business'.[4] Oliver LJ also alludes to the issue that conducting activities such as sending out advertisements and soliciting finance may indicate the establishment of a place of business.[5]

This summary of *Re Oriel Ltd* leaves the impression that it would not be unreasonable for a court to deem the location of a server as an established place of business for a company based abroad which conducts its business through and by that server.[6] This may be seen as confirmed by another Court of Appeal decision. In *South India Shipping Corpn Ltd v Export-Import Bank of Korea*[7] the court applied the decision from an older Court of Appeal case[8] to the question as to what is an established place of business. In that older case, Buckley LJ states,

> 'We have only to see whether the corporation is "here"; if it is, it can be served. There are authorities as to the circumstances in which a foreign corporation can and cannot be said to be "here"; the best test is to ascertain whether the business is carried on here and at a defined place.'

Buckley LJ's answer to the question, despite being over eighty years old, does suit the nature of the Internet. It is true that a server and a web site are not physical places like an office block. They can, however, operate like the facilities within an

20   [1985] 3 All ER 216.
1   *Lord Advocate v Huron and Erie Loan and Savings Co* 1911 SC 612.
2   In *Re Oriel Ltd* the Court of Appeal was considering the Companies Act 1948, s 106.
3   1911 SC 612 at 616.
4   [1985] 3 All ER 216 at 220.
5   [1985] 3 All ER 216 at 220.
6   This is not to say that *every* business with a server in England establishes a place of a business at that server: it depends greatly on the nature of the business and the use of the server in relation to that business.
7   [1985] 2 All ER 219.
8   *A/S Dampskib 'Hercules' v Grand Trunk Pacific Rly Co* [1912] 1 KB 222.

office block. In addition, a web site does occupy a space,[9] and as such, does fall within the Oxford English Dictionary definition of 'place'.

---

29. An Israeli airline operates a web site from England to serve Internet traffic from Europe. This site contains details of flights, special offers and availability of seats. Orders cannot be placed through the site, and the site is not specifically orientated to the English public. This site alone is not sufficient to indicate an established place of business within Great Britain. It is, in effect, little more than an advertising hoarding.

Service on servers

It has been mentioned that to serve a company based abroad one may leave the writ at, or send it by post to, any place of business established by the company in Great Britain.[10] Having argued that it is possible for a web server to constitute a place of business in Great Britain, one is left with the more practical issue of how can one serve on that place of business.

In *Boocock v Hilton International Co*[11] the Court of Appeal considered whether service can be deemed good service even if the plaintiff does not comply with the statutory requirement in the Companies Act 1985, section 695. In this case, the plaintiff served on a person different to that person filed at the registrar of companies. Neill LJ delivered the main judgment that was unanimously agreed to by Hoffmann and Mann LJJ.

Neill LJ was unconvinced that the word 'may' in section 695(2) may be construed not as 'must' but as opening up the possibility that some other form of service would be adequate.[12] Despite this, he was willing to exercise the court's general discretion under RSC Ord 2, r 1(2) to cure an irregularity in the course of beginning any proceedings.[13] This case opens up the possibility that a writ *could* be validly served on a web server where no other methods are feasible.

Of course, the safest route to serve on a web server is to attempt to seek leave from the court to do so; to hope that a court will remedy the irregularity *after* service is to take an unnecessary chance. A court will always be concerned to hear that the writ is likely to reach the defendant or come to his knowledge.[14]

In the realm of the Internet, if applicable, service by e-mail appears the most convenient and most appropriate method.[15] The e-mail should be addressed to the web controller of the web site, an e-mail address that is regularly included on a home page. If possible the e-mail should be sent with a deliver and a read receipt; these will facilitate proof that the writ has been read or, at the least, received. Sending an e-mail that consists purely of the text of a writ is, perhaps, to be

---

9   On a storage medium like a hard disk drive.
10   Companies Act 1985, s 695(2).
11   [1993] 4 All ER 19.
12   See also Kerr LJ's questioning of the same issue in relation to serving on a limited company in *Singh v Atombrook Ltd* [1989] 1 All ER 385 at 391.
13   In *Harkness v Bell's Asbestos and Engineering Ltd* [1966] 3 All ER 843 at 845 Lord Denning MR explains RSC Ord 2, r 1: 'This new rule does away with the old distinction between nullities and irregularities. Every omission or mistake in practice or procedure is henceforward to be regarded as an irregularity which the court can and should rectify so long as it can do so without injustice.'
14   See *Deverall v Grant Advertising* [1954] 3 All ER 389, especially Romer LJ at 394–395.
15   The Internet has been used to serve an injunction by e-mail. *Daily Telegraph*, 1 May 1996.

avoided; it is far easier to alter the details of a purely textual message. It is therefore better to create a paper-based writ and scan this to be sent as a graphic file.

Service out

There are two separate and distinct aspects to serving out of the jurisdiction.[16] The first aspect is jurisdiction: does the plaintiff's claim fall within one of the heads of RSC Ord 11, r 1(1)? This test does not need to be satisfied to any high degree of proof: a good arguable case that the claim is covered by the one of the heads is sufficient.[17] The second aspect, which will not be covered here in great detail, is one of discretion: no leave to serve out will be granted unless it is sufficiently shown that the case is a proper one for service out of the jurisdiction. This is specified by RSC Ord 11, r 4(2).

Jurisdiction under tort head

The most common head that will apply for torts committed over the Internet is RSC Ord 11, r 1(1)(f):[18]

'the claim is founded on a tort and the damage was sustained, or resulted from an act committed, within the jurisdiction.'

Until 1987 the provision used to relate only to a claim 'founded on a tort committed within the jurisdiction'. This was amended in the light of the *Bier* case[19] to require a plaintiff to satisfy two requirements. First, the claim must be founded on a tort. Second, the damage must be sustained in the jurisdiction or have resulted from an act committed in the jurisdiction. The second question has been discussed in relation to the Brussels Convention and it would appear that the reasoning given there is equally applicable.[20] What must be considered here, in contrast, relates to the first question: simply put, what is a tort?[1]

The answer to this question can be found by considering the main precedent in this area: *Metall und Rohstoff A/G v Donaldson, Lufkin and Jenrette Inc.*[2] In this case the defendants whilst in New York had sent to English persons inducements to break contracts which subsisted with other English persons. The tortious claim was for inducing breach of contract in which the damage was sustained in England. The court permitted service abroad, but not before making an analysis of this complex area.

---

16   See *Seaconsar v Bank Merkazi Jomhouri Islami Iran* [1993] 4 All ER 456.
17   See *Attock v Romanian Bank for Foreign Trade* [1989] 1 All ER 1189.
18   Of course, RSC Ord 11, r 1(1)(a) or (b) may be more appropriate in some circumstances.
19   See 'Location of harmful events', at page 112.
20   See 'Location of harmful events', at page 112. This said, the English courts appear keener to look for a 'substantial act' rather than merely *any* tortious act. See *Metall und Rohstoff A/G v Donaldson, Lufkin and Jenrette Inc* [1989] 3 All ER 14 at 25.
1   This was discussed in relation to the Brussels Convention but it is clear that the autonomous meaning under the Convention is inapplicable for an English court to adopt. See 'What is a tort?', at page 111.
2   [1989] 3 All ER 14.

Choice of law under jurisdiction

The court decided that to determine whether a 'tort' has been committed,[3] one had to consider the choice of law rule in *Boys v Chaplin* to ascertain whether the relevant events would have given rise to liability in tort under *English* law.[4] The court expresses this ruling as,[5]

> 'if [the court] find that the tort was in substance committed in some foreign country, they should apply the [*Boys v Chaplin*] rule and impose liability in tort under English law, only if both (a) the relevant events would have given rise to liability in tort in English law if they had taken place in England, and (b) the alleged tort would be actionable in the country where it was committed.'

In short, the court must consult the choice of law rules *first* to check that the 'wrong' is actionable here as a tort. But, as the following section explains, the choice of law rule for torts other than defamation, is no longer that expounded in *Boys v Chaplin*. It is contained in the Private International Law (Miscellaneous Provisions) Act 1995; section 10 of the Act abolishes the rules of the common law replacing them with the rules in sections 11 to 13.[6]

Proving jurisdiction under tort head

For a 'wrong' committed over the Internet, it would appear that the convoluted scheme for determining whether one can serve out is as follows.

1. Check whether damage was sustained within the jurisdiction or whether the damage resulted from an act committed within the jurisdiction.[7] If neither apply, the plaintiff will be unable to serve out under RSC Ord 11, r 1(1)(f).
2. Check whether, under English law, the claim relates to issues arising in any defamation claim, including claims for slander of title, goods or other malicious falsehood.[8]
3. Looking back over the series of events establish where in substance the cause of action arose.[9]

3　It should be noted that the (f) head refers not to a 'wrong' but to a 'tort'; this is therefore a legal question that is distinct from the question of where, in substance, a wrong is committed.
4　[1969] 2 All ER 1085. Apologies are made to those who are unfamiliar with the conflict of laws. It is correct but confusing that in *Metall und Rohstoff* the court conflated the usually distinct considerations of jurisdiction and choice of law. If a reader is unfamiliar with choice of law in tort it is advised, at this point, to read this chapter's following section on these rules. Normally one can, with certainty, consider jurisdiction separately from choice of law. For service out on a tortious claim, however, one must decide whether the 'wrong' is a tort in the first place and this is only achievable with recourse to English choice of law rules. The circularity of this section is regretted but unavoidable.
5　[1989] 3 All ER 14 at 32.
6　Readers unfamiliar with the operation of the new Act are advised to read the chapter's following section on choice of law. Issues arising in relation to defamation are still governed by the common law.
7　As confirmed by *Metall und Rohstoff A/G v Donaldson, Lufkin and Jenrette Inc* [1989] 3 All ER 14. See 'Location of harmful events', at page 112 to determine the sorts of issues that the English courts will consider for the various torts.
8　The Private International Law (Miscellaneous Provisions) Act 1995, s 13.
9　See *Distillers Co (Biochemicals) Ltd v Thompson* [1971] 1 All ER 694 at 699 per Lord Pearson and subsequent refinement in *Castree v ER Squibb & Sons Ltd* [1980] 2 All ER 589.

4.   If the cause of action arose in England, the plaintiff will have established jurisdiction under RSC Order 11, r 1(1)(f).
5.   If the cause of action arose outside England, the plaintiff will have to prove that the 'wrong' is actionable in England as a tort:
  5.1.   If the claim relates to a defamation claim (see 2) the plaintiff will have to apply the old common law test in *Boys v Chaplin* satisfying the court that both the relevant events would have given rise to liability in tort in English law if occurring in England, and that the alleged tort is actionable in the country where it is committed.[10]
  5.2.   If the claim does not relate to a defamation claim (see 2) the plaintiff will have to apply the Private International Law (Miscellaneous Provisions) Act 1995 satisfying the court that the 'wrong' is actionable under the law of the country where the tort occurs,[11] or if more than one country is involved, the law of the country in which the most significant element of the events occurred.[12]
6.   If points 1 and 4, or points 1 and 5 are satisfied, the claim falls within RSC Order 11, r 1(1)(f).

---

30. Revealing pictures of a British film director and his mistress are released onto the Internet by an American journalist. Under English law, the director has no legal redress against the journalist, but under American law a law of privacy would protect him. The director has a good arguable case that the dispute falls within RSC Ord 11, r 1(1)(f). Damage to the director's reputation has occurred in England, and the cause of action arose in America where the 'wrong' is actionable as a tort. The director may have the jurisdiction of the English courts to serve out to the journalist suing him under American law.

Discretion under service out

To serve out, it is not sufficient simply to satisfy a court of a good arguable case under one of the heads of RSC Ord 11, r 1(1). The claim must also be a proper case for service out under RSC Ord 11, r 4(2). The discretion to serve out includes, as a main factor, an assessment, perhaps not overtly, of whether England is the *forum conveniens*, the most suitable forum in which to hear the dispute. This will be considered briefly in the following section on staying actions.[13] This discretionary factor should not be overlooked by legal advisers: for a tort committed over the Internet it may be difficult to persuade a court to serve out. If

---

10   It is admitted, but ignored for the sake of simplicity, that the flexible exception in *Red Sea Insurance Co Ltd v Bouygues SA* [1994] 3 All ER 749 may be invoked allowing a defamation-type claim which is not actionable in England to be actionable here. This said, in the light of Parliament's intention to prevent the Act applying to defamation claims, a strong case would have to be put to invoke the *Red Sea* exception.
11   The Private International Law (Miscellaneous Provisions) Act 1995, s 11(1). This country will probably be the same as that decided for point 3.
12   Ibid.
13   The court's assessment is the same although for service out, the plaintiff must ask the court to exercise discretion; for staying service as of right, the defendant must persuade the court to stay the action.

the defendant, in contrast, is domiciled in Europe, the court has far less discretion over jurisdiction.[14]

Staying actions

It is always open to a putative defendant to apply to stay the *common law* jurisdiction of the English courts by pleading that it is not the most suitable forum in which to resolve the dispute. Whether a court stays an action is decided with recourse to the principle of *forum non conveniens*. This principle is clearly explained and stated in the House of Lords decision in *Spiliada Maritime Corpn v Cansulex Ltd*.[15] Although a full discussion of this case is beyond the scope of this chapter, an appreciation of its *implications* is worthwhile. Until courts approach Internet disputes with the familiarity and understanding that they approach, say the telephone, litigators must be prepared to argue that despite the transnational nature of the Internet, some forums are more suitable than others.

Lord Goff provided the leading judgment given in *Spiliada*. He set out a number of guidelines[16] that may guide a court as to whether England is a suitable and appropriate forum: the court must, in effect, balance the suitability of England against that of another forum. This forum must be clearly and distinctly more appropriate: one 'with which the action [has] the most real and substantial connection'.[17] Once this clearly and distinctly more appropriate forum has been found the court will stay the action unless the plaintiff can prove that he clearly will not be able to obtain justice there.

This discretion, unlikely to be disturbed on appeal,[18] may be of paramount importance in an Internet dispute. In contrast to most other means of communication, the Internet can make it appear that a defendant has little connection with any country. A server may be in a country far away from the defendant's domicile. A defendant may have mirror servers, identical web sites, scattered throughout the world. The information or product that is the root of the dispute may have passed through as many as one hundred countries. Worse still, it is a question of technical semantics to resolve whether the digital information moved from the server to the plaintiff or whether the plaintiff 'collected' the digital information from the server.

These issues, and many more like them, may cloud the answer to which is the *forum conveniens* for the dispute. Of course, one may take the more pragmatic approach and look at the dispute trying to ignore the Internet complexities. To describe computer virus damage, one may state that, at its heart, an individual's property in England was damaged as a result of the negligence of an individual, whose property was in America. While this may appear a précis of the dispute, it does not address the question before the courts: which is the suitable forum in the interests of all the parties and the ends of justice?

The answering of this question involves examining the mechanics of hearing the dispute as well as its geographical basis. In illustration, often it is important to know where the relevant evidence is held and where the relevant witnesses live.[19]

---

14 See the Court of Appeal's interpretation of the Civil Jurisdiction and Judgments Act 1982, s 49 in *Re Harrods (Buenos Aires) Ltd* [1991] 4 All ER 334.
15 [1986] 3 All ER 843.
16 The necessary details of these guidelines can be found in specialist texts.
17 *The Abidin Daver* [1984] 1 All ER 470 at 478 per Lord Keith.
18 [1986] 3 All ER 843 at 846 to 847 per Lord Templeman.
19 See [1986] 3 All ER 843 at 856.

For many Internet disputes, however, such factors may not be weighty enough to disturb the jurisdiction of the court. Computer files will often be the main evidence and often the plaintiff in England will be the sole human witness to the tort itself. So for an Internet dispute, the jurisdiction of the English court may be less easily upset. As a further illustration, the issue of convenience, often a factor for the court, may be less convincing when all of the actual evidence is in a digital format. Such evidence can be sent to England, over the Internet, cheaply, quickly and accurately. Again, the actual nature of the Internet may lead to the conclusion that little is lost by hearing the dispute in England.

A court will also consider the residence of the defendant. The plaintiff, no doubt, will attempt to persuade the court that the Internet allows persons to have no residence as such. In this sense, those who use the Internet have no claim over one country any more than another. The defendant's argument may take a more commonsense view: the Internet is a means of communication that operates from one fixed point to another. In addition, the defendant who would be forced into the English courts has a fixed residence; that the defendant is alleged to have committed a tort over the Internet which is difficult to locate may not be relevant as to where is the most appropriate place to litigate the dispute.

For the purposes of jurisdiction, the defendant's argument is the more realistic. If a tort committed over the Internet seems to have no geographical locus then, presumably, any court is equally suitable to gather evidence on the Internet aspects of the dispute. What will tip this finely balanced situation is the fact that the court is judging which is the natural forum: which is the forum with the closest and most real connection to the dispute. This is a relative not absolute requirement: the forum need not be close, but simply the closest out of many; the forum need not have a real connection, but simply the most real out of the other connections. The court is seeking, at times, the 'best out of a bad bunch'. The court must consider all the relevant factors, such as where the defendant and plaintiff are and which law will apply to this dispute. Under the Private International Law (Miscellaneous Provisions) Act 1995, except for defamation issues, the law that generally will apply to a tort dispute is the law of where the tort occurred. And Lord Goff in *Spiliada* notes that the law of the dispute will often be a relevant factor.[20] What can be concluded from all this is that presence of the Internet in a dispute will never create the situation where no court is appropriate to hear the case. All the Internet *may* complicate is the question of where the tort occurs; there are numerous other factors that will, despite this complication, prove that England is, or is not, the natural forum.

---

31. A publisher resident in Calcutta publishes an on-line newspaper. In one edition an Indian domiciled in England is gravely defamed. He seeks to serve a writ out of the jurisdiction against the Indian publisher. Evidence is adduced that the newspaper has 73,000 subscribers in India but only 15 in England. The court in deciding whether England, or Calcutta, is the appropriate forum may consider that the courts of the place where the publisher is resident, publishes and has the greatest distribution, has the most real connection with the dispute.

---

20   With reference to *Crédit Chimique v James Scott Engineering Group Ltd* 1982 SLT 131. In this Scottish case, Lord Jauncy goes further and asks that a court look not simply at the fact that foreign law will be applied, but to look deeper at the *nature* of the foreign law. It may be that it is trivial for an English court to turn its mind to the foreign law, but it also may be that the law is so alien that the most appropriate court to consider the legal issues is a court which regularly deals with them.

CONVENTION AND COMMON LAW JURISDICTION

The last scenario is included for two reasons. First, it relates to a real case involving not on-line newspapers, but paper newspapers.[1] The second reason is that it acts as a nice comparison with *Shevill* and other defamation claims heard under the Brussels Convention.[2] In *Shevill* the court seemed unable to factor in the small circulation in England; in *Pillai* the limited circulation was a significant factor in French J's reasoning that,[3]

> 'all the plaintiffs can hope to achieve here is success in respect of publications which can only be described as trivial in scale by comparison with the 73,000 copies which were published in India.'

This section has shown that, if a defendant of an Internet tort is domiciled within a contracting state, a plaintiff will have little difficulty in suing in the English courts. In contrast, if the defendant is not domiciled in a contracting state, a plaintiff will have to show more than merely a few downloads of a defamatory article in England; a substantial connection with England will have to be found and stressed to the court.

CHOICE OF LAW

Establishing that the English courts have jurisdiction over an Internet tort dispute does not determine which law they must apply to *resolve* the dispute. This is a separate issue decided by reference to English law's choice of law rules for foreign torts. It may be a complex issue because the court must determine where the tort occurs before deciding which law will apply. Over the Internet, such geographical issues may be difficult to resolve, but, it is submitted, of no increased difficulty over other transborder torts. What the Internet will increase is the frequency with which courts are pressed on these issues of choice of law.

Common law choice of law

The Private International Law (Miscellaneous Provisions) Act 1995 leaves in place the old common law rules to determine the law to apply to the determination of issues arising in any defamation claim.[4] Defamation claims include not only libel and slander but also slander of title, slander of goods or other malicious falsehood and their equivalents.[5]

---

1   *Pillai v Sarkar* (1994) Times, 21 July.
2   See 'Defamation', at page 115.
3   Unreported, judgment, at 6F–G.
4   Private International Law (Miscellaneous Provisions) Act 1995, s 13(1).
5   Private International Law (Miscellaneous Provisions) Act 1995, s 13(2).

DOUBLE-ACTIONABILITY TEST

The common law rules are well covered in specialist texts so what follows is a short introduction to their vestigial application to an Internet defamation claim. The basic rule is that the claimant must have a cause of action under English domestic law[6] and under the law of the place where the tort occurred.[7] Without this 'double-actionability' the claim cannot be brought unless it falls within the exception. This is that, in the interests of justice, single-actionability may suffice. In *Chaplin v Boys* the exception was 'created' and invoked by the House of Lords to permit a plaintiff to recover in England that which he could not recover under the foreign law.[8] More recently in *Red Sea Insurance Co Ltd v Bouygues SA* the Privy Council invoked the exception to allow the plaintiff to recover under the foreign law for a claim not actionable under English law.[9]

---

32. An Internet Service Provider in Spain publishes a web page for a known libellous sports commentator. As could be expected, this individual uses the web page to defame an English football player. The player seeks to sue the individual and Provider from England. The player has the jurisdiction of the court under Article 5(3) of the Brussels Convention. Under English law, the Internet Provider would be liable not having taken reasonable care considering the author's previous conduct. Under Spanish law, however, the Provider may be liable for defamation only where the publisher knew that the material was defamatory. Unless a court becomes convinced of the need to invoke the exception, the player will have no right of action against the Provider in the English courts.

Statutory choice of law

APPLICABLE LAW: GENERAL RULE

The Private International Law (Miscellaneous Provisions) Act 1995 introduces a new regime for choice of tort law. It abolishes the common law test of double-actionability[10] and instead looks primarily to the law of the place where the events constituting the tort occurred.[11] To aid the courts in assessing where this place is when events occurred in different countries,[12] the Act provides two rules of

---

6   See *The Halley* (1868) LR 2 PC 193.
7   See *Phillips v Eyre* (1870) LR 6 QB 1.
8   [1969] 2 All ER 1085.
9   [1994] 3 All ER 749.
10 Other than for defamation claims as discussed, Private International Law (Miscellaneous Provisions) Act 1995, s 13(1).
11 Private International Law (Miscellaneous Provisions) Act 1995, s 11(1).
12 Private International Law (Miscellaneous Provisions) Act 1995, s 11(2).

relevance to the Internet.[13] The first is that the applicable law for a cause of action in respect of damage to property is the law of the country where the property was when it was damaged.[14] The second is that in any other case, the applicable law is the law of the country in which the most significant element or elements of the events occurred.[15]

---

33. A controller of an American web site knowingly and maliciously allows virus code to be transmitted to its viewers' computers. One English corporation suffers huge data damage and sues the American controller in the English courts. The American seeks to prove that the law of the State of New York should apply as it is from there that the virus spread. This is incorrect. The property that is damaged is in England; English law will apply. There is no real conflict of laws.

---

34. A controller of an English Web site provides dubious financial advice on which reliance is placed by a Canadian company with offices around the world. The company suffers loss and decides to sue the controller in England. The applicable law for resolving the dispute will not be English law. The significant elements of the tort occurred in Canada. It is there that the company received, acted upon and was damaged by the negligent advice. Canadian law will be the applicable law. That the dispute is brought in the English courts is of no consequence to which law applies.

APPLICABLE LAW: DISPLACEMENT OF GENERAL RULE

A court is not entirely bound by the rules in section 11; it can displace the general rule where it appears from a number of factors that there is a substantially more appropriate law for determining the issues.[16] This is not meant to be invoked regularly, it is an exception and should be treated as such. Section 12 contains three factors to consider which are persuasive, not definitive, as to when it is appropriate to displace the general rule.

---

13   The Act provides three rules in total; the other rule is excluded from this discussion as it relates to personal injury (s 11(2)(a)). It is assumed, at least for now, that a rule relating to personal injury is generally irrelevant to the Internet. This said, the Act does specifically define 'personal injury' to include 'any impairment of physical or mental condition' (s 11(3)). Therefore, the recovery for nervous shock as a result of seeing or hearing about a tragedy provides a possibility that the Internet will be messenger of such bad news and that claims will be brought blaming the Provider or creator. Cf *Alcock v Chief Constable of South Yorkshire* [1991] 4 All ER 907 at 921 per Ackner LJ: 'I agree, however, with Nolan LJ that simultaneous broadcasts of a disaster cannot in all cases be ruled out as providing the equivalent of the actual sight or hearing of the event or its immediate aftermath.'
14   Private International Law (Miscellaneous Provisions) Act 1995, s 11(2)(b).
15   Private International Law (Miscellaneous Provisions) Act 1995, s 11(2)(c).
16   Private International Law (Miscellaneous Provisions) Act 1995, s 12.

Chapter four
Intellectual property

[T]he Internet is the world's biggest copying machine.
Marybeth Peters, *Register of Copyrights*, 1995[1]

The material stored and transmitted through the Internet is intangible and much of it can be protected by intellectual property rights. These rights can protect the intangible but important assets of companies and creative products of the mind from damage. This chapter focuses on two of these rights: trade marks and copyright.

A trade mark or a brand name is becoming increasingly important to businesses and consumers. For businesses the goodwill built up through sales under a brand can be extremely valuable. For consumers, a trade mark indicates the source of a product and so indicates its quality. It is therefore crucial that as commerce takes to the Internet, where it is easy to fake an identity, the law protects trade mark owners and consumers from impostors. This is crucial in the area of domain names.

Copyright can protect almost all the material used and transferred over the Internet and the World Wide Web. This right can protect e-mails, forum discussions, and web sites. It is therefore relevant for users and Service Providers to understand the ambit of these rights and what activities will lead to their infringement.

This chapter examines the following issues:

1. What is the relationship between trade marks and domain names?
2. What are the legal remedies against those who use another's trade mark as a domain name?
3. What is the best way to protect a domain name?
4. What are the legal issues involved in using trade marks on a web site?
5. What is the reach of the English courts' jurisdiction over trade mark infringers?
6. Where must an Internet work be created to be protected by copyright?
7. What is the nature of copyright protection over e-mails, forum threads, file collections, newsgroups, web sites, their text, graphics, applets and links?
8. What is the level of copyright protection for search engines, link lists and web broadcasts?
9. In what ways can the copyright in works on the Internet be infringed?

1   *US News and World Report*, 23 January 1995, page 59.

10. How may a Service Provider hosting a newsgroup or a forum be liable for infringing material posted to the collection?
11. What is the English courts' jurisdiction over those who deal with copyright works from abroad?

TRADE MARKS

Commerce is moving with remarkable speed onto the World Wide Web. Many television and newspaper advertisements detail not only conventional addresses, but also the web site address of the company. Sometimes this web site address, or domain name, is recognisable as the name of the company itself. For example, McDonalds can be reached at the address 'www.mcdonalds.com'. This domain name is provided by a central registry who allocate names on a first-come, first-served basis. In addition, the registry is able to provide only one user with a particular domain name. There is only one 'www.nabarro.com' and there will not be another until Nabarro Nathanson decides to release its rights over its domain name. This situation has resulted in and will continue to lead to many clashes between companies. This chapter considers when a domain name will infringe a trade mark and what a company should do to protect itself having registered a domain name.

The greatest use of trade marks is on a web site itself. Signs, sounds, animations and static graphics are all capable of being registered under the Trade Marks Act 1994. This chapter therefore examines whether there are any special conditions that may apply for the use of registered trade marks on the World Wide Web. Clearly related is this section's analysis of trade mark infringement using a web site as an infringing medium.

A registered trade mark in the United Kingdom placed on a web site in the United Kingdom can infringe a trade mark registered elsewhere in the world. Although trade marks protect only within a defined territory, the World Wide Web operates across all territories so permitting infringement in all. A corollary of this is that a trade mark registered in the United Kingdom may possibly be used to prevent a web site anywhere on the globe using that trade mark, if such use would infringe the United Kingdom trade mark. The advantages in reaching an audience in every country are in equal measure with the respect that must be paid to the legal regimes of those countries.

Rights in domain names

Every presence on the World Wide Web has a unique address called a domain name. Usually these domain names begin with the prefix, 'www' and end with a two- or three-letter suffix that indicates which type of organisation runs the site. For example, a business will usually have a 'com' or 'co' suffix. In addition, there may be a two-letter suffix that indicates the country of registration.

A full example of this is the domain name for *The Times* newspaper: 'www.the-times.co.uk'. This indicates that the owner of this web site is a company and that its name was registered in the United Kingdom. It does not mean that the company which owns the web site or the server computer storing the web pages are in the United Kingdom. The domain name address, once obtained, may be utilised from anywhere in the world. So, unlike a postal address which necessarily changes when one moves to another town, a domain name may remain the same wherever one moves; it is like a PO box address. This is possible because the domain name is actually an alias for a large, unique number called an Internet Protocol Address. It is this number that corresponds to the computer that stores the digital material. If that material is moved to another computer, the unique number will be altered but the domain name can remain the same. It only *refers* to the unique number. Just as the post office will forward any post from a PO box to a 'real' address, so the Internet forwards digital information from a domain name to the storing computer. This author uses clive@pobox.com.

Domain names are truly international. Not only can any domain name be reached from anywhere in the world, but the computer to which that domain name refers can be located anywhere in the world. Seeing the domain name, 'www.harrods.co.uk' gives a strong impression that it is an English web site, but this cannot be confirmed until the Internet Protocol Address is geographically located.

Domain names, like company names, are not simply taken; they are registered. The registration companies do not check that an applicant has the right to use a particular name as a domain name and so allocates them on a first-come-first-served basis.

TYPES OF DOMAIN NAME

There are various families of domain name each with different suffixes. Those with a suffix 'org' refer to charitable organisations; those ending 'gov' are governmental domains. There are also a number of different suffixes for companies. 'com' was the first and is mainly owned by American companies; 'co.uk' was the first United Kingdom domain name but there are now others such as 'uk.com' and 'com.uk'.[2] That there are many suffixes, and that more are created every month does not eliminate the fundamental legal problem with domain names: they are unique. This is considered below by comparing domain names with trade marks.

TRADE MARKS V DOMAIN NAMES

For every computer connected to the Internet from every country in the world there is only one 'www.apple.com'. It is obvious that Apple Computers and Apple Records would both like to use that name, but it is impossible for them to share the name. This creates serious conflicts because there is no compromise available. In contrast, the law generally allows two companies to own the same trade mark but in respect of differing products or service offerings. Trade marks are also protected only within a defined territory; there is no one system which provides worldwide rights. Two individuals in different countries may therefore own the same mark. This creates the situation where two users of a trade mark in the same class but in different countries may be fighting over the same domain name. The

---

2   The International Ad Hoc Committee (IAHC) has proposed expanding the number of generic top level domain names (gTLD), such as 'com'. *Proposed gTLD—Memorandum of Understanding*, 28 February 1997.

important questions in such a dispute are: who is entitled to the name and is it infringement for one to use the name within the other's territory?

This section also addresses the growing practice of trafficking in domain names. This is where a person registers a domain name purely to sell it. Comparisons will be drawn with those who register company names for similar purposes.

TRADE MARKING DOMAIN NAMES

One common issue concerning domain names is whether they are protected by an existing trade mark registration. The Trade Marks Act 1994 specifies that in order to be registered, a trade mark must be a sign capable of being represented graphically which is capable of distinguishing goods or services of one undertaking from those of other undertakings. Unless the mark has acquired a distinctive character through use before application, a trade mark cannot be registered if it has no distinctive character, or serves to designate the characteristics of goods or services. This basic background is useful to appreciate the tension between choosing a domain name and trying to protect that name by registering it as a trade mark.

Descriptive domain names

In some industries, it is often better to be listed under one's services than under one's name. For example, it may be more profitable for a chemist to be listed under 'pharmacies' than under his name. It may appear that the same is true for the Internet: the domain name, 'www.flowers.com', may appear to be worth far more than 'www.lindasflorist.com'. The legal difference between these two domain names is that one is descriptive, so probably unregistrable as a trade mark while the other, though less memorable, may be more distinctive so is more likely to be registrable. The advantage of registering a descriptive *domain name*, however, shall not be overstated: most viewers on the World Wide Web use search engines to find sites of interest.

Search engines, unlike, say directory enquiries for a telephone number, do not simply search for particular words within a domain name; they can search almost every word in every document that appears on the World Wide Web. So, searching for the word 'florist' would identify the sites which sell flowers, sites which contain an article about florists, and so on. For each of the sites, the viewer is presented with a collection of domain names and their site's descriptions to choose from.[3] Because of this common way of searching for information on the Internet, the advantages of acquiring a generic domain name are not as great as they might otherwise be.

Those individuals who are considering acquiring a domain name are therefore advised to use a distinctive name: this has no significant disadvantages on the web but has the obvious advantage of being registrable as a trade mark.

---

3   This author used Digital's Alta Vista search engine to look for the word 'florist'. Within ten seconds Alta Vista had found over 10,000 sites that included the word 'florist'.

Registered trade marks

There will often be occasions where an owner of a registered trade mark over a name seeks to use that name as a domain name. For a name to gain protection as a registered trade mark it must fulfil two tests.

Capable of being represented graphically

To be registered as a trade mark, the sign must be capable of being represented graphically. This is essentially a procedural requirement and is one always met by a domain name.[4]

Capable of distinguishing undertakings' goods or services

The Trade Marks Act 1994 requires that the sign is capable of distinguishing goods or services of one undertaking from those of other undertakings.[5] This sign must be registered within a particular class of goods or services.[6] It is important not to confuse uniqueness with being capable of distinguishing. Each domain name is necessarily unique. This uniqueness alone does not make the name capable of distinguishing its goods or services from those of another.

> **1. A data recovery company registers the domain name 'data-recovery.co.uk'. It is the only owner of this domain name; it is unique amongst not only all data recovery companies, but also all domain name owners. This does not mean that the name is capable of distinguishing the services of its owner from any other company. Without more the company will be unable to register a trade mark over the name.**

New trade mark classes

Practically, there will be few occasions when a registered trade mark proprietor will *need* to broaden his trade mark registration when using the name as a domain name. It is wrong to think that because the *medium* is a new telecommunications system that the trade mark registration needs to be expanded into this class as well.

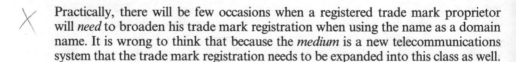

> **2. Artsake Ltd is a manufacturer and retailer of artist materials within the United Kingdom. It has a trade mark registration in class 16 to reflect the use of its name Artsake in relation to paper, cardboard goods and other artists' materials. It now wishes to expand its business by setting up a web site through which customers can place orders. It chooses the domain name 'artsake.co.uk' and is concerned that it will require additional trade mark protection for the domain. It does not; its existing registration will equally protect its domain name in respect of artists' materials sold over the Internet.**

---

4   Trade Marks Act 1994, ss 1(1) and 103(2).
5   Trade Marks Act 1994, s 1(1).
6   Trade Marks Act 1994, s 34.

There may be times where an individual already has a trade mark registration but is providing new goods or services through a web site. In this circumstance there may be a reason to broaden the number of classes or specification for which a trade mark is registered. Most web sites are little more than a digital billboard or leaflet. In contrast, new technologies which allow the site to obtain information about the viewer may lead to an increase in the *activities* provided through a web site. An illustration is where the proprietor of a paper newspaper releases selected stories on its web site. A change in the nature of the business takes place. This trade mark owner should simply rely on a registration for paper products, but should widen it to include electronic documents.

> **3. A car manufacturer that uses its trade mark as a domain name decides to make its web site more than merely a digital version of its paper brochures. To do this the dealer includes on its web site an ActiveX program that acts as a route finder: individuals may type in where they are and where they wish to go and the program generates a map of the quickest route. The map also includes the miles per gallon that the dealer's car would use on the same route so promoting the fuel economy of the car. The business now involves not only the sale of cars but also the provision of a route-finding service. It would be prudent to broaden the trade mark protection accordingly.**

Similarly there will be times where the trade mark owner continues to use the registered trade mark in a slightly different market of goods or services. For example, a travel agent may well have a trade mark registered in classes including class 39 for travel services. If, however, the agent expands its business to include taking bookings over its web site, it may want to consider carefully its existing *specification* on the trade marks register. In this situation it may be wise to ensure its registration covers the provision of travel services *by means of a global network*.

New trade mark

The Internet has spawned a great number of new businesses who are seeking to gain a foothold in the online facilities market. Because the barriers to set up a web site are so low, there is a need to differentiate oneself in that market and then to protect that differentiation. To register a trade mark that protects a domain name will provide substantial reinforcement. What follows are not the words of a lawyer touting for trade mark business, but that of Laddie J extolling the virtues of trade marks.[7]

> 'If a trader wishes to bring passing off proceedings he has to prove the existence of a reputation in his mark with potential customers. In the majority of cases this means that his common law rights will wither and disappear unless he continues to market and advertise his goods under the mark. Furthermore his rights are only breached if there is, or is likely to be, confusion in the marketplace which will cause him substantial damage. *This should be contrasted with the rights acquired*

---

7   *Mercury Communications Ltd v Mercury Interactive (UK) Ltd* [1995] FSR 850 at 864. Emphasis added.

by a proprietor who registers a mark. His registration gives him a true monopoly. Subject to certain statutory defences, the proprietor will be able to restrain any trader who uses the same or a sufficiently similar mark on the goods covered by the registration. This is so even if, in the marketplace, no confusion is being caused. Indeed he will be able to sue for infringement even if he is not using his own registered trade mark (subject to it being removed if prolonged non-use is proved). Furthermore, with little effort any competently advised proprietor will be able to keep his registration in force indefinitely.'

Little more needs to be said of the power of trade marks and their worth in such a fiercely competitive market such as the provision of Internet-related services. Companies, such as Yahoo Inc, have used a very distinctive name both as their company name and domain name. From a protection point of view, this is helpful to gain a trade mark registration over the domain name or the company name. It also allows for a broader 'brandwidth': Yahoo are now selling 'Yahoo magazines', and other merchandise; all using its strong brand name.

Registering a domain name as a trade mark

Some individuals and companies may wish to register as trade marks their actual domain name, prefix, suffix and all. This is opposed to registering as a trade mark only the name making up the domain name. For example, in America, MovieFone Inc has registered as a trade mark the domain name 'moviefone.com' as well as 'movielink.com'.[8] If all the registration criteria are met, there seems little that would prevent a domain name being registered as a trade mark. Indeed, America's PTO has notified its examiners to ignore the standard suffixes like '.com' and '.ac' when assessing whether or not two marks are confusingly similar: a clear indication of the *prima facie* registrability of a domain name. From a pragmatic perspective, there seems little reason to register as a trade mark a domain name including the suffix, rather than purely the name element of the domain name. Registering as a trade mark the name element of the domain name will also protect the name's use within a domain name.

> **4. Phillip Jones Ltd is a one-man company that specialises in repairing old hi-fi equipment. As the company grows in experience its owner realises that there is a market in repairing old computer equipment for a pre-determined quotation. The company sets up a web site on which restored equipment is offered for sale and on which viewers may enter details of their ailing equipment to receive an e-mailed repair quotation. The domain name for the site is 'www.compair.com'. To provide added protection for this sign, Phillip Jones Ltd may seek a trade mark registration over the word 'compair' in the appropriate classes.**

Computer software class

Software- and Internet-related firms need to consider the extent of the trade mark protection they require for the trade mark. It is too easy but wrong to suggest that

---

8   4 November 1994: applications 74/595, 293 and 74/595, 294.

the registration over a domain name that references a search engine should be within class 38 for telecommunications. Class 38 should be considered as only appropriate for the infrastructure providers for the Internet. AT&T as the owners of the Internet's conduits would be appropriately registered in class 38.[9] It is submitted that the owner of a web site that acts as a search engine may be more appropriately registered for computer programs and information services.

Authority to this effect can be found in the case *Mercury Communications Ltd v Mercury Interactive (UK) Ltd.*[10]

> '[T]he defining characteristic of a piece of computer software is not the medium on which it is recorded, nor the fact that it controls a computer, nor the trade channels through which it passes but the function it performs.'

Controllers of web sites need to consider carefully whether a registration *outside* the computer software class 9 is actually warranted or whether it is an incorrect understanding of their goods and services.

Computer software classification

Once it is decided in which class a trade mark should be obtained, an appropriate specification *within* that class must be provided. Here, again, those who provide a web site should rein in their delusions of grandeur: a specification that includes the generic term 'computer programs' is likely to be viewed as too wide. Electronic communication apparatus may be more appropriate.[11]

In *Mercury*, Laddie J was able to comment on the trade mark in Class 9 held by Mercury Communications Ltd. The specification was in broad terms including both 'computers' and 'computer programs'. Mercury Communications Ltd alleged that Mercury Interactive was infringing its trade mark as Mercury Interactive analysed and bug-tested computer software. Laddie J held that the term 'computer software' or 'computer programs' is normally far too wide as a specification. It would cover any set of digitally recorded instructions used to control any type of computer. This would include software in the medical diagnostic field, software for controlling the computers on the London Underground and software for designing genealogical tables![12] Clearly such a wide registration provides an excessively broad monopoly over goods and services that are unconnected with the true trading interests of the applicant.

It was Laddie J's opinion that such a registration is ripe for having its registration removed entirely on the grounds of non-use, or at the least, having the specification of the goods dramatically pruned during rectification proceedings.

The lesson that web site owners can learn from this case is clear. If the name within a web site domain name is registrable, a trade mark may provide additional protection against those who would seek to emulate the name of the site. But the

---

9   In contrast, a controller of a web site, without more, would not be appropriately registered in class 38. Similarly, the companies who rent out storage space on web servers will generally be inappropriately registered in class 38; they should be within class 42.
10   [1995] FSR 850 at 865.
11   In *Second Sight Ltd v Novell Inc and Novell UK Ltd* [1995] RPC 423 an overly wide specification in class 9 for 'computer software' was the cause of a clash between two rights-holders in *different* fields both asserting rights over the same trade name.
12   Examples provided by Laddie J in his judgment, [1995] FSR 850 at 864.

registration of the trade name must be in respect of a suitable specification in respect of goods and services.

---

5. BetaBlockers Ltd are the pioneer testing company for unreleased software, often called, beta versions. They establish a web site with the domain name 'WWW.BETABLOCKER.CO.UK'. They then discover that another site exists, also controlled by a beta-testing company, with the domain name 'WWW.BETABL0CKER.CO.UK'. Knowing that two identical domain names cannot exist, they investigate further to discover that the copy-cat site has used the number zero instead of the letter 'o'. If BetaBlocker was appropriately registered as a trade mark, this would permit an action of trade mark infringement; if no trade mark was registered, the company would have a harder and more expensive task proving passing-off.

Protecting domain names

This section contains numerous examples of clashes over domain names. The most common is where a person with a legal right to a trade mark seeks to use it within a domain name but discovers that someone already has registered that name as a domain name. More complex are the examples of companies already with a domain name who object to another domain name that has a different suffix. This section, with reference to the facts of actual American disputes, considers in detail the likely outcomes had these cases been between English litigants under English law over English facts. The section also considers future possible clashes such as where a trade mark and domain name owner objects to the use of its domain name as a link on another web site. Finally, this section prescribes the safest way of legally and technically protecting a domain name as well as the best way of resolving a dispute.

Infringement of a registered trade mark can occur where there is unauthorised use in the course of trade of a sign that is identical or similar to that trade mark. This use may be in respect of goods which are identical to or similar to the goods for which the trade mark is registered. This chapter considers two real examples of trade mark infringement with domain names: first, between a registered trade mark and an identical domain name in respect of the same services; second, between a registered trade mark and an identical domain name in respect of dissimilar services. The chapter also considers what rights of action the trade mark owners would have against the domain name owners if their trade marks were not registered.

TECHNICAL RIGHTS V LEGAL RIGHTS

In *MTV Networks v Adam Curry*, Adam Curry had beaten the famous Music Television Network to a domain name.[13] Before August 1993 he had registered and operated a web site with the domain name 'www.mtv.com'. This site provided information about the music business and dovetailed with the television business

13   867 F Supp 202 (SDNY 1994).

of MTV. MTV eventually realised the potential of the Internet and on 19 January 1994 sought to reacquire the domain name owned by Adam Curry. By Spring 1994 millions of Internet users had accessed the 'www.mtv.com' site.

This is a common scenario in domain name clashes. The only right which Adam Curry had over the site was a technical one: he was the owner of the domain name alias; he was not the owner of any *legal* rights to use the name MTV in relation to the same business. Under English law there are three main legal attacks that could be used to acquire the domain name: trade mark infringement; passing off; deliberate damage to goodwill.

Trade mark infringement

On the assumption that 'MTV' is registered as a trade mark under the Trade Marks Act 1994 in respect of music information and broadcasting, the use of the letters in a domain name of a site providing similar services seems a blatant infringement.[14] Section 10(1) states that it is an infringement for a person to use in the course of trade a sign which is identical with a registered trade mark and in relation to goods or services which are identical with the goods or services for which the trade mark is registered. The two relevant questions are therefore, is the use the domain name in the course of trade, and is the defendant's sign identical or similar to the registered trade mark?

Use of a sign in the course of trade[15]

A person uses a sign in particular when he,[16]

'(a) affixes it to goods or the packaging thereof;
(b) offers or exposes goods for sale, puts them on the market or stocks them for those purposes under the sign, or offers or supplies services under the sign;
(c) imports or exports goods under the sign; or
(d) uses the sign on business papers or in advertising.'

The relevant examples for this scenario are (b) and (d). Adam Curry was offering and supplying services under the sign 'www.mtv.com' where 'www' and 'com' are entirely generic or are not part of the name. In addition, the sign could be seen as advertising for Adam Curry's activities within the goods and services covered by MTV's trade mark registration.

14 A suitable defence may be that the domain name is the actual name of the defendant: Trade Marks Act 1994, s 11(2). See 'Misrepresentation by defendant', at page 140, for an example and the passing off equivalent of the defence.
15 Some have attempted to read into s 10(1) that the sign must be used as a trade mark. One argument is that s 9(1) states that exclusive rights in a trade mark are infringed by the *use* of the trade mark without consent. To this argument, Jacob J in *British Sugar plc v James Robertson & Sons Ltd* [1996] RPC 281 at 291 stated, 's 9(1) is really no more than a chatty introduction to the details set out in s 10, itself adding no more than that the acts concerned must be done without consent.' To this he added that the Directive, Article 5 does not use this language. 'For reasons which baffle me our parliamentary draftsman did not simply copy this. He set about re-writing it. So the argument based on s 9(1) involves a departure from the Directive. This is wholly improbable. I reject it.'
16 Trade Marks Act 1994, s 10(4).

'In the course of trade' should not be taken to mean 'in the course of taking money'. To be trading, money need not change hands; it does, however, imply the use of the trade mark in relation to the trading activities of the defendant. If the site is serving some commercial purpose, be it for money or money's worth, it may be classed as trading.[17] If the nature of the site is deduced to include 'trading' its domain name will, necessarily, be being used in the course of that trading. The first indication of the existence of a particular web site is its domain name; that surely must be viewed as being used in the course of trading *with* that web site. In this MTV dispute, the domain name is not only the attractive force that brings in viewers. It is also the sole mechanism for these viewers to see the site: the name 'www.mtv.com' must either be clicked on as a link or typed to reach the site.

This is the first test; next we must assess whether the defendant's domain name is identical or similar to the plaintiff's trade mark.

Identical sign to registered trade mark

For this case, let us assume that the registered trade mark is the letters 'mtv' and the defendant uses as its domain name 'http://www.mtv.com'. These two strings of characters are not identical character for character, but are they identical for the purposes of section 10(1)? It is submitted that the courts should consider them as identical. The characters both before and after 'mtv' are standard and do not form part of the sign. Just as the American PTO strip off the suffixes when comparing marks, so should the English courts when considering whether a mark is identical.[18] What is at issue is whether a consumer would consider the sign and mark as identical; it is submitted that every consumer familiar with the Internet would see them as identical.[19]

In relation to goods or services

The sign purportedly infringing the trade mark must be used in relation to goods or services. Like its equivalent in the 1938 Act, this requirement of use is interpreted widely and will generally be satisfied whenever used as a domain name. This is because most web sites are used in this way; they may appear to be purely providing information but increasingly they also have links to other pages that advertise or even provide goods or services. Few sites are no more than an electronic poster. If the site is used for interaction with customers then the domain

---

17   In *Panavision International v Toeppen* (CV 96-3284 DDP, 1 November 1996) the Californian district court held that the defendant's 'business' was to 'register trade marks as domain names and then to sell the domain names to the trade marks' owners.'

18   The issue of where two domain names are identical bar the prefix and suffix is discussed at 'Legal and technical rights v legal and technical rights', at page 144.

19   Indeed, the latest browsers now 'understand' the typed characters 'www.site.com' as 'http://www.site.com'. This is a further indication that the letters before and after the name should be discarded when comparing the plaintiff's mark with the defendant's sign.

name would appear to be used in relation to goods or services. There is no other route to access the web site than by using the domain name.[20]

Identical goods or services

The last test is that the use of the purportedly infringing sign must be in relation to identical goods or services for which the trade mark is registered. This is a question of fact, although in this scenario it appears likely that a court would deem Adam Curry's site to be in the identical services of MTV's registrations.[1]

Trade mark infringement remedies

Having established a prima facie case of infringement, MTV would have to think carefully about the remedies it seeks. Unlike usual trade mark infringement where an injunction and delivery up of infringing articles is possible, for a domain name the issues are more complicated. MTV would prefer that Adam Curry not only stop using the domain name, or any similar, but also allow MTV to *take over* the domain name.[2]

For this reason, in addition to any claim for damages and injunction, MTV should seek delivery up of the infringing materials.[3] These materials are essentially the domain name registration in the name of Adam Curry; the actual content of the site may, or may not, be infringing material. Section 17(4) defines 'infringing material' to include material bearing a sign identical or similar to the infringed mark which either is used for advertising goods or services in such a way as to infringe the registered mark, or is intended to be so used and such use would infringe the registered trade mark.

Under this definition it appears *possible* that a domain name registration could be delivered up. This said, a domain name does not fit comfortably into 'infringing materials'. Should a court take the view that a domain name cannot constitute 'infringing materials', the plaintiff should seek an Order that the defendant 'takes all steps as lie within its power to release or facilitate the release of the domain name' and appeal to the court's general discretion to grant 'all such relief' to the plaintiff under section 14(2).

20 Of course, *off* the Internet, the domain name may be used not in relation to registered goods or services. For instance, a designer of the Harrods web site may set up his own web site to advertise his previous commissions including Harrods'. The presence on his web site of the domain name 'www.harrods.co.uk' would not be the use of the trade mark in relation to goods or services for which Harrods had a trade mark. See *Harrods v Schwartz-Sackin* [1986] FSR 490. In contrast, Harrods were granted an injunction against defendants who registered the domain name 'harrods.com' when Harrods had already registered 'harrods.co.uk' (Unreported, Mr Justice Lightman, 9 December 1996).
1   It should be remembered that the services can be identical despite MTV providing its services over the television and the site providing the same services over the Internet.
2   The right to an injunction under the Trade Marks Act 1994, s 14(2), like all injunctions must be sought expeditiously. In the real facts of *MTV v Curry*, it would appear that MTV would have been too late to be awarded with an injunction. The MTV Network Vice President discussed Curry's use of the MTV site in June 1993 and allowed him to continue at Curry's expense. 867 F Supp 202 (SDNY 1994), at 203-204, Counterclaim 9.
3   Trade Marks Act 1994, s 16(1).

Passing off claim

If MTV does not have a registered trade mark that it can use as the basis of trade mark infringement proceedings, it may seek to rely on its common law rights: namely a passing off claim. The ingredients of passing off have been classified as a 'classical trinity': goodwill of the plaintiff; misrepresentation by the defendant; and, consequent damage.[4]

Goodwill of plaintiff

The concept of 'goodwill' is succinctly defined by Lord MacNaghten in *IRC v Muller & Co's Margarine Ltd*:[5]

> 'It is the benefit and advantage of a good name, reputation and connection of a business. It is the attractive force which brings in custom.'

If a company has customers who would think of using its name, or the name of a product, as a domain name, there appears little to suggest that the company does not have goodwill in the domain name. And as businesses pervade the World Wide Web it will become more common for businesses to advertise and provide goods and services to their customers using the Internet. This, in turn, will increase the chances of a company extending its goodwill from merely its name to the *domain* name of the company.

In the MTV case there is indubitable goodwill in the domain name 'www.mtv.com' by virtue of the existent goodwill in the name MTV. The plaintiffs should be able to prove this element of the passing off classical trinity.

Misrepresentation by defendant

The term 'misrepresentation' does not imply any malice or intention; it is more a statement of the perception of the public.[6] Using a domain name may therefore be bona fide. The court, however, will look to whether potential customers are misled into thinking that the defendant's goods are those of the plaintiff.[7] In a passing off case concerning the use of similar telephone numbers, Aldous J said:[8]

> 'The defendants are right that a misrepresentation must be established, but are wrong in believing that it requires an express statement. A

---

4   *Consorzio del Prosciutto di Parma v Marks & Spencer* [1991] RPC 351, per Nourse LJ. Cf the five characteristics of passing off presented (and followed) by Lord Diplock in *Erven Warnink BV v J Townend & Sons (Hull) Ltd* [1979] FSR 397 at 405. Advisers should be wary of using the three- (or five-) part test as the definitive answer whether one web site passes off a plaintiff's reputation. Lord Diplock warns, at 405, 'It does not follow that because all passing off actions can be shown to present these characteristics, all factual situations which present these characteristics give rise to a cause of action for passing off.'
5   [1901] AC 217 at 223–224.
6   Innocence does not provide a defence to an injunction. The court will simply assess whether on an objective basis injury was a reasonably foreseeable consequence of the misrepresentation. See *Taittinger v Allbev Ltd* [1993] 2 CMLR 741 at 751 [21]–752 [25].
7   *Frank Reddaway & Co Ltd v George Banham & Co Ltd* [1896] AC 199.
8   *Law Society of England and Wales v Griffiths* [1995] RPC 16 at 21.

person who adopts the mantle of another can by his silence misrepresent that he is that other. Thus a person who selects a confusingly similar telephone number or a similar name may well represent that he is that other by either saying so or by failing to take steps when telephoned or called to disabuse the person who is making the telephone call.'

This can be applied to domain names. If instead of Adam Curry setting up the copy-cat web site, Martin Trevor Vantram had established the site with his initials as a domain name, there may still have been a misrepresentation.[9] What is important is whether the misrepresentation, intentional or not, leads, or is likely to lead, the public to believe that goods or services offered by the defendant are those of the plaintiff.[10]

Without more, the domain name 'www.mtv.com' gives the impression that the site is under the control or licence of MTV networks. Of course, the suffix of the domain name may go some way to indicate the business of the owner: 'www.sheffield.ac.uk' *is* an academic institution as shown by the suffix 'ac'.

This raises the question as to whether anything could be done to disabuse the public of this misrepresentation. Certainly the defendant, in the knowledge that its domain name is confusingly similar to another's name, may seek to distinguish its site from the potential plaintiff's. It may be thought that, by using the words, 'Unofficial MTV Site' the misrepresentation is stopped. In certain circumstances this may be true. It is submitted, however, that often the misrepresentation is the domain name *itself*. *After* the domain name has been entered into a browser and the site is seen through the World Wide Web, information on the site may make clear the true nature of the site, but this may be too late to defeat the misrepresentation element of passing off.[11]

What is key to a passing off case is the influence of the defendant's representations *at or prior to the point of sale* not later.[12] The court will consider whether the 'public is moved in any degree to *buy* the article because of its source'.[13] It may be of no relevance that after entering the site the viewer is instructed that it is not the one expected.

To avoid litigation a defendant must seek to introduce 'true' distance between its site and that of the plaintiff by using disclaimers. Associations should be avoided. This said, there are limits to this distancing: any site that uses the domain name 'www.mtv.com' and features details of popular music will risk passing off, no matter how many and bold the disclaimers of unconnection. Of course, there will always be some individuals who will remain confused as to the source of a web site because of the domain name. Gibson LJ addresses this issue bluntly:[14]

---

9   That this may be a misrepresentation does not mean there is passing off. Indeed, it has been said, 'a man must be allowed to trade in his own name and, if some confusion results, that is a lesser evil than that a man should be deprived of what would appear to be a natural and inherent right': *Marengo v Daily Sketch* (1948) 65 RPC 242 at 251 per Lord Simonds.

10 A paraphrasing of Lord Oliver in *Reckitt & Colman Products v Borden Inc* [1990] 1 All ER 873.

11 Its effect may be to defeat the element of consequent damage, or at the least reduce the damages awarded if the plaintiff is successful at trial.

12 See *Bostik Ltd v Sellotape GB Ltd* IPD 17029.

13 *Crescent Tool v Kilborn & Bishop* 247 F 299 (1917), per Judge Learned Hand. Emphasis added. Cited with approval by Jacob J in *Hodgkinson & Corby Ltd v Wards Mobility Ltd* [1995] FSR 169 at 178.

14 *Taittinger v Allbev Ltd* [1993] 2 CMLR 741 at 751 [20]. See *Singer Manufacturing Co v Loog* (1882) 8 App Cas 15 at 18, per Lord Selborne LC.

'It is not right to base any test on whether a moron in a hurry would be confused, but it is proper to take into account the ignorant and unwary[.]'

Consequent damage

Misrepresentation in respect of another's goodwill does not provide the basis for a passing off action. The third aspect of passing off is that the plaintiff must show that he has suffered, or is likely to suffer, damage to the property in his goodwill because of the misrepresentation. This requirement to show damage, however, is not onerous in quality or quantity.

Quality of damage

If the infringing web site is selling goods or services, the test will be easy to satisfy. But the World Wide Web contains many sites that serve not as shops but as shop fronts. A web site under the domain name 'www.mtv.com' may not provide products and services for payment; it may merely provide useful information such as the latest releases and Top 20 sales. The damage therefore cannot be equated to lost sales but to a 'dilution' in the distinctiveness of the name MTV or harm to the reputation attaching to it. This will have the likely consequence that the goodwill in the name MTV will be reduced.

Quantity of damage

The level of damage need not be high. In fact, the level required is expressed in terms of a presumption that there will be damage unless proved to be below a *de minimis*.[15]

'The question is whether the relevant activities of the defendants are on such a small scale leading to such a small injury that it can be ignored.'

Passing off remedies

Like the remedies for trade mark infringement, the key order that the plaintiff should seek is to restrain the defendant from providing or describing any web site, e-mail access or other Internet access under or by reference[16] to the domain name 'www.mtv.com' or any other domain name colourably similar. The injunction will be unlikely to be awarded in a form wide enough to prevent the use of the material on the web site itself, as long as, subject to the main restraint, it does not use the domain name. This is, of course, unless it too passes off the plaintiff's reputation. Whether the court would order the domain name to be transferred to the plaintiff is a matter of debate. It is not *necessary* to restrain the passing off. The situation

---

15   *Taittinger v Allbev Ltd* [1993] 2 CMLR 741 at 753 [27] per Gibson LJ.
16   This will include the use of the domain name in a page of links on which viewers click rather than retype into their browser.

therefore may theoretically result in no one being able to use the domain name; the court may refuse to grant mandatory relief on motion.[17]

Deliberate damage to goodwill

Although not in the MTV dispute, there are occasions where an individual with no legal rights over a name acquires a domain name incorporating that name and then offers to sell the domain name to a more bona fide owner. This practice can work where the policy of the domain name registration company permits such arbitrage. Such a practice is common for company names[18] and a precedent from that area may be applicable for domain names. Before describing the case, a word of warning: the case turns on its facts; the court was clear that the defendants were dishonest. For occasions where the case is not simply one of obvious extortion, the courts may be more conservative.[19]

Glaxo plc and Wellcome plc v Glaxo-Wellcome Ltd

On 23 January 1995, a press release was issued announcing that if Glaxo plc's bid for Wellcome plc was successful, the new merged company would be called Glaxo-Wellcome. The next day a company registration agent filed an application for Glaxo-Wellcome Ltd. After Glaxo's bid was accepted the two companies discovered that the limited company version of the name had already been registered; they offered the going rate of £1,000 to buy the name. The agent together with his mother refused and demanded £100,000 with the implicit threat of exploiting the name of the newly merged company to its prejudice. The companies sought an injunction, urgently needing to resolve the issue before the adoption of the new name on 1 May 1995.[20]

Lightman J was convinced that the defendants were dishonest[1] and that they were abusing the system of company name registration by attempting to extort a substantial sum for not damaging the plaintiff's goodwill. As a result of this he not only granted the obvious injunction against the company and its subscribers to be restrained from continuing to be registered. He was also prepared to order an express mandatory injunction specifically requiring the company and subscribers to change or facilitate the change of the company name.

Many domain name disputes have parallels with this situation. An individual selects a domain name on the basis of selling that name to a company for an extortionate price. Joshua Quittner, a writer trying to prove a point, registered the domain name 'mcdonalds.com'. Proving the point, McDonalds donated thousands of dollars to a charity nominated by Quittner in return for the domain

17   In such a case, after a given time, the registration authority would reclaim the name at which point the 'truer' owner could register it.
18   See *Habib Bank Ltd v Habib Bank AG Zurich* [1981] 2 All ER 650; *Exxon Corpn v Exxon Insurance Consultants International Ltd* [1981] 2 All ER 495; *Fletcher Challenge Ltd v Fletcher Challenge Pty Ltd* [1982] FSR 1.
19   See *Ben & Jerry's Homemade Inc v Ben & Jerry's Ice Cream Ltd* (19 January 1995, unreported).
20   *Glaxo plc v GlaxoWellcome Ltd, Cullen, and McDonald* [1996] FSR 388.
1   The defendant's allegation that the choice of the name 'Glaxo-Wellcome' was 'merely an interesting combination of words' was sternly rejected. 'All I need say in regard to these suggestions is that there are limits to judicial credulity.' [1996] FSR 388 at 391.

name.[2] Mark Sloo registered the domain name 'bbb.com' and 'bbb.org' in an attempt to force the Council of Better Business Bureaus to buy the domain names.[3] The Council brought an action for unfair competition and for trademark infringement.[4] The case was settled. Carnetta Wong Associates registered the domain name 'avon.com'. Avon filed one of the first suits under the US Federal Trademark Dilution Act 1995. According to the complaint, Wong's representatives had admitted that[5]

> 'at least one of the defendant's purposes in registering 'avon.com' was to prevent Avon from establishing a domain using that domain [name] until Avon paid the defendant a sum of money satisfactory to the defendant.'

In these situations, where the defendant is clearly trafficking in a domain name with the intention of, in effect, holding to ransom the rightful owner of the name, it would appear that *Glaxo and Wellcome v Glaxo-Wellcome* is an appropriate authority on which to base an injunction.

LEGAL AND TECHNICAL RIGHTS V LEGAL AND TECHNICAL RIGHTS

Although there can be only one 'www.mtv.com', there may be many variations of that domain using different suffixes. For example, in November 1993, Merritt Technologies Inc was granted the domain name 'mit.com'. From 30 December 1993 Merritt used the domain to provide free Internet access to the handicapped, disabled and elderly. On 6 May 1996, Merritt received a letter from the Massachusetts Institute of Technology asking Meritt to select an alternate domain name. Their rights to insist upon this were based on their use of the MIT trademark since 1861, having a worldwide reputation and five registered trade marks in classes unrelated to Merritt's use of the mark. They also, like Avon, relied upon the amended US Trademark Act, section 43(c) providing rights for famous trade mark owners against those who might 'dilute' their marks. The Institute already owned the domain names 'mit.org' and 'lit.edu'. There was no cross-over in fields of activity: the Institute was simply worried that its trade mark was being used at all.

This is a scenario that will occur more and more frequently. This is because the naming committees both here and elsewhere are expanding the numbers of suffixes available. The latest policy document available from Nominet UK[6] lists five suffixes: 'co.uk', 'ltd.uk', 'net.uk', 'org.uk' and 'plc.uk'.[7] These are in addition to 'uk.com' and '.com' issued by other authorities. There are others such as '.biz', '.law' and '.sports' on the horizon. But as Jon Postel of the Internet Assigned Name Authority writes,[8]

2   See http://www.smartdocs.com/~migre.v/wired.com/1-22.html.
3   The Council is commonly referred to by those initials.
4   *Council of Better Business Bureaus Inc v Mark Sloo* (No 95-0473-CV-W-2) US District Court for Kansas City.
5   See http://www/infolawalert.com/stories/020996b.html. US District Court for Eastern District of New York (CV 96 0451).
6   Nominet UK has direct responsibility for the issuing of domain names with these suffixes.
7   Policy document dated 2 August 1996. See also fn 2 at page 130.
8   Information Law Alert, 02/09/96, '*Antidilution trademark law gets first court case*'.

'[T]he trademark issue is just a mess. McDonalds is going to want to have mcdonalds.com, mcdonalds.biz, and other domain names involving McDonalds.'

What follows, as for the MTV dispute, is an assessment of English law's reaction to the MIT dispute. Unless a mark is famous, English law does not provide a total monopoly over *every* use of a word.

Trade mark infringement

Unlike the MTV dispute where the domain name was used in relation to identical goods and services, Merritt's domain name is used in relation to dissimilar goods and services. The Institute has registered its mark in the UK only in relation to clothing; coffee mugs, cups, etc; pencils, notebooks, etc; computer programs and manuals; educational courses. With the assumption that these registrations were under the Trade Marks Act 1994, the use of 'mit' in Merritt's domain name seems possibly to be an infringement of a registered trade mark over the identical or similar name but with dissimilar goods or services.[9] Section 10(3) states that it is an infringement for a person to use in the course of trade a sign which is identical or similar with a registered trade mark[10] and in relation to goods or services which are identical with the goods or services for which the trade mark is registered.[11]

Use of a sign in the course of trade

As already discussed, section 10(4) provides four presumptions for when a person uses a sign.[12] The relevant presumptions in this scenario are again (b) and (d). Merritt was offering and supplying services under the sign 'www.mit.com' and advertising for Merritt's other business activities. Assuming that Merritt's use was in the course of trade, despite being for a charity, it is certainly arguable that the sign was used in the course of trade.[13]

Identical or similar sign to registered trade mark

The Institute's trade mark is the acronym 'mit' and the sign used by Merritt is 'http://www.mit.com'. It has already been discussed that despite these two strings, character for character, not being identical they may be identical for the purposes of the Act.[14] One reason for this is that the characters before and after 'mit' are generic for domain names or are not considered to be part of the sign at all.[15] But,

9 Here a suitable defence may be that the domain name is the actual name of the defendant used according to honest practices in commercial matters: Trade Marks Act 1994, s 11(2). Countering this, of course, the Institute may allege that the name of the defendant is not MIT, but Merritt Technologies Inc.
10 Trade Marks Act 1994, s 10(3)(a).
11 Trade Marks Act 1994, s 10(3)(b).
12 See 'Use of a sign in the course of trade', at page 137.
13 For deeper reasoning see, in relation to *mtv*.com, 'Use of a sign in the course of trade', at page 137.
14 See generally, 'Identical sign to registered trade mark', page 138.
15 When comparing marks the American PTO ignores the suffixes.

as this heading suggests, section 10(3) is wider than section 10(1): it may operate on more than purely an identical sign, but also a similar one.[16]

Similarity of sign to mark

The requirements in section 5(2) for non-similarity are generally considered to be equivalent to the 1938 Act's prohibition on registering trade marks that 'nearly resemble' another's mark.[17] The court's assessment of this section is notoriously dependent on the facts of each case, but if there is one common theme it is that the court is looking to establish the 'gist' of the two trade marks as the public would perceive them, not as the Registry lists them.[18] In this context, the sign 'www.mit.com' as compared with the mark 'mit' does appear similar if not identical. The millions of people who use the Internet and World Wide Web are unlikely to be aware of the conditions that must be met to be granted a '.com' domain name; they are likely to view the sign as similar to the mark despite the fact that as the Institute is not a company it could not use a '.com' domain.[19]

In relation to dissimilar goods or services

The difficult aspect to this test is not proving that the goods or services are dissimilar; Merritt's use of the domain name is clearly not covered by the Institute's registrations. The hurdle is that the trade mark must be used in relation to *some* goods or services. Certainly, Merritt was utilising its site as more than merely an information board: it was a self-promotional web site with a purpose not entirely altruistic. It will therefore be assumed that this aspect of the section was met. This brings us to the most uncertain aspect of a section 10(3) infringement: the defendant must have used the mark without due cause and by

---

16   One needs to identify the defendant's sign for the purposes of comparison. Occasionally, the sign will not be within the domain name, but within the hierarchical folders on the server holding the web site. For example, one could register a domain with the name, 'www.complete.com' with few complaints from the domain name registry. But, once the site is in use, one can create series of hierarchical folders that store the various pages on the web site. If the top level of these folders is named 'paq' and contains a page called 'computers', a link on a web site to that folder will look like 'http://www.complete.com/paq.computers'. Once the words 'compaq computers' are identified it becomes simple to allege that this sign is identical or similar to Compaq's trade mark. Similarly, one can use a domain name as an address for e-mail. Usually the 'www' is replaced with a person's name followed by an '@' sign. Bill Gates has the e-mail address, 'billg@microsoft.com'. Someone could also register the domain name 'soft.com' and publish the contact e-mail address as 'micro@soft.com'. Again, once the sign is identified it can be seen that the sign is identical or similar to Microsoft's mark. This said, one is humorously reminded by Jacob J that 'No one but a crossword fanatic, for instance, would say that 'treat' is present in 'theatre atmosphere': *British Sugar plc v James Robertson & Sons Ltd* [1996] RPC 281 at 294.
17   Trade Marks Act 1938, s 12(1). Also the similar infringement provisions under the 1938 Act, as amended, s 4.
18   See Kerly's *Law of Trade Marks and Trade Names* (12th edn), paras 17.08 and 17.09.
19   Such an argument can be tempered with the view that the mark should not be divided but viewed as a whole when being compared to another: *Bailey (William) Ltd's Application 'Erectico'* (1935) 52 RPC 136. This does not sit comfortably with the more common view that the marks should be assessed for their 'feel' rather than their strict spelling and syntax. See generally, *Wagamama Ltd v City Centre Restaurants plc* [1995] FSR 713.

doing so must have taken unfair advantage of or been detrimental to the distinctive character or repute of the trade mark.[20]

Due cause

The concept that the defendant must have had 'due cause' to use the sign is vague. The Act does not expand upon the term and its extent remains debatable. For a domain name dispute, this phrase may become pivotal. Merritt may well *also* have a trade mark over the letters MIT but in a different class altogether. It may be for this reason that they applied and used the domain name 'mit.com'.[1] The intention to use one's trade mark in relation to a domain name appears to be due cause.[2] It should be noted that the infringement is only made out by the plaintiff if the use is *without* due cause. It certainly does not appear to be *without* due cause to use one's trade mark as a domain name.[3]

It appears from the above discussion that, without strong opposing reasons, it will be due cause to use as a domain name one's own name for which one has a registered trade mark.

Unfair advantage or detriment

Even without due cause, the plaintiff must establish that the use of the sign takes unfair advantage of, or is detrimental to the distinctive character or repute of the registered mark. It is important not to overlook that this section is not available to all registered trade marks: they must have a distinctive character or repute.

Unfair advantage

Taking unfair advantage conveys a theme of free-riding: that one cannot reap the benefits of another's labour in building up goodwill in a trade mark. To defeat this in a domain name dispute, one would presumably be required to 'distance' one's sign from the registered trade mark. This should be achieved by using an opening disclaimer on a web site that this is not the 'Massachusetts Institute of Technology official site which can be found at *http://www.mit.org*'. It is submitted that, by doing this one is gaining little to no advantage, other than people passing through one's site on the way to another. To class this as an unfair advantage is perhaps to misconceive the World Wide Web. The very nature of the web is of a number of documents that are *interlinked*. Using a site as a thoroughfare to another is no more taking unfair advantage of the destination site as is walking into one shop on

---

20 The mark must also have a reputation in the United Kingdom; this contrasts with the situation where a trade mark is registered without a reputation in the United Kingdom. For the purposes of this English law analysis of the MIT dispute, it is assumed that the Institute does have a reputation in the United Kingdom.

1 These arguments justifying use are similar to those which can be put forward as a *defence* in s 11(2).

2 See *Fry's Electronics Inc v Octave Systems* (No C95-2525 CAL ND Cal). Frenchy Frys, a Seattle-based seller of french fry vending machines, registered the domain name 'frys.com'. Fry's Electronic alleged that Frenchy Frys wrongly appropriated the Fry's trade name. Fry's Electronics did not have a Federal trade mark. Frenchy Frys remains at 'frys.com'.

3 Under the Uniform Benelux Trademarks Law 1971, Article 13(2), 'due cause' has been construed narrowly, and even that Article embraces the idea of prior rights in the sign.

the high street while on the way to another. Clearly, any use of such a disclaimer must not be a sham; the courts will look beyond the words and coding and concentrate on any ulterior motives in choosing the domain name.

Until the courts provide further guidance, it is advised that those with a domain name registration similar to a well-known mark should be careful not to take unfair advantage of their domain name. They should make it clear to their site's viewers that they may be at the wrong site owing to a contingency of the domain name system, rather than any motive of the site controller. It will be a sign of good faith to include on the home page a link to the 'other' site.

Detriment

Far wider than the requirement that the domain name not take unfair advantage of a registered trade mark is the alternative requirement. A sign that is detrimental to the distinctive character or repute of the registered trade mark, all other conditions met, is infringement. It is submitted that to make out infringement under this section, a plaintiff will have to convince the court that the *content* of the site will be a detriment to the plaintiff's registered mark.

This was obvious in the dispute between Hasbro, owners of the Candyland trade mark, and Internet Entertainment Group[4] who owned the domain name 'candyland.com'. IEG used the domain as a web site offering sexually explicit material. Hasbro's trade mark was used in relation to children's toys and activities. The detriment to the trade mark is clear and was clear to the court who injuncted IEG from using the domain name.[5] In contrast, Warner Brothers, which had registered 'Road Runner' as a trade mark for toys, objected to Roadrunner Inc using the domain name 'roadrunner.com'.[6] Roadrunner Inc was a provider of Internet access services. In this situation it will be harder than in the Hasbro situation to suggest that the use of the Roadrunner sign will lead to the detriment of the trade mark. It may be more appropriate, but still hard, to allege unfair advantage.

For the present dispute, between MIT and Merritt, it appears that the Institute under English law would have a hard task to prove trade mark infringement. This reflects the commercial decision taken by the Institute on 23 July 1996 to withdraw its complaint and accede to Merritt's use of the domain on two conditions.[7] First, the rights should not be transferred to a third party. The second condition was that Merritt agrees to forward to the Institute all communications that are intended for the Institute.

This second condition was met by Merritt using a link on its web site to the Institute's. As indicated by this section, this forwarding link may not compromise either party; it is common to arrive at the wrong address on the Internet. Such a commercial solution should be contemplated before legal action is taken; John Gilmore of the Electronic Frontier Foundation sums up the issue well:[8]

4   After, IEG.

5   *Hasbro Inc v Internet Entertainment Group Ltd* (No C96-130WD, United States District Court, WD Washington), 9 February 1996.

6   Some may recall that this is not the first time that the Road Runner has been involved with litigation. In *Duracell International Inc v Ever Ready Ltd* [1989] FSR 71 one of the advertisements that was claimed to be infringing used a monochrome picture of the cartoon Road Runner 'and the Road Runner is going "beep-beep"' (at 74).

7   Letter dated 23 July 1996 from Director of the MIT Technology Licensing Office.

8   *The Economist*, Letters, 13 July 1996. Emphasis added.

'Trademarks are registered in a system that permits many companies to share a name legitimately without interfering with each other, such as Sun Photo, Sun Oil and Sun Microsystems. Domain names only permit one user of a name; there is only one sun.com, which Sun Microsystems registered first. *Neither lawyers nor governments can make ten pounds of names fit into a one-pound bag.*'

Trade mark infringement remedies

As for the MTV dispute, MIT would have to think carefully about the remedies it seeks. In the interest of balancing the conveniences it may be useful to allow a 'hand-over' period in any injunction order. For this the defendants should immediately remove all the content from the site, but post a referral notice on the site to the new location of the defendant's content. This notice should not be a hypertext link, thus cutting down the risk that viewers may unwittingly pass through the trade mark domain name site to the detrimental or unfairly advantageous site. This non-linked referral notice should remain for a fixed time after which the defendants should discontinue any use of the domain name or any similar to it.

This allows the intentional viewers of the infringing site to locate the new location, so not damaging too much the legitimate trade of the infringing site. It also stops dead any further infringement under the infringing sign.

Passing off claim

If the Institute did not have a registered trade mark on which they could base trade mark infringement proceedings, they may have sought to rely on a passing off claim. The 'classical trinity' has been discussed in relation to the MTV dispute.[9] What is different from that situation is the consequent damage.

Consequent damage

Assuming that the first two requirements of misrepresentation and goodwill are satisfied, the Institute must prove the final requirement of passing off: it must have suffered, or be likely to suffer, damage to the property in its goodwill because of the misrepresentation. Although the requirement to show damage is not onerous, as discussed,[10] it may be difficult to establish where the defendant's site is in a different field of activity.

The damage claimed cannot be equated to lost sales but to a 'dilution' of a trading name; a reduction in the distinctiveness and repute of the MIT name. In *Taittinger v Allbev* the Court of Appeal was of the opinion that the use of the name champagne in relation to an elderflower drink caused the requisite damage.[11] This was based on the fact that:[12]

9   See 'Passing off claim', at page 140.
10 See 'Consequent damage', at page 142.
11 [1993] 2 CMLR 741 at 762 [62]–763 [64].
12 [1993] 2 CMLR 741 at 763 [63].

'[a]ny product which is not champagne but is allowed to describe itself
as such must inevitably, in my view, erode the singularity and
exclusiveness of the description champagne and so cause the first
plaintiffs damage of an insidious but serious kind.'

Could the Institute, or any company with a distinctive name, claim similar
damage? It is submitted not. First, champagne is a special and unique product, 'a
reference to champagne imports nuances of quality and celebration, a sense of
something privileged and special'.[13] As such the goodwill can be damaged *merely*
by its use on other products. The same may not be true for a domain name. It is
understood by users of the Internet that domain names are limited; damage is
rarely caused by simply *using* another's domain name. Where there may be
damage is if the site using the plaintiff's name will somehow benefit from the
connection or prejudice the defendant.[14] This is a question of fact and of the cross-
substitutability of the plaintiff's customers with the defendant's. In this situation, it
is suggested that the Institute's goodwill in its abbreviated name suffers no such
damage as that in the *Taittinger* case.[15]

Deliberate goodwill damage

To rely on the *Glaxo-Wellcome* precedent it has been stated that the court will
have to find that the defendants abused the domain name system by attempting to
use it in their favour to extort from the plaintiffs.[16] This is not the situation with
MIT: both users of the MIT domain names are 'rightful' owners with prior legal
and common law rights in the name. For these situations, it is inappropriate to cite
Glaxo-Wellcome as authority that the domain name should be relinquished.

PROTECTIVE MEASURES

This examination of domain names allows the deduction of a series of measures
which may be beneficial to those who wish to register a domain name. As has been
discussed, registering a domain name which is protected by a registered trade mark
can lead to problems. Conversely, registering a domain name and then protecting
that domain name with a registered trade mark can provide additional security
over the domain name. Potential applicants for domain names should therefore
first perform some clearance exercise over the name they wish to register as a
domain name. Having registered a domain name they may then seek to protect it
from third parties and the registration authorities.

---

13   [1993] 2 CMLR 741 at 763 [64].
14   See 'Detriment', at page 148.
15   In *Panavision International v Toeppen* (CV 96-3284 DDP, 1 November 1996) the court stated
       that '[a]s a result of the current state of Internet technology, Toeppen was able not merely to
       "lessen [ ] the capacity of a famous mark to identify and distinguish goods or services" 15
       USC §1127, but to *eliminate* the capacity of the Panavision marks to identify and distinguish
       Panavision's goods and services on the Internet'. This is not strictly true: Toeppen had
       registered only 'panavision.com' leaving Panavision International able to register 'panavision-
       int.com' and any other unregistered domain name which is not exactly 'panavision.com'.
16   See 'Deliberate damage to goodwill', at page 143.

I. Check availability of domain name

Domain names are not simply taken. Like company names, they are registered. Network Solutions Inc, on behalf of InterNIC, registers the domains ending '.com'. For domains ending 'co.uk', 'ltd.uk', 'net.uk', 'org.uk', 'plc.uk', Nominet UK is the provider.[17] Both companies charge a small fee to register a domain name. The difficulty arises because neither company has the resources to check that an applicant has the right to use a particular name and so allocates them on a first-come-first-served basis. Because of this policy, many names are already registered. The first step is therefore to contact Nominet and InterNIC to check whether the intended name has been registered. Companies should try to consider variations of their names and attempt to register these also.

2. Clear use of domain name

Generally

Registering a domain name does not provide any legal rights over the domain, only technical rights. A company which seeks a particular domain name should search to see whether or not a third party is using the intended domain name as a trade mark. As far as practicable and economically justifiable, this search should be performed on an international basis to take account of the transnational nature of the Internet, and so the multinational nature of any rights claims.

Additionally, Network Solutions and Nominet insist that:[18]

1. the applicant has the right to use the domain name as requested in the application; and
2. the registration of the domain name by the applicant, to the best of the applicant's knowledge, does not interfere with or infringe the right of any third party. This applies to any third party in any jurisdiction;
3. the applicant is not seeking to register the domain name for any unlawful purpose. A previous policy[19] included explicitly tortious interference with contract or prospective business advantage, unfair competition, injuring the reputation of another, or for the purpose of confusing or misleading a person, whether natural or incorporated.

These representations appear onerous because they are not limited to trade marks but include 'the rights of any third party'. However, the representations need only be made to the best of the applicant's knowledge.

In the event of dispute over a domain name the registration company may withdraw the domain name with 30 days' notice.[20] 'Moving' the site material to a new domain name is not costly. What can be expensive is reprinting stationery that mentions the domain name, and informing contacts of the change of address. Applicants should therefore take seriously the right of withdrawal.

---

17   Operating under the European auspices of RIPE. See also fn 2 at page 130.
18   NSI Domain Name Dispute Policy Statement (Revision 02, Effective 9 September 1996) (ftp://rs.internic.net/policy/internic.domain.policy). As incorporated into Nominet's policy (http://www.nic.uk).
19   (Revision 1, Effective 23 November 1995).
20   Clause 4.

3. Protect domain name with trade mark registration

As described earlier, an applicant's domain name may already be protected under its existing trade mark registrations. If this is not the case, the domain name owner should seriously consider obtaining a trade mark registration in respect of the name within the domain name. It has been illustrated that a trade mark registration provides significant rights against a user of a commercially-impinging domain name. Even without a registration, the use of a domain name may build up trade mark rights in the name. To signify this to the 'world' the domain name can be followed with the ™ symbol on the web site content.[1]

A trade mark registration has additional justification.[2] In the event of a dispute where a complainant with a trade mark registration objects to the ownership of a domain name, the applicant for the domain name has to prove one of two conditions to keep the name.[3] It either must prove within 30 days that it registered the domain name prior to the complainant's trade mark registration. The alternative condition is that its domain name was activated after the complainant's trade mark registration, but it has an earlier trade mark registration in relation to the same name. For this purpose a trade mark registration in any class in any country is relevant.

If one of these two conditions is met, the status quo is maintained and the domain name holder may continue to use the domain. If neither condition is met, however, besides any legal action being taken by the objecting third party, the domain name holder will be provided with an alternative domain name to which its site must be moved within 90 days. The original disputed name is then maintained on a 'hold' status until the dispute is settled by the parties, arbitration or the court. Until this time, the domain name cannot be used by anyone, including the parties. If litigation is started in respect of the domain name, the domain name is not put on 'hold'; the incumbent owner of the domain name remains its holder.[4]

The domain name will be placed on 'hold' without recourse to evidence of infringement; the incumbent domain name can be 'held' with no more than evidence that one trade mark registration in *one* class in *one* jurisdiction. This clearly benefits those who have a prior registered trade mark in respect of the domain-relevant name.

4. Protect domain name from registration companies

Nominet and Network Solutions would prefer to remove themselves from any disputes as quickly as possible. Indeed their policy states that it 'cannot act as an arbiter of disputes arising out of the registration of a domain name'.[5] Because of this, and worries of liability, some domain name owners have found the

---

1   NB it is a criminal offence to use in relation to an *unregistered* trade mark any word, symbol or express or implied reference that the trade mark is so registered. Use of ® should be carefully monitored: it is not akin to misuse of © for which there is no criminal sanction. Trade Marks Act 1994, s 95.
2   Clause 5.
3   The domain name must be identical to the complainant's valid and subsisting foreign or US Federal trade mark registration in full force and effect. A certified copy must be available and prior notice must be given to the incumbent domain name holder: Clause 5(a).
4   Clause 7.
5   Clause 5.

registration companies a little too willing to 'hold' a domain name where there is an indication of a dispute. This may have served the registration companies but it can be extremely inconvenient if a domain name is suspended until a dispute is settled.

For this reason domain name owners have now taken to injuncting Network Solutions from suspending the domain name *until* the outcome of any parallel trade mark dispute is settled. Data Concepts sued both Network Solutions and Digital Consulting for attempting to interfere with its domain name, 'dci.com'.[6] On this basis, Data Concepts sought a declaratory judgment establishing its right to use the domain name and an injunction preventing Network Solutions from interfering with that use. Network Solutions has agreed to maintain the status quo by letting Data Concepts continue use of the domain name. Roadrunner Computer Systems and Clue Computing Inc have also sought to injunct Network Solutions on a similar basis.[7]

To counter this unwelcome litigation Network Solution has adopted a new policy where it will not hold a name if litigation starts first.[8] As seen from this section, the problem is not the policy on holding but the policy of equating the rights over a domain name with the ownership of a registered trade mark.

Trade marks on the World Wide Web

The World Wide Web can present text, pictures, sounds, music, and animations. The Trade Mark Act 1994 does not, of itself, prevent any of these items being protected by a trade mark. The only real limitation on the *nature* of a mark is that it must be,[9]

> 'capable of being represented graphically, and capable of distinguish-ing goods or services of one undertaking from those of other undertakings.'

The condition that the mark used on the Internet be capable of graphic representation is unlikely to present much of a hurdle, even in unusual cases.

---

6. To signify that a program is being used to secure web sites, its designer uses a small Java applet on every secure site. This applet shows an animation of a keyhole being sealed with a red thumb. The programmer can apply to register this applet as a trade mark. Both a frame-by-frame 'storyboard' of the animation and the applet code should be sufficient to represent the trade mark graphically.[10]

---

6 *Data Concepts Inc v Digital Consulting Inc* (MD Tenn, filed 8 May 1996).
7 *Roadrunner Computer Systems Inc v Network Solutions Inc* (DC Eastern District of Virginia, Civil Docket No 96-413-A); *Clue Computing Inc v Network Solutions Inc* (Colo Dist Ct, No 96 CV 694, filed 13 June 1996) – this was based on contractual claims.
8 Owners of registered trade marks should be careful in threatening those who apply a registered trade mark as a sign to a web site or as a domain name. This may fall within the 'groundless threats' provisions of the Trade Marks Act 1994, s 21. See *Bigsmith Global Ltd v Caterpillar* (11 July 1996, unreported) *ex parte* injunction.
9 Trade Marks Act 1994, s 1(1).
10 The Derbyshire Building Society has registered in Class 36 the gesture made by a person tapping one side of his or her nose with an extended finger, normally the index finger: No 2, 012, 603 on 28 February 1995.

Sounds or music can also, in appropriate cases, be registrable. A sound can be represented graphically both as a description and as a series of notes or frequencies. With the increased use of music on web sites, this may be a useful way of protecting the goodwill in a web site.

Apart from these new forms of trade mark, the use of symbols, graphics, and words remain registrable and will probably form the greatest number of trade marks on the World Wide Web.

It has already been explained that in registering a trade mark for use on the World Wide Web one needs to be careful about for which goods and services those registrations are made.[11] It has also been explained that for owners of existing trade marks often there will be no need to expand the scope of their protection, although there may be a need to encompass its use for electronic goods or services.[12]

Infringement on the World Wide Web

There are two stages to every trade mark infringement alleged to have been committed over the World Wide Web.[13] The first is whether the wrong complained of occurred within the jurisdiction of the English courts.[14] The second stage is whether the use of the sign constitutes infringement of the registered trade mark. For this section's analysis, however, the substantive issues will be taken first: what is infringement on the World Wide Web?

SCOPE OF INFRINGEMENT

On the World Wide Web sites can be used not only for advertising but also for actually providing goods and services. Sites can act as a billboard, an agent, and a shop and till. All these activities will involve the use of a variety of words, symbols and other signs that could potentially conflict with others' trade mark rights.[15] This section examines what activities on the Internet can constitute *trade mark* infringement. Another important issue to consider is the extent to which liability for such infringement may attach to the designers of web sites.

Offering or exposing

A person who offers or exposes goods for sale, or puts them on the market under a sign, or offers or supplies services under that sign, may infringe a registered trade mark if that sign conflicts with the trade mark in question.[16]

11   See 'New trade mark', at page 133.
12   See 'New trade mark classes', at page 132.
13   This chapter focuses on a trade mark that is infringed by a sign present on the World Wide Web, rather than a trade mark *on* the World Wide Web that is infringed on some other medium.
14   See page 156 et seq.
15   It is submitted that the Internet as a medium does not alter the legal tests needed to establish infringement of a trade mark by a sign on a web page. Trade mark texts should be consulted in this respect; but see 'Protecting domain names', at page 136 for illustrations of the scope of s 10(1) and (3).
16   Trade Marks Act 1994, s 10(4)(b).

> **7. A web site lists various programs for sale under the Microsoft logo and uses the Microsoft logo on the small icons that represent each program itself. The name of each program begins 'Microsoft' or 'MS'. Microsoft is not the developer of any of these programs. It is of little legal consequence that this is on a web site: this is use of a sign by exposing and offering goods for sale under a registered trade mark.**

Use in advertising

Section 10(4)(d) provides another example of the use of a sign that can constitute infringement, all other things being equal. This is where a person uses the sign in advertising. Trade mark owners will not be able to sue successfully all those on the World Wide Web who merely use their trade marks. Having proved 'use' the harder proof is that there was infringement.

Secondary infringement

Those who *use* infringing signs on the Internet are not the only individuals who may be sued for infringement; the designers of the web sites may also be liable.[17] The Trade Marks Act 1994, section 10(5) states that:[18]

'[a] person who applies a registered trade mark to material intended to be used for labelling or packaging goods, as a business paper, or for advertising goods or services, shall be treated as a party to any use of the material which infringes the registered trade mark *if* when he applied the mark *he knew or had reason to believe* that the application of the mark was not duly authorised by the proprietor or a licensee.'

The effect of this for web site designers is clear. If they satisfy the mental element, which will be considered below, they may be liable for designing a web site used to advertise goods or services that incorporates an infringing trade mark. It would seem to be a hard-fought case on semantics to suggest that creating a web site that incorporates a registered trade mark is not 'appl[ying] a registered trade mark to material' simply because the material is not physical and the attachment is performed not with glue or ink but by programming. It would also, it is suggested, be a losing case: the Trade Marks Act 1994 originated as a European Directive. It should be interpreted purposively and less literally than domestic legislation.

---

17   It is often reported that the American case, *Playboy Enterprises Inc v George Frena* 839 F Supp 1552 (MD Fla 1993) is an example of secondary trade mark liability of a bulletin board operator who held unlicensed copyright *Playboy* photographs. This is a misreading. The trade mark infringement found by the court was, if comparable, 'primary'. Frena removed *Playboy*'s trade mark text from the photos and placed his own advertisement on *Playboy*'s photos; a reverse passing off. This 'false suggest[ion of] affiliation with the trade mark owner in a manner likely to cause confusion constitutes infringement' (*Burger King v Mason*, 710 F 2d 1480 at 1492 (11th Cir 1983)). Again, in *Sega Enterprises Ltd v Maphia* 857 F Supp 679 (ND Cal 1994) the operator of a bulletin board distributing infringing software was liable under the Lanham Act for its 'primary' infringement of the trade mark by confusingly supplying it under the mark. See clarification in permanent injunction: No C93-04262 CW (ND Cal, 18 December 1996).
18   Emphasis added.

Knowledge or belief

For a web designer to be liable he must do more than type the appropriate 'tag' in HTML to incorporate the trade mark; he must know or have reason to believe that this is not authorised by the proprietor or a licensee. This level of knowledge is also required for secondary infringement under the Copyright, Designs and Patents Act 1988, section 23. Although the two statutes serve different purposes, it is nevertheless submitted that without other authority it is reasonable to rely on cases under section 23 to construe the meaning of section 10(5).

In *LA Gear Inc v Hi-Tec Sports plc*, Morritt J decided that 'reason to believe',[19]

> 'must involve the concept of knowledge of facts from which a reasonable man would arrive at the relevant belief. Facts from which a reasonable man might suspect the relevant conclusion cannot be enough. Moreover, as it seems to me, the phrase does connote the allowance of a period of time to enable the reasonable man to evaluate those facts so as to convert the facts into a reasonable belief.'

For trade marks in the Internet arena, this dictum may be viewed as meaning that web developers will be liable if they turn a blind eye to the facts. Those who will not be liable are those who have grounds to suspect but reasonably fail to appreciate the significance of the issues involved. The requirement of a period of time will often be present because of the time taken to code and test a web site. If, after designing the site and providing it to the client, however, the designer realises the significance of his actions, he will have no liability. His knowledge or belief must be present when 'he applied the mark'. He has a moral duty but has no corresponding legal duty.

The short points for web designers are simple. First, obtain indemnities from clients. Second, be particularly careful when asked to deal with well-known marks: the better known the mark, the higher the risk of litigation and the more likely a court will find the reasonable belief.

Jurisdiction over infringement

Private international law and intellectual property law have an uneasy coexistence. What is uneasy is that the older rules of jurisdiction and choice of law rely on tangible 'things' being dealt with by people in fixed locations. Intellectual property and the Internet in particular confuses this reliance. A web developer in America may knowingly put a United Kingdom trade mark on a web site maintained in Holland but accessible throughout the world. In this situation do the English courts have any jurisdiction to hear complaints of infringement from the United Kingdom trade mark proprietor? The proprietor may complain that the American web developer was a secondary infringer and that the Dutch controller was a primary infringer of the trade mark by using the sign in an infringing manner. Our courts will be faced with many problems like this; it is therefore important to

---

19   [1992] FSR 121 at 129. The Court of Appeal did not consider this aspect of Morritt J's decision. This said, it was applied in *Hutchison Personal Communications Ltd v Hook Advertising Ltd* [1995] FSR 365 at 378–379.

examine the issues for the judges who sit in those courts, and for the litigants who await reasoned judgment.

INFRINGEMENT OF UK TRADE MARKS ABROAD

This heading is legally impossible: infringement is a legal term in relation to a legal right granted within a territory. One cannot infringe a United Kingdom trade mark abroad because 'abroad' is outside the width of the monopoly granted by the United Kingdom legislation. So one may perform actions in relation to a United Kingdom trade mark that are the *descriptive* equivalent of infringement but those actions will not *be* infringement unless within the United Kingdom territory. One may also be sued in the UK for infringement of IP rights created in a state signatory to the Brussels Convention.[20] Courts, however, have sought to constrain intellectual property rights being sought to be enforced outside their granting territories in this way for many years.

> 'Each [action for breach of a trade mark] is separately derived from a statutory privilege which the trade mark holder has in the territory in question and is strictly confined to that territory.[1]
>
> As I have said, the United Kingdom trade mark has no effect outside the United Kingdom.[2]
>
> [T]he decision of Buckley LJ lends further support to the proposition that the question of validity, title to and infringement of a trade mark fall exclusively within the jurisdiction of the courts of the country by the laws of which the trade mark was created.'[3]

This author would not wish to stand in the way of such a long line of authorities. But, it is important that the authorities are not applied out of context: on the Internet many acts done in relation to United Kingdom trade marks, even though appearing to originate from overseas, *will* be actionable in the United Kingdom. The excerpts above consider the situation where the activity occurs *outside* the United Kingdom. The courts are attempting to resolve the conflict of laws where the intellectual property right is dealt with in a territory other than the one that granted the right initially. For example, to apply a United Kingdom trade mark to a product in America is clearly outside the jurisdiction of the English courts: the action that constitutes the infringement occurs outside the United Kingdom. In contrast to this, there are situations where the *action* takes place outside the United Kingdom, but the *infringement* occurs within the territory.[4]

---

20 See *Gareth Pearce v Ove Arup Partnership Ltd* (7 March 1997, unreported) interlocutory application *inter alia* to strike out.
1   *James Burrough Distillers plc v Speymalt Whisky Distributors Ltd* 1989 SLT 561 at 566.
2   *LA Gear v Gerald Whelan & Sons Ltd* [1991] FSR 670 at 676.
3   *Tyburn Productions v Conan Doyle* [1991] Ch 75 at 88.
4   For the purposes of service out under RSC Ord 11, r 1(1)(f), the tort (if infringement is classed as a tort rather than a breach of statutory duty) is committed within the jurisdiction. Also for the purposes of the Private International Law (Miscellaneous Provisions) Act 1995, s 11(2)(b)) the applicable law will probably be English. See also fn 19 at page 208.

Advertisement within the United Kingdom

In *R J Reuter Co Ltd v Ferd Mulhens*, the plaintiff was the registered proprietor of a number of English trade marks over the perfumes and associated products called '4711'.[5] The defendant, in Germany, was exclusively associated with the manufacture there and elsewhere of '4711' eau de cologne. On 23 October 1951, the defendant addressed a letter to the export agents for the plaintiff's product: the letter's envelope featured a '4711' that was in all respects identical with the plaintiff's trade mark. Reuter sued for trade mark infringement, inter alia, under the Trade Marks Act 1938, section 4(1)(b). Under this section if the registered mark is used in an advertisement issued to the public as importing a reference to some person having such a right, there may be infringement.

The Court of Appeal was convinced that sending the envelope, even from abroad, was an advertisement within the Act. The court disagreed that to infringe there must be an intention to use the mark in the United Kingdom in relation to goods in the course of some transaction in the United Kingdom.[6]

> 'Since, admittedly, the device on the envelope was advertising matter, the use of the envelope constituted ... an infringement of the plaintiffs' rights under section 4 if they are in other respects entitled to succeed.'

What this case illustrates is that the location that is vital for infringement by advertising is where the advert is received; the envelope was viewed as an advertisement under English law because it was received in England.[7] If the conclusion were otherwise, that the place of issuing the advertisement was the significant location one could avoid infringement merely by issuing all infringing advertisements from abroad. Instead, the section must be construed purposively: the law protects the trade mark from damage that *occurs* in the United Kingdom.

Advertising is not the only example of actions seemingly taking place outside the United Kingdom that are nevertheless actionable within the territory. In *Bigsmith Global Ltd v Caterpillar*, an injunction was sought against Caterpillar to prevent them making groundless threats in relation to a United Kingdom trade mark.[8] Jacob J agreed that the threats were groundless within the Trade Marks Act 1994, section 21. He also confirmed that what is relevant for jurisdiction over a threat is not from where it is issued or to where it is sent:

> 'You have to look at it purposefully. The substance is that there is a threat to take action in the UK. It does not make any difference where it is [communicated]. It would be an unfortunate position if people threatened infringement of patents and copyrights and trade mark

5   [1953] 2 All ER 1160. The case was complicated by the Trading with the Enemy Act 1939, s 7(1), but the court was able to divorce that Act from the issue of infringement.

6   [1953] 2 All ER 1160 at 1174. This aspect has been subject to academic criticism. If it is taken at 'face value' the case teaches that a periodical published abroad but with circulation in the United Kingdom may infringe a United Kingdom trade mark if it contains advertisements under the same trade mark: Kerly's *Law of Trade Marks and Trade Names* (12th edn), para 14.14.

7   The Advertising Standards Authority seeks to enforce its standards over Internet advertisers in the United Kingdom. See *Cable Communications Association* Adjudication, December 1996.

8   (11 July 1996, unreported) *ex parte* injunction.

proceedings from abroad and they could not do it once they came here. You just fax it across to a chum in Paris and ask him to fax it back.'

This reasoning is applicable to infringements of trade marks; for advertising, like groundless threats, the place from where a communication is despatched is irrelevant; what is relevant is where that communication is received.[9] This reasoning can be applied to the Internet.[10]

Merely because a web site is accessible within the United Kingdom and uses a sign identical or similar to a registered trade mark does not necessarily mean that there is infringement. To infringe, at the least, the use of the sign must be a use within the course of trade. Presumably one can infer that this requires trade within or with the United Kingdom. Were this not the presumption, in contradiction with the authorities, one would be regulating the use of a trade mark outside its granting country.

---

8. A French company uses a logo on its web site that appears identical to a United Kingdom registered trade mark. The web site is entirely written in French; no international dialling codes are detailed and orders are only shipped within France. This site, although able to be viewed in England, may not be *advertising* in England as, by definition, it does not give notice to the English public of the goods: the very nature of an advertisement.

Secondary infringement abroad

Web site developers situated abroad, in contrast to their employers, do not have so much to fear from infringing English trade marks. Developers' liability only fixes where they have designed an infringing web site *within the United Kingdom*. If a developer in New York affixes a United Kingdom registered trade mark to a web site also situated within New York, the English courts will have no jurisdiction over the developer's secondary infringement. This is because the fixing of the sign occurred outside the United Kingdom; it is only the viewing of the site that may occur within the United Kingdom.

---

9. WebMaster Inc in California is a highly regarded company of web site designers. The sites they design are hosted on their servers in California. One of their sites is alleged to infringe a United Kingdom trade mark. The English courts cannot have jurisdiction over them as secondary infringers as their 'application' of the trade mark to the site was made outside the United Kingdom.

---

9   See also *ABKCO Music & Records Inc v Music Collection International Ltd* [1995] RPC 657 in relation to authorising copyright infringement: 'Anyone contemplating the grant of a licence to do an act restricted by copyright would be able to avoid liability simply by having the document executed abroad' at 661, and 'I can see no satisfactory basis for placing a territorial limitation on the liability of a person who "authorises another to do" a restricted act', at 663.
10 See *Mecklermedia v D C Congress GmbH* (7 March 1997, unreported) interlocutory application *inter alia* to strike out.

Justification

The conclusion reached in this section that a web site owner anywhere in the world may infringe a United Kingdom trade mark may strike some as shocking and so false. It is perhaps not so shocking when one considers that trading on the Internet is growing at exponential rates. For software, in particular, it is almost possible to buy and download any software package over the Internet from anywhere in the world. The converse of this is that from a single location an individual can advertise to and trade with every Internet user in every country. Internet technology allows the individual to compete with local firms, despite being based abroad. The law that applies to these local firms ensures that they do not trade off each other's goodwill and allows them to build up a brand name.

If that law did not equally apply to companies acting from abroad, so permitting them to appropriate the goodwill and trade marks of others there would be two detrimental effects. First, the local firms would suffer and so may not invest in the creation of quality brands because of fear of their good name being misappropriated. The second effect is to the Internet. If users of the Internet were unable to trust a logo or a trade mark as an indication of rightful usage they would be less willing to trade using the Internet. It is legally right and commercially justifiable for the courts to protect brand owners from infringement on the Internet. Jacob J has made a statement to similar effect:[11]

> '[W]hen an enterprise wants to use a mark or word throughout the world (and that may include an Internet address or domain name) it must take into account that in some places, if not others, there may be confusion ... I do not think it is surprising that [the defendant] is met with actions in places where confusion is considered likely.'

TRADE MARK INFRINGEMENT OVER THE INTERNET

The American courts have recently illustrated that the potency of an injunction is not reduced by the ethereal nature of the World Wide Web. On 1 April 1981, Playboy Enterprises Inc, publishers of the magazine, *Playboy*, was awarded an injunction against an Italian company called Tattilo, the publisher of *Playmen* magazine. The injunction prevented Tattilo from using the word 'playmen' or any confusingly similar word anywhere on the cover of a 'male sophisticate magazine' that is published, distributed or sold in the United States. It should be noted that this injunction has no extra-territorial effect: it operates only against activities *in* the United States. Indeed, in Italy, the Italian courts had ruled that 'Playboy' was a weak mark and was not entitled to protection there. Tattilo continued, not breaching the injunction, publishing *Playmen* in printed form in Italy.

On about 22 January 1996, Playboy discovered that Tattilo had created a web site with the domain name 'www.playmen.it'. This site provided free access to moderately explicit images. By e-mail subscription, viewers were able to access the Playmen Pro version of the site. Playboy Enterprises Inc moved for a finding of contempt against Tattilo for violating the injunction.[12]

The court discovered that, as is true for most web sites,

11   See fn 10 at page 159.
12   *Playboy Enterprises Inc v Chuckleberry Publishing Inc* (DC SNY, 79 Civ 3525, 19 June 1996).

'[t]he Playmen Internet site is widely available to patrons living in the United States. More to the point, *anyone* in the United States with access to the Internet has the capacity to browse the Playmen Internet site, review, and obtain print and electronic copies of sexually explicit pages of Playmen magazine.'

The first issue for the court was whether the 15-year-old injunction could have been violated despite the fact that the Internet was not contemplated at the time. The court was under no doubt that the injunction still had force to prevent distributions by the Internet into America.

To decide that the injunction was violated, the court had to find three conditions. First, that the word 'Playmen' had been used as part of any trade mark, service mark, brand name, trade name or other business or commercial designation. This condition was met partly by the domain name and partly by the Playmen logo being present on each page of the web site. The second condition was also met: the use had to be in conjunction with an English language publication or related product. The final condition was the most analytically difficult for the court but the most pertinent for similar English disputes: the use had to be made in connection with a sale or distribution within the United States.

Sale or distribution within territory

Before continuing with the court's analysis, it is worthwhile reconsidering the UK position. Under the Trade Marks Act 1994, section 10(4), a sale or distribution of a product under a sign will constitute use of that sign. And as the sign 'Playmen' is similar to 'Playboy' and is clearly being used in the course of trade, there is a strong likelihood that such use would infringe *Playboy*'s trade mark in England. The court's analysis of whether the product was sold or distributed in the United States is therefore as relevant to whether it would have been sold or distributed in the United Kingdom.

Flying to Italy

Tattilo argued that it was not distributing the pictorial images within the United States. It argued that it was merely posting the images on a server in Italy. A computer operator who wished to view these images must, in effect, transport himself to Italy to view Tattilo's pictorial displays. The court summed up this analogy as,

'[t]he use of the Internet is akin to boarding a plane, landing in Italy, and purchasing a copy of *Playmen* magazine, an activity permitted under Italian law. Thus the defendant argues that its publication of pictorial images over the Internet cannot be barred by the injunction despite the fact that computer operators can view these pictorial images in the United States.'

This reasoning will undoubtedly be repeated by many defendants in cases involving the Internet. The logic of the argument works by stressing the passivity of those who host web sites. First, the technology must be explained: a web server does not broadcast information of its own volition. A web server will only distribute information if another person actively requests it. This explanation allows the controller of a web site to claim that he had no active role in distributing the information; the web site owner may even highlight to a court that the computers that view web sites are called 'clients' while those that store them are called 'servers'. The second limb of the argument is to suggest that this passivity indicates that it is the viewers of a site who move into the web site's jurisdiction, not the web site owner into the client's.

The court in this case was unconvinced by this passive bystander defence:

> '[the] defendant has actively solicited United States customers to its Internet site, and in doing so has distributed its products within the United States.'

The court was not legally concerned that the Internet site *can* be accessed from around the world; it is that the defendant accepted subscriptions from American customers that proved distribution in the States.

> 'While this court has neither the jurisdiction nor the desire to prohibit the creation of Internet sites around the globe, it may prohibit access to those sites in *this* country. Therefore, while Tattilo may continue to operate its Internet site, it must refrain from accepting subscriptions from customers living in the United States. In accord with this holding, an Italian customer who subsequently moves to the United States may maintain his or her subscription to the Internet site.'

Amongst other orders, the court ordered that Tattilo refrain from accepting any subscriptions from customers residing in the United States. The order was backed up with a fine for non-compliance of $1,000 each day.

Relevance under English law

This case illustrates two relevant issues for English law. First, English courts and plaintiffs must accept that the Internet permits access from any country in the world. This does not, without more, give the English courts jurisdiction over the contents of every server in the world. To gain jurisdiction under trade mark law, the owner of the server must infringe a United Kingdom trade mark *within* the United Kingdom. The first question is therefore whether the courts will accept a 'passive provider' argument. Reference to the Court of Appeal's decision in *R v Fellows* discussed in the chapter on crime indicates that using a web site to *allow* material to be distributed will be viewed as an active transmission. Then the courts must look to the use of the web site: if its content is focused on United Kingdom customers, there may be infringement. Similarly, even if its content appears non-partisan to United Kingdom customers but the site permits a United Kingdom customer to acquire goods or services, there may be infringement.

The second relevant issue is for foreign defendants. That the Internet, technically, permits worldwide distribution does not necessarily mean that this limitless dissemination must be utilised. The customers of certain countries can be blocked out by the suffixes of their e-mail addresses, and those who pass through this net can be warned to go no further if they are from a particular jurisdiction. Finally, if services or goods are provided over the Internet, consumers from certain jurisdictions can be screened out at the contractual stage. If defendants from foreign jurisdictions do this, not as a sham, but with deliberate intent not to use a sign in the course of trade in the United Kingdom, they may avoid the jurisdiction of the United Kingdom trade mark courts. If they do not, and freely advertise and sell goods throughout the world, they must appreciate that with profits of a worldwide distribution they are accepting the potential risks of litigation in every jurisdiction of the globe.

COPYRIGHT

Most material on the Internet is protected by copyright. It protects e-mails sent from one person to another and protects all the elements of an intricate web site including all its mini-programs or executable code. Copyright also can protect the underlying material *beneath* that which appears on a screen: it protects say the original drawings which were converted into a digital animation on a home page. This width and depth of protection means that everyone using the Internet should be aware of their rights as creators of copyright works and their obligations as users of others' works. Users must also be aware of new treaties, such as WIPO's on 20 December 1996, which address copyright and the Internet. The Copyright, Designs and Patents Act 1988 grants not only a 'right to copy and not be copied' but also certain 'moral rights'.

This section considers the exact extent of copyright's protection of material on the Internet. It examines the copyright in e-mails and postings to bulletin boards, and the copyright that protects web sites. This examination of web sites reveals that, although copyright protects the whole web site, its constituent elements are also protected: a separate copyright attaches to the text, the graphics, and more active elements such as animations and sounds. Copyright even protects the complex executable programs on a web site such as applets.

Having discussed that copyright protects most material on the Internet, this section goes on to show that most material on the Internet is copied on a regular basis. Through a clashing of technology with older legislation, all information retrieved by a computer is deemed to have been copied. This width of copying results in a simple conclusion. Copyright disputes involving the Internet will rarely turn on the existence of copyright or if copying took place: the key will be whether or not the copier was explicitly or implicitly permitted to copy the work.

The Internet works by copying. E-mails are not actually sent and web pages are not purely viewed; they are both broken into packets and copied from one computer to another. E-mails therefore are copied at least once: the original exists on the sender's computer and the recipient holds a copy; web pages are also necessarily copied: the server computer hosts the original and each client computer stores another copy. Service Providers who host bulletin boards do not simply store people's original postings: like e-mails, the Service Provider stores a copy of the posting. Even the executable code that makes web pages more sophisticated is automatically copied from its host to a client computer. Although this indicates that all those involved in the Internet copy copyright material, they do not all *infringe* those copyrights. Much of the copying that takes place on the Internet is impliedly authorised by those who hold the copyright: ie the law implies a licence. This section focuses on the types of copying that regularly occur on the Internet and attempts to partition that which is legitimate or defensible copying from that which is infringement of copyright or moral rights.

The final section on copyright considers the force of English law on a telecommunications medium which facilitates infringements around the world. It is as easy to copy an English copyright work on the Internet from Brazil as it is from England. This section therefore concludes by examining the conflict of copyright laws that exist on the Internet. It then summarises the disputes which will be actionable in the English courts and those which may have to be litigated elsewhere.

Copyright works

There are two important questions which must be answered at the outset. First, is the work itself protected by copyright at all? The second, who owns the copyright? This is a query that is always relevant to a copyright issue, but particularly relevant for the Internet. More than any other medium, the Internet allows many individuals to interact to produce a copyright work. Taking the most simple of examples: a Service Provider hosts a bulletin board to which members may post questions, to which other members reply. This is repeated over many days creating a 'conversation thread' that is stored on the Service Provider's central server. What rights have the individual members who have posted up their questions and answers? What rights has the Service Provider in relation to the entire conversation thread, and the individual postings? These questions, and many more like them, will be examined; initially there must be some analysis of what works are protected by copyright.

ELEMENTS FOR PROTECTION

Types of work

The Copyright, Designs and Patents Act 1988, section 1(1) states nine different types of work that can qualify for protection as a copyright work. These are:

'(a) original literary, dramatic, musical or artistic works,
(b) sound recordings, films, broadcasts or cable programmes, and
(c) the typographical arrangement of published editions.'

Before moving to discuss which categories of work encompass which aspects of the Internet, an important point should be noted. The work which appears on the screen of someone viewing a web site is not simply one copyright work: it is a collection of works, some side by side and some underlying the work shown on screen. For example, a home page consisting of graphics and text which plays a recorded tune has at least four discrete copyright works that are evident and others underlying those. Separate copyrights will attach to the text on the page, the graphics and the sound recording. In addition, the copyright which protects computer programs may protect the entire home page. But deeper than this is the protection that may attach to the musical score that was composed to play the recorded tune. Controllers of web sites in particular must therefore understand that their servers are not holding simply one copyright work, but a montage of works. They should ensure that they have the right to use all the works and understand that a visually small aspect of a web site may represent an entire copyright work.

Fixation

A requirement for most copyright works distributed over the Internet is that they are fixed in a material form; if a work is not fixed, even indirectly, then it is no more than an idea or concept. The Copyright, Designs and Patents Act 1988, section 3(3) provides a specific endorsement of this principle,

> 'Copyright does not subsist in a literary, dramatic or musical work unless and until it is recorded, in writing or otherwise[.]'

Copyright does not protect ideas; it protects the skill, labour and judgment exercised in converting an idea into something tangible. Merely recording an idea, however, does not provide protection over that idea.

> **10. Four individuals login to a special web site which allows them to type messages to each other in real time; they can see one another's typing on their own screen as each letter is pressed. The controller of the web site realises that one of the individuals is a famous actor and keeps a copy of everything typed by the actor with a view to publishing it. Without a licence or assignment, the controller does not have the copyright to do this; the actor's typing is a copyright work which was formed when he converted his ideas into expressions through his keyboard.**

Every copyright work has an author.[13] The person who is the author is who creates it. Generally, the first owner of a copyright work is its author.[14] This is, however, a general statement and those who work for others in creating web sites and on-line graphics should be aware that works made in the course of employment are first owned by the employer, subject to any prior arrangement.[15]

> **II. A designer is employed by a bank for general design work and is asked to create a web site for the bank: the site looks like the inside of a bank with graphics of cashiers counting money, help-desks and other features. Some months later the designer resigns from his post and starts working as a freelancer. He is asked to design a similar web site for a building society. He reuses the graphics of the cashiers and help-desks. Unless this is provided for in his contract, he does not own the copyright in those graphics. He may be the *author* of the works, but having created them during his employment, the bank is the copyright *owner.***

Original works

Most copyright works must be original to be protected. The term 'original' does not mean novel or new; it refers to the fact that the work must *originate* from its author. It will therefore not be original if it is purely copied from another work and no independent skill, labour or judgment was used to produce the copy.

13   Copyright, Designs and Patents Act 1988, s 9.
14   Copyright, Designs and Patents Act 1988, s 11(1).
15   Copyright, Designs and Patents Act 1988, s 11(2).

This requirement of originality has a second effect: because a work need not be novel or unique to acquire protection it is possible that two identical works are both protected by copyright. In most areas identical works are rare and are the result of copying; on the Internet, there are instances of works being identical without copying. The most common example of this is the use of search engines. These are programs that can search for a given word or phrase amongst all the web sites on the Internet. The engine produces a list of every occurrence of the searched term. Two different search engines but both searching for the same term may well both produce identical lists. That these lists are identical does not mean that the works are not original; it is simply a quirk of digital precision and both may attract a separate and equally valid copyright.[16]

> **12. A budding journalist 'cuts' an article he finds on a web site (by pressing two keys) and 'pastes' it into an e-mail. He sends this e-mail to an editor of a newspaper claiming to have written the article. The editor publishes the article without paying the journalist. The journalist, however, may not be entitled to payment: he had no copyright in the e-mail sent to the editor as it did not originate with him.**

Skill, labour or judgment

Until 1990 the phrase, 'what is worth copying is worth protecting' was much in vogue. This originates from Peterson J's statement in a 1916 case, *University of London Press v University Tutorial Press*.[17] It seems to suggest that if a person seeks to copy a work then the law will ensure that the work has sufficient protection to prevent that copying. This post facto attribution of rights has been doubted; the House of Lords in *Re Smith Kline & French Laboratories* said it was 'not the law'.[18] What English law requires is that *some* skill, labour or judgment must have been utilised to convert the idea into the fixed expression. Unlike the United States, which looks more for creativity than mere labour, the fact that an author expends 'sweat of the brow' is generally enough to be granted copyright's protection over that work.[19]

This has the legal result that most works which are original in the copyright sense will also have the minimal level of skill and labour required to enjoy protection. This becomes important where individuals on the World Wide Web have generated lists of useful sites for others to view. Under American jurisprudence there may be an argument that the list does not possess the 'minimal degree of creativity'.[20] Under English law, in contrast, copyright will be granted over such a list without the courts having significant recourse to the effort, or creativity of its author.[1]

---

16   See 'Search engines', at page 185.
17   [1916] 2 Ch 601 at 610.
18   [1990] 1 AC 64 at 106.
19   See *Feist Publications Inc v Rural Telephone Serv Co* 499 US 330 at 364 (1991).
20   *Feist Publications Inc v Rural Telephone Serv Co* 499 US 330 at 345 (1991).
 1   Cf *CCC Information Services Inc v Maclean Hunter Market Reports Inc* 44 F 3d 61 (2nd Cir 1994).

TYPES OF PROTECTION

Copyright provides copyright owners with protection in the form of economic rights. These differ slightly for each particular category of copyright work but can be broadly summarised as follows: the owner of the copyright in a work has the exclusive right to copy it, issue it to the public in any form and adapt the work.

In addition the authors of certain types of copyright work enjoy moral rights which protect the integrity of the work and the right to be identified as the work's author. The implication of these rights on the Internet will be discussed under each aspect of the Internet considered below.

QUALIFICATION FOR PROTECTION

This book considers only when English law will grant copyright and moral right protection. This section also only deals with the law as it applies to works created after 1 August 1989. The section is concerned with the rights afforded to copyright works created *for* the Internet, rather than the wider rights afforded to copyright works that can be *used* on the Internet.

There are three alternative routes for a work to qualify as protected under the Copyright, Designs and Patents Act 1988:

1. in relation to its country of first publication;
2. by reference to its author;
3. where applicable, by reference to the place from where it was broadcast.[2]

If any one of the routes is satisfied, the work benefits from protection.

Place of publication

The question of where the work is first published[3] is complicated in an Internet environment. It is made available simultaneously throughout the world; where is it published? To address this question it is initially important to understand the stages in creating and 'publishing' a web site.

When people speak of 'designing a web site' they are technically creating a computer program. Either the designer creates the program by typing commands or uses another program visually to design the site then allowing that program to generate the appropriate commands. These programs that represent web sites are written in a special computer language called HTML. This language describes to a computer what a particular web page should look like; it is a layout language. The program is then 'run' through a viewer's browser (maybe thousands of miles away) which interprets the HTML commands and converts these back into a visual layout for the web site. Similarly, any executable code embedded in the HTML is written on the designer's computer and then interpreted by the viewer's. For example, a designer may create some executable code in the form of a Java applet. This is stored on the designer's computer in Java Byte Code and interpreted on the viewer's computer by a program called a Java Virtual Machine.

2   Copyright, Designs and Patents Act 1988, s 153.
3   Copyright, Designs and Patents Act 1988, s 153(1)(b).

The 'publication' of a web site is only when a viewer's computer is provided with a copy of the HTML code from the server computer and the viewer's browser program converts this into a visual representation.

So a web site is not published as such; it is made available on a server for the public to access over the Internet. It is published by means of an electronic *retrieval* system rather than an electronic *distribution* system. The Act construes this as being 'publication'[4] but this still leaves open the issue of *where* that publication takes place. It is submitted that the old principles apply and that publication takes place not in the place of receipt of a copy but where the publisher invites the public to view the copies. Were this not the case, 'a periodical which is offered to the public by postal subscription and has 10,000 subscribers would have 10,000 places of publication'.[5] Applying this to the web, the relevant place is from where the site material is made available.[6] If this is located in the United Kingdom or in another country to which the section extends,[7] UK copyright will protect the site. This important question of place of publication for a web site is therefore answered by where the server is located. This will be the physical location of the web server which may be located by reference to its Internet Protocol Address (the unique number which has a domain name as its alias).[8]

---

13. An Iraqi company establishes a web site, physically based in Iraq, to publish anti-English propaganda aimed at Iraqis living in England. This propaganda is printed, verbatim, in a ridiculing newspaper article in an English newspaper. It will not be deemed to have been first published in England, even if the only accesses to the web site are from England. England is the place of receipt; Iraq is the place of first publication under English law.

Simultaneous publication

In view of the conclusion that the place of the server is the place of publication it is vital to address how this rule works for a web site on two servers. These are called 'mirror sites' and are server computers holding identical copies of the HTML code so allowing more people to access the code at once. Web site designers who wish to benefit from the English copyright regime must ensure that their porting of HTML code to two such servers will not constitute first publication *outside* the requisite countries.

Simultaneous publication, for the purposes of the Act, appears reserved for when two separate distribution channels exist in separate countries. This will be the situation for two or more mirror sites. The rule that applies to this situation is simple: as long as material on one server inside a requisite country was made

---

4   Copyright, Designs and Patents Act 1988, s 175(1)(a).
5   *British Northrop Ltd v Texteam Blackburn Ltd* [1974] RPC 57 at 66.
6   See *McFarlane v Hulton* [1899] 1 Ch 884; and *British Northrop Ltd v Texteam Blackburn Ltd* [1974] RPC 57 as applied in *Television Broadcasts Ltd v Mandarin Video Holdings* [1984] FSR 111. This also accords with the definition that both 'publication' and 'commercial publication' refer to the *issuing* of the work to the public: Copyright, Designs and Patents Act 1988, s 175(1)(a) and (2)(a).
7   Copyright, Designs and Patents Act 1988, ss 155 and 157.
8   There are web sites which will locate a server on the globe by simply typing in the IP address.

available within 30 days of the site's publication on another server, the site will qualify for copyright protection.[9]

---

14. An individual establishes a web site based on a server outside the requisite countries. After a couple of months the popularity of his site has grown so much as to warrant renting space on a server based in London. Unfortunately, one week after establishing this mirror site, a copycat site springs up also in London. The individual has missed by one month having his work qualify for protection.

The lesson of this is obvious: it makes little practical difference where a web site is *hosted*. The server can physically be based anywhere in the world. Those web designers outside the requisite countries can therefore be advised to publish simultaneously their site material on two servers, one within a requisite country. It is hard enough preventing world wide infringement, but it is easier if rights over the work are gained in as many countries as possible.

Author qualification

There is another method to fall within the Copyright, Designs and Patents Act 1988 for copyright protection: if at the time the work was created its author was a 'qualifying person'.[10]

A wide spread of people qualify, including:[11]

> 'a British citizen, a British Dependent Territories citizen, a British National (overseas), a British Overseas citizen, a British subject, a British protected person within the meaning of the British Nationality Act 1981, an individual domiciled or resident in the United Kingdom or a British dependency, a body incorporated under the law of a part of the United Kingdom or a British dependency.'

This is in addition to those citizens and subjects of the extra countries provided by the Copyright (Application to Other Countries) Order 1993.[12]

---

15. An American web designer does not get a chance to publish her work before it is copied onto a London-based server. The copyright work in question, the HTML code, has not been published but the author is resident and domiciled inside one of the requisite countries. The work is, therefore, protected here.

Broadcasts or cable programmes

The Copyright, Designs and Patents Act 1988, section 153(1)(c) includes a qualification for broadcasts and cable programmes which is the country from where the broadcast was made or the programme sent. It is this chapter's

---

9   Copyright, Designs and Patents Act 1988, s 155(3).
10   Copyright, Designs and Patents Act 1988, s 154.
11   A paraphrasing of the Copyright, Designs and Patents Act 1988, s 154(1) and (2).
12   SI 1993/942.

assumption that the Internet and the World Wide Web are not broadcasts or, as a rule, cable programmes.

Definition of 'broadcast'

Section 6(1) defines a broadcast as being, essentially, a transmission by wireless telegraphy of visual images, sounds or other information. Wireless telegraphy refers to sending electro-magnetic energy over paths not provided by a material substance constructed or arranged for that purpose.[13] The optical fibres and telephone wires that constitute the Internet clearly are arranged for the purpose of sending such energy: the Internet is not a broadcast.

Definition of 'cable programme'

A cable programme refers to any item included in a cable programme service; this is defined as a service which consists wholly or mainly in sending visual images, sounds or other information by means of a telecommunications system, otherwise than by wireless telegraphy, for reception in one of two ways. First, at two or more places whether for simultaneous reception or at different times in response to requests. The second way is for presentation to members of the public.[14]

Sending information

It is submitted that few web sites or presences on the Internet will be within this definition. First, a web site does not 'send' material; if anything it is collected. As with dialling someone's telephone number, the person answering the 'phone does not 'send' audio information back to the caller. In disagreement with this, Lord Hamilton, in a Scottish interim interdict, decided that a web site did send information.[15] He agreed that the information 'passively awaits access being had to it by callers' but stated that this did not preclude the information being 'conveyed to and received by the caller'. It seems semantic, but is important, to analyse this statement closely.

Material available over the Internet is retrieved by a viewer, not generally pushed to a viewer from the site server. To prove this one needs only to question what occurs when no one accesses a web site: no information is conveyed. In contrast, if no one accesses a television broadcast, the programme is still conveyed but it is not seen. So Lord Hamilton's description of a web site's operation is technically dubious: web sites do not 'send' information, it is drawn from them.

Two or more places

The second aspect of a cable programme is that it is intended to be received at two or more places whether for simultaneous reception or at different times in response to requests. Lord Hamilton did not consider that this definition of a cable

---

13   Copyright, Designs and Patents Act 1988, s 178. The Copyright and Related Rights Regulations 1996 alteration of this definition does not change its application to the Internet.
14   Copyright, Designs and Patents Act 1988, s 7(1).
15   *Shetland Times Ltd v Dr Jonathan Wills* (Scottish Court of Session, 24 October 1996).

programme service attempts to encompass multicasting or broadcasting. That is, it is defined in terms of 'two or more places'. The inclusion of these words eliminates one-to-one communication. But this is communication which is perfectly possible over the Internet, for example e-mails.

Interaction

So, without looking further in the Act, a cable programme service does not appear to encompass a web site or a bulletin board on the Internet. Subsection 2 of section 7, however, provides a number of exceptions which can be demonstrated clearly to exclude web sites from the definition of a cable programme service.

> '(2) The following are excepted from the definition of 'cable programme service': a service or part of a service of which it is an *essential feature* that while visual images, sounds or other information are being conveyed by the person providing the system there will or may be sent from each place of reception, by means of the same system or (as the case may be) the same part of it, information (other than signals sent for the operation or control of the service) for reception by the person providing the service or other persons receiving it[.]'

In the *Shetland Times* interdict, Lord Hamilton stated that '[w]hile the facility to comment or make suggestions via the Internet exists, this does not appear to me to be an essential element in the [web site], the primary function of which is to distribute news and other items'. Lord Hamilton did admit that final resolution of the legal issues 'may in the end turn on technical material not available ... at the hearing'.

Technically speaking, few sites on the Internet consist of only one page. They are a collection of pages and material referenced usually from the home page which acts like a contents page for the site. To move from this contents page to another page the viewer *must* so instruct the site's server – subsequent pages do not simply follow one another like the frames of a cable television film. The viewer interacts with the site by sending requests for new data.[16] Viewing a web site is therefore not a one-way experience, as believed by Lord Hamilton or as indicated by the definition of a cable programme. It is possible while downloading one page of a web site to select a link to commence downloading another page. This is what is special about the World Wide Web: viewers can select what they want to see. A web site therefore falls within the exception to a cable programme service.

Nevertheless, if a web site or bulletin board *is* classified as a cable programme, its services will qualify for protection if they were 'sent' from a qualifying country. Being a cable programme for qualification, therefore, has the same result as if publication only is considered. The place will be that of the location of the server.

It is now possible to consider the copyright protection which may vest in various aspects of the Internet.

---

16 Such interaction is over and above 'signals sent for the operation or control of the service'. This exception (to the exception) refers to checksums that are sent by the receiving equipment so the transmitting equipment 'knows' the material has been received correctly. Newer 'push' technologies do, however, broadcast material.

E-MAILS

Electronic mail will be protected as a literary work if it meets the hurdle of originality and the lower hurdle of the requisite skill, labour and judgment used in its creation. The Copyright, Designs and Patents Act 1988 defines, rather widely, a literary work as any work, other than a dramatic or musical work, which is written, spoken or sung.[17] E-mails are not generally spoken or sung,[18] they are typed. Typing, in any language, even using symbols, appears to fall within the Act's definition of 'writing' that includes any form of notation or code. And this may be by hand or otherwise regardless of the fixing medium. This presumably includes the use of 'emoticons' which are little pictures made up from the characters of the e-mail viewed from the side.[19] It will also encompass an e-mail which is not written but dictated to a voice recognition system.

If the author is an employee creating the e-mail in the course of employment, the first owner will be deemed to be the employer.[20]

To individuals and others

Unless there are agreements to the contrary, sending an e-mail to someone does not alter its copyright owner or its owner's rights over that copyright. So, for most e-mails sent to other individuals, the ownership and exclusive rights remain with the sender of the e-mail. Receivers of e-mails, therefore, unless they are aware of an implied licence or have an express one, should not forward the e-mail to others. By forwarding an e-mail one is not simply performing the equivalent of putting a letter in another envelope (which would not constitute a breach of copyright, but perhaps only one of confidence). By forwarding an e-mail one is involved in copying and therefore may infringe its copyright. This, and the issue of moral rights, is covered below.[1]

Term of protection

Copyright subsists in an e-mail as an original literary work, for the life of the author plus 70 years from the end of the calendar year in which its author dies.[2]

FORUMS

A 'forum' is the term used by this chapter to encompass Usenet newsgroups and commercial bulletin boards controlled by Service Providers. Forums contain a variety of digital information. Some contain only postings and replies from

---

17   Copyright, Designs and Patents Act 1988, s 3(1).
18   The e-mailing of digital recordings of messages is more appropriately protected as a sound recording under s 1(1)(b).
19   For example, ;-) is a smiling, winking man when turned sideways. Whether such a symbol would qualify as an *original* literary work is another question. See *Exxon Corpn v Exxon Insurance Consultants International Ltd* [1982] RPC 69.
20   See fn 15 at page 165.
1   See 'E-mail', at page 196.
2   Copyright, Designs and Patents Act 1988, s 12(2).

members, called conversation threads; others contain digital files such as pictures and sounds deposited by members. These two types of posting will be considered separately.

Conversation threads

A conversation thread is a collection of postings by individuals collected together as a written conversation. An individual, instead of sending an e-mail to another person, sends the e-mail to the forum and particular thread. Anyone else who also accesses the particular thread may then read this e-mail. And these readers can either reply to the public e-mail or can simply read the e-mails and their replies. Over time, sometimes minutes, a conversation thread emerges in which questions are asked and answered and those answers prompt other questions.

The controller of the bulletin board maintains this collection of e-mails in one of two ways. First, the conversation thread may be 'moderated'. This means that the controller, or his agent, takes an active part in the management of the thread: certain parts of messages or whole messages may be deleted and certain conversations may be 'steered' in their content. The controller acts as an editor. The second way is where the controller does not manage or oversee the content of the bulletin board in anyway. The controller, in such a system, is simply providing a storage system for a group of individual's e-mails.

Compilation of conversations

This collection of e-mails sent to the forum is a compilation. Compilations of e-mails may themselves be subject to protection as copyright works;[3] the Act explicitly mentions this.[4] But, it will be recalled, copyright does not protect 'literary works' but 'original literary works' for the creation of which the author expended skill, labour or judgment.[5] This raises the issue of whether a conversation thread is original and whether it has the requisite level of skill, labour or judgment.

It may be thought that the conversation thread falls at the first hurdle of originality; after all, the thread is simply a copy of others' e-mails. This is not the hurdle at which the work falls: what is the subject of protection is not the individual e-mails but *their collection*. The copyright protection extends to the collecting, the arrangement and the selection of the e-mails but not the e-mails themselves. For an unmoderated conversation thread, however, it is unlikely that there will be sufficient skill, labour or judgment to warrant copyright's protection.

It is admitted that the tests for skill, labour and judgment are not particularly onerous,[6] but it is nevertheless submitted that a conversation that operates without any human interaction cannot possibly be a copyright work. Of course, those who would wish to claim copyright in a conversation thread may seek to allude to their

---

3　'There will be copyright in the database as a compilation in the same way as there is in, for example, a street directory', Lord Beaverbrook for the government proposing the Copyright, Designs and Patents Act 1988, 489 HL Official Report (5th Series) col 1533, 12 November 1987.
4　Copyright, Designs and Patents Act 1988, s 3(1)(a).
5　See 'Original works', at page 165; and 'Skill, labour of judgment', at page 166.
6　See *University of London Press Ltd v University Tutorial Press Ltd* [1916] 2 Ch 601 at 609.

skill, labour and judgment in *setting up* the conversation thread.[7] Again, it is submitted that such underlying skill, labour and judgment are not that which is required to create a copyright work.[8]

This should be contrasted with the situation where a moderator has a hand in editing and guiding the stored conversations. In this situation, the moderator does add that element of human skill, labour and judgment. Moderated conversation threads therefore probably do have protection as literary works.

What is true for either type of thread is that, without an agreement to the contrary, the controller does not own the copyright in the individual postings. It will be examined below as to what rights the controller does have in the individual postings.[9]

---

16. A Usenet newsgroup is unmoderated and is published through many different Service Providers. One Service Provider objects to a particular competing Service Provider also publishing the newsgroup. One aspect to the Provider's objection is breach of copyright. This is groundless. The Provider has no copyright in the newsgroup unless it has input sufficient skill, labour and judgment into its creation; simply storing the postings is not enough to warrant copyright's protection.

File collections

In the same way as some controllers of bulletin boards simply store e-mails for members, others store files for members. Often these are pictures or sounds that a member wishes to share with others; often the pictures themselves are infringements of copyright. What is of concern here is what copyright a controller has over the collection of files. The fundamental question is whether the collection of files could constitute a copyright work at all; compilations, to be protected by copyright, must constitute literary works in their own right. Case law indicates that the concept of a literary work, however, is wide enough to embrace collections of pictures in certain contexts.[10] The widest point in this reading of a literary work came in *Anacon Corpn Ltd v Environmental Research Technology Ltd*.[11] The question facing Jacob J was whether a circuit diagram could constitute a literary work under the Copyright, Designs and Patents Act 1988. Like most people's initial reaction to such a question, Jacob J said,[12]

---

7   Another option is for the controller to claim that the conversation thread is a computer-generated work under the Copyright, Designs and Patents Act 1988, s 9(3). Even computer-generated literary works require a level of originality and it is submitted that this is not met by a Service Provider who purely 'hosts' a forum.

8   A Service Provider may allude to the protection afforded to the journalist in *Walter v Lane* who the court decided had copyright in his verbatim transcript of Lord Rosebery's speech: [1900] AC 539 (still good law, see [1990] FSR 359). Of course a written transcript is very different in character to the transcribed oral speech and also takes judgment and skill. A Service Provider who does not moderate a forum or newsgroup simply re-publishes the text typed by others, formatted by others. The Service Provider does not even select the order to re-publish the various postings; the poster decides whether to 'follow' a thread or create a new one. There is little that the Service Provider adds to alter the quality and character of the raw material (see *Macmillan & Co Ltd v Cooper* (1923) 40 TLR 186 at 188 per Lord Atkinson).

9   See 'Forums', at page 198.

10   *Geographia Ltd v Penguin Books* [1985] FSR 208.

11   [1994] FSR 659.

12   [1994] FSR 659 at 663.

'My first thought was that it would be absurd to regard a circuit diagram as a literary work ... [.]'

He continued to state that on further thought it becomes apparent that the Act's use of the expression 'writing' encompasses almost anything[13]

'provided it is all written down and contains information which can be read by somebody, as opposed to appreciated simply with the eye[.]'

This may well serve as a protection for a collection of meaningful symbols that are grouped together, or a series of instructions in the form of diagrams. It does not serve as any indication that the group of sorted pictures, sounds and messages found on bulletin boards benefit from protection as literary works. These pictures are simply to be appreciated with the eye.

It is certainly arguable, therefore, that controllers of collections of assorted files do not hold any copyright over the collection as such. If they wish to prevent others copying the *collection* they must rely on establishing a contract with their viewers that prevents this copying. Such a contract, as all, suffers from the limitation on privity: it may serve to restrict contractually primary copiers, but those who duplicate the copy will not be bound by the contract. They, and the controller, may also be restricted by the copyright vested in the individual files themselves.

Commercial forums and newsgroups

So far this section has discussed the copyright that subsists in the conversation threads as compilations. It is also important to highlight the issue of who owns the copyright in the individual postings to the conversation threads. As this section has stated, without prior agreement, the copyright to a posting is vested in its author. Certain commercial forums controlled by Service Providers ensure that all members to a particular forum accept a contract which grants a wide licence to the Provider over any postings made to the forum.[14] Often such licences permit Providers to 're-post' conversation threads on other Service Providers' forums or even further afield. Members of these forums should be careful to read the licence agreement if they are concerned that their postings may be read outside the forum.

Usenet houses the largest collection of bulletin boards on the Internet. Its bulletin boards are called newsgroups and there are many thousands of different varieties. But no one individual owns or controls any of the conversation threads. In fact, every Service Provider who seeks to provide its members with access to the newsgroups is only responsible for adding messages posted by its own members. Once posted the message is slowly and methodically copied to each of the other Service Providers who are also hosting that newsgroup. This so-called 'flooding' eventually reproduces the posted message on all the different Service Provider's copies of the newsgroup.

From a copyright point of view there are two conclusions from this. The first is that one Service Provider has no exclusive rights over the compilation. At best all

---

13 [1994] FSR 659 at 663.
14 See the *Guardian*, 24 October 1996, which reports that authors of software objected to Compuserve's assertion in its member agreement of its non-exclusive right to 'copy, distribute, display, perform, publish, adapt, modify and otherwise use' any software uploaded to Compuserve.

the hundreds of Service Providers who host the newsgroup are joint copyright owners.[15] In addition, it is this author's submission that with no skill, labour and judgment involved to produce the thread, there is no copyright over which to have joint ownership anyway.[16] The second conclusion is that the individuals who post their messages must be posting their messages with a very wide implied licence. This will be discussed in more detail below, but at present it is enough to state that individuals who are concerned that their postings may be copied into many different forums should not post them to a newsgroup. The system only works on the basis of implied licences to copy all the messages to anyone who wishes to host the same newsgroup.

Term of protection

If a conversation thread is deemed to be an original literary work, copyright subsists in the compilation for the life of the author plus 70 years from the end of the calendar year in which its author dies.[17]

WEB SITES

Web sites are the most legally complicated of all works on the Internet. Web sites consist of many overlapping and adjacent copyright works each of which may have protection separate from the whole and each of which may have a different owner. To appreciate these many copyright works it is perhaps useful to outline how one creates a web site.

Creation of a web site

To most web site designers what is important is how the site looks and how quickly it can be displayed.[18] The first stage is usually to create a scheme that shows how each of the different pages of a site fit together. For example, the first page, or home page, will generally link to many pages, rather like a contents page of a book. Each one of these connections will be drawn either on paper or on a computer screen. Eventually the designer will have built up a skeleton for all the various pages of the site. For the most complex sites, it is at this stage that a designer may draw in some frames within each one of the pages. Frames allow some information to remain on the screen even though the viewer chooses a new page. Candidates for frames are contents sections and legal disclaimers; these then remain on the screen for any page of the web site.

The second phase of the site's design is preparing the individual pages. A designer must be aware of where every element of a page will be placed. This is because the language used eventually to store the site eventually is a layout language, and like all computer programming languages demands certainty.

---

15   Copyright, Designs and Patents Act 1988, s 10(1).
16   See 'Compilation of conversations', at page 173.
17   Copyright, Designs and Patents Act 1988, s 12(2).
18   This section refers extensively to web designers in the sense of a person or company who creates HTML code to put on a server. The legal conclusions reached, however, are equally applicable to anyone who designs a web site whether for themselves or their company.

Designers do this 'story boarding' either on paper (converting it subsequently by eye into HTML commands), or on a computer screen using a special program that performs the conversion.

A page may consist of many discrete, individually-designed elements. The most basic of these is the text: this is the line of characters from the first letter to the last, rather than the layout which is how the characters are portrayed; in which typeface,[19] in which format. The other common element is graphics. These are digitally stored pictures, but it is crucial to realise that their digital nature refers only to the method of storage. A picture on a web site could just as easily have been an oil painting on canvas as a digitally *created* picture made using a computer painting package. Each graphic is stored on the web site and 'anchored' into the page at the correct place. Unlike a newspaper, the graphics are stored and are accessible separately from the main page. All the page holds is a link to the graphic.

Certain web sites use a Common Gateway Interface script; this allows interaction with the viewer of the site. At its simplest, viewers can enter their name and other details to receive information. More involved scripts allow certain areas of the screen to become 'hotspots' and to respond to a viewer's clicks on those parts.

The most complex and recent addition to web sites is executable code. These 'applets' and 'objects' are, in short, whole computer programs that are automatically run whenever a web site is viewed. Some executable code may perform a simple task such as playing a three-note tune. Other code is more intricate and displays animations and even allows viewers to play games. For instance, some web sites will allow their viewers to draw pictures, others to write letters. Of course the effort which goes into coding one applet may be extensive involving the work of many people including designers and programmers.

Having explained this factual background it is now possible to examine the copyright that will, inevitably, protect not only the whole web site, but also its constituent parts.

Preparatory material

Most web sites start life as a few sketches on paper or computer. The Copyright, Designs and Patents Act 1988 protects original artistic works being[20] any painting, drawing, diagram, map, chart or plan, engraving, etching, lithograph, woodcut or similar work, and photograph, sculpture or collage, irrespective of artistic quality. So, the visual chart of how the web site fits together, even though not on computer, if fixed and originating from its author, will be protected by copyright as an original artistic work. Each of the individual graphics, even as rough sketches, are protected as original artistic works.

This underlying protection cannot be ignored: if the designer is not the owner or the licensee of the underlying protected works, he will probably infringe their copyright by incorporating them into a web site. This is dealt with below. What should be noted is that those who design web sites cannot simply scan, say, a photograph from a magazine and legally use it on their web site without being the owner or licensee of the copyright in the photo. Web designers cannot hide their work: a web site is available for viewing by anyone who wants to type the

---

19 Or 'font' in computer parlance.
20 Copyright, Designs and Patents Act 1988, s 4(1)(a) interwoven with s 4(2)(a) and (b).

corresponding URL; their designers must be wary of using infringing works as they can easily be spotted.

> **17. Many web sites use a backdrop that gives each page a textured background. One designer decides that the patterned wallpaper on his office walls would be appropriate for a particular background. He uses a digitised version as the backdrop. Although he may have incorporated the graphic and designed the other portions of the site, he is not entitled to use the textured background to the site. The wallpaper can be protected as an original artistic work and he may face infringement proceedings for copying it.**

Constituent elements

The lesson that a web site may infringe copyrighted elements *underlying* the main site is even more serious for elements that are obvious to any viewer. This is because the more similar a work is to an alleged copy, the greater the inference of copying. This should not be taken to mean that a distorted copy that is unrecognisable as such is not an infringement; it simply may be harder to prove.

Text

The text that is used on a web site is clearly a literary work and as such will possibly be protected by copyright. The web designer, by simply retyping the text, gains no copyright over it unless a contract specifies this.

> **18. A web designer is employed to create a site for a law firm. As to be expected, the firm supplies a page of carefully drafted disclaimers to put on the site in a frame. Months later the designer is approached to design a site for an accountancy firm and offers them a site, 'including web-specific disclaimers'. If the designer uses the disclaimers on the accountant's site, without permission from the lawyers, he is copying a literary work protected by copyright. He may be stopped from doing so.**

Term of protection

If the text on a web site is an original literary work, copyright subsists in it for the life of the author plus 70 years from the end of the calendar year in which its author dies.[1]

Links

The *Shetland Times* case may be thought to indicate that there is copyright in a link to one's site.[2] The implications of this interim decision could be serious if it

---

1   Copyright, Designs and Patents Act 1988, s 12(2).
2   *Shetland Times Ltd v Dr Jonathan Wills* (Scottish Court of Session, 24 October 1996).

allows one site to prevent another linking to it. This is unlikely to be followed and will possibly be rejected on appeal.

The Shetland News is a web site, like many others, which provides its readers with access to web pages on other sites by including links to those pages. These included links to CNN's web site and other major newspapers. At no time did the Shetland News provide its readers with copies of the articles themselves. The links are simply listed on the web site as series of headlines from the other web sites.

The Shetland News had included among the links on its home page a number of headlines appearing in issues of the *Shetland Times*' web site. The headlines on the *Shetland Times*' web site were identical to those on the *Shetland Times*' list of links. If a viewer were to select one of these headlines from the list, the Internet would then connect the viewer to the *Shetland Times*' web site at the point of the headline. The Shetland News did not copy nor *provide* the copy of the relevant article. The *Shetland Times* sought declarator that the Shetland News' actions constituted an infringement of copyright in the headlines.

On 24 October 1996 Lord Hamilton granted the *Shetland Times* an interim interdict (the Scottish equivalent of an interlocutory injunction) for copyright infringement. Without being referred to any authority on the point, Lord Hamilton rejected the defendant's submissions that a headline was not an original copyright work. His opinion was that there was copyright in the newspaper headline and that it is infringement to copy it in an electronic form or to incorporate it in a cable programme. What is important here is to assess whether copyright vests in the headline and then to assess the relevance of this.

There are a number of cases which indicate that it will be rare for there to be copyright in a headline, or indeed any other single line of text.[3] This, perhaps, does not reflect the position accurately. A page of text on a web site may well be protected by copyright as a literary work. To infringe the copyright in the work one must copy the whole or a substantial part of the work.[4] One line of text, or one link, is clearly not a 'whole' copyright work. The question then is, is the line or link a substantial part of the copyright work of which it makes up a part? The House of Lords has addressed this question:[5]

> 'No doubt [headlines] will not as a rule be protected, since alone they would not be regarded as a sufficiently substantial part of the book or other copyright document to justify the preventing of copying by others.'

For the web a distinction should be made between including the *text* from another's web site in your own and including a *link* to that web site. A link is no more than a reference to other material, rather like the first footnote on this page. It is submitted that there is either no copyright in such a link by virtue of it not taking skill, labour and judgment to create, or that it cannot form a substantial part of its embodying copyright work.[6] Including the text from another's site is

---

3   *Dicks v Brooks* (1879) 15 Ch D 22; *Francis Day & Hunter Ltd v Twentieth Century Fox Corpn Ltd* [1940] AC 112.
4   Copyright, Designs and Patents Act 1988, s 16(3)(a). See 'A substantial part', at page 190.
5   *Ladbroke (Football) Ltd v William Hill (Football) Ltd* [1964] 1 WLR 273 at 286 per Lord Hodson.
6   In addition, there is a fair dealing defence that the justification for including a link to another's web site must have been for the purposes of the viewer *reviewing* that web site: Copyright, Designs and Patents Act 1988, s 30(1).

subject to all the usual checks and balances in copyright law. If a substantial part of that site is included on one's site, without defence, the copyright in the work is infringed.[7]

Graphics

Web designers are often approached by companies and firms who already have graphics to put on their site. These may include logos and photographs already used on the commissioner's paper literature. Sometimes the designer will have to go to considerable trouble to convert these paper graphics into a suitable format for viewing on a web site. For example, a web site may use just 256 colours, whereas a supplied photograph may be full-colour.[8] The labour and judgment expended by the designer in creating a new, 256-colour, artistic work may well lead to the designer having a new copyright over the digital version of the photograph. But this right should not be confused with the right to copy the original photograph: the designer's right is in the *fixed conversion* not in the underlying photograph. The designer should therefore seek explicit permission if he seeks to re-use the digitised photograph on another web site.

---

19. A well-known petrol company commissions a web designer to produce a web site for it. It supplies the designer with its logo which is a small yellow shell. The designer sets about writing a Java applet that will appear to rotate this shell in three-dimensions on the screen. Some time later the designer is approached by a high-class seafood restaurant which also wants a web site. The designer, rather than 'reinventing the wheel' colours the shell in grey and uses the same Java applet on the restaurant's site. If copyright subsists in the shell logo, the designer can be prevented from displaying the copy even though his skill, labour and judgment went into the production of the animating applet.

Term of protection

If the graphics on a web site are original artistic works, copyright subsists in them for the life of the author plus 70 years from the end of the calendar year in which its author dies.[9]

Music and sounds

Web sites now play music. They also allow a sound recording to be played. But the technical conversion from a musical score to a recording or MIDI file should not be confused with any legal rights over that underlying musical score. If original in the copyright sense, a musical score is protected as an original musical work.[10] That does not translate into having a legal right to reproduce the tune of a musical

---

7   See ' A substantial part', at page 190.
8   One can presumably imply license by the commissioner to make the adaptation (s 16(1)(e)) although the web designer should ensure that the commissioner has the right to grant this licence. The photographer may hold the copyright and have granted a limited licence to the commissioner that does not extend to its use on a web site.
9   Copyright, Designs and Patents Act 1988, s 12(2).
10   Copyright, Designs and Patents Act 1988, s 1(1)(a).

score on a web site. Again, therefore, a web designer must look to the owners of the rights in the underlying works for permission before reproducing them in another form on a web site.

It is more common on web sites to hear sounds than music, however. For example, a site advertising a new film set in space may open with the sound of laser fire. The 'sound' is recorded in a digital format called a 'sample'. This sample is sent from the web site server to the client computer. The browser program on that computer then interprets the sample's series of binary codes as pitch and amplitude variations and will play the sound back in perfect quality.

This sample will be a sound recording in a copyright sense. A sound recording means either a recording or sounds from which the sounds may be reproduced, or a recording of the whole or any part of a literary, dramatic or musical work from which sounds reproducing the work or part may be produced. This is *regardless of the medium on which the recording is made or the method by which the sounds are reproduced or produced.*[11] This definition is wide enough to protect both digital recordings on a computer, stored in a digital format, and a MIDI file, storing the music in a special musical notation that allows the computer to 'play' the music directly.

No rights subsist in a sound recording which is a copy of another.[12] This may also be an infringement of the copyright in the copied recording.

---

20. The owner of a news web site decides to use a sound recording of Big Ben chiming one o'clock. The owner digitally records BBC Radio's use of the same chime on its one o'clock news programme. The web site owner not only may have infringed the copyright in the BBC's own recording, but also, the owner has no copyright in his own recording. If the owner had stood beside Big Ben and digitally taped the chiming himself, he would have a copyright in the sound recording.

Term of protection

If the music used on a web site is an original musical work, copyright subsists in it for the life of the author plus 70 years from the end of the calendar year in which its author dies.[13] The copyright in a sound recording expires 50 years after it was released as long as this release was within 50 years of being made.[14] It seems acceptable to assume that when a sound recording is present on a server that is connected to the Internet, this will be its first publishing, and hence its release.[15]

Commercial point

This discussion of the individual elements of a web site serves two purposes. First, it shows that those who design web sites should be careful to form explicit arrangements with their commissioners. They should ensure that they are indemnified from any copyright infringement by virtue of using material supplied

---

11   Copyright, Designs and Patents Act 1988, s 5(1).
12   Copyright, Designs and Patents Act 1988, s 5(2).
13   Copyright, Designs and Patents Act 1988, s 12(2).
14   Copyright, Designs and Patents Act 1988, s 13A(2).
15   Copyright, Designs and Patents Act 1988, s 13A(3).

to them by those who commissioned them. They should, conversely, be sure to indicate what copyrights are to pass back to the commissioner and what is to remain vested in the designer. This is important to commissioners: programming a general purpose Java applet that, say, animates a graphic may be something that the designer would wish to use again. Without a contract stating this explicitly, the law can imply that the owner of the copyright is the designer.[16]

The second purpose of looking at the copyright that subsists in the elements of a web site is that it is trivial for infringers to copy only those elements. It is better to show a court that one owns the copyright in a graphic that is copied than to have to demonstrate that the graphic copied constitutes a substantial part of the whole web site so is an infringement.[17]

Encompassing aspects

Although a web site is built up from a number of smaller elements, the whole site is the code which is stored on the server computer. This is the web site absolute. This section explains its assumption that a web site is a computer program within the Copyright, Designs and Patents Act 1988.

Web sites as programs

The Copyright, Designs and Patents Act 1988, section 3(1)(b) states that computer programs should be considered as literary works. The same requirements of originality and skill, labour and judgment apply, and it will be assumed that they are met for most web sites that are created independently.

'Program or computer', for this section of the Act, is left wisely undefined by the draftsman; there are too many examples of legislation serving only a bygone technology. So, the term should be given its reasonable meaning. There would be few programmers or lawyers who would disagree that a program is a set of instructions that can be interpreted by a computer into a set of functions. So is HTML code a program? It is a set of instructions which when read by a browser program produces visual and or audible changes in the functioning of the computer.[18]

Protection for programs

In *Ibcos Computers Ltd v Barclays Finance Ltd*, Jacob J considered the extent to which copyright protects programs.[19] There are two critical aspects to his lucid

16　Cf Copyright, Designs and Patents Act 1988, s 11(2).
17　See the Copyright, Designs and Patents Act 1988, s 16(3)(a). This will be addressed in greater detail under 'Infringement', at page 187.
18　Some sites may also have protection for their typographical arrangement under the Copyright, Designs and Patents Act 1988, ss 1(1)(c) and 8. The reason that only *some* sites will benefit from this protection is that most web pages allow the area in which they are viewed to be reduced and allow the viewer's browser to re-align and re-set the information to fit inside this smaller area. For these cases, it would be difficult for the coder of the HTML to assert that the layout has been fixed and so is capable of copyright protection. For sites that do not allow such re-formatting, their term of copyright protection over the layout is 25 years from the end of the calendar year of first publication on the World Wide Web: Copyright, Designs and Patents Act 1988, s 15.
19　[1994] FSR 275.

judgment: first, the American case of *Computer Associates v Altai*,[20] relied on by a previous judgment,[1] is not 'particularly helpful' and its main concept 'merely complicates the matter so far as our law is concerned'.[2] The second aspect of the judgment of direct relevance is that copyright may protect not simply the whole program but also the sub-programs which make up the complete program.

Copyright protects the program at two levels: one, the actual words, symbols and numerals of the HTML code;[3] two, the compilation of the various smaller programs or elements within the whole. These are both literary works.

Protection of web sites

For a web site this is no mean protection. The entire coding from the first instruction to the last is protected as a pure literary work. In addition, the individual programming elements are also protected as smaller literary works. This becomes particularly important for web sites that use a considerable amount of executable code. If a person copied one small applet without licence there is an argument that, in relation to the whole HTML listing, the applet is insubstantial so its copying is not infringement.[4] If the programmer of the code can claim that the copyright work is not the whole web site but is the copied applet only, an argument of insubstantiality will fail. The whole work is copied.

---

21. A bank establishes a web site over which it conducts business. One aspect of the site is a form to fill in one's personal details. The web site has over 200 graphic-rich pages of information taking up 20 Mbytes of storage space; the form takes up half a page and less than one Mbyte. The form is copied, no doubt for its neatness and compactness. If the bank claims copyright only in the whole site, the taking of the form may be viewed as not substantial. The bank can, however, also claim a separate literary copyright in the code for the form for which the 'defence' of insubstantiality will surely fail.

Term of protection

If a web site is classified as a computer program, and then as an original literary work, copyright subsists in it for the life of the author plus 70 years from the end of the calendar year in which its author dies.[5]

---

20   982 F 2d 693 (2nd Cir 1992).
1   *John Richardson Computers v Flanders* [1993] FSR 497 at 526.
2   [1994] FSR 275 at 302. This author is in full agreement with this assessment: the United States Copyright Code 102(b) actively excludes from copyright protection any 'process, system, method of operation'. This is partly the reason why the court in *Altai* developed the 'filtration' of such aspects from protection, eventually to reduce the work to a 'core of protectable material'. The Copyright, Designs and Patents Act 1988 does not exclude these aspects of a work.
3   Some might use the word 'source code' to refer to this listing. This is perhaps not strictly accurate as the distinction between source and object code for HTML code is not as pronounced as for compiled programs such as executable code.
4   Copyright, Designs and Patents Act 1988, s 16(3)(a).
5   Copyright, Designs and Patents Act 1988, s 12(2).

Web site copyright by remote control[6]

Having examined the significant protection for web sites it is necessary to touch again on who benefits from that protection. It will be remembered that every copyright work must have an author, but a copyright work can have joint authors.[7] This is particularly relevant for web site designers who often work with their client's in-house designers. In illustration, a designer of a brochure may instruct a web site designer to create a web site like the brochure.[8] As the design of the web site progresses, the in-house designer may contribute to the design process, recommending different typefaces, providing extra illustrations and other input.

In providing this guidance, the in-house designer may allege that he provided skill, labour and judgment into the creation of an expression from a mere idea. In short, the designer is partially responsible in an 'investment' sense for the finished product. The web site designer, in contrast, could claim that copyright vests in an author who expends skill, labour or judgment in fixing an idea into an expression. On these lines, a helpful idea or suggestion from a third-party is not a copyright work; it is a mere idea to which copyright affords no protection.

Joint authorship of web site

The Act is of little guidance in this area, demanding only that joint authorship requires both collaboration and contributions that are indistinct.[9] The case law also, until recently, provided little binding dicta on the requirements for joint authorship.[10]

In *Cala Homes (South) Ltd v Alfred McAlpine Homes East Ltd* the requirements for joint ownership were examined.[11] Employees of Crawley Hodgson were the sole draftsmen of some architectural drawings. However, Mr Date, a designer who worked for the client, often provided the ideas for the drawings, even to very small details. The draftsmen of Crawley Hodgson worked to Mr Date's brief but, for the drawings in question, he did not 'move the pen on the paper'.[12] This should not detract from the fact that most of the design features of the drawings came from and were insisted to be included by Mr Date.

The question before Laddie J was whether Mr Date could be viewed as the joint author of these drawings. He was sure that he could.[13]

> 'In my view, to have regard merely to who pushed the pen is too narrow a view of authorship. What is protected by copyright in a drawing *or a literary work* is more than just the skill of making marks on paper or some other medium. It is both the words or lines and the skill or effort involved in creating, selecting or gathering together the detailed concepts, data or emotions which those words or lines have

6 A phrase seemingly coined by Mr Hobbs QC in *Cala Homes (South) Ltd v Alfred McAlpine Homes East Ltd* [1995] FSR 818 at 835. This case is discussed at length below.
7 Copyright, Designs and Patents Act 1988, s 10(1).
8 This is common practice for firms who wish to maintain some coherence between all their publicity and products.
9 Copyright, Designs and Patents Act 1988, s 10(1).
10 *Murray v King* (1983) 2 IPR 99; *Prior v Lansdowne Press Pty Ltd* [1977] RPC 511.
11 [1995] FSR 818 at 834–836.
12 [1995] FSR 818 at 833.
13 [1995] FSR 818 at 835. Emphasis added.

fixed in some tangible form which is protected. *It is wrong to think that only the person who carries out the mechanical act of fixation is an author.'*

The parallels with some web site designs are obvious. Where web site designers work together with another designer, to a considerable degree, they may not hold the copyright in the design as sole authors. They will always be *an* author of the site, but they may share that authorship with others. This, again, highlights the need for both parties in a web site design agreement to make explicit who owns what and what can be done with the works one owns.

SPECIFIC WEB SITES

This final section on protection examines the copyright considerations for special web sites. With the increased use of frames, there is little reason why these special types of web site will not, in time, simply become parts of a larger site. The same conclusions will then apply, but the protection that will be afforded will be in addition to the protection for the site as a compilation.

Search engines

Certain web sites are devoted to searching for other web sites. These sites allow a viewer to enter a string of words or even one word and then be presented with a complete list of every site containing the searched-for words. One created by Digital, called Alta Vista, can search the 16 million or so documents on the World Wide Web for one word within seconds.[14] When the word or words are found the search engine presents a list of all the sites and their addresses in which the word appears.

Computer-generated list

Clearly, the copyright to the program which searches the web is owned by or licensed to the search engine owners. But who owns the copyright to the outputted list of 'found' sites? The list is a literary work; it is a compilation like many other protected lists. If done by hand, its author would be the poor person who had to wade through the documents searching for the given word. But this searching, this labour and judgment, is performed by a computer program; who is its author, and owner, in this situation?

The Act states that a computer-generated work is one that has been generated by computer in circumstances such that there is no human author of the work.[15] This is the case with a list generated by a search engine. In this circumstance the Act provides that the author of the computer-generated work must be the person by whom the arrangements necessary for the creation of the work are undertaken.[16] This is probably the person who types the search terms into the search engine.

---

14 The engine is searching its own *index* of the web.
15 Copyright, Designs and Patents Act 1988, s 178.
16 Copyright, Designs and Patents Act 1988, s 9(3).

What is significant about this conclusion is that it means the controller of the search engine has no copyright over the *products* of the program. This may not be a problem, but there are instances where owners of search engines are resentful that users of their engine can establish a list of, say, flower shops in London, without having even to attribute the list to the search engine. The simple way around this problem is for the search engine owner to enter a licence with every user of the site. This may provide that the generated list is provided only on a non-commercial basis and that any list created by the engine must display also a link to the search engine that created it (in a non-copyright sense). Alternatively the owner of the engine may seek to impose an assignment back from each user.

---

22. A search engine is used to find every art gallery in Manchester that has a web site. The resulting list is simply ported onto a web site and advertising is sold on that web site to the galleries listed. The search engine site, without an agreement to the contrary, has no right to object to the use of the list and no right to claim a cut of the advertising revenue for the site.

Term of protection

If a search engine creates a computer-generated compilation, copyright subsists in it for 50 years from the end of the calendar month in which it was made.[17] This should be contrasted with the protection given to a human-made list that, as an original literary work, has copyright protection for the life of the author plus 70 years from the end of the calendar year in which its author dies.[18] Whether a web address will remain current for over even ten years is another issue.

Link lists

While some people prefer to search for web sites using a search engine, others prefer to use the equivalent of an index or contents page. The most famous example of this sort of site is Yahoo's. This site does not contain details of every site on the World Wide Web. Instead it lists selected sites in categories. For example, one may wish to look for lawyers who specialise in construction law. A list of suitable lawyers could be found under say both 'Professionals:Lawyers:-Construction' and under 'Building:Construction:Services'.

These sites, far from being boring, are colourful and are able to make huge profits through advertising and listing space sold on their site. They may therefore wish to protect the information on their site with the full force of copyright. And there seems little reason why this should not be possible. English law, in contrast to American law, has always protected lists of information where only a slim amount of skill and judgment is required to construct them.[19] The copyright in such a listing is in the compilation, the collection of the links. It is not in the links themselves. There is therefore nothing stopping an individual copying an interesting link or using a link from a link list. First, it is unlikely that copyright subsists in a URL; second, it would be unlikely that one link could form a substantial part of a list to form the basis for an infringement action.

17   Copyright, Designs and Patents Act 1988, s 12(7).
18   Copyright, Designs and Patents Act 1988, s 12(2).
19   See fn 19 at page 166.

The rights in a link list that is commercially available are the same as those that are publicly available.

---

23. Over a period of months, a Bonsai tree expert compiles a list of useful Bonsai-related sites on the Internet. He lists these on his personal site. A commercial link list receives a number of e-mails requesting a list of bonsai sites and a number of gardening centres indicate that they would be happy to pay for advertising near such a link list. The commercial link list copies the expert's list, reformats it in a different typeface and posts it up on their own site. They do not own the copyright in this list and may be infringing by copying it for this purpose. They would not have infringed copyright by simply providing a link to the expert's list.

Term of protection

If a link list is a computer-generated compilation, copyright subsists in it for 50 years from the end of the calendar month in which it was made.[20] If it is a human-made list then, as an original literary work, it has copyright protection for the life of the author plus 70 years from the end of the calendar year in which its author dies.[1]

Broadcasters

A recent advancement in Internet technology is the use of live and recorded radio programmes within a web site. Using special software, a viewer can 'tune into' a radio show being broadcast or 'streamed' from almost anywhere in the world. Recent advances are allowing a web site also to be able to show films and television shows in the same way.

What should be understood about these 'broadcasts' is that they have originated in the usual way: the radio shows are broadcast from a regular radio station and *then* converted into digitally compressed signals for the Internet; the same will probably occur with television shows initially. Because of this, the copyright that applies to the radio show is that which applies to radio shows generally. All that changes on the World Wide Web is that the owner of the copyright in the radio show permits it to be copied into a digital format and to be 'streamed' onto the Internet. If the owner of the copyright radio show does not permit this streaming, or is not permitted by his licensing authority, then the web broadcast may be in breach of copyright and other statutory regulations.

Infringement

Copyright works are protected in two main ways. First, certain ways of copying the work are deemed to be copyright infringement. The second way, for certain works, is to have moral rights that cannot be infringed.

---

20   Copyright, Designs and Patents Act 1988, s 12(7).
1   Copyright, Designs and Patents Act 1988, s 12(2).

COPYING AND INFRINGEMENT

It is vital to understand that not all copying is infringement and that not all infringement is copying.

Not all copying is infringement

To infringe[2] a copyright work by copying it one must, without licence of the copyright owner,[3] reproduce[4] at least a substantial part[5] of it in any material form.[6] Put another way, if one has the licence to copy a copyright work, one does not infringe it. Also, even without a licence, if one copies only an insubstantial part of a copyright work, one does not infringe the copyright in the work. These two non-infringing methods of copying are particularly relevant for the Internet. This is because, as will be explained, the only way to work on the Internet involves copying.

All infringement is not copying

It is not only unlicensed substantial copying that infringes a copyright; visually presenting a work in public may also infringe the copyright in the work.[7] One also infringes a copyright by authorising anyone to perform an act restricted by copyright.[8] In addition the law provides for secondary infringements where one deals in a restricted way with an infringing copy of a work.[9] This wider understanding of copyright infringement is essential to appreciate the ways that unwitting third parties such as Service Providers or web designers may be liable for copyright infringement.

COPYING AND THE INTERNET

Copying technically

A copy is made each time one views a web site, or accesses a bulletin board, or even forwards an e-mail. This is because, unlike the postal system, any material of any form that is sent over the Internet or viewed over the Internet is copied. What occurs is that the viewer's computer transmits a request to the server computer to forward a duplicate of some particular material it is storing. This duplicate material is not passed directly to the viewer's computer. It is broken into packets, each with a delivery address, and sent across the Internet. It is passed from one computer on the Internet to another until all the packets are eventually received at the viewer's computer. And, in reality, each of these intermediary computers has made a copy of the packet that it received and forwarded.

---

2   Copyright, Designs and Patents Act 1988, ss 16(1)(a) and 17(1).
3   Copyright, Designs and Patents Act 1988, s 16(2).
4   Copyright, Designs and Patents Act 1988, s 17(2).
5   Copyright, Designs and Patents Act 1988, s 16(3)(a).
6   Copyright, Designs and Patents Act 1988, s 17(2).
7   Copyright, Designs and Patents Act 1988, s 19(2)(b).
8   Copyright, Designs and Patents Act 1988, s 16(2).

When the material is finally received by the viewer's computer it is stored in the computer's memory; another copy. This transfer does not physically alter the information held by the server, rather it reproduces in the memory of the viewer's computer the material held by the server. The material on the server remains unchanged. The material now held in the viewer computer's memory is then 'interpreted'[10] or 'executed'.[11] This will allow the viewer to see the web site and hear its sounds if present. But this sight is the result of another copy. The computer's main memory translates the material received from the server into graphic images and these are sent to the screen memory; a further copy.

Copying legally

The Act defines copying widely. A copy is made by reproducing the whole, or any substantial part, of the work in any material form. This includes storing the work in a medium by electronic means.[12] And as has been examined, all material on the Internet and World Wide Web is, or has underlying it, a work protectable by copyright. The Act goes further and makes explicit that *any* reproduction will be deemed to be copying. This is even where the copying is indirect,[13] and even where it is transient or incidental to some other use of the work.[14]

This wide ambit of what is copying can be translated into one simple truth: using the Internet creates copies. When a web site is viewed, all the server computers on the Internet that pass on the packets will be deemed to have copied the site. Their copying is transient and incidental to another's use, but this still remains copying under the Act. The computer that finally receives the copies will also be deemed to have copied the site. The computer's copy may not be on paper, but storage by electronic means is sufficient to constitute copying under the Act. When e-mails are sent, received, even viewed, copies are made in a similar way as described above.

As almost all use of the Internet involves copying, the main legal issue in copyright actions will be whether the copying constitutes infringement.[15] The issues of licensing and substantiality will be generally discussed before addressing the infringement of moral rights.

IMPLIED LICENCES AND THE INTERNET

It will be recalled that it is not an infringement to copy the whole or a substantial part of a copyright work with licence from the copyright owner.[16] A licence does not need to take any particular form. Licences can be implied from statute[17] and by the courts from the circumstances in which the copyright work or part of it is

9   Copyright, Designs and Patents Act 1988, ss 22–26.
10   For pure HTML.
11   For executable code.
12   Copyright, Designs and Patents Act 1988, s 17(2).
13   Copyright, Designs and Patents Act 1988, s 16(3)(b).
14   Copyright, Designs and Patents Act 1988, s 17(6).
15   Of course, there may be many *factual* disputes as to whether the defendant actually *did* copy the work.
16   Copyright, Designs and Patents Act 1988, s 16(2).
17   Copyright, Designs and Patents Act 1988, s 50.

transferred.[18] What will be at issue in most Internet cases is the existence, scope and duration of these implied licences.

Some licences can be readily implied for dealings over the Internet. For example, the intermediary computers involved with an Internet dealing are impliedly licensed to copy the packets being passed to the end user. This can be inferred from the fact that the copyright owner made the information available over the Internet, so, surely a licence must be implied for business efficacy. If the owner of every server computer on the Internet infringed any packet that passed through it, the Internet would collapse because no one would want to connect to it. It seems also fair between the parties that the licence is implied only to the extent that the intermediary can pass on the packets. It would be outside the scope of the implied licence to retain copies of the packets after they are confirmed to have been accurately sent.

The Copyright, Designs and Patents Act 1988, section 50C provides that it is not an infringement of copyright for a lawful user of a copy of a computer program to copy it provided that is necessary for his lawful use and is not prohibited by contract. As a web site is a computer program and the only way to 'use' the web site is to copy it, it is implied that a lawful viewer of a web site is entitled to copy it to memory and screen memory. It will be examined below whether a user may also store a copy on a disk and for how long this copy may be stored. Similarly, it will be examined whether a third party is entitled to store copies of many different web sites, so allowing people easier access to them without having to access the individual servers. Both these sorts of copying are coined 'caching'.

A SUBSTANTIAL PART

To infringe a copyright work by copying it one must not only have no licence so to copy the work, but also the copy must be of a substantial part of the *plaintiff's* work.[19] There is no statutory definition of what constitutes a 'substantial part'. This absence is complicated further by the two senses of the word 'substantial'. The Concise Oxford Dictionary defines the word both qualitatively as 'of real importance or value' and quantitatively as 'of considerable amount'. The courts have chosen not to specify whether the test is one of quantity or one of quality but it appears that even aspects of a plaintiff's work that are quantitatively small may still constitute a substantial part.[20] What constitutes a substantial part of a

---

18   *Springfield v Thame* (1903) 89 LT 242; *Hall-Brown v Iliffe & Sons Ltd* (1928–35) Macq Cop Cas 88; *Blair v Osbourne & Tomkins* [1971] 2 QB 78; *Solar Thomson Engineering Co Ltd v Barton* [1977] RPC 537 at 560–561; *Barnett v Cape Town Foreshore Board* [1978] FSR 176; *Roberts v Candiware* [1980] FSR 352; *Anvil Jewellery Ltd v Riva Ridge Holdings Ltd* (1985-87) 8 IPR 161.

19   Copyright, Designs and Patents Act 1988, s 16(3)(a). 'The question is whether the defendants' [work] reproduces a substantial part of the [plaintiff's work], not whether the reproduced part of the [plaintiff's work] forms a substantial part of the defendant's [work]': *Warwick Film Productions v Eisinger* [1967] 3 All ER 367 at 385 per Plowman J.

20   '[T]hough it may be that it was not very prolonged in its reproduction, it is clearly, in my view, a substantial, a vital, and an essential part which is there reproduced': *Hawkes and Son v Paramount Film Service* [1934] Ch 593 at 606, per Slesser LJ; '[I]t is quite clear that the question of substantiality is not determined solely by any process of arithmetic': *Joy Music v Sunday Pictorial* [1960] 2 QB 60 at 68, per McNair J; '[T]he question whether he has taken a substantial part depends much more on the quality than on the quantity of what he has taken. It will, therefore, depend not merely on the physical amount of the reproduction but on the substantial significance of that which is taken': *Ladbroke (Football) Ltd v William Hill (Football) Ltd* [1964] 1 All ER 465 at 469, per Lord Reid, and at 473 per Lord Evershed.

conversation thread may be a familiar issue for a court to assess; what constitutes a substantial part of web site may be more difficult.

A web site may consist of 200 individual instructions to the computer and a copier may copy 100. But whether this quantitatively substantial taking is substantial in a copyright sense may depend on how the 100 lines appear on interpretation. If the lines are part of some executable code that merely animates a small graphic on a many-page website, this may not be substantial. This said, the courts must not forget that copyright protects not the expression itself but the skill, labour and judgment that was expended in creating that expression. So, if the animation of the graphic was a very complex and time-consuming piece of programming it may be a substantial part of the whole copyright work.[1]

Assessing substantiality is a question that will always rest on the facts of a case. The last word on its determination is left for Jacob J from *Ibcos Computers Ltd v Barclays Finance Ltd*:[2]

> 'Even in the case of technical drawings it is possible to examine the parties' drawings to see whether a substantial part of the plaintiff's work is to be found in the defendant's. *In a computer program case, however, the court cannot so readily assess the question of substantial part unaided by expert evidence. I believe I should therefore be largely guided by such evidence.*'

In illustration, a large parcel delivery company sets up a web site. It consists of information about the company, parcel-tracking facilities and lists of all its services. It amounts to over 30 pages of web pages and just under 1,000 lines of code. It features animations, sound jingles and forms to be filled in where appropriate. One such form was copied from a newspaper's site on the Internet. The form takes up one-third of one page and the coding is about 30 lines. The company admits unlicensed copying but deny that it is a substantial part when the form amounts to only 3% of the code on their page and 1% of the visual reproduction of the site. This is focusing on the wrong work and the wrong concept. The question should be how much of the *newspaper's* site has been lifted (even this question should not be answered with percentages); the *significance* of the form in *programming* terms should determine its substantiality.

INFRINGERS SUING INFRINGERS

It is the nature of the Internet that on a frequent basis copying and inevitably infringement occurs. This raises an issue more relevant to the Internet than any other medium: can an infringer of a copyright work sue for infringement of *his* copyright work?

The fundamental points to make are that even if a work infringes another, the work may still benefit from copyright protection.[3] Conversely, it is not a defence

---

1   In such a case, the plaintiff should not overlook the issue that the web site, although a computer program, is also a compilation. He may therefore be advised also to plead infringement of the Java applet by itself. This then eliminates the question of whether the taking is a substantial part of the web site. This can be compared to the approach used in *Ibcos*. See 'Protection of web sites', at page 183.

2   [1994] FSR 275 at 301.

3   *Redwood Music Ltd v Chappell & Co Ltd* [1982] RPC 109 at 120.

for a defendant to claim that the plaintiff's work is a copy.[4] What is proposed by Lightman J, and accepted by the Court of Appeal in *ZYX Music GmbH v Chris King* is that where there is no obvious public policy ground[5] the plaintiff can pursue infringers of his work with an obligation to account to the original author for his share of the recovery.[6] Infringement of a third party's copyright is not sufficient to refuse to enforce the copyright on public policy grounds. Lightman J added that the court[7]

> 'may require that the copyright owner whose rights the plaintiffs have infringed should be notified of the proceedings and given the opportunity to be joined, make representations or otherwise protect his rights before judgment is given or enforced.'

---

24. A software developer uses some executable code on his web site to make the viewer's mouse cursor appear to shine a beam of light on his web pages like a torch. A retailer of high-durability torches copies the code and uses it on its site. It does not credit nor pay for its use of the code. Some time later a smaller competing retailer copies the majority of the other retailer's site substituting its details on the contact page. This retailer is sued for infringement of copyright and passing off. It should not rely on a defence that the first retailer has also copied a copyright work; so long as the first retailer has notified the software developer and undertakes to account for the developer's proportion of the damages, the plaintiff has a valid claim of copyright infringement.

MORAL RIGHTS AND THE INTERNET

The Copyright, Designs and Patents Act 1988 does not purely provide economic rights to copyright *owners*. It also provides certain 'moral' rights to the *authors* of copyright works.[8] These rights include the right to be attributed as author of a copyright work, the right to object to derogatory treatment of a copyright work and the right not to be falsely attributed as the author of a copyright work. This section considers the first two of these rights: the so-called rights of 'paternity' and of 'integrity'.

The two rights do not apply to computer programs or computer-generated works, so excepting from protection much of the work on the Internet. The rights attach only to literary, artistic, musical and film works. This does not mean that a

---

4   *British Leyland Motor Corpn v Armstrong Patents Co Ltd* [1982] FSR 481 at 502.
5   For example, a 'dishonest and misleading work' (*Slingsby v Bradford Patent Truck and Trolley Co* [1906] WN 51) or an exploitation of a breach of confidence 'reeking of turpitude' (*A-G v Guardian Newspapers Ltd (No 2)* [1990] 1 AC 109 at 262H, 276H–277A and 294A–D).
6   [1995] FSR 566 at 576–578 and Court of Appeal (20 February 1997, unreported). This issue had been the subject of much academic debate, and Lightman J chose to endorse the view taken in Laddie, Prescott & Vitoria *The Modern Law of Copyright and Designs, Volume One* (Butterworths, London, 1995, 2nd edn).
7   [1995] FSR 566 at 577–578.
8   The rights do not apply where the work was created by an employee in the course of employment: Copyright, Designs and Patents Act 1988, ss 11(2), 79(3), 82(1)(a).

site on the World Wide Web cannot *infringe* a work's moral rights. What this means is that those who construct web pages, and those that control conversation threads, should be wary of infringing the moral rights in one of the works that they are using.

Paternity

The author of a literary work has the right to be identified as the author of that work whenever it is published commercially, broadcast or included in a cable programme service.[9] The author of an artistic work has the right to be identified as the author of that work whenever the work is published commercially or exhibited in public.[10] It has been discussed that putting a work on a web site will constitute commercial publication; money does not need to change hands.[11]

Assertion

To rely on the right, an author needs first to assert it.[12] This is achieved in relation to general or specific acts on an assignment of copyright or by an instrument in writing signed by the author.[13] A relevant question for those who see their works commercially published on the Internet is, therefore, whether this right can be asserted *over* the Internet.

Certainly, an e-mail can constitute a written instrument. The term 'writing' is widely defined as *including* any form of notation or code, whether by hand or otherwise and regardless of the method by which, or the medium on, in or on which it is recorded.[14] Whether a signature can be included within an e-mail is another, and more difficult question. What is certain is that the term 'signature' is interpreted widely by the courts[15] as a means 'as personally to authenticate the document'[16] and 'any mark which identifies it as the act of the party'.[17] This broad interpretation, no doubt, may, in certain circumstances, permit an encrypted message to serve as a written signed instrument.[18] But it is a risk. If authors truly are concerned that their moral rights on the Internet are respected, they should revert to paper and pen to make their assertion.

---

9 Copyright, Designs and Patents Act 1988, s 77(1) and (2)(a).
10 Copyright, Designs and Patents Act 1988, s 77(4)(a).
11 See 'Place of publication', at pages 167 to 168 especially, fn 6.
12 Copyright, Designs and Patents Act 1988, s 78(1).
13 Copyright, Designs and Patents Act 1988, s 78(2).
14 Copyright, Designs and Patents Act 1988, s 178. Cf Law of Property Act 1925, s 40 which is silent on what may constitute 'writing' forcing a court to rely, therefore, on the Interpretation Act 1978, Sch 1. This provides that '[w]riting includes typing, printing, lithography, photography and other modes of representing or reproducing words in a visible form ...'.
15 See also *Baker v Dening* (1838) 8 Ad & El 94; *Cohen v Roche* [1927] 1 KB 169.
16 *Goodman v Eban (J) Ltd* [1954] 1 All ER 763 at 766.
17 *Morton v Copeland* [1855] 16 CB 517 at 535.
18 See *Clipper Maritime v Shirlstar Container Transport, The Anemone* [1987] 1 Lloyd's Rep 546 in which there are dicta that the 'answerback' of the sender of a telex would constitute a signature.

> **25. An individual posts an e-mail to a commercial forum and ends the e-mail with the words 'This author asserts his right to be identified as the author of this work under the Copyright, Designs and Patents Act 1988.' This is unlikely to be a valid assertion and, subject to copyright infringement, the forum and others using the forum may reproduce his e-mail without reference to his authorship.**

Artistic works may have their paternity right asserted simply by being identified on the original or copy of the work in relation to a public exhibition.[19] For this method of assertion it appears likely that the assertion may be made over the Internet. Most web sites that show artistic works may be considered as public exhibitions and it is easy to include on a digital copy of a work a typed or 'signed' name.

> **26. A commercial forum serves as an advertising medium for young artists. One artist posts up on the forum a computer-generated graphic that he designed. He includes on the graphic his name and is perturbed when he sees his work republished on a web site without payment and without acknowledgment. He may well have a strong case of copyright infringement. He would have a similarly strong case of infringement of his moral rights but there are no moral rights over computer-generated artistic works. A hand-generated work *digitised* and posted on the Internet, in contrast, could be protected by a paternity right.**

Infringement

The right of paternity applies to the whole or any substantial part of the work.[20] This right is infringed where the work is commercially published or exhibited without the author's identity being brought to the notice of a viewing person.[1]

Integrity

In appropriate circumstances, the author of any literary or musical work has the right not to have the work subjected to derogatory treatment.[2] Similarly, in appropriate circumstances, the author of any artistic work has the right to object to any derogatory treatment of a copyright artistic work in a commercial publication or public exhibition.[3] In comparison to the right of paternity, the right of integrity is far more powerful: it does not need to be asserted; it applies to any part of the work not merely substantial parts;[4] and, it has far wider scope for infringement.

---

19   Copyright, Designs and Patents Act 1988, s 78(3)(a).
20   Copyright, Designs and Patents Act 1988, s 89(1).
1   Copyright, Designs and Patents Act 1988, s 77(7)(c).
2   Copyright, Designs and Patents Act 1988, s 80(1).
3   Copyright, Designs and Patents Act 1988, s 80(4)(a).
4   Copyright, Designs and Patents Act 1988, s 89(2).

Infringement

Treatment on the Internet

A 'treatment' of a work means any addition to, deletion from or alteration to or adaptation of the work. It does not include a translation of a literary work or a transcription of a musical work involving no more than a change of key or register.[5] As should be apparent, this is a very wide definition. It may include the re-colouring of an artistic image to look appropriate on a web site with a limited palette.[6] It will also include the reduction in size of an artistic work, or cropping of an artistic work to fit in a particular space on a web site. More technically, an artistic work will also be 'treated' where it is converted into a digital format with a lower resolution so that the picture appears more grainy or 'pixelated'. Literary works may be treated by over-zealous editing or 'snipping' as it is termed in conversation threads. Obviously, literary works are also 'treated' when they are blatantly altered.

Derogatory treatment

A treatment is derogatory if it amounts to distortion or mutilation of the work or is otherwise prejudicial to the honour or reputation of the author.[7] This has not been tested at full trial, so it is difficult to guess how favourably the courts will interpret the phrase. Some indication can be provided by a summary judgment given by Rattee J. In *Tidy v Trustees of the Natural History Museum*, Bill Tidy, a well-known cartoon artist, objected to a 16% reduction in size of his cartoons when displayed.[8] The plaintiff claimed that this reduction constituted derogatory treatment as a distortion of the work or by being prejudicial to his honour or reputation.

Rattee J decided that it would be difficult to decide that a treatment was prejudicial to an author's honour and reputation without recourse to evidence from the public as to how the reduction affected the plaintiff's standing in *their* eyes.[9]

If anything can be drawn from this summary judgment it is that the opinion of the author, while sometimes persuasive, is not the final arbiter of whether treatment is derogatory. What can outweigh the author's opinion, when reasonably arrived at, is the reaction of the public. On the Internet, therefore, the public may well know that a computer screen does not always faithfully represent the artistic works it portrays. And often this lack of quality is as a result of the quality of the viewer's screen or computer specifications; something for which the owner of a server or web site cannot be legally responsible.

For literary works, the result is less than clear. Those who edit conversation threads should therefore be careful to treat with respect the postings made by others.[10]

5   Copyright, Designs and Patents Act 1988, s 80(2)(a).
6   See the analogous French judgment of *Angelica Houston v Turner Entertainment* [1992] ECC 334.
7   Copyright, Designs and Patents Act 1988, s 80(2)(b).
8   [1996] 3 EIPR D-81, 29 March 1995.
9   Rattee J was not clear that the opinion of the author was essential to decide the point, so doubting the application of the Canadian decision *Snow v Eaton Centre Ltd* (1982) 70 CPR (2d) 105.
10 It is unlikely that a forum may be excepted from the obligation of non-derogatory treatment. If one exception is closest it would be that the right does not apply in relation to the publication in a newspaper, magazine or *similar publication*: Copyright, Designs and Patents Act 1988, s 81(4)(a). Infringement by possessing or dealing with an infringing article will be considered throughout the remaining section.

Waiver of rights

The uncertainty and scope of moral rights should make every user of another's copyright on the Internet think carefully about obtaining a waiver from each contributing author. It is not an infringement of the moral rights if the author waives those rights.[11] Unlike assertions, a waiver does not have to meet any formal requirements and can be in relation to any works for any purposes.[12] The waiver can also be made unconditional.[13]

Web designers would therefore be wise to obtain such a waiver in respect of any work that they use for a site; Service Providers can also be advised to obtain a waiver on all works submitted by their members; finally, the terms and conditions for any conversation thread or forum should include an express waiver in relation to any posting.

E-MAIL

Infringement by recipient

This section considers what might be infringement of the copyright in someone's e-mail. It is assumed that there is copyright in the e-mail. When an e-mail is received, it has already been copied; it is copied into the memory and probably hard disk drive of the receiver's machine. That much copying will certainly be implied by the common law not to be infringement: it is necessary for business efficacy and can be implied by sending it over the Internet rather than, say, by post.[14] What is not implied is to forward the message without either an express or implied licence to do so. A good example of this is any e-mail that is headed 'Private & Confidential'.

---

27. Paul sends an e-mail to Robbie. It ends, 'Actually, you should tell Charlotte about this.' Robbie forwards the e-mail to Charlotte who then replies to Paul. Paul is upset that Charlotte read the e-mail, but he has no legal redress in copyright. His end-note was an implied licence that Robbie would not infringe the copyright by copying the whole message to Charlotte. Charlotte also does not infringe Paul's copyright; her licence is implied by the common law.

Infringement by Service Provider

It has been described that a Service Provider holds a copy of all its member's e-mails until they are collected by the member. But there are times, say for backup purposes, that the e-mails are retained for longer. Service Providers would be advised to alert members to this additional copying by including such a statement in their terms and conditions with each member. The legal difficulty is that, while a member can provide a licence to her Service Provider in respect of e-mails authored by her, she cannot provide a licence on behalf of *others* for e-mails sent to her. A Service Provider can rely on an implied licence from the sender of the

11   Copyright, Designs and Patents Act 1988, s 87(1).
12   Copyright, Designs and Patents Act 1988, s 87(3)(a).
13   Copyright, Designs and Patents Act 1988, s 87(3)(b).
14   See 'Implied licences and the Internet', at page 189.

e-mail, in the same way as its recipient does.[15] It can also shore up its protection by seeking an indemnity from each of its members in respect of infringement allegations made by senders of e-mails to the member in relation to this backup facility.

Infringement by forums

There are two discrete issues concerned with controllers of bulletin boards infringing copyright. The first is the issue of what the controller can do with copyright material owned and posted by its members. This will be discussed presently. The second issue is what liability has a controller of a forum in respect of copyright material *not* owned by its members but nevertheless posted on the forum. This issue of secondary infringement is discussed in the section below.[16]

Every e-mail posted by its author to a forum, bulletin board or conversation thread carries with it an implied licence. This licence permits the copying of the e-mail on the server itself and also onto any other viewer's computer that is legitimately permitted *by the controller* to access the e-mail. This much is implied by business efficacy and the implied intention of the sender of the e-mail to so distribute the copyright work.[17] What is uncertain is the extent to which the controller may re-post or authorise re-posting to other forums. This uncertain issue can be more easily addressed by considering separately commercial forums from Usenet newsgroups.

Usenet newsgroups

A Usenet newsgroup can be republished by any service provider. Consequently there is an implied licence by those who post e-mails to a newsgroup that their work is free from publishing restriction.[18] This is implied from the course of trade with Usenet. This might not mean that the e-mail is free to be published in newsprint or in a medium other than the Internet. It is clear that authors of newsgroup postings wish their work to be distributed as widely as possible. Of course, any implied licence can be rebutted by an express provision to the contrary within the e-mail.

> **28. A contributor to alt.female.erotica ends all his postings with 'Not for re-posting or redistribution on any other newsgroup.' Someone re-posts his messages to a forum dealing with women's exploitation. That re-posting constitutes an unlicensed copy of the whole of a copyright work; it is an infringement of the author's copyright.**

---

15 Contracts should be drafted to allow for the fact that many companies provide their employees with e-mail accounts but the employees will not be the owners of the copyright in any work-related e-mails: Copyright, Designs and Patents Act 1988, s 11(2).

16 See 'Forums', at page 198.

17 There are clear analogies with the implied licence of an editor to publish an article submitted to him: *Hall-Brown v Iliffe & Sons Ltd* [1928–35] Macq Cop Cas 88.

18 Licences to 'all the world' have been upheld as valid. See *Mellor v Australian Broadcasting Commission* [1940] AC 491.

Commercial forums

A controller of a commercial forum will attempt to assert copyright in the compilation that constitutes each conversation thread,[19] and generally by express agreement, a licence over any individual's postings. As a result of such an express agreement it is likely that there will be terms that prevent any re-postings by individuals of *others'* e-mails. An individual is unlikely to be contractually restricted from posting his own message elsewhere.[20]

To re-publish an entire conversation thread to another forum may be an infringement of the copyright over the compilation. This depends on whether the conversation thread as a compilation is actually protected by copyright.[1]

---

29. A member of the Mechanics Forum is also a member of the Engineers Forum. These are operated by two rival Service Providers. The member re-posts from the Mechanics Forum to the Engineers Forum a conversation between him and another mechanic. This lasts about 15 lines out of a thread that is made up from over 200 lines from 40 different contributors. The controller of the Mechanics Forum threatens the mechanic with an action for copyright infringement. The controller has three significant legal hurdles. First, it must be proved that there is a copyright in the compilation; second, that it, rather than all the 40 contributors jointly, own the compilation; and third, that the taking is a substantial part of the copyrighted conversation thread.

Even if the conversation thread is not protected by copyright, for want of skill, labour or judgment, the Service Provider may still be able to assert its *contractual* rights. This is achieved by ensuring that every person who is allowed to access a conversation thread enters a contract which stipulates that no material, other than the member's own, will be re-posted elsewhere. A person that does re-post the material will be in contractual breach. Re-posting a thread from a commercial forum to a Usenet newsgroup will almost always be a clear copyright infringement of the compilation right, if present, and more certainly of the rights held by the individual author of the posted messages.

FORUMS

This section considers the occasions when a controller of a forum or host of a Usenet newsgroup will be liable for infringing material put on the forum. In the same way as someone can post an e-mail to a forum or bulletin board, a person can equally as easily post a file. This file may be a work in which the poster owns, or has a licence over, the copyright. In this situation, the controller of the forum has little to fear; the guidelines above will be applicable.[2] There are other times where the poster of the work is depositing an infringing copy of the work on the bulletin board. This section concentrates on this situation.

---

19   See 'Forums', at page 172.
20   Or rather, such a contractual term would have to be drawn to the attention of a new member to be enforceable as it would be unusual.
1   See 'Forums', at page 172.
2   See 'Infringement by forums', at page 197.

Secondary infringement

Reproducing without licence a substantial part of a copyright work is a copyright infringement. The Copyright, Designs and Patents Act 1988, sections 22 to 26 also provide circumstances where other dealings with a copyright work with a 'guilty mind' will constitute secondary infringements of copyright.[3] These dealings include the possession in the course of business of an article which is an infringing copy of a copyright work; a dealing that may be satisfied by a bulletin board storing a copy of an infringing work. The requisite guilty mind is where the defendant knows or has reason to believe that the article is an infringing copy. These two aspects to a secondary infringement are discussed below with specific reference to the controllers of forums and bulletin boards.

Dealings

Sections 22 to 26 of the Copyright, Designs and Patents Act 1988 provide the types of dealings in a copyright work that, together with a guilty mind, will constitute a secondary infringement. This section details those dealings that will be applicable to a forum or bulletin board.

Section 23 provides four situations where, with the requisite guilty mind and without licence of the copyright owner, a person will infringe the copyright in a work, as follow.

1. In the course of business he possesses an article which is an infringing copy of the work.
2. He sells or lets for hire, or offers or exposes for sale or hire an article which is an infringing copy of the work.
3. In the course of a business he exhibits in public or distributes an article which is an infringing copy of the work.
4. Otherwise than in the course of a business, he distributes an article which is an infringing copy of the work to such an extent as to affect prejudicially the owner of the copyright.

Infringing copy

An article is an infringing copy if its making constituted an infringement of the work in question.[4] It is presumed that an article was made at the time that copyright subsisted in the work if it is shown that the article is a copy of the work and that copyright subsists, or has subsisted, in the work at any time.[5] This will rarely be at issue in a case and a controller of a forum certainly should not hope to rely on there being no copyright in the alleged infringement unless there is a strong indication otherwise.

---

3 It is not dealt with here, but it also should be considered that there can be secondary infringement of a derogatorily treated copyright work: Copyright, Designs and Patents Act 1988, s 83.
4 Copyright, Designs and Patents Act 1988, s 27(2).
5 Copyright, Designs and Patents Act 1988, s 27(4).

Course of business

A business is defined by the Act to include a trade or profession.[6] A question arises as to under what circumstances will a person 'dealing' with an infringing copy not be seen as doing so in the course of business. The cases which have considered the meaning of 'course of business' all point to the conclusion that a Service Provider hosting a forum or even a newsgroup will do so in the course of business.[7] It is less likely that an individual who hosts a bulletin board purely as an amateur does so in the course of business; of course, even if he does not, he may still be caught under section 23(d) where his distribution is to such an extent as to affect prejudicially the owner of the copyright.

Exhibit, distribute and possess

The four subsections of section 23 use the words 'exhibits', 'distributes' and 'possesses' in relation to infringing articles. There appears to be little doubt that the word 'possesses' carries a wide connotation; the presence on a hard disk drive or memory of a computer would seem to constitute possession. It is for this reason that even if a Service Provider is able to show that no person downloaded a particular file, so that there was no distribution, there may still be secondary infringement by virtue of its storage of the file. Of course, with no distribution any damages will probably be minimal. Section 23(a) will therefore probably be appropriate for any infringement in the course of Internet business.[8]

Where the defendant is operating otherwise than in the course of business, the plaintiff must show distribution. There is no case on what constitutes distribution, but for the Internet two questions will be relevant. Is it distribution to *allow* another person to download a file from a bulletin board? If it is, the next question will be whether the defendant *did* so distribute the infringing article. In this situation, a defendant may allege that the term 'distribution' denotes an active action by the defendant whereas a file is not actually distributed by the bulletin board but by the requester of the file.

Courts and plaintiffs should be careful to unpick such a defence. First, there is nothing to suggest that distribution cannot be passive: the activity is *allowing* the article to be distributed. The second point is more important. When a file is downloaded technically the server is *not* passive: the server responds to a request from another computer. It can deny a request or it can permit downloading of a file to occur. This choice may be compared with deciding or not deciding to put on a van an infringing article to be delivered. In such a situation, there is still distribution even though it may appear that the article has actually 'been collected' by the requester.

Knowledge or reason to believe

This is the most important aspect of secondary infringement: the plaintiff must prove that the defendant knew or had reason to believe that the article is an infringing copy of the work in question. The proof, for the purposes of this

6   Copyright, Designs and Patents Act 1988, s 178.
7   *LA Gear Inc v Hi-Tec Sports plc* [1992] FSR 121 (re copyright); *Davies v Sumner* [1984] 3 All ER 831 (re trade descriptions).
8   It is perhaps an anomaly of the digital world that it is impossible to distribute a digital file without first possessing it.

chapter, can be rephrased as: did the controller of the digital depository know or have reason to believe the file is an infringing copy of the copyright work?

Clearly, in most cases, a plaintiff will be seeking only to show 'reason to believe'; proving knowledge is more onerous than proving a reason to believe. In *LA Gear Inc v Hi-Tec Sports plc*, Morritt J decided that 'reason to believe',[9]

> 'must involve the concept of knowledge of facts from which a reasonable man would arrive at the relevant belief. Facts from which a reasonable man might suspect the relevant conclusion cannot be enough. Moreover, as it seems to me, the phrase does connote the allowance of a period of time to enable the reasonable man to evaluate those facts so as to convert the facts into a reasonable belief.'

On appeal the court upheld this decision for, in Nourse LJ's words, substantially the same reasons as those given by Morritt J. The principle has again been applied by the Court of Appeal in *ZYX Music GmbH v Chris King*.[10] The test would be applied as follows: the plaintiff should prove that the facts known by or brought to the attention of the controller would have made the reasonable *controller of such a bulletin board* believe that the file is infringing. This need not be immediate; a period of time may elapse during which the reasonable controller may come to the belief. If this is satisfied, the actual controller may rebut the allegation by proving that facts in his knowledge made him believe that the article was not infringing.[11]

Reasonable belief on the Internet

The application of this test to the Internet is vexed. On the one hand, bulletin board operators are fully aware that pirated software and copyright infringing images are posted on their servers. In some situations this will be enough to indicate that a posting is an infringing article. On the other hand, this general knowledge may not be enough to prove a reasonable belief: the very 'work in question' must have been reasonably thought to be infringing.[12] Also, knowing that many postings on a bulletin board *are* infringing does not translate into a reasonable knowledge that a *particular* posting is an infringement.[13]

Three American cases have considered, under a different copyright law to our own,[14] the position of a bulletin board operator who has distributed infringing copyright material.[15] At the outset it should be understood that in each of these

---

9   [1992] FSR 121 at 129.
10 Court of Appeal (20 February 1997, unreported).
11 The reversal of the burden is suggested in Laddie, Prescott and Vitoria's *The Modern Law of Copyright and Designs* (Butterworths, London, 1995, 2nd edn) at para 10.6.
12 Copyright, Designs and Patents Act 1988, s 27(3)(b).
13 See *Columbia Picture Industries v Robinson* [1986] FSR 367.
14 There is no statutory rule of liability for infringement committed by others under American law. Instead, the American courts have sought to rely on principles of contributory liability. (See *Sony Corpn v Universal City Studios Inc* 464 US 417 at 435 (1984).) Liability for participation in infringement will be established where the defendant, 'with knowledge of the infringing activity, induces, causes or materially contributes to the infringing conduct of another': *Gershwin Publishing Corpn v Columbia Artists Management Inc* 443 F 2d 1159, 1162 (2d Cir 1971). This is clearly a different and more arduous test. Under English law secondary infringement concentrates on the knowledge that an article is infringing; American law focuses on the role of the secondary infringer *in that infringement*.
15 This author has not considered under copyright law the case brought by the United States against David LaMacchia. 871 F Supp 535 (D Mass 1994).

cases the operators of the board either actively encouraged the posting of copyright images and files or actually took an active role in the copying personally. It is submitted therefore that little of the legal reasoning is capable of importation to an English case where the bulletin board operator has no active role.

Playboy Enterprises v George Frena

In *Playboy Enterprises Inc v George Frena*, Frena operated a bulletin board on a subscription basis.[16] The board stored copies of *Playboy*'s pictures but these were not posted there without Frena's reasonable belief: he actually removed from the photographs *Playboy*'s own text and substituted his own name and contact details. Under English law, any reasonable operator who did such an activity would then certainly have (or be deemed to have) the requisite reasonable belief that the uploaded images infringed *Playboy*'s copyright. Frena admitted that every one of the alleged images that infringed is substantially similar to the *Playboy* image from which the copy is produced.[17]

Sega Enterprises Ltd v Maphia

In a similar case, *Sega Enterprises Ltd v Maphia*, the defendants Maphia and Scherman operated a bulletin board that actively solicited the uploading of infringing Sega computer games.[18] Information on the board included the following notice:[19]

> 'Thank you for purchasing a Console BackUp Unit [copier] from Parsec Trading [the defendants]. As a free bonus for ordering from Dark Age, you receive a complementary Free Download Ratio on our Customer Support BBS. This is if you cannot get a hold of SuperNintendo or Sega Genesis games. *You can download up to 10 megabytes, which is equal to approximately 20 normal-sized Super-Nintendo or Genesis games.*'

Again, like the *Frena* case, the operators of this bulletin board were in full knowledge of their infringements. Indeed, the operators even encouraged the posting of other infringing files in return for other such goods such as copiers.[20] Under English law the defendants would also be found to have the requisite guilty mind. However, the extreme circumstances of the case must not be forgotten at the expense of the decision. This is not akin to a forum controller who does not encourage or solicit the posting of infringing files.

---

16   839 F Supp 1552 (MD Fla 1993). This case is more akin to a *primary* infringement suit: it was demonstrated by *Playboy* that Frena, himself, copied the images (at 1556).
17   Under English law, a comparison that reveals two identical images can lead a court to infer the reasonable belief of infringement. See *LA Gear Inc v Hi-Tec Sports plc* [1992] FSR 121; *A P Besson Ltd v Fulleon Ltd* [1986] FSR 319.
18   Preliminary injunction: 857 F Supp 679 (ND Cal 1994). Permanent injunction: No C93-04262 CW (ND Cal, 18 December 1996).
19   Keene Decl Exh 5B at 2.
20   857 F Supp 679 (ND Cal 1994) at 683–684.

Religious Technology Centre v Netcom Online Communications Services Inc

In the well-publicised summary judgment *Religious Technology Center v Netcom Online Communications Services Inc*, a member of the centre left the religion and then published the centre's materials through a Netcom connection on a Usenet newsgroup: alt.religion.scientology.[1] The centre sued Netcom for both direct and contributory infringement of copyright. While the court was sure that there was no direct infringement, it was clear that the plaintiffs[2]

> 'raised a genuine issue of fact regarding whether Netcom should have known that Erlich [the former member] was infringing their copyright after receiving a letter [fixing them with notice] from plaintiffs, whether Netcom substantially participated in the infringement, and whether Netcom has a valid fair use defense. *Accordingly, Netcom is not entitled to summary judgment on plaintiffs' claim of contributory copyright infringement.*'

This Netcom case is probably the closest that a court has come to ruling on the liability of a controller of a forum in relation to postings made without solicitation. And the court decided that the issue should be decided at full trial. Even at full trial,[3] it is submitted that the difference between American and English law for both infringement and defences[4] will make little of the judgment applicable to a similar English dispute. This said, there are two rough statements that can be drawn from this analysis of English law and American cases.

One main infringer for newsgroup

There are two types of server that are involved with any infringing posting made to a Usenet newsgroup. First, the server, generally the Service Provider, through whom the posting was made; and second, all the other servers who also host that newsgroup who will automatically receive copies of the posting. The secondary servers will only be secondary infringers for an infringing posting where they are provided with specific notice of this, or the newsgroup as a whole is so obviously designed for infringing material that one would have to turn[5]

> 'a blind eye to an inquiry which he should have known he ought to have made.'

An example of this is a newsgroup that has an obviously dubious title such as 'alt.copyright.infringements'.

The primary server (that is the server on whose system a file was initially posted) can be liable for secondary infringement in a wider set of circumstances. First, if alerted to an infringement by being fixed with the facts; it is a foolhardy controller

---

1 No C-95-20091 RMW (ND Cal, 21 November 1995).
2 Emphasis added.
3 The action was entirely settled on 22 August 1996.
4 For infringement see fn 14 at page 201; as to defences, under American law the exclusive rights under 17 USC section 106 are limited by the section 107 defence of 'fair use'. This 'permits and requires courts to avoid rigid application of the copyright statute when, on occasion, it would stifle the very creativity which that law is designed to foster': *Campbell v Acuff-Rose Music Inc* 114 S Ct 1164 at 1170 (1994). This, together with Congress's four non-exclusive factors, differs greatly from the defences under the Copyright, Designs and Patents Act 1988, Chapter III.

who continues to store a file after he has been put on such notice. The second source of liability is where a particular member is known or is justifiably accused of posting copyright infringements. No court could demand that a Service Provider screen every message and every file, but, if the reasonable controller would have suspected the activities of a certain member, the actual controller should act to check at least some of the member's postings. Very often the name given to the posting will be indicative of the nature of the file.

Commercial forums

Commercial forums, as opposed to Usenet newsgroups, have a far tighter control over the postings made to their service. This is because, first, they are the ultimate judge of any type of forum set up on their system. If they choose to allow a forum called 'Star Wars Clips' it is more than likely that its contents will infringe copyright. It is also likely that a court will deem that the title alone provided sufficient facts to put the controller on notice of infringements. The owner of a commercial forum should therefore choose carefully the forums that he permits to be stored on his server. The second rein of control is over each member. Rogue members can be cut off from access to the forum unless they agree to a method of practice; indeed, certain services now provide extra usage credits for members who 'whistle-blow' on copyright infringers.

If, despite these two protective mechanisms, a copyright infringement is posted on a forum, it is submitted a controller will not be deemed to have reason to believe that the article is infringing *unless*: notice is already provided to the controller; or, the controller has a moderator of the forum. All moderators, therefore, should be given the authority to remove any potentially infringing posting immediately. As a mirror to this, agreements with members should include a term that the moderator has the ultimate right to purge a posting.

Not reasonable care

As a final point, Service Providers and controllers of forums should be aware that the Copyright, Designs and Patents Act 1988 does not impose any minimum standard of care. In each individual case a court will assess whether a controller had reason to believe that a particular posting infringed copyright. If controllers do not become involved through either moderating or actively soliciting such material it will be difficult to prove the belief unless it is obvious from, say, the forum name. In contrast, the Defamation Act 1996 demands that, to benefit from the defence of publishing defamatory material, one must not have a guilty mind *and* must have taken reasonable care. Providers and controllers may therefore be better advised to concentrate their vetting procedures on defamatory material rather than copyright infringements.

WEB SITES

This section now looks to the other side of the coin and considers how the copyright in a web site may be infringed. This is an issue often overlooked by those who deal with the World Wide Web; merely because a site is available for all to view does not mean that all the images and applets and text can be used at will.

Backup copies

Some users believe that a web site comes complete with an implied licence to take a backup copy, on disk rather than the normal memory only.[6] This is unlikely to be implied by either the courts or the law. It has been discussed that a web site is a program for the purposes of copyright. Under the Copyright, Designs and Patents Act 1988, section 50A(1) lawful users of a computer program do not infringe copyright by making a backup copy of it *which it is necessary for him to have for the purposes of his lawful use*. It will rarely be necessary to take a backup copy of a web site. The material that is being backed up is already available 24 hours a day on the web site that originally supplied it. It may be *convenient* not to have to re-access a web site but is seldom *necessary*. And as more owners of web sites sell advertising on their pages they will be increasingly aware of the need to have viewers re-accessing their pages. The more 'hits' on a page each hour, the more one can charge advertisers for space.

Increasingly, however, web sites have explicit restrictions on copying in certain situations. Viewers and users of web sites should be cautious of these restrictions which may be found in the context of a positive licence. Some prevent viewers from even making a printed copy of a site.[7] Other sites prevent the use of their graphics.[8] These explicit licences are not added on site as rhetoric. If contravened it will have the result that the viewer has infringed copyright. If this infringement is then 'advertised' by, say, posting a copied graphic on one's *own* web site, the copyright owner may well take action.

Caching

Related to backup copies are 'caches'. A web cache is a computer with vast storage capacity which holds copies of the most popular pages on the World Wide Web. If this cache is located on the local network, users can be saved the delay of gaining access to the over-burdened site. It also means that the network can restrict access to the Internet, thus reducing the risk from hacking and viruses.

Commercially, a web cache may be unwelcome for a web site owner. Few companies publish on the web out of charity; they wish to advertise, to sell and to find the demographics of those who visit their site. A web cache hides this information from companies. Companies whose sites are cached are unable to establish exactly how many people are 'hitting' their site, and also they cannot find out who makes up their audience. These statistics are one of the aspects of the Internet that are so attractive.

Caching can also adversely affect companies whose income comes from selling advertising space on their pages. To increase this income, these companies often show a different advertisement each time the site is viewed; they 'roll' a number of adverts. This multiplies each page's earnings. Unfortunately, the caching computer stores just one copy of the popular pages. So there will be just one advertiser who

---

5   *Infabrics v Jaytex* [1978] FSR 451 at 464–465.
6   A web site viewed but not saved will not be available for re-viewing after the computer is switched off and then on again. A web site saved to disk will be re-viewable even after the computer has been switched off.
7   Online newspapers are a prime example of this sort of restriction.
8   The popular browsers allow users to copy a graphic to be used as the computer screen's backdrop. This may be infringement by the viewer.

is getting their money's worth. Clearly then, these companies have a commercial objection to caching.

Caching a web page is certainly copying a substantial part of a copyright work. If the site cached has an explicit licence that prevents such copying, that may be the end of any inquiry of infringement. If the licence restricts the storage of the site for access by others, the controller of the caching server may be a primary infringer of copyright. If the site has no express licence it will be difficult for the owner of the web cache to imply an appropriate licence to permit the copying. As has been discussed, the Copyright, Designs and Patents Act 1988 does not allow the copying of a computer program for backup purposes unless this is necessary. Copying the page then to provide it to others on the network is not necessary; it is purely convenient and perhaps safer. Section 50A of the Copyright, Designs and Patents Act 1988 is unlikely to be of much avail.[9]

To be safe, the rights to cache a site should be based only on the express permission of the owner of each site. The courts and the law will not imply this permission so a licence must be sought to avoid infringement.[10]

In-line graphics

The World Wide Web was created to link together documents in a seamless fashion. Like a 'live' footnote, a link on one document can be clicked on and the linked document is then retrieved. The browser replaces the linking document with a freshly retrieved document; this new document may have been stored on an different web server. A browser can also be instructed to display on one screen a collage of images and text all from different web servers *at the same time*.[11] This will appear to the viewer as one document from one source; in fact and at law there are a number of different owners of the copyright in these images and some of them may see this selective copying as an infringement of copyright.

The copyright owner of a computer graphic used within a web site has the right to license, or choose not to license almost any use of the image.[12] What is questionable is whether it is an infringement, not to copy another's graphics, but instead to include a command that instructs the *viewer's* computer to copy those graphics. Although this is untested in the courts, it is submitted that, inclusion without permission of the owner of these in-line graphics may infringe their copyright. It was mentioned above that copyright is not only infringed by the copying of a work.[13]

The Copyright, Designs and Patents Act 1988, section 24(1)(a) provides that it is a secondary infringement to make an unlicensed article specifically designed or adapted for making copies of the copyright work when the maker knows or has reason to believe that it is to be used to make infringing copies. It is submitted that a line of code can be an article and that as the URL refers to a specific graphic on

---

9   Caching is also unlikely to benefit from a fair dealing defence. A court is unlikely to view as 'fair' wholesale copying of a commercial creation justified purely on the grounds of making it 'easier' to access this information. This said, universities who restrict access to their caching server to students may be able to claim a defence under the Copyright, Designs and Patents Act 1988, s 29 (research and private study) or s 32 (things done for the purposes of instruction or examination).

10   Copyright, Designs and Patents Act 1988, s 16(2).

11   Cf 'Constituent elements', at page 178.

12   See 'Graphics', at page 180.

13   See 'All infringement is not copying', at page 188.

a specific web site this article is specifically designed for making copies of a work.[14] The final requirement is a guilty mind that the article would be used to make infringing copies.[15] This also is satisfied. Unless the viewer turns off the automatic loading of images, the programmer of the code knows that a copy will be made of the graphic. As the programmer is the person who has electronically contacted the graphic's true site, this person will *know* that the copy will infringe. It will be outside the bounds of most implied or explicit licences on web sites. It is clearly arguable that using in-line graphics without a licence is secondary copyright infringement.

Jurisdiction over infringement

This section considers the type of situation where a United Kingdom copyright work on the Internet is dealt with abroad in a way that would be an infringement if here. The sort of situation considered is where a web developer in America uses a United Kingdom copyright graphic on his web site that is maintained in Holland but accessed throughout the world. In this situation do the English courts have any jurisdiction to hear complaints of infringement from the United Kingdom copyright owner?

INFRINGEMENT ABROAD

The English court's approach to foreign infringement of English intellectual property has already been met in relation to trade marks.[16] The conclusions reached there are equally applicable here. For the sake of completeness, at the sacrifice of brevity, they will also be repeated here. Infringement is a legal term in relation to a legal right granted within a territory. One cannot infringe a United Kingdom copyright abroad because 'abroad' is outside the width of the monopoly granted by the United Kingdom legislation.[17]

> 'The owner of the copyright in a work has, in accordance with the following provisions of this Chapter, the exclusive right to do the following acts *in the United Kingdom* ...'

One can perform actions in relation to a United Kingdom copyright work that are the *descriptive* equivalent of infringement but those actions will not *be* infringement unless within the United Kingdom territory. Courts have been restraining the rights of copyright holders in this way for many years.

> 'It is therefore clear that copyright under the English Act is strictly defined in terms of territory. The intangible right which is copyright is merely a right to do certain acts exclusively in the United Kingdom:

14 Unlike a tape recorder that makes copies per se rather than makes copies of specific CDs.
15 It is the requirement of this element that ensures that the Service Providers who store such a web site will not be secondary infringers for possessing the article in the course of a business. Few plaintiffs will be able to show the reason to believe that a web site uses unlicensed in-line graphics unless they have put the Provider on notice.
16 See 'Jurisdiction over infringement', above.
17 Copyright, Designs and Patents Act 1988, s 16(1). Emphasis added.

only acts *done* in the United Kingdom constitute infringement either direct or indirect of that right.'[18]

The dicta above are with reference to an activity carried on *outside* the United Kingdom that is purported to be an infringement *inside* the United Kingdom. The courts are attempting to resolve the conflict of laws where the intellectual property right is dealt with in a territory other than the one that granted the right initially. To illustrate, to copy in America a United Kingdom literary work is clearly outside the jurisdiction of the English courts: the action that constitutes the infringement occurs outside the United Kingdom. But these are not the only types of infringement. There are situations where the *action* takes place outside the United Kingdom, but the *infringement* occurs within the territory.[19]

Authorise to infringe

In *ABKCO Music and Records Inc v Music Collection International Ltd* the Court of Appeal was faced with an authorisation to infringe made from abroad.[20] ABKCO claimed a British copyright over certain sound recordings made by Sam Cooke. The second defendant was a Danish company that carried on no business in the United Kingdom but that did grant a licence to the first defendant to manufacture and sell copies of the sound recordings in the United Kingdom.

ABKCO sued under the Copyright, Designs and Patents Act 1988, section 16(2) that,[1]

'[c]opyright in a work is infringed by a person who without the licence of the copyright owner does, *or authorises another to do*, any of the acts restricted by copyright.'

The restricted act complained of being authorised was the copying and issue of copies of the work to the public.[2] The Court of Appeal had to consider two discrete legal issues: was an authorisation made abroad within the jurisdiction of the English courts? The second issue was the substantive one: was the granting of a licence an authorisation under the Act?

Hoffmann LJ was clear, even in the face of the general authority,[3] that for authorisations of infringement the Copyright, Designs and Patents Act 1988 did apply to foreigners.[4]

'It does not matter that the acts which preceded that consequence [of infringement] all took place abroad. It is I think sufficient that the definition of a tort requires an act and that that act is performed within the United Kingdom, however it may be linked to the preliminary act performed abroad.'

18   *Def Lepp Music v Stuart-Brown* [1986] RPC 273 at 275.
19   It is also possible that, because of the Brussels Convention, Arts 2 and 6(1), an infringer is sued in a contracting state other than the state which vested the copyright in the plaintiff. See fn 20 at page 157.
20   [1995] RPC 657.
1   Emphasis added.
2   Copyright, Designs and Patents Act 1988, s 16(1).
3   *Clark (Inspector of Taxes) v Oceanic Contractors Inc* [1983] 2 AC 130 at 144–145.
4   [1995] RPC 657 at 660. Agreed to by Neill LJ.

As a final indication of the common sense of this approach Lord Justice Hoffmann added,[5]

> 'I think that a territorial limitation on the act of authorising would lead to anomalies. Anyone contemplating the grant of a licence to do an act restricted by copyright would be able to avoid liability simply by having the document executed abroad.'

This case teaches that for authorisation the place of communication is irrelevant so long as the authority is to do an infringing act within the jurisdiction. This reasoning can be applied to the Internet, specifically, the World Wide Web.[6]

Bounds of authority

An authorisation has been defined as,[7]

> 'a grant or purported grant, which may be expressed or implied, of the right to do the act complained of.'

This raises an interesting issue which can best be raised with an illustration.

---

30. A programmer in Brazil copies an entire Applet from an English web site. As the copying takes place outside the United Kingdom, the UK copyright is not infringed. The Brazilian then places the Applet onto his own web site which can be accessed around the world. An individual accesses the web site from the United Kingdom. Necessarily the applet is copied onto the individual's own computer. This will constitute a copy under the Copyright, Designs and Patents Act 1988. As the applet's copyright owner has not provided a licence to copy this work the Brazilian is actually providing an authorisation to infringe a United Kingdom copyright. This is an infringement within the jurisdiction of the English courts.

This illustration indicates that one who copies a United Kingdom copyright work from elsewhere but then allows it to be retrieved over the Internet will be providing authority to infringe the copyright. The reason for this is that the Internet does not transport copyright works; it allows them to be copied. So to put an infringing work on the Internet should always be viewed as an authorisation to copy the work, infringing it once more. To counter this, a foreign defendant would have to resist the court's jurisdiction, or prove that the work was not copied within the United Kingdom.[8]

---

5   [1995] RPC 657 at 660–661.
6   There is a risk that infringement actions based on the Copyright, Designs and Patents Act 1988, ss 17, 18, or 19 will be viewed by the courts as 'occurring' outside the jurisdiction.
7   *CBS Songs Ltd v Amstrad Consumer Electronics plc* [1988] AC 1013 at 1054 per Lord Templeman, HL.
8   The mere existence of the infringing work on a web site that *can* be accessed from the United Kingdom should be enough on which to base a *quia timet* action unless the site is blocked access from the United Kingdom.

This may strike some as being a conclusion that strikes at the heart of the Internet itself. To intellectual property owners, on the other hand, it is serious and worrying if a work can be copied without permission outside the United Kingdom but then freely distributed within the United Kingdom without fear of litigation. The law will apply to the individual abroad where that individual seeks to erode, using the transnational scope of the Internet, the rights that an owner has over a work within the territory. The law will certainly apply to those domiciled in contracting states who seek to infringe UK copyright works.[9]

Other 'foreign' infringements

The reasoning used in relation to authorisations may also apply to other types of primary infringement. A plaintiff may allege that the issuing of copies occurs where the copies are received. By this reasoning, a web site holding material infringing a United Kingdom copyright can be construed as issuing the copies within the United Kingdom, so within our courts' jurisdiction.[10] This author doubts the strength of such a pleading.[11] The location of the activity of issuing copies is more likely to be construed as being the place *from where* copies are issued, rather than where they are received.[12]

ENFORCEMENT OF COPYRIGHT ABROAD

To sue the authoriser of the infringement over the Internet is simply a case of viewing the authorisation as a tort and proceeding on the basis of a tort committed within the jurisdiction. The defendant will have to be served with the writ outside the jurisdiction.

9   See fn 19 at page 207.
10   Copyright, Designs and Patents Act 1988, s 18(2).
11   It is submitted that it is also a weak allegation that a visual or acoustic presentation, a primary infringement, occurs where it is seen or heard: Copyright, Designs and Patents Act 1988, s 19(2)(b).
12   See fn 5 at page 168. Cf the concept of 'distributes' in *Playboy Enterprises Inc v Chuckleberry Publishing Inc* (DC SNY, 79 Civ 3525, 19 June 1996). The reasoning in this case would be applicable to a secondary infringer under the Copyright, Designs and Patents Act 1988, s 23(c) or (d).

Chapter five
Crime

Unauthorised access to property, damage to property, theft, distribution of obscene and indecent material are all familiar crimes. Under new guises all are possible using the Internet. This chapter considers these crimes in the context of present and future developments on the Internet.

Unauthorised access to computer material is becoming more prevalent, and with our increasing reliance on computers, more serious. The United States' General Account Office discovered that, in 1995, hackers using the Internet broke into the US Defense Department's computer more than 160,000 times.[2] The Office's report stated that:

> 'At a minimum, these attacks are a multimillion-dollar nuisance to Defense. At worst, they are a serious threat to national security.'

It is also predictable that the proliferation of commerce on the Internet will be matched by an expansion of crime on the Internet. The rise in the use of digital cash and credit cards over the Internet provides a greater incentive to hack than ever before. Even the rise of password-protected web sites will be a lure for hackers; simply to wreak havoc.[3]

This chapter envisages a corresponding rise in the spread of computer viruses also. This is because of a technical change in the material being sent over the Internet. There has always been a threat from computer viruses which are spread over the Internet. However, the growth in transmission of executable code over the Internet provides an increased number of hosts from which viruses may be contracted.

What is more distasteful is that the Internet is also being extensively used by paedophiles who take advantage of the ease with which images and movies,

---

1   UNIX operating system security. *AT&T Bell Laboratories Technical Journal*, 63(8, Part 2):1649–1672, October 1984.
2   *Financial Times*, 24 May 1996.
3   A large number of web sites use a version of server software which leaves their systems very vulnerable to hacking. 'It is not the case that you can stick up a web site and assume it will be secure forever.' Netcraft Web Consultants, http://www.netcraft.com.

encrypted from the prying eyes of the authorities, can be transmitted in a matter of seconds. The case most shocking in this area is of a Roman Catholic priest who admitted to having built up a library of over 11,000 paedophilic digital images and communicating with an international paedophile ring using e-mail. In passing a six-year sentence Moses J said to the convicted priest:[4]

> 'you lived up to your fantasies, fuelled by pornography to which you had access through the Internet.'

All these crimes, and the evidence needed to prosecute them, are examined as follows.

1. When does one commit the computer misuse crime of unauthorised access using the Internet?
2. How does the more serious computer misuse offence of unauthorised access with ulterior motive address the wrongful interception of digital cash?
3. What are the laws and how do they control the electronic spread of viruses, logic bombs and other malicious code?
4. For crimes committed over the Internet, what is the special significance and difficulty of adducing computer-generated evidence?
5. Those who gain unauthorised access to computers often follow the same pattern; what are the key legal issues involved in their techniques?
6. What is the English courts' jurisdiction over criminals who use the Internet and how may they be extradited?
7. What are the criminal laws that apply to obscene digital articles, and more serious indecent photographs?

TYPES OF COMPUTER MISUSE

Broadly, there are three main types of computer misuse. First, there is unauthorised access, or 'hacking'. This is where a person without authority physically or electronically penetrates a computer system. This may be compared with breaking and entering, where no further offence is intended or then committed. The second type of digital crime is the more serious form of unauthorised access. This is where a person without authority accesses a computer with the intention to commit a further offence such as theft. Distinct from unauthorised access is the third type of digital crime: destruction of digital information, or the impairment of access to digital information. A common example of this is a computer virus which may prevent a computer from working.

The unique legal question in relation to all these three crimes is who or what is actually the victim? Everything which exists in a computer is represented as zeros and ones. These binary digits, or bits, are generally stored using a magnetic medium. So, to destroy a computer file a person may only have to change the state of, say, 100 bits from one, on, to zero, off. Before the Computer Misuse Act 1990, courts were forced to wrestle with older statutes which concerned physical property to fit the misuse of new technology before them.[5] Even where this was

---

4   (1996) Times, 13 November.
5   Eg Forgery and Counterfeiting Act 1981 in *R v Gold and Shifreen* [1988] 2 All ER 186.

successful, there was an obvious need for legislation to take account of computers. Prosecutions were troublesome.[6]

The legislative solution

To counter the distrust of computers which was emerging, stemming from the ineffectiveness of the criminal law to deal with computer viruses and hacking, Parliament introduced the Computer Misuse Act 1990; an Act:[7]

> 'to safeguard the integrity – what I call the trustworthiness – of computers'.

The Act introduced three new criminal offences:[8]

1. digital browsing through a computer without authority;
2. such unauthorised browsing with intent to commit or facilitate the commission of further offences;
3. unauthorised modification of computer material.

This section takes a split approach to examine the role and strength of this legislation in practice. First, the prohibitions are dissected in relation to the Internet in particular. Second, a typical hacking scenario is analysed.[9]

UNAUTHORISED ACCESS

The discussion of hacking in relation to the Internet necessarily focuses on the Computer Misuse Act 1990. It is crucial to understand that it is often easy to prove the conduct aspect of the offence, the *actus reus*. The structure of the Act is such that, where the Internet is involved, it is almost impossible for a defendant to interact in any way with a victim computer without satisfying the physical requirements of the section of 'causing the performance of a function'. The tough burden on the prosecution lies elsewhere. It is proving the necessary intention and satisfying the rules to admit computer-generated evidence. Before considering these burdens it is necessary to appreciate the ambit of the activity required to satisfy the conduct aspect of the offence.

---

6   In an obvious signal to Parliament, Lord Brandon in *R v Gold and Shifreen* said, 'there is no reason to regret the failure of what [Lord Lane CJ] aptly described as the Procrustean attempt to force the facts of the present case into the language of an Act not designed to fit them.' [1988] 2 WLR 984 at 991.
7   Michael Colvin MP, *Hansard* HC volume 166, column 1134.
8   Computer Misuse Act 1990, ss 1, 2 and 3. Recently the CPS has broadened the scope of the Act by bringing cases of conspiracy to commit an offence 'with persons unknown'.
9   See Cheswick WR and Bellovin SM, *Firewalls and Internet Security* (Addison-Wesley Publishing Company, Wokingham, 1995).

Section I conduct or *actus reus*

Section 1 creates the summary offence. The details of the *actus reus* are set out in full below: the first subsection of section 1 of the Computer Misuse Act 1990.

> '1. (1) A person is guilty of an offence if –
> (a) he causes a computer to perform any function with intent to secure access to any program or data held in any computer;
> (b) the access he intends to secure is unauthorised; and
> (c) he knows at the time when he causes the computer to perform the function that that is the case.'

There are two main questions which must be addressed in relation to this section. First, what is required to cause a computer to perform a function? Second, what is entailed in securing access to any program or data?

Computer, data and programs

The conduct element of a section 1 offence is causing a computer to perform any function with intent to secure access to any program or data held in any computer. At an early stage it should be noted that the words 'program', 'data' and 'computer' are not defined by the Act.[10]

COMPUTERS ON THE INTERNET

The Computer Misuse Act 1990 does not define 'computer'. This will no doubt cause problems for the prosecution seeking to prove, say, that a car's computerised braking system which has been tampered with has been the victim of a section 1 offence. The absence of the definition will not cause any difficulties, however, for proving unauthorised access over the Internet. For a machine to be a victim or conduit of hacking over the Internet, that machine must be a computer within any reasonable definition. The very nature of the Internet is that it joins together networks of computers.[11] For the purposes of this chapter, therefore, where the hacking is conducted over the Internet, the functioning 'machine' and accessed 'machine' will both be considered as computers within the ambit of section 1.

---

10 Mr Harry Cohen MP did attempt to amend the Act at the Committee Stage with a definition of the word 'computer'. This was unsuccessful. Cf Law Commission No 186 on the Computer Misuse at para 3.39: 'it would be unnecessary and indeed might be foolish, to attempt to define computer . . . We cannot think that there will ever be serious grounds for arguments based on the ordinary meaning of the term "computer".'

11 It is not doubted that the *future* of the Internet is away from the conception of simply linking computers as such but more towards connecting together 'intelligent appliances'. 'Movies, television programs, and all sorts of other digital information will be stored on "servers", which are computers with capacious disks. Servers will provide information for use anywhere on the network.' Gates B, *The Road Ahead CD-ROM* (Penguin, 1995), on screen 67.

PROGRAMS AND DATA ON THE INTERNET

The terms 'program' and 'data' within section 1 are also left undefined by the Act. As with 'computer' these terms were left undefined for fear of a definition becoming outdated by technological developments. That said, it remains crucial for a computer misuse prosecution that the conduct element of the offence, the *actus reus*, is proved and, therefore, that the two terms are understood in a reasonable context.

The main difficulty with these terms is understanding what, other than 'a program' or 'data', *can* be accessed in a computer. The answer is that the terms program and data do encapsulate all that can be accessed *digitally* in a computer. But if the terms were absent from the section, one could commit a section 1 offence by turning off a computer before prising open the casing. Turning off the computer causes it to perform a function, and opening its metal casing would be accessing the computer in the physical sense.

In summary, the absence of definitions should not concern a court where the accused has used the Internet to gain access to information which resides in a digital form. In this form, the information will constitute data or a program within the ambit of the relevant section.

I. **A company runs a home page with details of relevant news stories. Users pay a subscription and, in return, are given a password to grant them access to the page. A hacker attempts to use a password which he has not paid for in order to enter the home page to read the stories. Home pages are constructed using a computer language called HTML, and much of a home page's content is data. The hacker is intending to secure access to a program and its associated data without authority.**

Held in any computer

Before examining the remainder of section 1 and its application to the Internet, this section analyses the notion of data or programs being 'held in a computer'. A computer can be reasonably thought as to include the processing unit, its memory and storage devices. Computers are simple machines; they are so simple that they can purely store and work with two numbers: a zero and a one. But that sentence illustrates one division which exists within a computer: it *stores* and it *works*; it executes instructions on those numbers. The central processing unit of a computer is able to store very few of these numbers at one time but is able to process them very quickly: it is where all the real work is performed. However, certain other physical parts of the computer cannot process or work with these numbers: they can only store them. Examples of these are the computer's hard disk drive and its memory. These are purely components of a computer that can store vast quantities of digital information.

Section 17(6) clarifies the phrase 'held in a computer' by providing that it includes references to data or programs held in any removable storage medium which is in the computer for the time being. This particular inclusion refers to the possibility of obtaining access to the data or program which is stored on a floppy disk: these allow the storage of small quantities of data, but are physically small and portable. A CD-ROM is a further example of a removable storage medium. Section 17(6) does not define the term and seeks only to clarify the phrase 'held in a computer' with one example, one inclusion. 'Held in a computer' may therefore also be reasonably read to include data or programs which are stored away from the processing unit of a computer, but accessible by it.

> **2. A hacker uses an authorised person's password to login to a UK insurance company's computer. The hacker is hoping to gain access to the company's customer details. The computer to which he logs into stores these details in a huge data storage unit which is located elsewhere. The data itself is stored on a magnetic tape. The processing unit of the computer retrieves this information through fibre-optic cables. The computer would be thought to include the magnetic tape, and so the data would still be considered as being 'held in a computer'.**

Performing any function

If it is concluded that any machine which is connected to the Internet will fall into the category of 'computer' in section 1(1), it is then necessary to establish how one causes that computer to perform a function. The word 'function' is also undefined within the Act, but the interpretation section of the Act provides some indication of the wide scope of the term. It appears that there is no activity which one can perform in relation to a computer which does not cause a function to be performed. Even typing on a computer's keyboard or using an input device, such as a mouse, will alter the state of the computer's processor. This alteration has been effected by the person causing the computer to perform a function.

FUNCTION ON ANY COMPUTER

The computer performing the function does not need to be the same computer on which the data or programs are stored. So, a client computer, being made to perform a function, which is intended to secure access *to the server computer*, falls within the ambit of section 1(1). Section 1(1) also encompasses the use of a home computer to login to an Internet Service Provider from which the user intends to penetrate another computer. The home computer is caused to perform a function, and so is the Internet Service Provider's computer.

Where a hacker uses the Internet to attempt to gain access to a victim computer, signals may pass through many computers, as described in this book's introduction, before reaching the victim. What is important to the prosecution though, is that each of these intermediary computers is caused to perform a function. And the cause of the performance of this function is the instructions which the hacker has provided to the first computer in the chain. This allows the prosecution to rely on the functioning of *any* computer in the chain to establish this aspect of the *actus reus*. What is difficult for the prosecution to prove is that the *accused* was the cause of the performance of this function. This difficulty is considered in greater depth below.[12]

---

12   See 'Evidence' at page 233.

> **3. A hacker uses a stolen mobile phone to access an unauthorised account at an Internet Service Provider. For a section 1 offence, the prosecution does not need to prove that the hacker's own computer was made to function: the Internet Service Provider's computers will suffice. The prosecution may have a problem in proving that it was the accused who caused this function.**

UNSUCCESSFUL ATTEMPTS

The broad drafting of section 1 and its application to the Internet has the effect that even unsuccessful hackers can be guilty of the offence. Usually to gain unauthorised access a person must enter a login procedure, and masquerade as another, or attempt to bypass the login procedure altogether. In the first instance, if the victim computer rejects the unauthorised login, the person has caused at least two computers to function: his own, and the victim computer. The victim computer has performed a function: it rejected the hacker. Where the hacker attempts to login with the requisite intention, a guilty mind, despite being unsuccessful the hacker may have committed the offence.

Of course, the difficulty for the prosecution in such a situation is proving that the victim computer did foil the attempt, and proving that the attempt was made by the accused. This will be hard unless the victim computer maintains a log of all unsuccessful logins as well as successful ones.[13] It is more technically complex to prove the source of an unsuccessful login, weakening further a prosecution.

If the person is somehow able to bypass the standard login procedure, this bypassing itself will constitute the function. If the standard procedure for the victim computer is to ask for login details from each person wishing to gain access, by avoiding this the person must be causing the computer to perform a function.

> **4. A hacker oversees a password being entered by someone logging-in to a remote computer. The login prompt specifies that you must be authorised to access the computer. Later, the hacker then attempts to use the password himself. Because the remote computer only allows one login each day, the unauthorised login attempt is rejected by the computer. This would still constitute a section 1 offence: the rejection constitutes a function and this function was caused by the hacker using a password at the wrong time.**

AUTOMATIC CAUSATION OF A FUNCTION

Most hackers will automate part of the process of unauthorised access. For example, a home page may require two items of information from each of its users to allow them to enter the site. The first may be the person's name, followed by the second, their password, which is say a number seven digits long. To penetrate this site digitally a hacker may write an automatic login program. Its first task is to enter a common name, 'John Smith'. The hacker's program then tries to enter the

---

13   Evidence used to convict one hacker consisted of a log which *his computer* maintained of all functions!

password. First the password 0000001 is tried. If the victim computer rejects this as being incorrect, the login program will simply increase the password number to 0000002. Often after a number of unsuccessful attempts, the victim computer will reject the attempting client. If this occurs, the hacker's program will simply re-enter the URL into the browser and repeat the attempts starting, now of course, from 0000003.

As automation usually plays some part in hacking, it is necessary to address whether this may constitute a section 1 offence.[14] The key question is whether a computer has been caused to perform a function. The running of the hacker's program would constitute the conduct element of the offence. It is at the point of executing that code that a computer is caused to perform a function, so the physical element of the offence can be made out. Establishing the intention for this automated hacking is less straightforward.

Securing access

The Computer Misuse Act 1990 prescribes that securing access to a program or data is established where the defendant, by causing a computer to perform a function:[15]

'(a) alters or erases the program or data;
(b) copies or moves it to any storage medium other than that in which it is held or to a different location in the storage medium in which it is held;
(c) uses it; or
(d) has it output from the computer in which it is held (whether by having it displayed or in any other manner)'.

The purpose of considering this aspect of section 1 is to establish the *intention* of the defendant to secure access to any program or data held in any computer.[16] That the defendant actually *did* secure such access, a question of fact, may bolster the case that the defendant has the requisite intention; it is not a prerequisite of proving this intention.

---

14   A similar program can be used to search automatically for the vulnerable hosts on the Internet, which, once discovered, may be probed further. See Cheswick WR & Bellovin SM, *Firewalls and Internet Security* (Addison-Wesley Publishing Company, Wokingham, 1995) at page 145. A similar program can be used to scan a range of telephone numbers to test whether they are connected to a modem, and are thus potential targets. Such a program is described in the now deleted book, *The Hacker's Handbook* by Hugo Cornwall (Century Communications, London, 1985).
15   Computer Misuse Act 1990, s 17(2).
16   The author submits that no emphasis should be placed on the Act's use of the word 'secure'. It is the author's understanding that this verb is introduced because, while using the word 'access' as a verb is grammatically dubious, it also makes the word ambiguous. Cf USC, Title 18, Part I, Chapter 47, 1030(a)(1).

WHICH COMPUTER?

It is helpful to consider to which computer section 1(1)(a) refers. Section 1(1)(a) states 'to secure access to any program or data held in *any* computer'.[17] The access does not need to be directed at the computer on which the hacker caused performance of the function. It will now be illustrated that the Computer Misuse Act 1990 leaves very little scope for interacting with a computer over the Internet without that interaction being classified as securing access.

---

5. A hacker uses a Telnet connection to attempt to gain unauthorised access to a company's Intranet. Three main computers are used to attempt the access: the hacker's own computer and the computer to which he connected to by Telnet. This 'distance' alone will not prevent a successful hacking prosecution. The computers that are caused to function are two: the hacker's own, the Telnet computer. That the hacker sought to secure access to data held on a third computer is not a bar to a conviction: it is still 'any computer'.

Copying or moving programs and data

Section 17(2)(b) defines securing access as a person copying or moving data or programs to any storage medium other than that in which it is held or to a different location in the storage medium in which it is held. The word which widens this section dramatically is 'copies'. Computer data and programs cannot even be viewed on a screen without there being copying. To show characters on a screen, the characters making up the program or data are copied from the storage unit, be that memory or a hard-disk drive, to the video memory of the computer. The same is true of a hacker who uses the Internet to view the content of programs or data which are held on a victim's computer. By being able to view their content, a part of those data must have been copied into the memory of the hacker's computer. It therefore appears that viewing files which are held on any computer will constitute securing access to those files.

---

6. A hacker makes a connection to a secured part of a server. Once within this portion of the server the hacker views the contents of a password data file. To avoid drawing attention to the breach in security, the hacker does not make a digital copy of the data file. Nevertheless the hacker has secured access to the file by having read it: to view the file it must have been copied from the storage unit on the server to the memory of the hacker's computer.

Using a program

Section 17(2)(c) states that one secures access to a program if one 'uses it'. The Act elaborates on the meaning and context of this word 'use'. Section 17(3)(a) explains, first, that one uses a computer program if the program is executed. This is, pragmatically, covered by subsection (2)(b). One cannot execute a program without moving or copying it from its original storage medium. This aside, section

17   Emphasis added.

17(3) explains that running a program indicates the gaining of access to that program.

> **7. An employee uses her firm's Intranet to attempt to read the online diary of her supervisor. She is unable to read the diary because the program requests her to enter a password which she does not know. That the diary program is able to reject her attempt shows it had, at the least, been executed. The employee did intend to access the diary program.**

Output of programs or data

It will be remembered that to execute a program one needs to copy that program into another storage medium.[18] Section 17(1)(d) expands the term 'access' by not only including executing a computer program, but also *reading* a computer program. A computer program is made up from a list of instructions. Each instruction tells the computer to perform a function. Some functions are imperceptible, such as moving a byte from one storage area to another. Others make a perceptive difference, for example clearing the screen. Section 17(1)(d) defines securing access as including 'ha[ving the program or data] output from the computer in which it is held . . .'. Section 17(4)(a) refines this section by further defining 'output' as including the instructions of the program being output. So, executing a program over the Internet is deemed to be securing access to it. This was explained above.[19] In addition, merely looking at the instructions which make up the program will also be securing access.

It is crucial that a court appreciates the mischief at which this section is aimed. It is concerned with the 'integrity'[20] of programs and data. It is not directed at subsequent use, or utility, of the digital information compromised. For this reason, section 17(4)(b) clearly expresses that the form of output, whether executable or otherwise, is immaterial. This expression applies also to data: it is of no concern that, say, the data is unusable. The fact that it has been output per se is sufficient to constitute securing access.

> **8. A company, worried about data security, encrypt all data held on their network. Each individual who is permitted to gain access to the data is provided, on disk, with a de-encrypting program. The network security is breached and a hacker prints out some of this data. The hacker has still gained access to that data despite the issue that the output is unreadable. In addition, the data will be deemed to have been copied onto the hacker's computer for printing; this also denotes securing access.**

Erasure or alteration

Subsection (a) of section 17(2) illustrates the final type of access to programs or data: alteration or erasure of programs or data. This would constitute a 'classic'

18   See 'Copying or moving programs and data' at page 219.
19   See 'Using a program' at page 219.
20   See fn 7 at page 213.

hack: data are deleted and programs are altered. Complex issues of proving the program has been altered, where the program itself is the source of that proof (an activity-logging program for example), are covered below.[1]

Section I: intention or *mens rea*

The prosecution must prove the two limbs of the intention aspects of the offence. The first, that the defendant intended to secure access to any program or data held in any computer, has been considerably examined above.[2] Nevertheless, a few additional points are mentioned below. The second limb is that at the time of causing the computer to perform the function the defendant knew that the access intended to secure was unauthorised. This can be a difficult intention to prove where the defendant had limited authority, but is accused of operating outside this authority. A common example of this is where the defendant is an employee of a company and is accused of using the company's Intranet outside their authority.

INTENTION TO SECURE ACCESS

Any computer

Much has been explained about what constitutes securing access; a little needs now to be added to what is an *intention* to secure access. First, it should be reiterated that this intention can be directed at *any* computer. The defendant does not need to have been aware of exactly which computer he was attacking. This suits the Internet: often it is complicated to prove that a person intended to login to a specific computer. This is particularly true where the defendant used a program to check automatically the security, or otherwise, of a computer.

Any program or data

The intention to secure access also does not need to be directed at any particular, or particular kind of, program or data. It is enough that an individual intends to secure access to programs and data per se. The section encompasses the hacker who intends to access a computer with no clear perception of what data or programs will be held on the computer.

UNAUTHORISED

The second limb of intention is focused on the authority of the defendant to secure access. Section 1(1)(b) prescribes that the access the defendant intends to secure be unauthorised. Section 1(1)(c) makes it clear that the person must have the relevant knowledge that the access is unauthorised at the time the computer is forced to perform a function. One can envisage arguments arising as to whether a defendant had the relevant knowledge but it seems that the subsection is relatively restricted in operation.

---

1   See 'Proof of modification' at page 239.
2   See 'Securing access' at page 218.

Outsider

The question of authority is generally not difficult to prove when an 'outsider' to a system uses the Internet to attempt to secure access to any programs or data on the system. Where a person must resort to using 'techniques' to gain access to programs or data, it can be readily inferred that an insecure defence is to claim he did not know he was unauthorised.

Partial authority

The concept of authority is elaborated, but thinly, by section 17(5). This section states that access is unauthorised if the person is not entitled to control access of the kind in question, and the person does not have the consent of the person who does control access.

A person must *know* that he is unauthorised in this sense. The question of fact as to whether the individual knew the limits of his authority will often be a finely balanced one.

> **9. An art gallery uses a web site to advertise forthcoming displays. On its home page it states that the graphics which follow on subsequent pages may not be downloaded to a storage medium. A person saves one of the graphics to his hard disk. The person has authorised access to copy the file to memory, but not to his hard disk. Access was unauthorised; the issue would be whether the evidence would be strong enough to prove that he did not see the limitation to disprove he had the necessary intention.**

This raises an issue of relevance for advisers to server operators. Where a server seeks to provide limited authority, say with an ftp site, the boundaries of this authority must be clearly stated.[3] If not, it will be doubtful an offence has been committed. If publicly available but subject to a limitation, a court will be unenthusiastic to hold that an offence has been committed. What is more, because the intention must have been formed at the time of causing the function, the stipulations of any limitations should be obvious at all times. An ftp site appears to a user as a catalogue of the files and directories on the particular computer. Unless security is in place, a user can secure access to any file without having to pass through any limitations statement. Similarly, with the World Wide Web, it is possible that a person may select a single page of the web site to view, missing the opening page altogether.[4] A viewer may not have seen a limitation statement.

3   A Microsoft web site states the following on its copyright notices page: 'Permission to use, copy and distribute documents and related graphics available from this World Wide Web server ('server') is granted, provided that . . . (2) use of the documents and related graphics available from this Server is for informational and non-commercial purposes only . . . (4) no graphics available from this Server are used, copied or distributed separate from accompanying text.' Accessing the site with the intention to use the graphics in a commercial brochure would therefore constitute a section 1 offence, if these disclaimers were known at the time of downloading the graphic. In this case, the copyright notice appears after the first graphics are shown.
4   This is a very common occurrence where a person uses a search engine to search for a particular term. If the term is found the engine returns not only the site which features the term, but also the exact *page*. It is a regular occurrence that a site's pages will not be viewed in their sequential order.

Insiders

The proliferation of Intranets within organisations creates a potential arena for insiders to secure unauthorised access to programs and data. Disgruntled employees, temporary staff and even happily employed staff may all attempt to read information which is actually out of their authority to view. This is possible where there are various strata within an Intranet each for different users of the network. For example, personnel files may be uploaded to the Intranet but only made available to the personnel department. Before considering the problems of an insider's unauthorised access it is necessary to mention how an insider may access the files.

Direct access to server

An insider can secure access to unauthorised information held on an Intranet through a connected computer, or through the actual server on which the information is held. A legal point must be made about this second technique; it is covered by the Act, despite only one computer being involved. In the early case, *R v Cropp*,[5] Sean Cropp, without authority, entered a discount into a computerised till to obtain key-cutting equipment at 30% of cost. This is a straightforward example of unauthorised access.

Aglionby J, after consulting the statute, held that there was no case to answer. Section 1(1)(a) refers to:

> 'causing a computer to perform any function with intent to secure access to any program or data held in any computer'.

He construed this wording did not apply where only one computer is used; he felt the word 'any' referred to any *other* computer. To confirm this interpretation, Judge Aglionby considered section 17 of the Act. Here, a section 3 offence is described as only addressing:[6]

> 'the computer concerned or *any other* computer . . . It seems to me to be straining language to say that only one computer is necessary'.

Concern at this decision was so widespread that an opinion on a point of law was sought from the Court of Appeal.[7] The question was asked, to commit an offence under section 1(1) does the computer caused to perform a function have to be a different computer to the one in which unauthorised access is intended? The Court of Appeal set the Act back on course.[8]

---

5   *R v Cropp*. Unreported although see [1991] 7 *Computer Law & Practice* 270.
6   Per Aglionby J in *R v Cropp*. Transcript of Shorthand Notes, page 9F. Emphasis added.
7   *A-G's Reference (No 1 of 1991)* under s 36 of the Criminal Justice Act 1972 [1992] 3 All ER 897. Today, the presiding judge may have consulted *Hansard* under the ruling in *Pepper (Inspector of Taxes) v Hart* [1993] 1 All ER 42. While explaining s 1 offences to the House of Commons, Michael Colvin MP added, '[The section] is also aimed at insiders who try to get into parts of the system where they know that they should not be.' *Hansard* HC volume 166, column 1138. Parliament's intention is confirmed by the unanimous opposition to and later withdrawal of Harry Cohen's amendment proposing that 'any computer' be replaced by 'another computer'.
8   [1992] 3 WLR 432 at 437.

'In our judgment there are no grounds whatsoever for implying, or importing the word "other" between "any" and "computer" ...'

This leaves no doubt that, all things being equal, insiders who gain access to unauthorised files through the computer on which they are stored can commit the offence.

So, an insider may be as culpable as an outsider. It should be noted that it is easier for an insider to gain unauthorised access. By definition an insider is behind the firewall so already beyond security measures. In court, proving an insider was acting outside of their authority can be arduous.

Authorisation

For an insider to be convicted the prosecution has two hurdles to prove intention. The first is that the person intended to secure access to any program or data. This may not be disputed. What will often be disputed is the second, higher hurdle, that the insider knew that he was unauthorised to secure this access at the time of causing the computer to perform a function.[9]

In a perfect organisation the boundaries of each employee's actions are clear and known. In practice, an employee's role changes over time. This is especially the situation for a temporary worker who may work for many different sectors of an organisation within a short period. It will therefore often be important for the prosecution to show clear guidelines which were made known to the employee at the time of causing the computer to perform the function.

On this point the Law Commission has provided the following guidance.[10]

'We think there is some importance in requiring the court, in a case where there is a dispute about authorisation, to identify, and to be clear about the status of, the person alleged to have authority to control the access which is in issue.'

Unclear guidelines, or none at all, in relation to the use of the Intranet can only weaken the prosecution's case that a person knew they were acting outside of their authority. Conflicting authorisations will also weaken any case.

---

10. An employee secures access to the personnel section of her company's Intranet. She copies her personnel file using a stolen password. Clearly the employee does not have authority to enter the personnel section of the Intranet, but, her intention was to gain access to her own personnel file. The relevant knowledge and intent may be inferred from her stolen password.

---

9   A 'bootstraps' approach to this question is to assess whether the ultimate purpose of the access was unlawful. As unlawful, it must, necessarily, have been unauthorised by the controller of the programs or data. That this was *known* by the defendant remains a question of fact but, an unlawful purpose, will indicate such knowledge.

10 Law Commission No 186, para 3.37.

Without a clear indication of boundaries, the defence is at liberty to question whether the defendant actually *knew* of these limits.[11]

This discussion highlights the theoretical applicability of the Computer Misuse Act 1990 to insider access, but also the practical difficulty of satisfying the criminal standard of proof in such a case.

HACKING TO OFFEND FURTHER

The section 2 offence applies to someone seeking to access a computer for a further criminal purpose. That is, where a section 1 offence has been committed with the further intent to commit a serious criminal offence.[12]

It is envisaged that the growth of commercial activity over the Internet will lead to an increase in the reliance on this section. It will be discussed below that this section applies to interception of digital cash. It also applies to the interception of goods or services which are sent over the Internet, for example software.

Further offence

If a section 1 offence is made out, the section 2 offence may be proved by establishing that the defendant committed that offence with the intention to commit a further offence. This type of further offence is defined as one punishable by at least five years' imprisonment. This covers theft and fraud, and most other dishonesty offences.[13] Importantly it now covers an offence of dishonestly obtaining a money transfer by deception.[14]

---

11   This said, the defence should be wary that 'it is always open to the tribunal of fact, when knowledge on the part of a defendant is required to be proved, to base a finding of knowledge on evidence that the defendant deliberately shut his eyes to the obvious or refrained from inquiry because he suspected the truth but did not want to have his suspicion confirmed.' Per Lord Bridge, *Westminster City Council v Croyalgrange Ltd* [1986] 2 All ER 353 at 359. This 'wilful blindness' approaches a subjective recklessness threshold of intention. It is the author's opinion that this lower level of intention was not intended by Parliament. Miss Emma Nicholson's Bill, proposed but rejected, included recklessness; the Computer Misuse Act 1990 does not. Further, the proponent of the Act explained, '[Section 1] is also aimed at insiders who try to get into parts of the system where they *know that they* should not be.' *Hansard* HC volume 166, column 1138. Emphasis is added to indicate the use of the qualifier, 'they know that', rather than solely, 'should not be'.

12   No exhaustive list of these further offences is provided by the Computer Misuse Act 1990. The offence must carry either a fixed sentence penalty, such as murder, or be punishable with imprisonment of five years or more. This appears to cover the majority of serious offences.

13   In illustration, although Cropp was acquitted for other reasons (discussed at 'Direct access to server' at page 223), Aglionby J stated, 'There is no doubt that false accounting contrary to s 17(1)(a) of the Theft Act 1968 falls within the statutory definition of "further offence".' *R v Cropp*. Transcript of Shorthand Notes, Page 7G.

14   Theft Act 1968, s 15A as inserted by the Theft (Amendment) Act 1996.

> **II. A hacker gains unauthorised access to a computer and takes a copy of an encryption key used for Internet-safe digital cash transfers. The hacker then uses the key to pay for services without the permission of the account owner. The hacker may be convicted of the section 2 offence because the section I requirements are met and the defendant intended to commit the further offence of obtaining a money transfer by deception.**

INTENTION

The hacker is not required actually to commit the further offence. Simply committing a section 1 offence with the *intention* of committing the further offence is sufficient. Where the hacker is accessing encryption keys to digital cash accounts, it seems probable that the secondary intention will be inferred. Gaining access to another's e-mail account though, with no other evidence of intent, would not appear to provide sufficient evidence to make out a conviction.

If a hacker is found not guilty under section 2, the jury may still find the defendant guilty under section 1.[15] Of course, where this takes place in the Crown Court, the powers of sentencing are those which the magistrate would have under section 1.[16]

FUTURE INTENTION

Section 2(3) states:

> 'It is immaterial for the purposes of this section whether the further offence is to be committed on the same occasion as the unauthorised access offence or on any future occasion.'

This eliminates difficult issues for the prosecution of whether the subsequent offence was sufficiently connected in time with the section 1 offence. It also creates a wider frame of culpability for the defendant: the intention may be to use the data at some time in the future.

IMPOSSIBLE FURTHER OFFENCE

Similar to the House of Lords' ruling in *R v Shivpuri*[17] in relation to the Criminal Attempts Act 1981, 'objective innocence' does not save a hacker who attempts a factually impossible crime. A hacker may be guilty of an offence under section 2 even though the facts are such that the commission of the further offence is impossible.[18] But the Computer Misuse Act 1990 is wider than the existing provisions under the Criminal Attempts Act 1981 and, say, the Theft Act 1968. This is because, even under the *Shivpuri* wider reading of the Criminal Attempts Act 1981, the defendant must still have done 'an act which is more than merely

15   Computer Misuse Act 1990, s 12(1)(a).
16   Computer Misuse Act 1990, s 12(2).
17   [1987] AC 1, especially at 21.
18   Computer Misuse Act 1990, s 2(4).

preparatory to the commission of the offence'.[19] In contrast, under the Computer Misuse Act 1990, an act *less than* merely preparatory may suffice as evidence of the additional intention needed for a section 2 offence.

> **12. A hacker uses a computer to obtain another person's encryption key with which he intends to access the owner's online bank account. The hacker does not know that the bank will only allow access from one phone number: that of the owner. The hacker's attempt would fail. Despite this the hacker may have committed a section 2 offence, although he would probably not have made sufficient preparation for a statutory attempt.**

This illustrates two crucial issues for would-be hackers and their lawyers. Almost any unauthorised dealing over the Internet with digital cash or other secure electronic transmissions will fall within section 2 of the Computer Misuse Act 1990. As a result of a conviction under this section, hackers may face up to five years' imprisonment. The same warnings extend to almost any dealing with intent to gain services or products using the Internet.

UNAUTHORISED MODIFICATION

In 1865 Mr Fisher was convicted of damaging a steam engine by plugging up the feed-pipe and displacing other parts to render the engine useless.[20] There was no removal of any part, no cutting and no breaking. Pollock CB upheld the conviction stating,[1]

> 'It is like the case of spiking a gun, where there is no actual damage to the gun, although it is rendered useless ... Surely the displacement of the parts was a damage ... if done with intent to render the machine useless.'

Malicious computer code is similar to Mr Fisher's feed-pipe plug. Often the victim computer program remains intact, as does the data it generates or uses; what alters is the computer's 'usefulness'. Before the Computer Misuse Act 1990 courts were forced to rely on the Criminal Damage Act 1971 to reason that the value of a computer's storage medium was impaired by altering the storing magnetic particles.[2]

Prosecutions are more straightforward under section 3 of the Computer Misuse Act 1990.

> '3. (1) A person is guilty of an offence if –
> (a) he does any act which causes unauthorised modification of the contents of any computer; and

---

19   See Lord Bridge, [1987] AC 1 at 21; cf *Anderton v Ryan* [1985] AC 560 at 582–583.
20   (1865) LR 1 CCR 7.
 1   (1865) LR 1 CCR 7 at 9.
 2   See *Cox v Riley* (1986) 83 Cr App Rep 54; also *R v Whiteley* (1991) 93 Cr App Rep 25. The Criminal Damage Act 1971 is no longer applicable owing to the Computer Misuse Act 1990, s 3(6).

    (b) at the time when he does the act he has the requisite intent and the requisite knowledge.

    (2) For the purposes of subsection (1)(b) above the requisite intent is an intent to cause modification of the contents of any computer and by so doing –

    (a) to impair the operation of any computer;

    (b) to prevent or hinder access to any program or data held in any computer; or

    (c) to impair the operation of any such program or the reliability of any such data.'

This section 3 offence is triable either way. The section covers a vast range of acts and programs. That is the first key point to the section: it covers both a person who directly impairs the workings of a computer and also the distribution of a program which does such an activity. It is worthwhile appreciating the range of modifications which can be made by rogue programs. Each type of modification has acquired a suitably descriptive tag which will be used in the remainder of this chapter.

VIRUS   A computer virus is actually a generic term for computer code which replicates, not only throughout the storage medium in which it incubates, but also across the network to which that computer is connected. Without anti-viral software a computer connected to the Internet poses a threat to all other computers also connected, and risks infection from those other computers. The ability to infect a home page with a virus, and even a word processing document, makes the Internet capable of spreading malicious code widely and rapidly.

WORM   A worm is a program which replicates and grows in size.[3] This reproduction and expansion can cause a computer storage system to run more slowly and can also cause the computer itself to slow down. Legally it is important to note that it does not attach itself to the operating system of the computer it infects; it does not *directly* impair the workings of a computer. The most infamous example of such a program is Robert Morris's Internet Worm. This was released on 2 November 1988 and within a couple of days had almost crashed the entire Internet which existed at the time including NASA and the US Defense System. Morris was convicted of violating the Computer Fraud and Abuse Act.[4]

TROJAN HORSE   A trojan horse is a seemingly innocent program which, true to its name, carries something more sinister. It harbours a further sub-program which is usually used for a special purpose such as capturing passwords or secretly copying and forwarding data. The vital legal issue is that the main program is executed by the user of the computer not the writer of the trojan horse. The 'Inner Circle', a sophisticated group of hackers, hid a trojan horse inside a chess program which was used in a large computer in Canada.[5]

---

3   Not to be confused with the acronym WORM. See Glossary.

4   *US v Morris* 928 F 2d 504 (2nd Cir 1991). For additional details see Hafner K & Markoff J, *Cyberpunk*, (Corgi, London, 1993).

5   For additional details see Landreth B, *Out of the Inner Circle* (Microsoft Press, Washington, 1985).

LOGIC BOMB A logic bomb, like a trojan horse, is a hidden program which, when triggered by a particular event, performs a function. Often this function is something rather destructive, such as wiping a storage medium, or crashing the computer on which it resides. Again, a significant legal factor is that such a program remains dormant until the triggering event. The most famous, still rife, is the PLO virus which is triggered on each anniversary of Israel's Declaration of Independence. It can destroy the files on the computer on which it is stored.

Unauthorised modification: conduct or *actus reus*

Any act which causes an unauthorised modification of the contents of a computer can be the necessary conduct for a section 3 conviction.[6] As for a section 1 conviction, it is useful to examine the pivotal words in this section. It will be shown that the *actus reus* aspect of the offence is quite wide, but the scope of the offence is tightened because specific intent must be proved.

MODIFICATION

Modification is exhaustively defined as taking place where, by the operation of any function, any program or data held in a computer is altered or erased or is added to.[7] The concept of this is widened by defining 'any act which *contributes* towards causing such a modification shall be regarded as causing it'.[8]

> **13. A programmer is commissioned to write a Java applet which will show an animation on a home page. Without authority he also includes a logic bomb which downloads to each client computer and wishes them 'Happy Christmas' on 25 December. The logic bomb will not directly alter any program or data as it does not attach to other code stored on the computer. On the set date, however, the program will alter the contents of data held in the computer. The applet causes a modification.**

Proving modification

Defence counsel should be alive to the fact that it is not unlawful to possess virus code. Further it is not prohibited to write malicious code.[9] The hard task for the prosecution is therefore to prove that the defendant distributed or contributed to the release of malicious code. This is the case for two reasons.

First, viruses are often spread by people other than those who wrote them initially. It can therefore be difficult to prove to the high burden of criminal proof that the source of the infection on the victim computer was the defendant's action. The existence of the virus on other systems *prior* to the alleged infection can

6   Computer Misuse Act 1990, s 3(1)(a).
7   Computer Misuse Act 1990, s 17(7)(a) and (b).
8   Computer Misuse Act 1990, s 17(7).
9   Use of inchoate offences to prosecute virus writers, while possible, has never been tested in court.

weaken the prosecution's case by suggesting someone other than the defendant caused or contributed to the modification. The second difficulty for the prosecution is that, at present, there is no equivalent of a DNA fingerprint test for computer code. It will often be impossible to state categorically the source of an infection other than by extrapolating the code's dissemination. Occasionally, though, the prosecution will be able rely on evidence gained from the defendant's own computer. In *R v Pile* the defendant surreptitiously stored programs on his computer which he used to write and distribute the viruses.[10]

UNAUTHORISED MODIFICATION

The second aspect to the *actus reus* is the issue of authority. As for sections 1 and 2, lack of authority is rarely a difficult factor to prove when the malicious code is spread from outside an organisation.[11] Under section 3 a modification is unauthorised if two conditions are met. First, the person who causes the act must not be entitled to determine whether the modification should be made.[12] The second condition is that the person must not have consent from any person who is entitled to provide the authority.[13] Sometimes within an organisation the malicious code and tampering are so obvious that the defence can raise no serious questions of authority. Two real case examples should suffice. A male nurse pleaded guilty to two charges under section 3. He had altered prescriptions and treatment of various patients in his hospital.[14] In *R v Spielman* the defendant, a former employee of an online financial new agency, tampered with and deleted employee e-mails.[15] He pleaded guilty to the charge under section 3.

There can be other situations where the modification of code over an Intranet does not pose a difficult question of authority. As stated previously, the more vague the internal guidelines on such authority, the more difficult it may be to prosecute an individual who is regarded to have acted outside such authority.[16] Of course, employers may not resort to calling the police when the employee can be dealt with internally for gross misconduct.[17]

Section 3(I): intention or *mens rea*

There are two limbs of a 'guilty mind' for section 3: the defendant must have the 'requisite intent' and the 'requisite knowledge'.[18] Logically requisite knowledge must be considered first.

---

10   Unreported, Plymouth Crown Court, May 1995. See the *Guardian*, 16 November 1995.
11   See 'Unauthorised' at page 221.
12   Computer Misuse Act 1990, s 17(8)(a).
13   Computer Misuse Act 1990, s 17(8)(b).
14   *R v Rymer*, Liverpool Crown Court, December 1993. See the *Guardian*, 21 December 1993.
15   Unreported, Bow Street Magistrates Court, March 1995. See *Computer Weekly*, 2 February 1995.
16   See 'Authorisation' at page 224.
17   In *Denco v Joinson* an employee's unauthorised access was stated by the Employment Appeal Tribunal to be gross misconduct [1992] 1 All ER 463.
18   Computer Misuse Act 1990, s 3(1)(b).

REQUISITE KNOWLEDGE

Simply put by the Act, the 'requisite knowledge' under section 3(1)(b) is that any modification intended to be caused is unauthorised. The examination under section 1 of the degree of 'knowledge' is equally relevant for this section.[19]

REQUISITE INTENTION

The defendant must not only have intended to modify the contents of a computer, but also this modification should have at least one of four results set out below.[20] This does not indicate that the defendant must have intended one particular kind of modification: an intention to modify is sufficient.[1] These results are considered below with specific reference to potential rogue code which may be spread over the Internet. It is not a defence that the results were intended to be merely temporary.[2]

Impair the operation of any computer (section 3(2)(a))

To impair the operation of a computer per se, without impairing the operation of any program, would suggest that this subsection caters for a worm. As explained, this type of code does not need to attach itself to a program or data.[3] Its presence in a computer, in multiple copies, alone may be enough to slow down a computer's processing speed.

It should be stated that, in certain circumstances, the prosecution may have problems in establishing that the worm's presence constitutes a modification. A worm may operate adequately without actually altering or adding to a program or data held in the computer. Too much should not be made of this technicality. Counsel should take expert evidence concerning both the nature of the worm, and also of the range of computers which it may infect. It may be that for one type of infected computer, programs and data *are* altered. The range of computers connected to the Internet and the increasing compatibility of these machines increases the likelihood that the operation of a computer is modified for the purposes of the Act.

Prevent or hinder access to any program or data (section 3(2)(b))

A worm will hinder access to a program or data, indirectly, but there are three other types of code which will cause this. A virus which obstructs the use of a computer will certainly fall within this section. One of Christopher Pile's viruses, Pathogen, after infecting a computer 32 times would at a particular time on a Monday evening show a message, 'Smoke me a kipper, I'll be back for breakfast. Unfortunately some of your data won't.'[4] This virus certainly hinders the access to the program being used at the time.

---

19   See fn 11 at page 225, the dicta of Lord Bridge, *Westminster City Council v Croyalgrange Ltd.*
20   Computer Misuse Act 1990, s 3(2).
1   Computer Misuse Act 1990, s 3(3)(c).
2   Computer Misuse Act 1990, s 3(5).
3   See 'Worm' at page 228.
4   See the *Guardian*, 16 November 1995. See also fn 10 at page 230.

This type of result is also satisfied where a programmer seeks to use a logic bomb to 'lock out' an individual from accessing a program or data. Again, disgruntled employees appear to be the prime candidates for causing this. Mr Hardy, an IT manager, added a program to his company's system which encrypted stored data, and de-encrypted it on retrieval. One month after he left the firm the program stopped unscrambling the data. This left his former company hindered from accessing its stored information. He pleaded guilty.[5]

---

14. As a joke a person attaches a virus to a word processing document which he forwards to a friend at work. The virus was intended simply to play a musical tune when the machine was next switched on. Owing to a special sound device attached to the friend's machine, the computer, and then the entire network, crashed. The more limited result intended by the joker is not relevant to the issue of culpability; it may be relevant for sentencing.

Impair the operation of any such program (section 3(2)(c))

This subsection focuses on how a program executes when some code has run. The 'operation' can be taken to mean how the program should function without the malicious code. It should not be read narrowly to mean the use which the victim makes of the program.

---

15. A web site has a virus which is downloaded secretly and automatically to any computer which accesses the site. This virus reduces the security of any credit card transactions which the user makes using their browser. It is of no importance that the only victims of the virus do not use their browser for such a purpose. The operation of the browser, as it was originally designed, has been impaired by the unauthorised modification.

Impair the reliability of any such data (section 3(2)(c))

This result should be viewed by defence counsel as an objective notion of reliability. It is not enough for an infected-computer owner to claim that he now cannot rely on the data because he feels it may be unreliable. The prosecution must prove the alteration or reduction in quality of the data on an objective basis.[6]

---

5   *R v Hardy*. Unreported, Old Bailey, November 1992.

6   This approach is confirmed in *A-G's Reference (No 1 of 1991)* [1992] 3 All ER 897. Lord Taylor stated obiter that it is questionable whether it is correct to 'giv[e] the word "reliability" the meaning of achieving the result in the printout which was intended by the owner of the computer. It may not necessarily impair the reliability of data in the computer that you feed in something which will produce a result more favourable . . . than the [owner] intended.' [1992] 3 WLR 432 at 438.

Any program or data

The intention to modify does not need to be directed at any particular computer, or particular program, data or kind of program or data.[7] It is enough that an individual intends to modify the contents of a computer in general. The drafting of section 3(3) was essential to encompass fully the mischief which it addresses. Computer viruses and other malicious codes are disseminated in a random manner. The initial release of the code then results in it being passed to, and perhaps replicated by, any number of computers anywhere on the Internet. The prosecution would not be able to show a defendant had the intent to infect each victim of his code.[8]

EVIDENCE

The defence counsel of any alleged computer misuser must focus his attention on the weaknesses of the evidence put before the court. Almost all relevant evidence will be computer-generated evidence. This evidence is treated differently from other evidence.[9] It is trusted less and requires a certificate as to the authenticity of the evidence. The prosecution should be aware that the existing rules on computer evidence are not easily applied to an Internet case.

The Police and Criminal Evidence Act 1984

Like the Civil Evidence Act 1968, section 69 of the Police and Criminal Evidence Act 1984 will only admit computer evidence that satisfies certain requirements. Section 69 has two tests which must be satisfied before evidence from a computer can be admissible as a fact recorded by the evidence.

First, there must be no reasonable grounds for believing that the statement is inaccurate because of improper use of the computer.[10] Second, the computer must have been operating properly at all material times or at least the part that was not operating properly must have not affected the production of the document or the accuracy of its contents.[11]

High authority on the operation of section 69 is given in *R v Shephard*.[12] Mrs Hilda Shephard was alleged to have stolen some items from a Marks & Spencer store. She admitted to having thrown her receipt away, but every item in a Marks & Spencer's branch has a Unique Product Code. So, a store detective was able to

7 Computer Misuse Act 1990, s 3(3)(a) and (b).
8 This is confirmed by the conviction in *R v Pile*. Mr Pile's viruses were placed on bulletin boards and then spread by other people. Unreported, Plymouth Crown Court, May 1995. See the *Guardian*, 16 November 1995.
9 The Law Commission Consultation Paper 138 at para 14.32 proposes repealing the special rules on computer evidence without replacement. Before such repeal, the defence may take the benefit of the special rules alluded to at para 14.20: 'The complexity of modern systems makes it relatively easy to establish a reasonable doubt in a juror's mind as to whether the computer was operating properly. Bearing in mind the very technical nature of computers, the chances of this happening with greater frequency in future are fairly high.'
10 Police and Criminal Evidence Act 1984, s 69(1)(a).
11 Police and Criminal Evidence Act 1984, s 69(1)(b).
12 [1993] 1 All ER 225.

ascertain whether those items had been sold by examining all the codes on a till roll from the day in question. As a central computer issued a date on each till roll the question was whether this evidence should satisfy the Police and Criminal Evidence Act 1984, section 69(1).

The Lords answered this with clear statements as to what evidence falls within the section, who can certify that evidence, and how.

CERTIFIABLE COMPUTER EVIDENCE

Lord Griffiths made the following statement:[13]

> 'if the prosecution wish to rely upon a document produced by a computer they must comply with section 69 in all cases'.

Examples of computer evidence

Evidence of a fact which is generated by a computer must clear the section 69 hurdle. Moreover, a critical analysis made of the types of evidence used in a digital crime case reveals that there will be little evidence which will *not* be required to meet the criteria of section 69. This evidence may include logs stored on the client's, host's, victim's or accused's computers.[14] It will also possibly include data or programs to which the prosecution alleges the defendant gained access. In this situation, the prosecution may, unwisely, also rely on 'date stamps'. As their name suggests, these dates show the last time that a computer file was modified or even viewed.[15] These date stamps may appear useful to the prosecution to show the exact time and date when, say, a program was infected with a virus. The evidential difficulty with these stamps is that they are notoriously unreliable and this can be challenged by the defence.

---

16. The prosecution seek to adduce as evidence of unauthorised modification a computer file which is alleged to have a date stamp showing an alteration during the weekend. All employees are forbidden from logging in outside office hours. Two discrete pieces of evidence are being adduced: the file itself with the modification apparent and, second, the date stamp of the file indicating the time of modification. To adduce this latter, temporal, evidence the prosecution must satisfy section 69. Adducing the file is not evidence of any recorded fact, but the actual fact itself: no certificate is needed.

---

13 Per Lord Griffiths, [1993] 1 All ER 225 at 230. This is not strictly correct. Some computer evidence may be adduced not for 'any fact therein', but as actual fact. Professor Smith gives the example of a bank statement showing an entry of £100 into a bank account: [1983] Crim LR 472. This evidence is not a statement that the account is credited, rather the fact. As will be discussed, under a section 3 prosecution a computer program which is alleged to have been modified may be brought before the court without clearing the section 69 hurdle. In such a circumstance the code is adduced not as evidence of the fact therein, but as the fact itself.
14 This author has been informed of one prosecution where the *accused's* computer held a log of all the attempted and actual hacking which took place!
15 See Haber S and Stornetta WS, *How to time-stamp a digital document*. Advances in Cryptology: Proceedings of CRYPTO '90 (Springer-Verlag, 1991).

The defence and prosecution should remember that section 69 poses a negative requirement: *unless* the evidence sought to be adduced meets the criteria it is inadmissible. Section 69 is therefore a powerful tool to ensure that the other side relies only on appropriately reliable evidence.

How to certify

There are two ways to prove that the generating computer is reliable for the purposes of producing a certificate: call oral evidence, or tender a written certificate in line with the Police and Criminal Evidence Act 1984, Schedule 3, paragraph 8.

Signed certificate

A certificate must be from a 'person occupying a responsible position in relation to the operation of the computer'.[16] To rely on this certificate, Lord Griffiths stated that,[17]

> 'it should show on its face that it is signed by a person who from his job description can confidently be expected to be in a position to give reliable evidence about the operation of the computer.'

If the defendant is not satisfied by the certificate, he can ask the judge to require oral evidence which can be challenged in cross-examination.

Oral evidence

Where oral evidence of the reliability of computer evidence is given the court does not need to insist on hearing the testimony given by an expert in the 'proper workings of the computer'. Indeed, in *R v Shephard* the court instead was prepared to accept the testimony of the store detective as proof that the central computer was working. Lord Griffiths went on to indicate that the burden of section 69 may vary from case to case.[18]

> '*The evidence must be tailored to the needs of the case.* I suspect that it will very rarely be necessary to call an expert and that in the vast majority of cases it will be possible to discharge the burden by calling a witness who is familiar with the operation of the computer in the sense of knowing what the computer is required to do and who can say that it is doing it properly.'

Degree of reliability

The final question which must be addressed, particularly in oral evidence, is what is the necessary level of reliability of computer evidence? This is of paramount

16   Police and Criminal Evidence Act 1984, Sch 3, para 8(d).
17   [1993] 1 All ER 225 at 230.
18   [1993] 1 All ER 225 at 231. Emphasis added.

importance in hacking cases where very often a hacker will attempt to 'clean up his fingerprints' by tampering with logs of his activities. It is also important where a modification is alleged to have occurred, but it is the time of this modification which is disputed. On these questions the House of Lords indicated that the simpler the computer, the less technically qualified the witness needs to be. In all but the most straightforward Computer Misuse Act 1990 prosecutions it is suggested that no less than an expert familiar with the system should be accepted as having the requisite understanding of the computer's trustworthiness.[19]

Certainly, vigilant counsel for a computer misuse defendant should be more pressing than those in *R v Shephard*. In evidence in chief Mrs McNicholas, the store detective, was asked, 'And what about the master computer? Did that malfunction?' Her reply was less than convincing, 'Touch wood, no. I have never known it to break down since we have had it.' She was not cross-examined on the point.[20] It is submitted that such a weak affirmation in a computer misuse case should certainly be tested under cross-examination.

This background understanding of the interaction between the Computer Misuse Act 1990 and the Police and Criminal Evidence Act 1984 is fundamental to the following examination of the evidence used in a computer misuse case.

Evidence of computer misuse

There are two main issues prevalent in a computer misuse case that may create an evidential burden on the prosecution. First, there must be continuity of evidence from the first computer used by a hacker to the final victim computer; second, hackers rarely use their own names and addresses to login to a victim computer.

CONTINUITY OF ACCESS EVIDENCE

To prove beyond reasonable doubt that the defendant was responsible for the unauthorised access of the victim's computer, the prosecution can be forced to prove continuity of evidence. That is, the prosecution should be able to 'follow' a line of access from the hacker's own computer to the victim's. Any discontinuity may raise the court's reasonable doubt that the defendant in the court was not the person responsible for the final unauthorised access. Only the most simple Internet hacking cases will feature two computers and an identifiable abuser. More regularly a hacker's commands to his computer will pass through many different computers spread across the Internet. It is also usual that a hacker will attempt to disguise his true identity: he is unlikely to attempt unauthorised access using an

19   The defence should also be conscious of the ease of manipulating digital data without trace; this is sometimes called 'chain of custody' evidence. The Committee of Experts on criminal procedural law problems connected with information technology notes honestly, 'Adequate safeguards must be taken by the investigating authorities to guarantee the integrity of data between its copying during the investigation and its presentation at court proceedings . . . [C]ourts may demand that the proponent of a digital picture, for example, be ready to establish a complete chain of custody. A hand-to-hand chain from the photographer to the person who produced the printout may, in some circumstances, be the only way to adequately ensure the integrity of an exhibit' Final Activity Report, Recommendation No R(95) 13 Concerning Problems of Criminal Procedural Law Connected with Information Technology (Strasbourg, 2 October 1995) at para 161.

20   (1991) 93 Cr App Rep 139 at 143.

electronic signifier which can identify him. This poses an evidential difficulty for the prosecution.

Fragmentation of Internet hacking

It has been explained that messages and commands sent over the Internet do not pass directly between the sender and receiver computer. Instead the message is broken into small packets, each with a destination address. Each packet is shunted from one computer on the Internet to another, and from that computer to the next; gradually moving the packet towards its destination. Eventually, all the packets arrive at their final resting computer in a matter of seconds.

Hackers' messages and commands are no different. Each message will be broken into packets and shunted through many different computers. The prosecution will have to establish that a hacker's message did travel to an unauthorised computer.

In addition, hackers rarely attempt to gain access to their victim computer directly. Their preferred method is to login to one computer on the Internet and from there to login to another. This process is repeated many times; it is the digital equivalent of turning many corners to shake off a chasing police car. And each new login made by the hacker presents another piece of evidence which the prosecution may have to prove to establish continuity from the first to the final unauthorised access.[1]

FALSE IDENTIFICATION – SPOOFING

The situation for the prosecution may be more complex. A hacker logging in to a computer on the way to his victim will often login under a different identity. This is called 'spoofing'. The hacker is able to do this by having previously obtained actual passwords, or having created a new identity by fooling the computer into thinking he is the system's operator. Whatever the technical method, the legal result remains the same. The prosecution must establish that the hacker at his own computer was the person who has logged into countless other computers.

EVIDENTIAL IMPLICATIONS

There are many section 69 implications of fragmented and spoofed access. Many certificates from many jurisdictions can be required. Also, hackers will often tamper with the evidence which recorded the details of their activities.

Obtaining certificates

Multiple certificates

Unlike the one certificate in *R v Shephard*, a hacking prosecution may have to rely on numerous certificates, and possibly produce the witnesses for oral examination.

---

1   *R v Cochrane* [1993] Crim LR 48 illustrates the utility of focusing on one computer in a chain to 'break' the continuity.

While this, in itself, is not a bar to a conviction, each certificate must adequately verify the proper workings of the computer. Each certificate is therefore potentially a weak link in the continuity chain.[2]

Multiple jurisdictions

The computers which a hacker may journey through to arrive finally at the victim computer will be scattered throughout the world. It will be recalled that there is one cost of accessing a computer anywhere on the Internet; there are no financial restraints on crossing borders and continents. Again, this is not a bar to a conviction but it does raise the possibility of a judge requiring that one of these witnesses be orally examined.[3]

Refusal to certify

This author has been informed of at least one UK Internet Access Provider who has refused to supply details from any log for a computer misuse investigation. The prosecution needs only one such stubborn system operator to produce a flaw in the continuity of evidence.[4]

Not working reliably

A hacker will often not only spoof his identity but also attempt to tamper with the logging software actually used by the system. This poses two problems: first, technically it may be impossible to prove that the defendant in the court was the hacker modifying the log. Second, to admit that the log has been tampered with *at all* raises the suspicion that the computer was not operating properly at the material time.[5] Any admission by the prosecution of tampering should be met by

---

2   '[F]orging computer logs is trivial. The same commands that let us obscure the names of attacking sites for [the referenced] book would let us insert any names we wished in our logs, including yours ... [E]ven assuming an absence of malice on our part, computer systems have a less-than-sterling reputation for reliability. The hardware is almost certainly working properly; the software though, is another matter entirely.' Cheswick WR & Bellovin SM, *Firewalls and Internet Security* (Addison-Wesley Publishing Company, Wokingham, 1995) at page 200. Cheswick and Bellovin designed AT&T's Internet gateway and are established experts.

3   Subject to the Criminal Justice Act 1988, ss 23 and 24. Often a log of accesses will have been prepared for the purposes of the trial. In such a situation, s 26 may be applicable. See Tapper C, *Cross & Tapper on Evidence*, (Butterworths, London, 8th edn, 1995) at pages 699–706. Section 29 assists both sides in obtaining evidence from a witness residing abroad. Section 32 allows a witness from abroad to give evidence using a video conference.

4   The Computer Misuse Act 1990, s 10, as amended by the Criminal Justice and Public Order Act 1994, s 162, now ensures that law enforcement officers will not be committing a s 1 offence by gaining unauthorised access to programs or data for investigation purposes.

5   The defence should, however, note that Lord Hoffmann, giving judgment for a unanimous House of Lords, stated: 'A malfunction is relevant if it affects the way in which the computer processes, stores or retrieves the information used to generate the statement tendered in evidence. Other malfunctions do not matter': *DPP v McKeown* [1997] 1 WLR 295.

the defence with a question as to whether the evidence still deserves a certificate, or at least that the operator should be orally examined.[6]

PROOF OF MODIFICATION

The prosecution of a section 3 offence may be faced with similar difficulties under section 69. To convict a person under section 3 the prosecution may seek to show that, following modification, the operation of a computer is impaired.[7] Evidence of this impairment, that the unauthorised modification caused the improper operation, must satisfy the Police and Criminal Evidence Act 1984, section 69(1)(b): the computer must have been operating properly at all material times. But this may be the very fact that the prosecution cannot prove because of the modification itself. This loophole has been addressed by the Law Commission, who provide a less than satisfactory solution for the Crown.[8]

> 'We see no reason in such a case for exempting the prosecution from the general requirement imposed by section 69 of showing that the computer was, apart from the alleged interference of which evidence will be given, *otherwise* operating properly.'

It is submitted that this may sometimes be impossible. A malevolent piece of code or modification can affect the very aspect of the computer which allows it to produce reliable data. For example a program which corrupts all time-stamps on files, including its own, will make it impossible for the prosecution to rely on any time-stamp. The defence should be aware that the more serious the modification alleged, the more likely it is that the prosecution will find their evidence unreliable.

In *R v Vatsal Patel*,[9] a section 3 prosecution, the Crown wished to rely on file time-stamps which were admitted to be inaccurate. The defence properly objected to the admission under the Police and Criminal Evidence Act 1984, section 69. After hearing expert evidence from both sides Slack J ruled that the evidence was admissible. He stated that any doubts as to its reliability should go to weight. Under the cross-examination of prosecution witnesses it was heard that other members of the team used the defendant's computer and that these members knew how to alter time-stamps. The jury found Mr Patel not guilty on all three counts under section 3. This case indicates that even where modification evidence is ruled admissible, the defence may still successfully challenge the evidence.

---

6   For commercial logging programs, often the software writer will be the most appropriate witness to testify as to the log's authenticity. He knows the weaknesses of a particular system and may be able to give evidence that, 'yes' the log has been modified, but 'no', this modification or unreliability 'was not such as to affect the production of the document or the accuracy of its contents'; Police and Criminal Evidence Act 1984, s 69(1)(b).

7   Computer Misuse Act 1990, s 3(2)(a).

8   Law Commission Paper 186 para 4.9. Emphasis present in original text.

9   Unreported. Aylesbury Crown Court, July 1993. See Turner M, *Case Report* Computers and Law, May 1994. See also *DPP v McKeown* at fn 5, page 238.

COMMON DIGITAL CRIME

What follows is a brief legal analysis of the ploys used by hackers in gaining unauthorised access to computers over the Internet.[10]

Destroy evidence

Having gained unauthorised access to a computer, a common hacking goal is to destroy the evidence of this access. This itself is an offence under section 3 of the Computer Misuse Act 1990. It will make more onerous the burden on the prosecution to prove the unauthorised access occurred, when it occurred and who was responsible. Nevertheless, a section 69 certificate or oral testimony of the workings of the computer does not need to prove that the computer was operating properly *in all respects*. It is open to the prosecution to admit that the computer's reliability has been reduced, but not in respect of the evidence relied upon. In illustration, an activity log which is stored on a Write Once Read Many[11] (times) device is far less likely to have been adversely modified.

Obtain further passwords

Obtaining further passwords is the first step to being able to 'spoof', to pretend you are someone else. To do this a person must be acting out of his authority because he *knows* that he is not the person whose password he obtains. The person is therefore within the ambit of a section 1 offence by making the computer perform a function to gain this password. Where it is a commercial system, his use will be charged to the real owner of the password. This may be enough to permit the prosecution to bring charges under section 2 also.

Evidentially, the prosecution have to prove that the hacker, not the rightful owner, was using the password. This will pivot on the facts, but it should be remembered that a log from the rightful owner's computer showing he was *not* connected shows merely that. It does not show that the hacker wrongly using the password was the defendant.

Open security holes

A hacker will often attempt to open up new security holes in the attacked system in case their present 'entrance' is discovered and sealed. Doing this necessarily involves both unauthorised access under section 1 and unauthorised modification under section 3. The interesting legal point is to consider which subsection of section 3(2) will be intended by the hacker. It is submitted that the hacker *necessarily* must intend to restrict access or impair the operation of at least the program or code he has introduced into the system. The very reason for

---

10   This metastasis is reproduced with kind permission from William Cheswick and Steven Bellovin. For their technical examination see Cheswick WR and Bellovin SM, *Firewalls and Internet Security* (Addison-Wesley Publishing Company, Wokingham, 1995) at page 152.

11   WORM. As the source of this acronym suggests, this device permits data to be stored but does not allow it to be altered thereafter. A good example of this is a CD-ROM. On this medium, like a music compact disc, one can record only once; users are able to retrieve but not modify its contents.

introducing the hole is that, without it, the present entry point may be discovered. The introduced code therefore impairs the operation of the program which would have discovered his entry.

Little more needs to be said about the evidential difficulties in proving a modification where the very program which is to be used to prove this fact has itself been modified.[12] It is enough to reiterate that the Law Commission saw no reason why the section 69 evidential burden should be lifted for the Computer Misuse Act 1990, section 3; the court and defence should also be cautious before lowering it.

Obtain root access

The ultimate goal of any hacker is to burrow to the root of a computer system, giving him as many rights as the authorised system operator. Gaining access to this level of power clearly steps into unauthorised territory and any modifications will, as above, be designed to secure that position for the hacker. As such, the modifications will be intended to hinder access to programs or data, namely the programs or data which establish the hacker with system operator rights.

The caveats of computer-generated evidence apply even more strongly to penetration to this level. With the same rights as the system operator, a hacker can delete any trace on a log, or otherwise, of his presence on the system.

JURISDICTION AND EXTRADITION

Jurisdiction and extradition can be fundamental to an Internet-based case. The Computer Misuse Act 1990 operates within tight jurisdictional confines. Computer misusers do not. It has been discussed that a hacker will often login to computers across the globe in a bid to disguise his true location and identity. Malicious code, such as viruses, can spread across the whole Internet, and are therefore capable of modifying any data or program in any jurisdiction.

The physical location of the hacker is not an indication of where the crime is committed. And what may not be legal here, may well be caught by the laws of another jurisdiction. These other laws are not considered in this chapter, but the rules on extradition *to* those countries are.

Jurisdiction

The Computer Misuse Act 1990 provides its rules on jurisdiction in sections 4 to 7.[13] They are complex and they apply differently to each of the three offences. If the English court does not have jurisdiction over the offence the offender may still face charges from abroad.

---

12   See above, 'Proof of modification' at page 239.
13   Readers unfamiliar with rules as to jurisdiction are warned not to conflate the assessment of jurisdiction with assessment of culpability under the offence itself. The rules described below are necessarily wider than the rules for a conviction. It is perfectly possible that the courts have jurisdiction over a person, who at trial, is found not to be guilty of the offence itself. Nevertheless, the defence should be prepared to fight on jurisdiction, without which there will be no trial in England at all.

SECTION I JURISDICTION

The court will have jurisdiction over a computer misuse offender under section 1 where the offence has at least one 'significant link' with England.[14] For a section 1 offence, a significant link can be either:[15]

1. that the accused was in England at the time when he did the act which caused the computer to perform the function; or
2. that the computer containing any program or data to which the accused secured or intended to secure unauthorised access by doing that act was in England at that time.[16]

Location of accused

> **17. A French postgraduate at university in England logs in to his former university computer in France. From this computer he runs an automated hacking program which fails to gain access to a further computer in America. The English court has jurisdiction even though the computer caused to function was outside England, as was the victim computer. The act causing the function was made while the postgraduate was in England.**

Location of victim computer

The nub of this subsection is that the hacker secured access or intended to secure access to *any* computer situated in England. It is of no consequence that the hacker was only using an English computer as a 'stop' on the way to a victim computer outside the jurisdiction. Jurisdiction can result from the victim computer or any computer through which the hacker journeys being within England.

> **18. A programmer based in America has for some time been plotting to hack into an English government computer. He is caught by American police having secured access to an American computer which has a secure line to the English computer. The English court, perhaps not alone, has jurisdiction over the American. It is sufficient that his intentions were directed to an English computer.**

SECTION 2 JURISDICTION

The jurisdiction over section 2 offences is wider than that for section 1. Either or both of two rules give the court jurisdiction:

---

14   Computer Misuse Act 1990, s 4(2).
15   Computer Misuse Act 1990, s 5(2).
16   A 16-year-old pleaded guilty to twelve s 1 offences. All the unauthorised accesses were performed from his north London home. The victim computers were top security military computers based in the USA. The Senate said that 'he had caused more damage than the KGB': *R v Pryce*, Bow Street Magistrates, 21 March 1997.

1. subject to 'double criminality' below if the accused intended to do or facilitate anything outside England which would be a section 2 offence if it took place in England *and* the offence has a significant link to England for a section 1 offence;[17]
2. if the accused gained unauthorised access to a computer abroad with the intent to commit the further offence in England.

Double-criminality

Not only the English courts must view the conduct as falling within the ambit of the offence, but also the relevant country abroad must also view the conduct as criminal, although the offences here and abroad need not be the same.[18] The further offence must involve the commission of an offence under the law in force where the whole or any part of the further offence was intended to take place.[19]

Defence counsel must note that the onus is on them to serve a notice on the prosecution stating that the double-criminality is not satisfied. Full facts and grounds for that opinion must be included in the notice.[1]

---

19. An American bank protects its records by storing them with an English data warehouse, fully encrypted. From a mobile phone, a hacker, at the time in Switzerland, gains access to this data warehouse and appropriates a number of confidential files, still encrypted. After cracking the encryption, the hacker intends to steal electronically from the American bank. The English court has jurisdiction over the hacker having both a significant link with England, constituting an offence if in England and being punishable in the United States.

SECTION 3 JURISDICTION

The court will have jurisdiction over section 3 computer misuse where the offence has at least one 'significant link' with England.[2] For a section 3 offence, a significant link can be either:[3]

1. that the accused was in England at the time when he did the act which caused the unauthorised modification; or
2. that the unauthorised modification took place in England.

It has been mentioned on numerous occasions that a virus may spread throughout the entire Internet. It is possible to affect computers in multiple jurisdictions. An effect of the 'significant link' is to allow the English courts to prosecute a person who disseminates malicious code from England, even if no computer in England is modified. Also, the significant link contemplates a computer modifier from

---

17　Computer Misuse Act 1990, s 4(4).
18　Computer Misuse Act 1990, s 8(4).
19　Computer Misuse Act 1990, s 8(1).
 1　Computer Misuse Act 1990, s 8(5) and (9).
 2　Computer Misuse Act 1990, s 4(2).
 3　Computer Misuse Act 1990, s 5(3).

anywhere in the world being prosecuted for a computer in England being modified.

Location of accused

> **20.   A schoolboy in England uses his school computer to post on a French Internet bulletin board a logic bomb which corrupts an important part of any computer it infects. It is of no consequence that the logic bomb is 'defused' before it reaches a computer in England. The act constituting the offence was committed within the jurisdiction.**

As previously stated, executable code which is on a web site may cause an unauthorised modification. The act of uploading this code to the web site will constitute the relevant act for the purposes of jurisdiction.

Location of victim computer

The jurisdiction of the court is triggered by any computer situated in England affected by an unauthorised modification. It does not matter that the modifier had no intention to infect an English computer.

Extradition

The law concerning extradition is involved and it is considered more appropriate that readers consult a specialist text in the field before proving or acting on any advice. The following is a brief indication of the aspects of digital crime over the Internet which should be factored into any extradition evaluation.

The Extradition Act 1989 defines an 'extradition crime'. This is conduct which is both an offence in England and in the other country which has a minimum sentence of 12 months' imprisonment.[4] As for the rules of double-criminality for jurisdiction,[5] it is irrelevant how the offence is defined in the other country.[6] In addition to the application of the Extradition Act 1989, the Extradition Act 1870 remains in force in respect of countries with which Britain has established extradition treaties.

The Extradition Act 1989's requirement of a maximum sentence in excess of 12 months excludes any extradition for a section 1 offence, but sections 2 and 3 offences are covered. The Extradition Act 1870 is also suitably amended to include sections 2 and 3 offences.[7]

EXTRADITION FOR HACKING

The following discussion of an actual extradition case illustrates the way a hacker from abroad may be extradited to a place where his actions were illegal.

---

4   Extradition Act 1989, s 2.
5   See 'Double-criminality' at page 243.
6   Extradition Act 1989, s 2.
7   Computer Misuse Act 1990, s 15.

In *R v Governor of Brixton Prison, ex p Levin*, the United States government sought the extradition of a Russian expert computer programmer who had gained access to Citibank's computer in New Jersey, America.[8] Levin, using his skill as a computer programmer was able to monitor the transactions of substantial customers and insert unauthorised instructions to make payments from those accounts into those of a Russian accomplice. If the scheme had been successful, sums in excess of $10m would have been obtained. Levin was detained on 3 March 1995 in execution of a warrant under section 1(3) of the Extradition Act 1989 at the request of the United States government. He was accused of having committed in the United States offences of wire fraud and bank fraud and of conspiring to commit those offences. No single criminal offence under the law of England and Wales equates to the offence of wire fraud or bank fraud.

The prosecuting authority gave details of acts and conduct which translated into 66 offences under the criminal law of England and Wales including unauthorised access to a computer with intent to commit or facilitate further offences, conspiracy to commit offences under the Computer Misuse Act 1990 and unauthorised modification of computer material.

The applicant challenged his committal on the main grounds that the computer print-out records could not be admitted under section 69 of the Police and Criminal Evidence Act 1984 since that section did not apply to extradition proceedings, because they were not criminal proceedings within section 72 of the Act.

The court held that as the extradition proceedings had conduct punishable under the criminal law, they were criminal proceedings for the purposes of the Police and Criminal Evidence Act 1984. Evidence of the computer print-outs in extradition hearings should be, and was rightly in this case, admitted in evidence under section 69 of the Act.

One of the other grounds was that as the appropriation took place in Russia, where the computer keyboard was situated, the English courts have no jurisdiction. For the purposes of the Theft Act 1968 the court had to decide where the actions of Mr Levin took place. They said:[9]

> '[T]he operation of the keyboard by a computer operator produces a virtually instantaneous result on the magnetic disk of the computer even though it may be 10,000 miles away. It seems to us artificial to regard the act as having been done in one rather than the other place. [T]he fact that the applicant was physically in St Petersburg is of far less significance than the fact that he was looking at and operating on magnetic disks located in [America]. The essence of what he was doing was done there.'

8   [1996] 4 All ER 350.
9   [1996] 3 WLR 657 at 671.

OBSCENE AND INDECENT MATERIAL

It has always been possible to acquire by mail order obscene and paedophilic material from abroad which would be illegal in England. The Internet has made this process easier, it may have also made this activity more prevalent; it has not, however, altered the legal ramifications of the activity.[10]

Obscene Internet material

The Obscene Publications Act 1959, as amended by the Criminal Justice and Public Order Act 1994, covers material which has the effect of depraving and corrupting.

PUBLICATION OVER THE INTERNET

An offence is committed if a person publishes an obscene article: merely possessing an article is not an offence.[11] Possessing an obscene article for publication for gain is an offence.[12] Often those who use the Internet for these purposes do not pay money for obscene articles, rather, they exchange them for other articles. This too will be seen as 'for gain'.[13] It is for the possessor of the article to prove that it was not for gain.

A recent amendment to the Obscene Publications Act 1959 has introduced the concept that it is publication to transmit electronically stored data which is obscene on resolution into a viewable form.[14]

> **21. A person sends an e-mail attached to which is an encrypted graphics file depicting an obscene activity. Only the recipient has the unlocking key. The person will have transmitted the obscene material: it does not matter that the data is encrypted; when de-encrypted it will be obscene.**

Transmission or retrieval

Often obscene material is not transmitted to an individual. It is uploaded to a web site or an ftp site. Interested parties download this material by instructing their computer to issue a command to the holding site. It is clearly an important question whether this constitutes transmission, and thereby constitutes publication.

This question was addressed by the Court of Appeal in *R v Fellows; Arnold*.[15] The appellants appealed that publication within section 1(3) requires some form of active conduct and that providing the *means* of access to a web site or ftp site is

10   See also Telecommunications Act 1984, s 43 and Indecent Displays (Control) Act 1981.
11   Obscene Publications Act 1959, s 2.
12   Obscene Publications Act 1959, s 2.
13   Obscene Publications Act 1959, s 1(5). See *R v Fellows; R v Arnold* (unreported, Court of Appeal, 27 September 1996).
14   Obscene Publications Act 1959, s 1(3). As amended by Criminal Justice and Public Order Act 1994, s 168 and Sch 9.
15   Unreported, Court of Appeal, 27 September 1996.

passive only. In short, putting obscene pictures on a web site, although no doubt *seen* by many people, is not publication of those pictures; technically it is each viewer who retrieves the picture.

The Court of Appeal was prepared to accept that some form of activity is required for publication. In this case they thought that there was ample evidence of such conduct: the first appellant:

> 'took whatever steps were necessary not merely to store the data on his computer but also to make it available world-wide to other computers via the Internet. He corresponded by e-mail with those who sought to have access to it and he imposed certain conditions before they were permitted to do so.'

This 'activity' prior to the actual offence appears to have satisfied the court that the storage of the material alone would be distribution.[16]

Publication by Internet Service Providers

That publication can be 'passive' may be of considerable relevance for Internet Service Providers. A Provider who facilitates, by storing, the transmission of an obscene file may be culpable as the publisher of that material. It is a defence to show that the defendant did not examine the material *and* had no reasonable cause to suspect that its publication would be an offence under the Act.[17]

This double-barrelled defence can place a high burden on Internet Service Providers, Bulletin Board operators and any other intermediaries who store data.[18]

On notice of obscene material

Internet Service Providers who store newsgroups now have a high burden because New Scotland Yard has attempted to put all Providers 'on notice' of those newsgroups which contain illegal material.[19] Providers have been supplied with lists of newsgroups containing dubious files. The Internet Watch Foundation, which represents most Service Providers, has announced, in conjunction with the police, a newsgroup rating scheme and unified national hotline.[20] This will allow Internet Service Providers to co-ordinate deletions of any indecent material and to help police track down offenders.

Only the bravest Internet Service Provider will now store a newsgroup on which notice from the police has been provided. In such a situation it will be difficult for the Provider to meet the defence that it had no reasonable cause to suspect it was an offence.

16   See also *R v Pecciarich* (1995) 22 OR (3d) 748 at 765.
17   Obscene Publications Act 1959, s 2(5).
18   The Internet Access Providers who allow access to the Internet and the World Wide Web but not newsgroups are rarely going to be liable under the Act. This is because, they act only as a conduit for digital data and this data is sent in short packets which are assembled by the client computer. It is therefore close to being impossible for an Internet Access Provider, as distinct from an Internet *Service* Provider who stores information, to know the contents of a requested data file until it is finally depicted on the user's computer.
19   *Independent*, 20 December 1995.
20   *Daily Telegraph*, 1 October 1996.

Indecent material

The Protection of Children Act 1978 as amended by the Criminal Justice and Public Order Act 1994 makes it an offence

> '(a) to take, or permit to be taken, an indecent photograph of a child (meaning in this Act a person under the age of 16); or
>
> (b) to distribute or show such indecent photographs or pseudo-photographs; or
>
> (c) to have in his possession such indecent photographs or pseudo-photographs with a view to their being distributed or shown by himself or others ...'

PHOTOGRAPHS AND PSEUDO-PHOTOGRAPHS

Photographs

The changes brought by the Criminal Justice and Public Order Act 1994 have been implemented to address the use that paedophiles make of computers. The term 'photographs' includes data stored on a computer disk or by other electronic means which is capable of conversion into a photograph.[1] This includes digital graphic images. The court will take a 'purposive approach': if the data can be converted into an indecent image, the data will be classed as a photograph.[2]

Pseudo-photographs

This means an image, whether made by a computer graphic or otherwise, which appears to be a photograph.[3] This inclusion, apparently, reflects the practice of paedophiles who use pornographic images of adults and then digitally alter them to look like indecent photographs of children.

TRANSMISSION OR RETRIEVAL

As in the case for obscene material, *R v Fellows* indicated that it will be distribution simply to *allow* such images to be transmitted. Similarly, having been warned that certain newsgroups contain indecent material it will be difficult to rely on the defence that one had no knowledge or reason to suspect that the material was indecent.

1　Protection of Children Act 1978, s 7(4)(b) as amended.
2　See the US Court of Appeals for the Sixth Circuit, *US v Thomas* 74 F 3d 701 (1996).
3　Protection of Children Act 1978, s 7(7) as amended.

Chapter six

Data protection

Vast amounts of information about everyone are stored on computers, capable of instant transmission anywhere in the world and accessible at the touch of a keyboard. The right to keep oneself to oneself, to tell other people that certain things are none of their business, is under technological threat.

Lord Hoffmann, *R v Brown*[1]

The Internet and its constituent parts facilitate the transmission of personal data, often around the world. Necessarily, these data are stored, sent by, and received by computers. It is for this reason that, where the data fall within the scope of the United Kingdom's data protection legislation, users of the data may have to register with the Data Protection Registrar.

The Data Protection Registrar has the power to regulate the transfer of personal data. It is this possible prohibition on overseas transfers that makes the Internet a closely watched medium for transferring personal data. There are few aspects of the Internet that someone cannot access from anywhere else in the world. Potentially therefore, personal data that are readily accessible over the Internet are necessarily accessible from an unsafe data area.

The Registrar also ensures that data users comply with eight data protection principles. One of the most salient for the Internet is that all personal data must be kept secure. This is in stark contrast to the Internet, which is inherently open to all to access. Without specific security measures in place, the Internet does not discriminate between different people accessing its data. Without, say, password control, it is difficult for a controller of a web site to prevent access by a particular person. This is in contrast to the controller of an ftp site, who can provide passwords to selected users. The data protection legislation therefore imposes minimum levels of security on Internet users of personal data.

This chapter deals with the following issues concerning data protection and the Internet.

1. What types of data are regulated?
2. What types of activity over the Internet are regulated?
3. Are Internet Service Providers, controllers and users of web sites classed as data users or computer bureau operators?
4. What are the obligations of registration for Internet data users and computer bureau operators both in the United Kingdom and abroad?

---

1   *R v Brown* [1996] 1 All ER 545 at 556.

5.   What are the recommended principles for obtaining personal data over the Internet?
6.   What are the recommended principles for keeping personal data up to date and accurate?
7.   With the Internet often lacking security, what are the principles for adequate data security over the Internet?
8.   What is the extent of the Data Protection Registrar's jurisdiction over United Kingdom and overseas data users and computer bureau operators?

BACKGROUND

History

The Council of Europe's Convention for the Protection of Individuals with regard to the Automatic Processing of Personal Data[2] sought to eradicate the hazard of a data-haven operating data banks outside national jurisdictions. To do this, ratifying countries of the Convention can withhold personal data from countries who do not have equivalent protection. In fear of this information exile, the United Kingdom signed the Convention.

FIRST EUROPEAN CONVENTION ON DATA PROTECTION

The Convention consists of three main parts: general principles; rules on transborder data flow; and mechanisms for mutual assistance and consultation between contracting states. The central aspect of the Convention are the 'common core' principles.[3] These ensure that all individuals in all signatory countries have the same minimum protection from misuse of automated personal data.[4] In theory, this eradicates the fear of data havens and decreases possible conflicts over data protection between states. There are clear practical difficulties in preventing personal data transmitted over the Internet, however, from passing to an unsafe domain.

THE DATA PROTECTION ACT 1984

The Data Protection Act 1984 came into force on 1 October 1985. The Act fixes new civil rights for individuals on whom computerised data are held; it also creates complementary civil and criminally sanctioned responsibilities for those persons who use that data. A Data Protection Registrar oversees these new rights and

---

2   European Treaty Series, number 108. Edition January 1981. After, First European Convention on Data Protection.
3   See Article 5, Quality of data; Article 6, Special categories of data; Article 7, Data security; Article 8, Additional safeguards for the data subject.
4   The European Parliament recommended that the Convention should cover both automated and manual data, but the Council rejected this suggestion. See Official Journal of the European Communities, number C 140/37, 5 June 1979, paragraph I.1. and European Council Explanatory Report on the Convention for the Protection of Individuals with regard to automatic processing of personal data, Strasbourg, 1981, paragraph 1.

responsibilities and may verify that registered users of data comply with the eight data protection principles.

Two types of computer user are required to register: any United Kingdom data user who automatically holds or processes personal data; and any United Kingdom computer bureau providing services in relation to personal data. If the data user does not qualify for exemption, and still does not register, the user will be guilty of an offence.[5] It is crucial to understand that the register does not contain the actual data, but *types* of those data. In illustration, data users must register particulars of the personal data held, the purposes for holding them, the sources of the data, any person to whom they may disclose the data, and overseas countries to which the data may be transferred.[6] By contrast, computer bureau operators need only register their name and address.

Recent developments

The European Council has now adopted a new Data Protection Convention. In relation to Internet-specific matters, it makes little change to the existing regime. Relevant changes proposed by the Convention are referred to in footnotes throughout this chapter.

TYPES OF DATA

Before investigating the application of the Data Protection Act 1984 to the Internet, it is vital to set out the main aspects to the legislation. It is unfortunate that the Act is particularly definition-based: to appreciate the responsibilities of a data user one must appreciate no less than four separate concepts: data, personal data, processing of data, and holding. For ease of understanding, therefore, this chapter attempts to simplify the legislation by referring to three issues: type of data; activity in relation to the data; the person performing those activities. This chapter describes each of these three issues with specific Internet examples; the remainder of the chapter considers the application of these issues to commonplace activities on the Internet.

Personal data

DATA

The Act applies only to personal data and those dealing with it. Assessing whether digital information is personal data is the starting point for all data protection questions. The word, 'data', is defined widely as meaning:[7]

---

5   Data Protection Act 1984, s 5(5).
6   It is these two last requirements that are under the greatest strain when the data user is using the Internet for its data transfer and processing.
7   Data Protection Act 1984, s 1(2).

'information recorded in a form in which it can be processed by equipment operating automatically in response to instructions given for that purpose.'

The important concept is that the data must be *recorded*.[8] For the Internet, this will generally be the case. Any data that is flowing through, or stored on, the Internet must necessarily be recorded in this way. E-mail is stored on a host computer; ftp sites store data also. Even a page on the web that features sound, music and animation has these data stored at the server, and then downloaded and stored on the accessing computer. The short point is that all data that can be accessed via the Internet will be classified as data for the purposes of the Act. It is not always true that these data are *personal* data; this is considered next.

PERSONAL DATA

The word 'personal' refers to the data consisting of information[9]

'which relates to a living individual who can be identified from that information (or from that and other information in possession of the data user).'

This definition is fundamental to whether a user of data has obligations under the Act, and thus to a data subject's rights under the Act. What follows is a set of four tests that can establish whether data could be personal data. These are provided with reference to use and availability of data on the Internet. Before using data over the Internet, computer users should initially check, using these four tests, whether the data could be personal data:

1. living individual;
2. subjectivity of personal data;
3. possession of other information;
4. opinions on individuals.

I. Living individual

The Act focuses on the data, not the individual to whom it relates. As long as the individual is living and is not a body corporate, the Act can apply. This includes all individuals whether resident abroad or of foreign nationality.

> **I. A UK software supplier forms contracts with Internet users and distributes software to them over the Internet. When considering the Data Protection Act 1984, the supplier need not ascertain the residence or nationality of each customer. The Act will apply to all the customers if the data held are classed as personal.**

---

8   See Fifth Data Protection Report, at paragraph 243.
9   Data Protection Act 1984, s 1(3).

> **2. A foreign national enters his personal details into an on-line form required to access a UK newspaper's web site. The individual is now concerned that these personal data are being misused. All things being equal, he has rights under the Act to prevent this misuse because he is a living individual and the data held are personal. The individual's nationality is largely irrelevant to the newspaper's obligations.**

2. Subjectivity of personal data

For data to be personal is a subjective notion, not an objective one. To one data user the data may be personal, but to another data user, who possesses less 'other information', the data may not be personal: the data user may be unable to identify the individual. This has the commercial consequence that one data user who regularly accesses a directory web site may be accessing personal data, whereas another data user may not be classified as accessing personal data. In this respect, one resolves whether data are personal by examining the relationship between the data user and the data themselves.

3. Possession of other information

The definition of 'personal' refers to identification in conjunction with other information in *possession* of the data user.[10] Users should contrast this with the identification being easy or, say, cheap. On the Internet it is simple to download vast quantities of information about an individual.[11] Where the information found relates to a living individual, but is not sufficient to identify that person, it is often possible to identify the person by re-searching using the acquired information. The *ability* to identify the individual from such third-party servers, located with additional searches for example, would not reclassify the data as personal.

4. Opinions on individuals

The final test to establish whether data are personal data is to ascertain the nature of the data: if the data are an expression of opinion about an individual, then the data can be personal. At the opposite end of the spectrum is an expression of intention about an individual; this does not, in itself, make the data personal.

To fall within the exception of not being personal data, the intention being expressed must be the intention of the data user and not a third party. For this reason, repeating the intention of another with respect to a living individual will not benefit from the exception; the data may still be personal. It is worthwhile noting that the Registrar will use a purposive analysis of the data. Framing an opinion as an intention will not make the data non-personal.

---

10   Data Protection Act 1984, s 1(3).
11   Indeed, one can use particular web pages to search for someone's e-mail address. With this, one may then 'finger' the host and check the last time that user logged in to his account.

> **3. A UK bulletin board operator monitors conversation threads in its forums. Where one user states their dissatisfaction with a particular software package, the operator may earn commission by passing the user's details on to the competing software manufacturer. The Act does not classify these details as an intention for two reasons. First, the opinion of the user is being clothed as an intention, so is not excluded. The second reason is that, if the user's dissatisfaction is viewed as an intention to buy a replacement, it is not the intention of the operator. These data would therefore be a third party's intention and so not excepted.**

DATA PROTECTION ACTIVITIES

It will be recalled that the Act only impinges on certain activities in relation to data with a particular quality, it must be personal. Having defined personal data, it is possible to consider two main activities regulated by the Act. These are processing and disclosure.[12] These two terms are vital to decipher the main restrictions on dealing with personal data over or from the Internet. Although the restrictions will be explored in greater depth below it is worthwhile setting the terms in their applied contexts.

Processing

The Act defines processing as not only performing one of a defined set of operations on the data but also performing these operations with reference to a data subject. It is not enough simply to perform the digital processing unless combined with reference to a data subject.[13] These two distinct aspects are examined below.

PROCESSING OPERATIONS

Section 1(7) states that processing data is

> 'amending, augmenting, deleting or re-arranging the data or extracting the information constituting the data ...'

---

12   'Transfer' is also crucial but its definition turns on the definition of 'holding'. As this is defined below at page 258, 'transfer' is also defined below.
13   Under the Second Data Protection Directive, subject to narrow exceptions there is a bar on using automatic processing as the only basis for making a decision. Processing of personal data will be legitimate only in specified situations. The first of these is where 'the data subject has unambiguously given his consent'. Consent must be given freely in knowledge of the purposes for which the data is to be used. Without consent, processing may be carried out in the performance of a contract with the data subject or if it is necessary to protect the subject's vital interests. These interests have to be weighed against those of the data subject. Data subjects have the right either to object to the processing of data for the purposes of direct mailing or to be informed of the fact that processing is to be carried out for this purpose. They must have the expressly offered right to object free of charge.

The above list of what constitutes processing is exhaustive. It does not, for example, include storing, so using a server simply to store data is not processing data. Similarly, the definition does not specifically include transmitting data as a form of processing. So it may not be processing within the Act to download a data file from an ftp site.[14] It is when the data user manipulates the data, as defined above, that the activity is processing.[15]

Reference to data subjects

As previously mentioned, Internet data users will only be seen as processing where their activity focuses on the data subject itself.[16] That *part* of the data is personal data is insufficient for the entire activity to be classed as processing. It is also insufficient that an operation is carried out on data in relation to a set, or class, of individuals unless in relation to each individual. The Act refers to 'processing by reference to *the* data subjects' not 'to data subjects'.[17]

Disclosure

The most relevant activity on the Internet for data protection is disclosure: the Internet, especially the World Wide Web, is heralded for the ease with which information can be disclosed to others. The novel legal issue for the Internet is whether there is disclosure when information is not actively distributed but is merely 'left' on a server for collection.

Disclosure of data occurs where information is divulged to another person, to the extent that that person can identify the individual to whom the data refers.[18] Where the data user can identify an individual only from other data in his possession, if these identifying data are not divulged along with the data, no disclosure has taken place.

---

4. An Internet Service Provider maintains a log of its members' login times. The Provider allocates each member a unique number and stores login times in conjunction with this number; in another database the Service Provider stores a list of the unique numbers for each member.

The Service Provider seeks to use this log to inform the local telephone networks of the most popular access times. It will not be disclosure for the Service Provider to supply only the log to the network, but not the members' numbers database. Without these data, the telephone networks cannot reveal the identity of the individuals.

---

14 An argument certainly exists that transmission of part of the data will be seen as 'extraction'.
15 The Data Protection Registrar has requested that the definition of processing be extended to cover both the storage and the transmission of data. Fifth Data Protection Report at paragraph 250.
16 Data Protection Act 1984, s 1(7).
17 Emphasis added.
18 The use of the word 'person' means that there will not be disclosure where the discloser and recipient are two branches or divisions of the same legal entity.

DISCLOSURE ON A HOME PAGE

One of the keys to the commercial success of the Internet is that it is very cheap to 'distribute' information to many recipients. There are two main ways: first, using a mailserver to e-mailshot[19] a list of e-mail addresses; the second way is to 'leave' information in a readily accessible area of the Internet, be that as an upload on an ftp site or published on a web site. The commercial difference is that in the second scenario, it is the receiver of the information who acts to retrieve that information; the provider remains passive. Receivers pay the online charges to locate and download the posted information. By contrast, when e-mailing the provider takes the active role, by sending the information; the recipients cannot help receiving it, they remain passive.

Disclosure or dissemination

This distinction may make a difference for the purposes of the Data Protection Act 1984. Is posting personal data on a web site 'disclosing' those data or is it merely disseminating? Technically, the data are not provided to a third party when uploaded onto the web site. Data are copied onto a second computer, called a server. It is only after *the third party accesses* the site that the data may be revealed to an outside source, and by no action of the data user. The data user has no active role in the reading of and reacting to those data.

Definitions of disclosure

There are strong reasons to conclude that disclosure is effected by publishing personal data on a web page or uploading it to an ftp site. The justification for this reasoning is that the statutory definition of 'disclosing' is not exhaustive. The definition at section 1(9) merely *includes* two possible definitions as:

> '"Disclosing", in relation to data includes disclosing information extracted from the data, and where the identification of the individual who is the subject of personal data depends partly on the information constituting the data and partly on other information in the possession of the data user, the data shall not be regarded as disclosed or transferred unless the other information is also disclosed or transferred.'

In the House of Lords decision in *R v Brown* Lord Goff considers the scope of this definition.[20] In this obiter dictum, Lord Goff states:[1]

---

19   It is common to find that the information technology industry elides nouns and verbs. This example, 'to e-mailshot' should be read to mean, 'to send a mailshot of e-mails'.
20   For the sake of academic completeness it should be noted that Lord Hoffmann, also one of the majority, was unprepared to indulge in any obiter analysis of the word 'disclose'. He referred to the speech of Lord Goff saying, 'I [agree with the judge at first instance and] also agree with the reasoning of my noble and learned friend Lord Goff of Chieveley . . . [b]ut I add . . . I express no view about the scope of the other words [than "use"] which the Act uses in relation to data, such as "disclosing and transferring". "Transferring" clearly includes transferring the data in its binary form. Whether this can also constitute disclosing or *whether disclosing requires that it should actually have come to someone else's knowledge is a question which I prefer to leave open*': [1996] 1 All ER 545 at 561. Emphasis added.

'Although there is a particular reference to the meaning of "disclosing" in section 1(9) of the Act, to which I shall shortly refer, disclosure as such is not defined in the Act, and the word "disclose", like the word "use", should where it appears in the Act be given its natural and ordinary meaning.'

The Oxford English Dictionary defines the verb 'to disclose' as, 'remove cover from, expose to view; make known, reveal'. With this definition it becomes clearer that publishing personal data on a home page or uploading them to an ftp site will be disclosure for the purposes of the Act. There can be little doubt that publishing data on a web site is exposing to view or revealing those data.

In the case, Lord Goff goes on to address whether an unauthorised transferral of data from one database to another would constitute disclosure. His reason for questioning this is that section 5(2)(d) specifies that one must disclose to 'any person' not referred to in the register. Thus, if one takes section 5(2)(d) literally, transferring to a second *database* may not fall within section 5(2)(d) as for that section the transfer must be to a *person*. The same argument could be adduced that to disclose personal data to a web server, being a computer not a person, no offence could be made out under section 5(2)(d). As to these arguments he says,[2]

> 'I however incline to the view that such a transfer would not of itself amount to disclosure of data ... contrary to section 5(2)(d), *although it may be readily inferred that the person effecting the transfer was inevitably therefore disclosing the data to another person or persons who, as he well knew, would retrieve the information from the second database and so have the information disclosed to him.*'

The Data Protection Registrar provides further persuasive, admittedly less powerful,[3] support to the conclusion that it is disclosure to publish on the World Wide Web information extracted from personal data. In the Data Protection Registrar's statement in the Guideline Number 2 it is noted that disclosure may be affected by 'showing someone a printout'. Providing information on a web site is arguably analogous to this situation. Those data users who make available personal data over the Internet will be seen as disclosing those data. Even if the viewer must enter a password to read the data, it is the actions of the web site controller that permit the viewing or disclosure.

---

5. A UK firm of advisers to wealthy individuals seeks to advertise its work for clients. It chooses to use a web site featuring lists of clients, each with a link to a further page describing the nature of the work undertaken for the person. Notwithstanding issues of professional conduct and confidentiality, the firm will be disclosing this personal data. Without a sufficiently wide description of transfer in the register, the firm will therefore be committing an offence under section 5(2).

---

1   [1996] 1 All ER 545 at 549.
2   Ibid. Emphasis added.
3   The Data Protection Registrar, while influential and knowledgeable, does not decide or conclude legal issues relating to the Act. At most, the Registrar may decide on certain questions of fact. Legal questions are only conclusively answered by the courts both of the United Kingdom and, possibly, the European Court of Justice.

DATA PROTECTION REGISTRATION

The application of the Data Protection Act for users of the Internet has been shown to be great. All information sent over the Internet will constitute data, and if personal, providing those data over the Internet will be viewed as either processing or disclosure. Those persons falling within the Act's ambit are required to register with the Data Protection Registrar. If a person should register but does not, this can constitute a criminal offence.[4]

The Data Protection Act 1984 regulates two types of computer users: data users and computer bureau operators. It is important both for users of data and for individuals concerned over their personal data to understand this distinction. This does not mean that a person cannot fall into both categories: often a computer bureau operator will, on closer inspection, fall within the category of a data user *as well*. The Registrar encourages that computer bureau operators register under both categories if they are unsure over their potential use of data; better this than acting as an unregistered data user.

The requirements for computer bureau operators and data user registrations differ. Persons who are acting as computer bureau operators are required to register only their name and address; data users are required to register a greater range of information related not only to themselves but also related to the type of data being held and their intended use.

Data user

To define a data user, the Act uses a further term, 'holding' data.[5] If a person holds data, they are a data user.

HOLDING DATA

A person holds data where each of three conditions are met:

1. the data must be part of a collection of data which has been processed or is intended to be processed by the data user or on behalf of the data user; and
2. the data user, whether jointly or in common with others, controls the contents and the use of the data in the above collection; and
3. the data are in the appropriate form having been or being able to be processed, or after processing the data are in a converted form with the view to being further processed.

It is necessary to deconstruct two of the conditions listed above. First, control over contents and use of data; second, actual or potential processed data.

Control

The second of three conditions to hold data is that the data user controls the contents or use of the data. This control may be jointly or in common with others.

4   Data Protection Act 1984, s 5(5).
5   Data Protection Act 1984, s 1(5).

Control of contents and use

Control can be distinct from processing. It is possible that one person compiles personal data, another processes it and a third person then uses the data. This differentiation separates data users from computer bureau operators: data users must use and control the contents of data; computer bureau operators only process personal data. Because the obligations on data users are more onerous than those on computer bureau operators it is important to understand what the Act means by 'control'. If an Internet Service Provider, registered as a computer bureau operator, is doing more than only processing personal data and is actually using and controlling it, he may be committing a criminal offence by acting as an unregistered data user. This said, it is not easy to distinguish between controlling the contents of data and processing them. It is especially difficult because 'processing' is such a broad term and includes 'augmenting' the data.

> **6. A UK bookseller maintains a web site which allows customers to read rated reviews of selected books online and then place an order if desired. The bookseller seeks to establish whether there is any correlation between placing an order and reading a highly rated review. To establish this, the bookseller divulges all the data to a market researcher. The bookseller has control over the contents of the data and their use. The market researcher has no control over contents and subsequent use.**

Jointly or in common

The terms 'jointly' and 'in common' broaden the ambit of control not only by including data that are under the absolute control of the data user, but also by including the data partially under the control, or instruction, of the data user. Similarly, where many persons control one collection of data, each person will be classed as controlling that collection in common. The inclusion of these terms is particularly relevant to the Internet because it is rare that a single-entity will deal on the Internet with data: most organisations use one person to design a web site, another to host it and perhaps even a third to provide access to the server.

> **7. A UK business rents space on a web site to a number of retailers and services providers, rather like a shopping mall. The web site collects personal data on each of the entrants to the mall. At the end of each day, the business provides to its 'tenants' a full list of each of the entrants to the mall. Each of the tenants uses the data at its discretion. The business and each of its tenants are data users in common.**

> **8. An organisation maintains a web site that allows any person's name to be entered and provides the e-mail address for the person, where applicable. This information is extracted from UNIX 'white-pages' which maintain a register of any postings to the Usenet. While the owner of the web site does not absolutely control the data on the site, the owner does hold the personal data as a data user.**

Of course, the control exerted over a collection of data may vary with time. It is conceivable that a person who previously had no control over the content of data, merely by processing them, could begin exerting control over the types of data supplied. The varying involvement of a web designer who takes an administrative role is one example. This variance of control does create uncertainty: those individuals who consider that they only process data should maintain careful records of their activities to ensure that they can justify their position as a mere computer bureau operator.

> **9. An airline already using an online reservation system seeks to research the use of its system. To do this, it provides a list of its users' e-mail addresses to a market researcher for the purposes of sending out a questionnaire. The market researcher reasons that geographical and age data will be useful to focus the questions. If the reasoning is accepted, the researcher has contributed to the content of the data and so may have inadvertently controlled and used the data jointly with the airline.**

Actual or potential processed data

After processing data, where a data user has a specific intention to re-process the data he will continue to hold that data even if the data are converted into another format.

If the Registrar would class say, a web controller, as holding personal data but the controller is not registered as a data user, the controller may be prosecuted. The scope of holding is therefore significant and should also not merely be considered once; a change in control may change an activity into holding. To be safe, data users should consider that they are holding the data if the data *can* be processed; destroying or converting the data into a non-processable format, such as a printout, will probably be the only sure way of not being classed as holding the data.[6]

> **10. An organisation uses a central server to allow its employees to communicate using the Internet. As with the use of telephones by its employees, the organisation accepts that its employees will use the e-mail system not only for business correspondence but also personal e-mails. The organisation maintains a database of the sender and recipient for each message. If this database is used to locate specific e-mails, but the individual's identity is not relevant to the purpose of locating the e-mail, the organisation is not holding personal data. If, instead, the organisation uses the database to 'monitor' certain recipients *or senders* of e-mails, it will be holding personal data.**

---

6   This presupposes that, respectively, the data user has no intention to resurrect the destroyed data from a backup, or scan the printouts by optical character recognition.

Computer bureau operators

As discussed, the Data Protection Act 1984 applies to data users who process personal data. The Act also applies, less onerously, to individuals who either allow users access to their equipment to process data, or perform the processing for them. More specifically, a person is a computer bureau operator if he:[7]

1. acts as an agent for other persons to cause data held by them to be processed; or
2. allows other persons to use equipment in their possession for the processing of data held by them.

Before considering the scope of this legal definition of these persons, it is useful to appreciate the types of storage and manipulation of data over the Internet.

REMOTE ACCESS

Data-warehousing

The ease of transmitting data over the Internet provides an opportunity to store information not on a client computer, but on a remote computer. Certain members of the Internet industry consider that, in the future, users will store information not on a home or office computer, but in a 'data warehouse' which will charge a rent for the amount stored.[8]

Large corporations, fearing data corruption, already store backups of their data with a data-storage corporation. Similarly for ftp sites, an owner of data can rent space on an ftp server, rather than investing in his own hardware.

Service Providers already perform a data-warehousing function for their members by storing e-mails until they are collected. Home pages are stored on servers, but there are often occasions where the owner of the home page only rents space on the storing server. Indeed, many of the Service Providers rent a fixed amount of storage space for each user to create and store his home page.

Remote manipulation

Certain corporations provide facilities for remotely manipulating data. Clients may choose this because the remote computer is extremely powerful and is able to perform tasks far more quickly than the client computer. There are two ways in which this manipulation can be performed: one, where the client computer communicates directly with the remote computer, giving instructions over the Internet or direct line; for the second way, owners of the remote computer are actually given instructions as to how to manipulate the data. It should be clear that the risk of a security breach is lower in the first way than the second.

---

7   Data Protection Act 1984, s 1(6).
8   This is the basis for the network computer having almost no storage capacity.

REGULATION OF DATA-WAREHOUSING

This chapter divides data warehousing into two sections: archives and servers. The archives section contemplates the legal regulation of organisations who simply store backups for data users. The servers section contemplates the Internet industry's widespread use of servers to store data, usually e-mails, or web sites.

Archives

A provider of equipment for backing-up a data user's data will be a computer bureau operator. This is because it is usual that the data are stored and are also accessible by the data user if there is a breakdown or emergency. This access is likely to fall within the broad scope of processing; as such, the owner of the data warehouse is allowing 'other persons the use of equipment in his possession for the processing of their data'.

Another common scenario is that the owner of the data warehouse, on request, will perform actions on the data on the data user's behalf. For example, where a data user urgently requires a list of names and addresses from a particular database, the owner of the data warehouse will usually, on request, provide these data to the data user. In doing so, that person is taking on the role of computer bureau operator. The person is performing processing on behalf of the data user.

The short and important point is that when storing another's data one should carefully assess whether one is acting as a computer bureau operator. The difficulty with such an assessment is that processing, as has been discussed, is a subjective term. And the subject is the data user, not the operator of the computer bureau. The result is that it is complicated to ensure that when a data user simply accesses its stored data, it is not processing those data; it may have other information in its possession which turns what could appear to be non-personal data into personal data.

Servers

The following discussion considers a few examples of server warehousing.

Internet Service Providers

Internet Service Providers such as Compuserve and MSN provide each member with an area of storage space which members can use to store e-mail messages, their file attachments and, more recently, an area of digital space for the storage of a home page. This storage potentially classes a Service Provider as a computer bureau operator. The main consideration is whether the Provider merely *stores* the information and does not allow the member to process data while in storage.

E-mail and e-mail addresses

If a Service Provider allows a member to alphabetise, or in any other way manipulate, e-mails *while stored on the Provider's server*, the member may be processing personal data. As a direct result, by using the Provider's computer to perform this processing the Provider may be viewed as a computer bureau operator.

> **11. An Internet Service Provider holds e-mails for each of its members until the member logs in. At this point the member is informed that mail is being stored and is given a choice: either continue to store the mail, or, download the information. On choosing to download the mail, the mail is deleted from the Provider's server. One copy only ever exists. Because the Service Provider does not permit its members to process their e-mail using, or on, its servers the Provider will not be a computer bureau operator.**

> **12. An Internet Service Provider prides itself on allowing its members to access their accounts from anywhere in the world, on any computer they choose. To facilitate this, one of the features of the system is that its members do not store their address book of e-mail addresses on their own computer, but on the Provider's server. This has the result that its members can process personal data using the Provider's equipment. This makes the Provider a computer bureau operator in respect of these personal data.**

Home pages

Many Internet Service Providers provide their members with space on their server to store an HTML document for access over the World Wide Web. As before, the Providers should carefully assess whether they are providing facilities to their members to process data.

Where home page construction is carried out using software run on the member's computer and the finished product is simply stored on the remote server, the Provider is unlikely to be a computer bureau operator.

REGULATION OF REMOTE MANIPULATION

Remote processing

Access to the Internet allows use of some of the most powerful computers in the world. Under certain conditions the owners of these and other computers will permit remote usage. Where the owner of a computer does permit remote access and manipulation, it may fall within the ambit of a computer bureau operator. The most common scenario is that a data user provides a batch file to a remote computer together with instructions for its processing. This arrangement will make the owner of the remote computer a computer bureau operator under the Act.

Search engines

The above situation differs from the use of *search engines* on a remote web site. In this instance, the search engine is searching data that is unlikely to be in the control of the person requesting the search. As a result, the owner of the search engine is not acting as a computer bureau operator. If anything, it is more likely that the owner is acting as data user.

REGISTRATION FORMALITIES

Time of registration

In keeping with the cliché, 'don't call us; we'll call you', applicants should consider themselves registered after submitting their registration until the Registrar tells them otherwise.[9] The Registrar is under an obligation to inform the applicant within six months as to the success, or otherwise, of an application.[10] Even if the Registrar refuses a registration, the applicant may lodge an appeal, and the applicant will remain registered until that appeal has been withdrawn or has been decided against the applicant. When in doubt, therefore, potential data users and computer bureau operators should submit a registration. By default a registration has a duration of three years, but applicants can choose a shorter one- or two-year duration.

Use of the registration

The Data Protection Register is a public document. Any member of the public can access a specific entry using the Data Protection Registrar's home page on the World Wide Web. This right differs from the right of a data subject to see his personal data. The register contains details of the computer bureau operator or data user and the use of the data, but not the actual data.

Format of register

Data users holding personal data must complete a registration form. This provides the Registrar with details of the data user, the data held, and the purposes of intended processing, sources of disclosure and transfers. Basic details about the data user are held in Part A of the form, details about data are held in Part B. This allows a data user to complete one Part A and then multiple Part Bs; one for each additional purpose. Computer bureau operators should complete Part A only. As has been mentioned, it is a criminal offence to hold personal data without an adequate registration.

---

9   If a form does not even meet the requirements of an application though, the applicant will not be registered. When this happens, the Registrar's office will inform the applicant of the errors or inadequacies of the form for appropriate amendment.
10 Data Protection Act 1984, s 7(1).

DATA USER DETAILS: PART A

Data user or computer bureau operator

The first choice is whether to register as a data user or a computer bureau operator, or both. It should be clear that, sometimes, there is a fine distinction between a data user and a computer bureau operator. For this reason, when a person who is dealing with personal data is in any doubt as to their status, they should register as both. This will not increase the cost of the registration, and if inappropriate, is not an offence.

Legal entity

The register must contain the actual legal identity of the data user or computer bureau operator. Companies should include not only the name and address of their registered office, but also include their number in the Register of Companies. Where the data user or computer bureau operator is not a company, it should include an appropriate address, such as a home or business address. It is a criminal offence not to update the register with any change in this address.[11]

Overseas element

The Data Protection Act 1984 has wide jurisdiction including not simply those persons who process in the United Kingdom data on United Kingdom subjects. First, the nationality or residence of the data subject is not relevant. Second, the geographical location of the data user is also of little relevance. In a reflection of the transnational nature of data processing, what is important is the place from where the data are controlled. This includes where an agent or servant in the United Kingdom effects that control.

> **13.** **A US company with no presence in the UK establishes a web site in America and, on that server, processes personal data relating to individuals living in the UK. The company does not need to register under the Data Protection Act 1984. The company then chooses to use a UK maintainer of a mailserver to e-mail all the individuals stored on its US server. The UK maintainer should now register under the Act; the US company remains free of obligations under the Act.**

Care should be taken when deciding that the foreign element is sufficient to remove the need to register data. This is because it is difficult to establish who controls data and from where that control is exercised; the inclusion of joint and common control has a blurring effect on the control's precise location. This 'blurring' is particularly true where the Internet is involved. It is difficult to ensure that some control exercised over the Internet is not being exercised from within the UK.

---

11 Data Protection Act 1984, s 6(5).

Subject access address

Data users are asked to provide the Registrar with a current contact address.[12] Applicants may include a physical address, and in addition the Registrar has expressed no problem with including an e-mail address. These addresses do not need to be those held by Companies House. Supplying an incorrect address can be an offence under section 6(6): it is prohibited to mislead the Registrar.

DATA DETAILS: PART B

All data users and computer bureau operators who also are data users must complete Part B of the Registration. This describes the types of data held, the purposes of intended processing and the sources of disclosure and transfers. Data users must complete Part B of the form for each purpose for which they hold data.

Purpose

Data users should pay much attention to the partially completed template received from the Registrar: Part B delineates the responsibilities of the data user to its subjects. Data users should be especially conscious that their application includes 'free-text' references to the Internet, where appropriate. If this section does not accurately describe the ambit of a data user's purpose for holding the data, at the least that data user may face a refused application; at worst, a prosecution under section 5 or 6.

The accompanying notes to Part B contain a large number of possible purposes for which a data user is holding data. Each purpose-type has an identifying code prefaced with the letter P and a full description of that purpose. Because there are a limited number of purposes to choose from, there will be some purposes that, while envisaged by the data user, are not encompassed by a standard purpose.

The Registrar has only provided *typical* examples of each purpose in its corresponding description. It is perfectly feasible that a data user's intended purpose, while appearing to fall within one of the purposes, is not specifically mentioned in the descriptions. This is currently the situation where a data user wishes to highlight the use of the Internet to achieve a particular purpose.

Part B permits a data user to expand on a particular purpose by amending its description. It is vital that data users provide the Registrar with the fullest account of their purpose for holding data. In this respect, it is open for a data user to define a personalised purpose to complete the form. This said, the many pre-defined purposes should cover the majority of anticipated purposes, especially where a data user amends slightly the corresponding description. Data users should also be aware that the processing of an application with standard purposes will be quicker than one with unique self-defined purposes.

Internet purposes

An example of needing to amend the description of a purpose is where the Internet is involved with that purpose. The justification for this is simple: providing data

12   Computer bureau operators are under no corresponding duty.

over the Internet, potentially, provides data to every computer in the world. The Data Protection Act 1984, however, was enacted particularly to watch and control transborder transfers; something trivial over the Internet.

> **14. A UK company currently uses one free-standing computer to store and process the biographical details of its staff. Now that the company is expanding out of the UK, it wishes to port these data onto a web site, to allow any member of the overseas operation to access the details. The company's Part B registration should reflect this. For, say, the purpose of 'Maintaining and publishing biographical details of staff', the description should be expanded to stress this is 'over the Internet's World Wide Web'.**

Often it will not be as straightforward as simply including the words 'over the Internet' to expand properly the description. Data users should be specific as to exactly what aspects of the Internet they will use. An anonymous ftp site with personal data is clearly less secure than a web site with password protection. Highlighting to the Registrar these distinctions ensures that the Registrar can properly assess the merits of an application. It also ensures that the Registrar will not be misled by the data user's purposes.

> **15. A UK car retailer has always sold its customer details to car insurance companies; appropriately, its registration included the P018 purpose of Trading in Personal Information. Previously, it provided on disk its lists of personal data to the insurance company. To keep the lists more up to date, it now has installed a server which acts as an ftp site for any person with the correct password. Despite this purpose remaining the same, the retailer should update the relevant description to reflect the change in provision.**

Data

Each purpose in Part B refers to a type of data. Data users should include in their application the description of the data, not the actual data. For this, the form provides standard species of data. Again, the form also allows data users to expand the descriptions of any particular type of data. Data users should attempt to make their completion of this section as accurate as possible: if their registration is too narrow to include the data that they are holding they will be unregistered data users concerning that data. The use of the Internet should not affect a data user's assessment of the data it is holding.[13]

Sources

The sources section, as with the above sections, allows a data user to select the most appropriate source of the data referred to above. As throughout the application, it is in a data user's interest to be as truthful and comprehensive as is possible. Where a data user is in doubt as to exactly which category describes a

---

13 This said, it is worthwhile noting that a person's e-mail address or home page URL should be classed as a C001 personal data identifier.

source, the data user should either include more than one category or hone the category by adding additional descriptions.

Disclosures

The disclosures section, at first blush, appears a mirror of the sources section. The form uses the same list and data users may tick the list for sources or disclosures. For data users on the Internet, the difference may be vast, however. Where a data user publishes personal data on a web site, notwithstanding any password control, the possible disclosures are effectively to any person with access to the Internet.[14] Where technical barriers are in place, such as passwords or client identifiers, there is an obvious reduction to the scope of disclosure. Without this 'technical tightening' of the potential disclosures, the Registrar may consider that the personal data can be distributed too widely.

Internet-wide disclosures

For data users, the choice to publish on the Internet is not only a technical one, but also a legal one. Data users have a special responsibility to safeguard personal data relating to data subjects. They should question whether it is justifiable to disclose this personal data to, in effect, the world.[15] Expensive technical improvements are occurring all the time over the Internet, but there are simple measures that a data user can take to restrict, to focus, its disclosures. For example, rather than using a web page to distribute personal data, a data user can use a mailserver. In this way, the data user can control to whom it will provide personal data. The defining quality of this list of e-mail addresses can be specified on the form, rather than having to specify, 'any person having access to the World Wide Web' as would be appropriate for World Wide Web distribution.

> **16. A university with multiple campuses decides that a cheap method of connecting the campuses is by simply establishing a common web site. Any personal data held on this site will be available to the entire Internet community. The university's Data Protection Registration should include with reference to each purpose, 'Personal data held for this purpose are accessible over the Internet's World Wide Web. Disclosure may therefore be made to any person having access to the Internet's World Wide Web.'**

Shared e-mail addresses

Data users should not overlook that more than one person may share one e-mail address. It is therefore possible that a data user's disclosures are more numerous than a list of e-mail addresses portrays. To allow for this, like sending confidential information, data users should check whether the disclosing e-mail is available to more than one person, be that a legal or natural person.

14   Also, as mentioned, there is no disclosure where the information is passed between two parts of the same company. This will be seen as one person. See fn 18 at page 255.

15   Especially as the data subject may have similar access to the data being published. The subject will therefore be able easily to see the true purpose for which his personal data is being used by the data user.

> **17.** A recruitment agency is concerned that one of its larger clients has a central e-mail address, allowing all employees in the organisation to access its e-mail. The agency wishes to e-mail to the personnel officer a list of potential candidates for a new position. To avoid broadening its disclosure section of its registration the recruitment agency encrypts the e-mail with public-key cryptography. This ensures that disclosure is solely to the personnel officer who controls the unlocking private key.

Overseas transfers

If personal data are able to be freely exchanged with territories where data protection safeguards are weak, the effect is that the domestic regime is compromised. It is essential for data protection that 'data havens' are exiled from any personal data transfer. In this respect the Act introduces protective measures to prevent personal data from being transferred into an impotent jurisdiction.

The first protective measure is that data users must complete section B4 which describes the scope of their overseas transfers. This is described in greater detail below, but it is worth noting at this point that the section provides some 56 options including a world-wide choice. The consequences of choosing the world-wide category, as will be inevitable for most Internet data users, are considered below also. The second protective measure to prevent personal data seeping into data havens is the Registrar's power to issue a transfer prohibition notice. The Registrar may address these notices to any registered data user and failure to comply with their restrictions is a criminal offence. Details of the effect of the reach and effect of these notices is explained below.[16] Before this section looks into registration of overseas transfers though, the term 'transfer' is defined and, in particular, distinguished from 'disclosure'.[17]

Transfer

'Transfer' is undefined by the Act. It is essential for Internet users, though, to appreciate the ambit to the main section of the Act that incorporates this term. Section 5(2)(e) states that it is an offence directly or indirectly to transfer data held by a data user to any country or territory outside the United Kingdom other than one named or described in its entry in the data protection register.

Meaning of section 5(2)(e)

This section uses two terms, previously defined, that must be correctly interpreted to appreciate the significance of the section. The term 'data' refers to information recorded in a form in which it can be recorded automatically.[18] It has been mentioned that the necessary digitisation to transmit material over the Internet has the result that the information will be recorded in the appropriate form.[19] So, any transmission over the Internet will involve the type of data as required under

---

16   See 'Overseas transfer prohibition' at page 296.
17   See 'Disclosure' at page 255.
18   Data Protection Act 1984, s 1(2).
19   See 'Data' at page 251.

section 5(2)(e). The next requirement of the section is that the data be 'held'. To hold data is a complex action, referring to the data being processed or processable.[20]

> **18. A recruitment agency holds curricula vitae on all its job candidates. It now wishes to publish these on its web page, to allow firms with vacancies to peruse the suitable candidates on the home page. If the agency, before publishing, strips out all the identifying information from each curriculum vitae, the publishing will not be a transfer. The data are not capable of being processed because the recipient is not identifiable from the transferred data; the data are not personal data.**

It is worth noting that disclosure is wider than transfer; disclosure *includes* transfer. The key to a transfer is that data must be ported in a processable form. As will be recalled, this requires that the identity of the data subject can be deduced. A disclosure, in contrast, includes porting the information extracted, or gleaned, from the data.

This distinction illustrates that the disclosures section of the registration form may, or may not, overlap with the overseas transfers. It is possible that a non-UK organisation is in the disclosures section, but that non-UK jurisdiction is not in the overseas transfer section of the form.

A further distinction between transfer and disclosure is in section 5(2)(e) and 5(2)(d) respectively. Section 5(2)(e) expresses its prohibitions in terms of transferrals to 'territories', whereas section 5(2)(d) states disclosure prohibitions with reference to 'persons'. This subtle distinction has ramifications for multi-national organisations. A seemingly internal transfer of personal information between an English and overseas branch of a company will not be covered by section 5(2)(d) as it is not between two *persons*.[1] The same exchange, if seen as a transfer, will fall within section 5(2)(e) as this focuses on the place of receipt not identity of recipient. This is particularly relevant for transnational companies who utilise a company-wide Intranet to transfer personal data.

Internet-wide transferrals

It has been mentioned that the choice to publish on the Internet is not simply a technical one, nor even solely a commercial one; there are also important legal considerations. These legal considerations are most evident where the law specifically addresses jurisdictional issues. The Data Protection Act 1984 does precisely this at section 5(2)(e) stating,

> '[A data user shall not] directly or indirectly transfer [personal] data held by him to any country or territory outside the United Kingdom other than one named or described in the entry.'

Like 'disclosure', making personal data available over the Internet will probably be a transfer of that data. At the least it will be an 'indirect transfer'. Therefore, also like disclosure, without appropriate security measures in place, any territory in the world can access any page on the World Wide Web, any file on an ftp site,

---

20   Data Protection Act 1984, s 1(5).
1   See fn 18 at page 255.

any computer on Telnet. So, if the data that identifies a living individual is retrievable by these methods the data user must be making world-wide transferrals.

Once a data user has identified that its personal data are being transferred throughout the world, for the purposes of the Act, two choices are available: a legal one, and a technical one.

World-wide transfer registration

The registration form allows for data users to select a 'world-wide' category for potential transferrals. It is suggested that data users without security measures in place do select this category. They cannot predict where in the world their data are being accessed from or in which territory the data are being retrieved.

The Registrar, in other circumstances, attempts to warn data users from selecting this category. This is for a simple reason. If the Registrar feels there is just one territory within the world that is not sufficiently data-safe for the personal data, the registration can be refused unless narrowed. In the world-wide category it is all or none. Selecting a world-wide category seems justifiable for Internet data users, even according to the Registrar's following guidelines.

World-wide transfer guidelines[2]

> '[T]hat transfers may be made to a relatively large number of overseas countries should not itself cause use of the "world-wide" category *if the destinations are predictable ...*'

The controller of a server without security cannot predict from where the accesses to that server will originate. It is also technically extremely difficult to restrict access from a particular territory to a particular server. The nature of the Internet is that data packets are routed around the world making it complex to predict the final destination of a retrieval. The presence of a firewall en route makes it impossible to establish from where a retrieval will finally be made. These security devices can act like a one-way door, allowing data packets to move in one direction, but preventing the data's final destination being divulged in the opposite direction. Even if requests from certain territories could be prevented, there is nothing stopping an individual from that territory accessing through Telnet a computer in an acceptable territory: the data would appear to be retrieved to an agreeable jurisdiction when this territory is simply the *penultimate* stop before the unacceptable territory. On similar principles, there is little preventing an individual dialling long-distance from an unfit territory to an Internet Service Provider based in a more appropriate territory. For these reasons, it cannot be predicted to where data on the Internet will be retrieved. By the Registrar's guidelines, therefore, use of the 'world-wide' category may be justifiable.

The Registrar also considers where the transferral situation is mainly predictable.

> '[I]f the situation is mainly predictable, but very rarely other transfers may occur, *with some notice*, then again this should not cause use of the "world-wide" category. A registration can easily be amended to add other transfers from time to time.'

2   At AX.1. in the Registrar's Guidelines. All emphases added.

The data user's inability to predict the destinations of data transfers over the Internet is discussed above in that most Internet disclosures are passive: the data user, and controlled server, have little regulation over the retrieval of data. The retriever of the data, the client, accesses and instructs the server to transfer the data; the data user is not directly involved in this process. A data user's knowledge of transfers is, necessarily, at best historic, not predictable. Clients do not give any notice of their access to a web site or login at an ftp site. The registration could therefore, at best, reflect each transfer post facto, making the registration inaccurate, and potentially making the data user an offender under the Data Protection Act 1984, section 5(2)(e). For the data subject's and the data user's safety, a data user should include on the registration all the potential territories of Internet transfers: the world.

Finally, the Registrar outlines consequences of unpredictable transfers:

> '[I]f the situation *is not predictable* and transfers occur relatively often or *at a short notice* to a *number of different countries*, use of the "world-wide" category would be appropriate.'

Putting personal data on the Internet, without security measures, allows any person, from any place in the world, at any time, to gain access to those data. The situation is unpredictable, with no notice and can be throughout the world: Internet data users must select the 'world-wide category'; anything narrower may leave them open to committing offences under section 5(2)(e).

Consequences of world-wide transfers

Where a data user selects the world-wide category there is a theoretical risk that the Registrar may begin an investigation into the safety of one of the countries in the world. This investigation may impinge on all data users with world-wide transfer registrations. They may informally or formally be compelled to prevent all transfers to the dubious territory.[3] In effect, data users are stopped from transferring *any* data over the Internet as it is so difficult, without security measures, to prevent flow of data to one particular jurisdiction. So far the Registrar has avoided this potential bar on one jurisdiction.

Restricting world-wide transfers

When a data user uses the Internet there is no simple method to avoid the extreme inconvenience of having to close access to a World Wide Web site because of one country's weak regime. Technical mechanisms can be introduced which *reduce* the chance that certain jurisdictions will access certain data.[4] No security measure will ever eliminate the possibility that data accessed over the Internet is *indirectly* being transferred out of the registered territories.[5]

3   See 'Overseas transfer prohibition' at page 296.
4   Of course, additional security can restrict the data access to certain *persons* using passwords and public-key cryptography. Unfortunately, the transferral offences are, strictly speaking, in relation to territories and even a person with the correct password may be using a computer in an unsafe region. In practice, the Registrar's approach has been to look at transfers case-by-case not by jurisdiction.
5   Section 5(2)(e) expresses transfers must not be made out of the registered territories whether direct or indirect. It is discussed below that, if a data user contravenes a transfer prohibition notice the data user can utilise a defence of 'all due care' to avoid being found guilty of the criminal offence.

CONSEQUENCES OF REGISTRATION

The previous sections provide the information to decide how and when an Internet user is a data user or a computer bureau operator for the purposes of the Act. If a person is a data user holding data or a computer bureau operator he must discontinue that role or activity until he registers under the Act.[6] Indeed, the Registrar has the power to prosecute for the offence of holding personal data as an unregistered person.

Obligations after registration

For both data users and computer bureau operators there are three main obligations which ensue after registration. First, the person must keep accurate the registration details held by the Registrar. The level of disclosure for the registration is substantially less for a computer bureau operator. The second obligation is for the registered person to comply with the Act's regulation of processing, disclosure and holding of personal data. Related to this is the third obligation to comply with the Registrar's notices. A vaguer, over-arching, obligation is that all registered persons are indirectly required to abide by their relevant data protection principles: data users must keep all eight; computer bureau operators only the last. The remainder of this chapter concentrates on the principles.

Data users under section 5(2)

This section states that registered data users will not act outside their stated registration. They must not obtain data from any source that they do not specify in the sources section of the registration.[7] Concerning the type of data, they must not hold personal data of a description outside the data entry.[8] The registered user must also not hold this, or any data, for a purpose not covered by the purposes section of the registration.[9] Finally, registered data users must not disclose the data to any person not described in the entry,[10] or transfer the data to a territory or country outside the geographical ambit of the registration.[11]

COMPUTER BUREAU OPERATORS UNDER SECTION 5(4)

In comparison with a data user, a computer bureau operator has more straightforward obligations. He must not provide services in respect of personal data unless there is a corresponding entry already on the register.[12]

---

6   Data Protection Act 1984, s 5(1).
7   Data Protection Act 1984, s 5(2)(c).
8   Data Protection Act 1984, s 5(2)(a).
9   Data Protection Act 1984, s 5(2)(b).
10   Data Protection Act 1984, s 5(2)(d). Unless an exempt disclosure.
11   Data Protection Act 1984, s 5(2)(e).
12   Data Protection Act 1984, s (5)(4).

PRINCIPLES OF DATA PROTECTION

As mentioned, following registration data users and computer bureau operators not only need to keep accurate their registrations and act within the ambit of their registration, but also they must abide by the principles of data protection.[13] Data users must comply with all eight; computer bureau operators, only the final eighth. The Registrar has the duty of ensuring the observance of these principles.

Eight principles of data protection

1. The information to be contained in personal data shall be obtained, and personal data shall be processed, fairly and lawfully.
2. Personal data shall be held only for one or more specified and lawful purposes.
3. Personal data held for any purpose or purposes shall not be used or disclosed in any manner incompatible with that purpose or those purposes.
4. Personal data held for any purpose or purposes shall be adequate, relevant and not excessive in relation to that purpose or those purposes.
5. Personal data shall be accurate and, where necessary, kept up to date.
6. Personal data held for any purpose or purposes shall not be kept any longer than is necessary for that purpose or those purposes.
7. An individual shall be entitled:
   (a) at reasonable intervals and without undue delay or expense, to be informed by any data user whether he holds personal data of which that individual is the subject; and to access any such data held by a data user; and
   (b) where appropriate, to have such data corrected or erased.
8. Appropriate security measures shall be taken against unauthorised access to, or alteration, disclosure or destruction of, personal data and against accidental loss or destruction of personal data.

Consequences of breach

On a strict view, breach of one of the eight principles is not an offence under the Act, nor is it sufficient grounds for a civil action. Although breach of a principle is not an offence per se, the Registrar has the power to serve an enforcement notice on any registered person to comply with the principles.[14] Non-compliance with an enforcement notice is an offence. Subject to a limited defence, non-compliance with such a *notice* can result in prosecution or being served with a de-registration notice.[15] Continued holding of data will then constitute an absolute offence under the Act.

---

13 Data Protection Act 1984, Sch 1, Pt I. Limited interpretation is found in the Data Protection Act 1984, Sch 1, Pt II.
14 Data Protection Act 1984, s 10.
15 Data Protection Act 1984, s 11.

Reach of principles

For the two reasons given above, it is worthwhile for potential applicants and individuals to understand what is entailed in complying with the principles. Data users must consider all eight principles while computer bureau operators need comply with the eighth solely.

I. OBTAINED AND PROCESSED FAIRLY AND LAWFULLY

> 'The information to be contained in personal data shall be obtained, and personal data shall be processed, fairly and lawfully.'

This principle will be particularly relevant for Internet data users who use their World Wide Web home page to obtain information from those who access the site. In short, the principle attempts to ensure those individuals who access a service or send information understand, and consent to, what will happen to their personal data. It is important for Internet data users to appreciate the true scope of this principle; well-established companies have been served with notices under this principle, damaging both consumer confidence and profitability. The Act protects data subjects, not users of these data.[16]

The Registrar makes the assessment of fairness on an objective basis; the main concern is the perception to the data subject and the use of the information, rather than the intention of the data user.[17] This is also a factual assessment taking into account all the circumstances of the obtaining and actual method of obtaining.

Information obtained fairly

There is no one test to establish that a data user has fairly obtained information from personal data, but there are a number of factors that the Registrar will take into account. The key factor is that the individual was not deceived or misled about the purpose of holding, disclosing or processing the data. A data user should try to indicate to the data subject the full potential use of that information. It is not enough to direct the subject to the registration or to assume that the subject knows the scope of a data user's registration. To be safe a data user must make explicit the purpose to each potential data subject: a data user may breach this principle even where the data subject was misled unintentionally.[18] Unless it is obvious from the method to obtain the information, data users should inform their subjects of the potential disclosures and transfers of the information, and the purpose for holding, using or disclosing that information.

---

16 'The Tribunal has taken the view that, in deciding whether processing is fair, the most important single consideration is the interests of the data subject': the Data Protection Guideline 4, para 1.24. The Registrar cannot enforce the principle where this would be likely to prejudice: the prevention or detection of crime; or the apprehension or prosecution of offenders; or the assessment or collection of any tax or duty: the Data Protection Guideline 4, para 1.26.
17 Data Protection Guideline 4, para 1.25.
18 This was decided in the *Innovations (Mail Order) Ltd v Data Protection Registrar* Data Protection Tribunal Case DA/92 31/49/1. This case will be examined in greater depth below.

Identity of data user

Potential data subjects should be made aware of to whom they are providing their personal data. The seamless way that a viewer of a web site can move between different web sites may cause data protection problems. For example, many commercial sites out-source any payment mechanisms to a third party who also operates a web site. A viewer of the commercial site will be taken through the various stages of choosing a product to purchase. The final stage in this process is for the viewer to enter his personal details and payment particulars. To do this the viewer will often be instructed to click a certain icon, one say labelled, 'Payment'. At this point, unbeknown to the viewer, the viewer is connected with the *payment* web site. The only way for the viewer to discover this, unless made clear, is to watch the URL alter at the top of their browser.

It is likely to be unfair obtaining of data where the provider of that data is not alerted to the identity of the person obtaining that data. Controllers of web sites that interact with others for the collection of personal data should make it clear to their viewers that this is the case.

Non-obvious purposes

Often a data user will have more than one contemplated purpose for personal information. Where a purpose could not reasonably be expected, the data user must inform the subject prior to holding the data. Data users must give each individual the informed chance to refuse to become a data subject.[19]

> **19. A search engine web site earns revenue by selling advertising space. Users are not charged to access the site, but they must complete an online form to use the site. This form asks many personal details including the person's e-mail address. The online form must specifically mention if, say, the site will pass these data to the advertisers. This would be a non-obvious purpose and, without such specific mention, may be a breach of the first data protection principle.**

It is a subtle distinction, but data users should assume that there is a need to inform the data subject of the intended use. Data users should alert their data subjects to any potential disclosure, transferral or use. This is the case even where the data, once obtained, will be used solely by the data user.

> **20. A UK magazine publisher provides free access to selected articles that it publishes on a home page. To gain access, a user must obtain a password by completing an online form. The publisher should inform each user if the personal data in the online form will be used to market the other magazines, or allow them to disallow such use.**

Changed purposes

Often a data user will obtain personal data with one intention in mind, and then later decide to use the information for another purpose. Unless this new purpose is

---

19   This is specifically discussed below at 'Prior consent', page 277.

within the scope of the purpose reasonably contemplated or disclosed to the data subject, strictly speaking, the data user should seek new consent.

Prior consent

In a growth industry such as the Internet, it is important to keep open one's options for future business ventures. Unfortunately, it is not advisable to attempt to keep open one's options of dealing with personal data. Data users must make their intentions clear to potential data subjects before soliciting their personal data.

The *Innovations* case

In *Innovations (Mail Order) Ltd v Data Protection Registrar* the appellant took individuals' names and addresses for completing order requests by the customer. After completing the order Innovations sent an acknowledgment on the back of which was a statement informing the customer that Innovations rents out its names and addresses. The company gave an address to its customers to write to if they objected to their data being used in this way. The Data Protection Tribunal held that this was too late: to be fair, data users must give their subjects the chance to consent to the use of personal information *before* it is taken. It upheld the Enforcement Notice served by the Registrar on 9 April 1992.

HELD

> **21. A successful version of browser software allows each site visited to store a small quantum of data about the visitor accessing the site. This data, or 'cookie', is stored on the visitor's hard disk and is used to compile data about each visitor when they revisit any site. If the visitor has no knowledge of this surreptitious method of obtaining information, be it stored at the client or server, it may be unfair obtaining of data. If the server then processes the information, again, without the client's consent, this also may be a breach of the first data protection principle as unfair processing.**

Opting out

It is likely to be unfair obtaining where a data subject has no choice but to provide consent to additional uses of his personal data. This is the situation where the data user informs all potential subjects that their order or transaction will not be processed unless they agree to the secondary uses of the data. While the data subject does still have a nominal choice, to stop dealing with the data user, for certain dominant data users it will not be a genuine choice.

> **22. A major Internet Service Provider states that it will trade all new customer details with companies who offer services on its system. Unless each customer is, at the least, given an opt-out option from this trading, the personal information may be unfairly obtained. The less substitutable the data user, the greater risk of a breach of the first data protection principle.**

Incentive in

The converse situation of opting out is where a data user offers potential data subject incentives *to* divulge personal data. Such a policy also runs the risk of breaching the first data protection principle. Indeed, the Registrar's guidelines specifically mention that a relevant question to ask in assessing fairness is whether any 'unjustified . . . threats or inducements [were] offered'.[20]

Information obtained lawfully

The first hurdle for the Registrar to prove unlawful obtaining is to prove that the obtaining of the information was in breach of a law. Possible candidates for grounds for unlawful obtaining in the normal course of dealing with personal data are breach of confidence and breach of contract. In the Internet sphere the most likely law to be broken is not civil, but criminal: the Computer Misuse Act 1990.[1] Unauthorised access, an offence under this Act may result in the obtaining of information unlawfully under the Data Protection Act 1984. Along with these more general laws by which data users must abide, certain data users are bound by rules specific to their industry.

Whatever the unlawful activity alleged, it will always be open to the data subject or Registrar to argue that, in the alternative, even if the obtaining was not unlawful, it was nevertheless unfair.[2] The protection for data subjects under the first principle of data protection is certainly broader when the accusation is unfair obtaining as compared with unlawful obtaining.

Data processed fairly

Fair processing is directed at protecting data subjects from treatment that may be described in a data user's registration but is, nevertheless, prejudicial use of the personal data. It is vital that data users view this principle holistically though: being unfair is not enough to breach the principle; one needs to have unfairly *processed*. The definition of processing is limited. The first question is necessarily to establish that processing itself has occurred. Only then can there be a meaningful investigation into whether this processing was unfair or otherwise. An example used by the Registrar is below:[3]

> 'It would also be unfair for a data user to process personal data with the result that unsolicited marketing material is sent to an individual who has informed the data user that he or she does not wish to receive such material.'

---

20   Guideline 4, para 1.1.
1   See the chapter on crime.
2   There will be many situations where obtaining is both unfair and unlawful. An explicit example is examined in the 11th Data Protection Report: the Unfair Terms in Consumer Contracts Regulations 1994 which make unenforceable against a consumer certain unfair contractual terms. A contracting party which by its unequal bargaining power is able to coerce a consumer into agreeing to supply personal data may be acting unfairly under the Regulations. The obtaining of those data may be outside the enforceable terms of the contract and classed as unlawful and, by virtue of the disparity in bargaining strength, unfair.
3   Guideline 4, para 1.15.

Unfair processing of mailservers

This example is particularly applicable to the Internet. Where a data user is using a mailserver, marginal costs can be close to zero for sending e-mails to individuals. It can be administratively more expensive to remove a name from a mailserver than to allow the mailserver to contain the extra name. It may be unfair to inundate a data subject's e-mail in-box with unsolicited e-mails. This will be a likely conclusion where the data subject has already made requests to the data user to stop the mailings. It makes little difference to the question of fairness whether the data user either refuses to remove the address from the mailserver, or where the user absolves responsibility by suggesting that the data subject should unsubscribe from the mailserver himself. Although this suggestion may appear the simplest solution, the data user's initial processing may still be unfair.

> **23. A manufacturer creates a sophisticated home page that records the number of hits to its site and the e-mail addresses of the individuals who view the site. This information is then analysed and certain addresses are targeted with 'follow-up' e-mails. Without a method for an individual to avoid being included in the e-mailout, the processing, and obtaining, may be unfair, and therefore a breach of the first data protection principle.[4]**

Data processed lawfully

An obligation to process lawfully, like its counterpart, the obligation to obtain lawfully, is narrower than fair processing. Also like its counterpart the term 'lawful' includes both criminal and civil legality. The Registrar has indicated three areas of law particularly relevant to breaches of the first principle of data protection.[5]

'Confidentiality, arising from the relationship of the data user with the individual;

The *ultra vires* rule and the rule relating to the excess of delegated powers, under which the data user may only act within the limits of its legal powers;

Legitimate expectation, that is the expectation of the individual as to how the data user will use the information relating to him.'

---

4   It is a moot point whether processing simply an e-mail address can constitute processing under the Act as processing must be directed to personal data which relates to a living individual. An e-mail address *may* not actually relate to an individual and *may* not permit identification of the living individual. A similar point was raised by Equifax in a Data Protection Tribunal inquiry. Equifax processed purely in relation to an address. The Tribunal gave a purposive solution to the point saying that one should look to the purpose of the processing. Where that processing was to determine information in relation to the living individual, the processing will fall within the definition of the word in the Act. It is submitted that this approach, while uncertain for a data user, is correct and in line with the European intention underlying the legislation.

5   Data Protection Guideline 4, para 1.18.

> **24. A data subject supplies to a data user personal data encrypted using a public key. This encryption may be enough to give the subject the legitimate expectation that the personal data will be used by only the holder of the private key. Wider processing may be unlawful and constitute a breach of the first data protection principle.**

2. HELD FOR SPECIFIED AND LAWFUL PURPOSES

'Personal data shall be held only for one or more specified and lawful purposes.'

Held for specified purposes

To comply with this second principle is simply a matter of ensuring that all purposes for which a data user holds data are properly and accurately registered. Data users should be vigilant over their databases and appreciate that including an additional field against a set of personal data or using a database in a new way may constitute a new purpose which their registration must reflect. A data user must also be aware that holding is widely encompassing: newly received personal data may alter the capacity in which other data are being stored. These other data may then become part of a collection of data which are intended to be processed. As such, these data will fall within the scope of data held.

> **25. A university has compiled a list of academics who may be suitable for a new post. To gain more information on them, it enters each academic's name into a search engine that searches both the World Wide Web and Usenet. From these additional data, the university appends to its database two new entries: first, personal details gleaned from the search; second, opinions on the nature of each academic's postings on Usenet. To comply with the second data protection principle the university must check that their current registration covers the newly held data.**

Held for lawful purposes

As for the first data protection principle, the word, 'lawful', relates both to criminal and civil laws. Depending on the intention for holding the data, it is feasible that an accurate registration is still in breach of the second data protection principle for being unlawful. It would, for example, be unlawful for a travel agent to compile names and addresses of its customers to provide those details to criminals to burgle the customers' properties while they are abroad.

3. USED OR DISCLOSED IN COMPATIBLE MANNER

'Personal data held for any purpose or purposes shall not be used or disclosed in any manner incompatible with that purpose or those purposes.'

As with the second data protection principle, the surest way for data users to comply with this principle is to use data for purposes only as described in their register, and to disclose data to persons only as described in their register. Data users should keep their register entries accurate always and their disclosures section should reflect the persons to whom the data user *may* wish to disclose data.

There will be circumstances where a data user may use or disclose data and that their registration does not cover. In this situation there will not necessarily be a breach of the third principle. The Registrar will assess as an issue of fact whether a data user's use or disclosure is so far from that described in the Register that it is incompatible with the entries.[6]

4. ADEQUATE, RELEVANT, NOT EXCESSIVE

> 'Personal data held for any purpose or purposes shall be adequate, relevant and not excessive in relation to that purpose or those purposes.'

The Act does not define the limits of this principle and does not interpret it. The Registrar suggests that one method of determining the correct quota of data is to decide the absolute minimum amount of data needed to achieve the registered purposes. The Data Protection Tribunal has established that it will look closely at exactly what information is necessary for the specified purpose.[7]

> **26. An online magazine requires all its readers to complete an online registration form. The magazine is to be sent only by e-mail, but the publishers are considering trading the personal data with other traditional print publishers. For this reason the magazine requires each individual to include his e-mail *and* physical contact address. Without this potential trading purpose registered, the data user will be holding excessive personal data in breach of the fourth data protection principle.**

Living individual focus

It is wrong to assume that the necessary quotum of data can be assessed purely in relation to the purpose. The principle applies to each living individual on which the data user holds personal data. What might be the minimum quantum of data for one individual may be excessive for another. The term 'personal data' does not refer to the defined data, as contained in the register, but rather the actual personal data held by the data user.[8] To establish a breach, the Registrar can examine the data held on *each* individual for *each* purpose as specified. This assessment is conducted from an objective viewpoint; it is of little relevance to a breach whether a data user had reasoned it was holding acceptable amounts.[9]

---

6   Certain types of disclosure are exempted from this principle.
7   The Tribunal held that it was excessive for the Community Charge Registration Officers of the local authority of Rhondda to hold the date of birth of an individual. This seemingly innocuous piece of datum was sufficient to warrant the Tribunal deciding that the local authority had breached the fourth data protection principle; Case DA/90 25/49/2.
8   See Part A of Guidance Note 25.
9   See Part A of Guidance Note 25.

> **27. An online software supplier uses a standard online form for its customers to complete their order details. Owing to programming technicalities each field of the form must be filled in before the user can select the 'Okay' button to complete the order. This has the result that all users are required to include their home address, even users who will be sent the software by e-mail. The supplier will be holding excessive data on all customers who wish their software to be delivered online: a breach of the fourth data protection principle.**

5. ACCURATE AND UP TO DATE

'Personal data shall be accurate and, where necessary, kept up to date.'

Accurate personal data

The interpretation section for this principle refers the definition of 'accurate' to the Data Protection Act 1984, section 22(4).[10]

'Data are inaccurate for the purposes of this section if incorrect or misleading as to any matter of fact.'

This definition excludes a mere opinion which does not include, or purport to be, a statement of fact. Data users must not confuse this with the definition of personal data which can include an opinion.[11]

This may appear to be an onerous requirement for data users, especially using the Internet, where one search engine may provide links to reams of personal data, each of which would have to be checked independently. However, the interpretative schedule to this principle excludes the data obtained from a third party, including the data subject, under two circumstances.[12] These are that, the source of the information is recorded as being the third party from whom the data are received or obtained; and, if relevant, the data user includes in the data an appropriate indication of the data subject's notification of alleged inaccuracies. So, where both these conditions are met, a data user need not check the accuracy of data himself and will not be liable for any inaccuracies.

Conversely, where data users do not mark personal data 'as received' they can be in breach of the fifth data protection principle and possibly liable to the data subject for compensation for the inaccuracy.

---

10   Data Protection Act 1984, Sch 1, Pt II, para 4.
11   See 'Personal data' at page 251.
12   'Any question whether or not personal data are accurate shall be determined as for the purposes of s 22 of the Act but, in the case of such data [which accurately record information received or obtained by the data user from the data subject or a third party,] as are mentioned in subsection (2) of that section, this principle shall not be regarded as having been contravened by reason of any inaccuracy in the information there mentioned if the requirements specified in that subsection have been complied with': Data Protection Act 1984, Sch 1, Pt II, para 4.

Internet data sources and locations

Particularly on the World Wide Web, the location of data may be only one aspect of its source. For example, the data held on the home page at http://www.compuserve.com/ourhome/coolhome are stored on the Compuserve server in the coolhome directory that is within the parent directory, ourhome. This is its location. Its source, in contrast, will include the *person* who uploaded that data onto the home page. This will probably be the owner of the Compuserve account, coolhome. This person's identity, together with the URL, will form the source of the information.

The reason for insisting on this distinction is two-fold. First, the relevant section refers to receiving or obtaining data from the 'data subject or a third party'.[13] Both these terms refer to natural or legal persons. The source required under the section is therefore not the place where the data are stored, or from where they are retrieved, but the person who supplied the data to the data user. In illustration, if a data user obtains personal data from a particular book, it will not be enough to include as its source its location in a library; the publisher and author will be its source. By analogy, if personal data are obtained from a particular home page, it will not be enough to include as the source the URL on the Internet; the controller and creator of the home page will be the source.

The second justification for the source to be the person not the URL is that it is trivial to alter a URL. Indeed, the greatest difficulty for home pages on the web is that their links to other sites may become outdated. The person who created the site is therefore a more stable and certain source than the location of the data in question.

Notification of inaccuracy

If a data subject finds personal data inaccurate or misleading he may inform the data user of his concerns.

Remedying breach

By the Registrar's admission there is an element of discretion involved in deciding whether to deal formally with any breach under the data protection principles.[14] In relation to the fifth principle, the Registrar has indicated that a number of factors will be considered before taking any action against the data user.[15]

1. *The significance of the inaccuracy.* Has it caused or is it likely to cause damage or distress to the data subject?
2. *The source from which the inaccurate information was obtained.* Was it reasonable for the data user to rely on information received from that source?

---

13   Data Protection Act 1984, s 22(2).
14   '[W]hen considering whether to take formal action to remedy a breach, the Registrar will not merely seek to establish that there is a factual inaccuracy but will also wish to see whether the data user has taken all reasonable steps to prevent the inaccuracy': Data Protection Guideline 4.
15   Data Protection Guideline 4.

3. *Steps taken to verify the information.* Did the data user attempt to check its accuracy with another source? Would it have been reasonable to ask the data subject, either at the time of collection or at another convenient opportunity, whether the information was accurate?
4. *The procedures for data entry and for ensuring that the system itself does not introduce inaccuracies into the data.*
5. *The procedures followed by the data user when the information came to light.* Were the data corrected as soon as the inaccuracy became apparent? Was the correction passed on to any third parties to whom the inaccurate data may have already been disclosed? Did the inaccuracy have any other consequences in the period before it was corrected? If so, what has the data user done about those consequences?

Reliability of Internet sources

It is perhaps only the second consideration listed above, the reliability of the source, which has particular implications for Internet data users. One of the advantages of the Internet over other information sources is that it is quick and simple to retrieve vast quantities of data about almost any subject, including living individuals. There is no quality control, however, over this data. It is as easy for individuals to publish unsubstantiated personal data on the World Wide Web as it is for organisations who prudently vet their data. It is therefore unwise, and probably unreasonable, for a data user to compile data about individuals using unsubstantiated material from the Internet. This reinforces the issue that the important details about data extracted from the Internet are the actual sources, which can be checked for their reliance, not simply the URL of the material on the Internet.

Up to date, where necessary

The fifth data protection principle does not require that data users keep all their data up to date at all times; they must do this if it is *necessary*.

There will be circumstances where data held on an individual does need to be updated. The Registrar includes data used to decide whether to grant credit or to confer or withhold some other benefit.[16] These are examples where what is required is a reflection of the data subject's *current* status or circumstances.

---

28. An online cinema-ticket agency establishes an account for each new customer. To set up an account a data subject must enter, among other details, his age in years and months on 1 January next. If the purpose of these data are to ensure that customers do not attend films under the required age, it must be updated each month to ensure that these data do not exclude individuals who have had a recent birthday.

---

16   Data Protection Guideline 4, para 5.3.

6. HELD NO LONGER THAN NECESSARY

'Personal data held for any purpose or purposes shall not be kept any
longer than is necessary for that purpose or those purposes.'

Data users should be diligent in deleting data when they have already served their
purpose. Each set of data should have a life-span. At the end of this time, the data
should be reviewed and assessed against the specified purpose for holding that
data. If the data no longer appear necessary to complete or continue the purpose,
data users have one of two options. They can either delete the data, or they can
amend their registered purposes to reflect the reason for extending holding the
data.

Multiple purposes

There will be many occasions when one set of data is held for more than one
purpose. Consequently, there will be occasions when, for one purpose, a data user
should delete data, but for the other purposes the data remain necessary and
relevant. The principle's use of both the singular 'purpose' and the plural
'purposes' clearly envisages this situation. The solution is to attempt to segregate
the use of the data into their various purposes and to ensure that all data which are
not necessary for a purpose are deleted.

> **29. A firm publishes biographical data about its employees on its home
> page. One of these employees leaves the firm. The firm is able to hold on
> an internal database the necessary information about the former
> employee for, say, legal claims. In contrast, it should, to comply with
> the sixth data protection principle, remove the personal data being
> held on the home page as soon as the employee leaves.**

The ease with which data may be published on the World Wide Web acts also as a
reason continually to check the relevance of data published on the World Wide
Web. Data users should regularly check their web site and other Internet sites to
delete data which has served its purpose and is past its life-span. It is therefore not
simply good commercial practice to update one's web site; it may be required
under data protection, and possibly other, laws.

Holding historical data

Data users are at liberty to hold indefinitely data that they will purely use for
historical, statistical or research purposes. These data may not be used in any way,
however, that is likely to cause distress to any data subject.

7. AVAILABLE TO DATA SUBJECT

'An individual shall be entitled:
(a) at reasonable intervals and without undue delay or expense, to be
informed by any data user whether he holds personal data of

which that individual is the subject; and to access any such data
held by a data user; and

(b) where appropriate, to have such data corrected or erased.'

Data subject informing and access

Part (a) of this seventh data protection principle is essentially enacted by the rights
accorded to data subjects in the Data Protection Act 1984, section 21.[17] This
section is relevant for data subjects whose data is stored on or off computers
connected to the Internet.[18]

A data subject may enforce the rights under the principle only where the data
user has failed to honour the obligations set out in section 21, 'Right of access to
personal data'. Even then, the Registrar has a discretion over what is a reasonable
interval between requests. Clearly, a web site attracting over 500,000 individuals
each day, and holding information on each of them, would be unable to satisfy the
requirements of the principle if each individual made a request each week. The
Registrar is instructed by the interpretative schedule to the principle to consider
three factors when evaluating what is a reasonable interval: the nature of the data;
the purpose of holding the data; and the frequency of altering those data.

Be ready to provide data

Little of the Data Protection Act 1984 forces an Internet data user to act in a
particular manner with personal data. Generally the Act simply prohibits acting in
that manner without having previously registered to that effect. The consequence
of a request under the seventh data protection principle, however, does force the
data user to act. He must supply to the data subject the relevant information under
section 21. And data users must supply this information within 40 days from
receiving a request.[19]

Often, all data required may be published on the Internet. In this case, Internet
data users should pay respect to this principle by ensuring that, on constructing
and programming their data subject database, there is a simple way of extracting
all the data relating to one individual. It is important for data users to note that
merely because a particular record has no reference to an individual's name does
not mean that the information should not be provided to the subject. If the data
user possesses sufficient information, wherever held or stored, to identify the
individual, then the data can be classed as personal data, and so be requested by its
subject.[20] Where the data held on individuals are spread throughout many
databases, throughout many buildings, it can be expensive and time-consuming to
locate all the necessary data within the period set by the Act. The Act sets a
maximum which a data user can charge for such a request.

---

17   Data Protection Act 1984, Sch 1, Pt II, para 5.
18   Readers should consult specialist texts on these general rights.
19   Data Protection Act 1984, s 21(6). This duration is subject to s 21(4)(a) and (b) which deals
      with the situation where a data user is not supplied with the information reasonably required
      to identify the data subject and the information requested, and the second situation where the
      disclosure to the data subject would also disclose information relating to another non-
      consenting individual.
20   See 'Possession of other information' at page 253.

> **30.** A data subject requests from a data user relevant information under the seventh principle and section 21. The data user duly retrieves the pertinent data from the various relational databases and then realises that more data are held than has been registered. If the data user supplies all the data to the subject the user is admitting holding unregistered data, an absolute offence under section 5(1). If the data user supplies the data only mentioned in the registration, the user can be forced to comply with section 21 which demands that all the data held by the user must be supplied to the subject. The data user must immediately contact the Data Protection Registrar to amend the registration or otherwise rectify the scope of data held.

Data correction and deletion

Part (b) of the seventh data protection principle does not give data subjects the *absolute* right to demand that a data user deletes aspects of personal data. The obligation to delete or correct is qualified by the word 'appropriate' in the principle. This qualification refers to where the correction or deletion is necessary to comply with other data protection principles. A data subject has no right to demand deletion because he is embarrassed or would prefer the information not to be known; the Act does not grant a right to privacy.

8. KEPT SECURE

> 'Appropriate security measures shall be taken against unauthorised access to, or alteration, disclosure or destruction of, personal data and against accidental loss or destruction of personal data.'

This final eighth data protection principle applies both to data users and computer bureau operators. It is part of the Data Protection Act 1984 that demands lawyers understand, at the least, the basics of computer security. Complying with this part of the Act can be expensive for data users and computer bureau operators. It is, however, essential that these controllers of personal data employ appropriate technological and supervisory methods to secure their subjects' data.

Security under the eighth principle

This principle tackles one of the most obvious tensions between the Internet and data protection. In the Data Protection Registrar's 1995 annual report it is stated that,

> '[i]n connecting to the Internet [data users and computer bureau operators] are entering an open environment which exists to facilitate the exchange of and the publication of information. It is inherently insecure.'

In contrast, data protection legislation attempts to ensure that personal data are not left in open environments but are stored in controlled, private environments.

The eighth principle takes the idea of a controlled environment to its logical extreme by demanding that data are not simply secure from unauthorised access and disclosure but also alteration, destruction and loss.

Appropriate

In the abstract it is difficult for a lawyer or security consultant to advise on the appropriate level of security for personal data. The level of the security should be in proportion to the nature of the data and the harm which would ensue should there be a breach in security. The Registrar distinguishes between personal data compiled from readily available sources, such as a list of names and addresses, and data which are more sensitive[1] or are acquired in confidence.[2] It is submitted that even a list of names and addresses may warrant a high degree of security, for example where the list is of elderly home owners who do not have a burglar alarm on their property.

Data users and computer bureau operators must make their own decisions as to the adequacy of their data security, but they should consider their obligation to the data subjects and the possibility of a compensation claim by a data subject.

Authorisation

The eighth data protection principle stresses that security measures must be in place preventing *unauthorised* changes in personal data. This does not refer solely to outsiders such as hackers; it is referring also to insiders who are acting outside the scope of their authority. Data users and computer bureau operators should consider this authority from two angles: technical authority and social authority.

Technical authority

All equipment which stores, processes, transmits or discloses personal data must have passwords which only authorised people know. These passwords must not be the same for all aspects of data security within the organisation. Data users and computer bureau operators must treat distinctly those aspects of their equipment which they will use for activities relating to personal data.

To stop as early as is possible any security compromise it is advisable that each person granted the authority to access the personal data has an individual password. This, combined with an audit trail of all personal data, can permit a data user or computer bureau operator to 'trace' the human source of compromised data, and so prevent its reoccurrence. It is essential that this technical authority is granted by providing individuals each with a unique password, not by allocating one password for 'all personal data activities'. This latter method does not allow a data user to trace the source of a security leak as easily and results in one password being known by more people.

1   Personal data which may be seen as more sensitive are defined in section 2(3). This is: racial origins; political opinions, or religious or other beliefs; physical or mental health or sexual life; and criminal convictions.
2   Data Protection Guideline 4, para 8.3.1.

Social authority

Establishing a strict regime with passwords is not adequate unless there is also a strict regime over who has these passwords. Data users and computer bureau operators must give proper weight to the discretion and integrity of members of staff who are to have these passwords. They should be given adequate technical *and* data protection training; they should be made aware of the seriousness of their responsibilities. If the unfortunate event occurs where a member of staff leaves the department, or is found to be unreliable, the data user or computer bureau operator must immediately 'lock out' that member from the system. There should be no 'old' or 'general' password for accessing personal data.

Alteration

The obligation to take appropriate measures to prevent alteration to data can be readily met by ensuring that certain data are 'read-only': that is, the data cannot be altered or even deleted without appropriate authority. This authority is generally in the form of a password that allows the password-user to alter the 'read-write' properties of the data.

---

31. An Internet Service Provider allows its members to sign up to various services using an online form. As well as address and surname, one field of this form is the forename of the member. Unless it is clearly appropriate this particular field should retain a 'read-only' status. If it is freely able to be overwritten, it is feasible an accidental alteration will result in another member of the same family, at the same address, being treated as the data subject.

As is stated below, the safest solution is to have 'read-only' status where possible along with regular, archival backups. If the backup is archival it will highlight any changes in data since the previous backup, so alerting a data user to a potential alteration. It will also allow the data user to regenerate an unaltered copy of the data, if necessary, from the previous backup.

Entitled deletion and backups

To comply with one of the other principles, the seventh data protection principle entitles a data subject to delete data which it is inappropriate for a data user to continue holding.[3] This required deletion will include both the personal data on the usual storage system and any backup copies of the data on whatever medium. Data users must therefore ensure that their archival backup system is sufficiently sophisticated to allow them to remove data fields without compromising the security of the remaining data which may breach the eighth data protection principle.

Destruction

The same security considerations apply to avoiding destruction, accidental or not, of data and avoiding alteration of data. Data users should classify as much data as

---

3 See 'Data correction and deletion' at page 287.

possible as 'read-only' and maintain regular and frequent backups of the data. In this way, if data are destroyed on the main system, it is an easy task to regenerate those data. As above, data users should ensure that their backup facilities, while secure, do not prevent the deletion of personal data where this will be necessary to comply with a data subject's request.[4]

Internet security issues

Connecting a computer to the Internet is easy and commonplace. But, with present levels of standard Internet security, going onto the Internet will result in the personal data held on the computer online becoming less secure. Data users and computer bureau operators must not rely on the inherent security on the Internet if they wish to avoid possible breaches of the eighth data protection principle. Some of the various ways that a data user or computer bureau operator may tighten security are considered below.[5]

Automatic-answer modems

A modem connected to the Internet that is set to accept incoming calls will weaken security. The mere fact that an outsider can access a computer which is holding personal data reduces the security of that data. Data users and computer bureau operators should take expert advice from the manufacturers of their automatic-answer software on how to partition securely certain aspects of their storage system from third parties. They should also investigate how to encrypt the personal data left on the connected system.[6]

Remote access

One of the advantages of the Internet and related networks is that it has made it possible for individuals easily to access computers from remote locations. This may be through a bulletin board; an ftp site; a Telnet connection; or a standard dial-up connection. All these methods, without tight security measures, can as easily allow an individual to *leave* data on the remote computer as to *copy* data from the computer.

Security should therefore be in place which, unless it can be justified otherwise, does not permit remote users to access all the personal data on the system: a firewall. The passwords and logins used by remote users should be 'rolled' on a frequent basis. Remote users should not use an automated login procedure that stores the login details and password on their computer. With this set-up, if someone steals the computer the entire security of the personal data are at risk.

---

4   See 'Data correction and deletion' at page 287.
5   Data users and computer bureau operators should take specialist advice; the comments on data security within this chapter are intended only to illustrate possible methods of improving security. The comments should not be implemented before checking with a security adviser that they are appropriate for the equipment and data in question.
6   The key to de-encrypt the data must not be stored on the computer storing the encrypted data.

E-mail transactions

If a data user or computer bureau operator uses the e-mail system to send personal data he should be aware that a standard e-mail system is not completely secure. He must not rely on the security of the Internet itself. Again, a good policy is to use public-key encryption on all e-mails which contain personal data. It must also be remembered that any e-mail is both a transferral and a disclosure of personal data or information. Data users should appropriately register for such an activity.

Web servers

By definition a web server is connected to the Internet. As much as is possible, these computers should not be used for storing data collected from the World Wide Web. The use of an online form on a home page to collect personal data from, for example, customers, should generate data which is either encrypted on the server or is transmitted automatically to a further computer beyond a firewall.[7] Users of the web to collect personal data must also enlist expert advice to ensure that while such an online form is being transmitted to the server from the customer-client, the most stringent safety measures are in place. The transferral of personal data between the subject and the data user is the most insecure time for the subject's personal data. Subjects must be informed of this risk *before* they transmit the data to a web site. Some sites 'pop up' a window allowing the subject to choose to transmit the data or to disconnect from the web site.

Viruses

The Internet allows its users to 'view' documents on their screen, but it is increasingly being used to download material into the client computer. Sometimes this is with the knowledge of the user: he requests a file to download. At other times, the user may be unaware that the site on the Internet is accessing the user's computer and may be storing files and running programs on his computer. There is a real risk that with any file downloaded there will have been a computer virus in tow. Viruses generally attach to programs, but have been found incubating in word processing documents and even pictures. There have also been growing concerns that there is an increased risk of viruses being spread over the Internet owing to the more sophisticated, 'client-side' methods of presenting information on the World Wide Web such as Sun Microsystem's Java and Macromedia's Shockwave.[8]

To take appropriate security measures, data users and computer bureau operators must install virus scanning software set to screen regularly for viruses. Where possible the computer should be installed with anti-virus software which checks files as they are being downloaded into the connected computer.

---

7   There have been reports that the use of Java language on a web site can open up the site to hacking: 'Sun working feverishly to fix Java Internet security flaw', Reuters, March 1996.
8   '[Digital signatures] are clearly of great importance for executable code on the web': Tim Berners-Lee, W3C Director, viewed as the creator of the World Wide Web; 'Industry embraces Microsoft's Internet digital signature', Microsoft Press Release, PR1382/14 March 1996.

Network or intranet

All the above security issues are equally, if not more, relevant to where an internal network or intranet is connected to the Internet. This may be through one computer connected to one modem or an established gateway, available to all users. The two scenarios pose risks to any personal data held on the network or Intranet.

One computer to Internet

The ease with which one may connect a computer on an internal network to the Internet is almost inversely proportional to the risk involved with such a connection. That the connected computer does not hold or process personal data does not greatly reduce the threat to the personal data stored on the network. Because the computer is connected both to the Internet *and* the internal network it can act as a conduit for hacking attempts and the promulgation of viruses, network-wide. Data users and computer bureau operators should therefore periodically check that no computer on an internal network is connected to the Internet. If one computer is to be connected, an appropriate technical and social security regime must exist.

Technically, the single computer should be appropriately firewalled from the main network; if it is not, it can form a very weak link in the data security of the network. The social security measures relate to the responsibility of those persons who will use the connected computer. Employers should give employees clear guidelines about whether they are permitted to download software; it is safer not to download. Employees should have clear instructions never to divulge any internal passwords to any other individual using e-mail or any other means.

Network hacking

Hacking into the internal network from the Internet is only a great threat where the connected computer has automatic-answer modem. In this situation, a hacker can phone directly into the connected computer and, from there, may be able to penetrate the internal security of the network. Clearly this poses a substantial risk to any personal data on the network, previously treated as being secure. The risk from hacking is currently not as significant, however, as the threat from viruses and other rogue programs.

Network viruses

Every user who has access to the Internet will be tempted to download a file. In doing so, as described above,[9] the user risks introducing a virus to the client computer. But where this computer is connected to an internal network, the virus can spread throughout the network threatening the destruction and alteration of any personal data held within the network. Data users and computer bureau operators should install and update anti-virus programs throughout the network, and where possible install virus antidote software which checks for viruses as software is being downloaded from the Internet.

9   See 'Viruses' at page 291.

JURISDICTION OF DATA PROTECTION

The global reach of the Internet makes it vital that its users are aware of the English law that may impinge on them. There are two aspects to this awareness with the Data Protection Act 1984. First, the conditions required to be within the territorial reach of the Act. Second, the power of the Registrar to limit the transfer of personal data out of the jurisdiction.

Territorial reach of the Act

Section 39 contains details of those to whom the Act does *not* apply. It does not apply to data users in respect of data held outside the United Kingdom. It also does not apply to a computer bureau operator in respect of services provided outside the United Kingdom. These complex statements need to be substantially unpacked.

JURISDICTION OVER DATA USERS

There is a two-stage test to assess whether the Act applies to situations with a foreign element. Both tests must be met: first, not all the data must be processed and used outside the United Kingdom; second, the data users must exercise control from within the United Kingdom.

Processed and used wholly outside UK

The initial test to apply is to establish where the processing takes place and where the use of the data takes place. The Act does not apply where data are processed wholly outside the United Kingdom *and* that data are not intended to be, or are not, used in the United Kingdom.[10]

Place of control as place of holding

If the data user uses or intends to use the data within the United Kingdom the first stage is met and the user may be within the jurisdiction of the Act. To confirm this, he should establish whether he holds data within the United Kingdom. As discussed above, holding is inextricably linked with control.[11] The relevant question is, therefore, does the data user exercise control over the data from within the United Kingdom?

Personal control

To exercise the requisite control from within the United Kingdom a data user does not physically need to be present in the United Kingdom. The data user may be a

---

10   Data Protection Act 1984, s 39(5).
11   See 'Control' at page 258.

foreign company with a branch in the United Kingdom; this will be sufficient for the jurisdiction of the Act if that branch exercises control from the United Kingdom.

Servant or agent control

In addition to exercising personal control, a data user may exercise control over personal data through an agent or servant in the United Kingdom. If the data user is not present in the United Kingdom but exercises control over personal data through an agent or servant in the United Kingdom, a registration in respect of the data must be completed. It is not, however, the data user who must complete the registration. The servant or agent must register under the Act as though a data user himself; the Act applies as though the servant or agent is exercising control within the United Kingdom.[12]

Automatic servant or agent

One of the advantages of the Internet and online technologies is that it allows a person to manipulate a computer from across the globe as easily as sitting at the computer's keyboard. In a great number of instances it can remove the 'middleman'. It allows data users to remove the servant or agent through whom they would previously have exercised control, substituting remote access. This creates a problem for data protection jurisdiction.

A data user who appears to be non-resident within the United Kingdom may wish to use personal data within the United Kingdom. The first jurisdiction test is therefore met. To control this personal data they may use a server which is physically located in England and has a domain address suffixed with co.uk.[13] This server is accessed only from outside the United Kingdom and always by a remote connection; no person acts on behalf of the United Kingdom non-resident data user. On one reading of the Act, this data user is not within the jurisdiction of the Data Protection Act 1984.

This conclusion is based on the Act's referral to a 'servant or agent' as being a 'person' and 'holding office'. Section 39(4) states:[14]

> '[A] servant or agent ... treated as a data user or as a person carrying on a computer bureau ... may be described for the purposes of registration *by the position or office which he holds*; and any such description in an entry in the register shall be treated as applying to *the person* for the time being *holding the position or office* in question.'

'Holding' an office or position and references to a 'person' clearly eliminate the possibility that a server, without any human input but from the data user, can be classed as a servant or agent under this section. However, even servers that can be accessed remotely require human maintenance and support. The Data Protection Registrar would be looking to these humans, based in the United Kingdom, to check whether *they* were acting as servant or agent for the data user overseas.

---

12   Data Protection Act 1984, s 39(3)(b).
13   It is important not to assume that a server with 'co.uk' domain *is* physically present in the United Kingdom. The 'co.uk' indicates only with which authority the domain was first registered.
14   All emphases added.

In addition, the Registrar has stated that,[15]

> 'Overseas companies operating in the United Kingdom *which carry on business from a fixed place of business* [*in the United Kingdom*] would normally be considered resident for the purposes of the Data Protection Act [1984].'

By paying for, maintaining, and using a server within the United Kingdom, a data user is arguably carrying on business within the jurisdiction. By the fact that the remote worker can locate the server to connect to it suggests that the server has the properties of a location, a place. That a server is a fixed place of business is less certain, but there are compelling arguments suggesting that it is fixed. That it is fixed probably depends on the facts of the individual issue under consideration. The physical aspects of the server are fixed; in contrast, the data stored on the server can be simply ported to another URL or server. This is true for all data under the Act, its ability to be recorded on computer allows this ease of transferral.

With this reasoning, a court could feasibly view that a server in the United Kingdom, controlled from abroad, gave the controller the degree of residence to fall within the jurisdiction of the Act.

JURISDICTION OVER COMPUTER BUREAU OPERATORS

The rules of jurisdiction over computer bureau operators differ slightly from those for data users. The first point to note is that the Act can apply to a computer bureau operator even if the processing takes place abroad. The two suggested tests to establish whether a computer bureau operator falls within the jurisdiction of the Data Protection Act 1984 follow.

Resident personally or vicariously

It is submitted that the conclusions about residence are equally applicable to computer bureau operators as to data users. If the computer bureau operator does not appear to have residence in the United Kingdom even with the suggested wider reading of 'residence', one must check whether the operator is acting through a third party servant or agent. If this servant or agent is resident within the United Kingdom, the Registrar may have jurisdiction over him.[16] If no residence can be established by these two tests, the Data Protection Registrar has no jurisdiction over the computer bureau operator.

Causing or allowing processing

After residence is established the computer bureau operator must have performed one of two types of conduct for the Registrar to have jurisdiction. The computer bureau operator must have either:[17]

---

15   Registrar's Guidelines, AX.7. Emphasis added. See also 'Presence of companies' at page 117.
16   Data Protection Act 1984, s 39(4). Servants or agents must register as if acting on their own account.
17   Data Protection Act 1984, s 39(2)(b).

1. acted as an agent for other people to cause data held by those people to be processed automatically; or
2. allowed other people the use of equipment in his possession for the automatic processing of personal data held by those people.

As previously, computer bureau operators will be assessed under the two headings of archives and remote manipulation.

Archives

As concluded earlier, a provider of equipment for backing up a data user's data will be a computer bureau operator.[18] The scenario following illustrates the regulation of archiving in an international context.

> **32. An American Internet Service Provider prides itself on allowing its members to access their accounts from anywhere in the world, on any computer they choose. The Provider has a server in every major jurisdiction of the world, each with a complete set of data. One of the features of the system is that its members do not store their address book of e-mail addresses on their computer, but on the Provider's servers. This has the result that its members can process personal data using the Provider's equipment. If one of the servers is in the United Kingdom, the Provider will be resident here and will be governed by the Data Protection Act 1984.**

Remote manipulation

Where the owner of a computer permits remote access and manipulation, he may fall within the ambit of a computer bureau operator. The most common scenario is that a data user provides a batch file to a remote computer together with instructions for its processing. This arrangement will make the owner of the remote computer a computer bureau operator under the Act.

As for archives, if the remote computer is based in the United Kingdom, or instructions are provided to the remote computer through a servant or agent in the United Kingdom, the owner of the computer will be under the jurisdiction of the Data Protection Act 1984.

Overseas transfer prohibition

The second main jurisdictional issue for data users is when a transfer prohibition notice[19] can be served to prevent their transfer of data to a particular jurisdiction which is outside the Registrar's jurisdiction.[20] In theory a TPN can be served

---

18   See 'Computer bureau operators' at page 261.
19   After, TPN.
20   The Registrar may serve a transfer prohibition notice only on a registered data user, or a computer bureau operator which is also registered as a data user: Data Protection Act 1984, s 12(1)(a). For a transfer prohibition notice, a data user is treated as registered if 'deemed' registered under s 7(6). An unregistered data user may suffer sanctions simply by not being registered but by holding data.

against any registered data user who proposes to transfer personal data to a place outside the United Kingdom. If a data user contravenes the TPN, he will be guilty of a criminal offence unless he can prove he used all due care in abiding by the notice.[1]

There are two aspects to the Registrar's decision to serve a TPN: safety of proposed transfer, and discretion over service. For transfers over the World Wide Web the Registrar may decide that the proposed territory of transfer is unsafe.[2]

SAFETY OF TRANSFER

The Registrar's decision on safety consists of three main questions. Where is the intended place of transfer? Is this place with one of the Convention states? Is it likely the transfer will lead to a contravention of one of the data protection principles? These questions will be addressed in turn.

Place of transfer

The Registrar must establish to where the data user may transfer the data. Evidence of this is contained in the data user's registration. The Registrar will also consider the locations of any secondary transfers. Where a data user is transferring personal data over the World Wide Web or by ftp, the data user will generally have selected the 'world-wide' option in Part B of his form. This suggests that any jurisdiction which is connected to the Internet, practically now all, will be capable of receiving the data. The issue of where any subsequent transfers may be made is also probably world-wide. Without security or encryption in place, any data published on the World Wide Web or ftp site can be easily downloaded and e-mailed or electronically published in any other territory. Once data are published on the Internet, they can technically be transferred to any territory.

> 33. An English school publishes on the World Wide Web personal details of all its alumni. It stresses that this information is purely as information for potential English parents. Without sophisticated security to prevent foreign accessing, the school will be transferring these personal data into almost all the jurisdictions of the world.

Convention state or not

The second question that the Registrar must consider is whether the place of proposed transfer is bound by the European Convention on Data Protection. These are currently: Austria, Belgium, Denmark, Finland, France, Germany, Iceland, Ireland, Luxembourg, the Netherlands, Norway, Portugal, Slovenia,

1   Data Protection Act 1984, s 12(10).
2   The Registrar takes into account factors such as the nature of the data, to whom specifically the data will be sent, and what is the likelihood and type of harm possible. Under the Second Data Protection Directive third party provisions must be considered 'adequate'. In determining the adequacy of the level of protection provided by a third country, account must be taken of 'all the circumstances surrounding a data transfer operation'. Where inadequate, member states may authorise a transfer if safeguards are provided in other ways including a contract between the data users concerned.

Spain, Sweden and obviously the United Kingdom. These countries are presumed to have laws on data protection which are broadly similar to those in force in the United Kingdom. If the proposed territory of transfer is not bound by the European Convention on Data Protection a stricter test is imposed.

For most transfers over the Internet, asking this question is a formality. By common means of Internet publishing, it is likely that at least one country of transfer will be outside the Convention. This is because servers connected to the Internet can not presently ascertain the final place of data retrieval.

The Registrar must appraise each data user's security arrangement. Although a data user's Registration may mention the Internet, he may have jurisdiction-specific software. For example, he may have a server, or bulletin board which, when connected, telephones back the user. This allows the software to restrict users to those within acceptable jurisdictions.

Transfer to a non-Convention state

If data are to be transferred to a state which is not within the European Convention on Data Protection, the transfer must be assessed as to whether it is likely to contravene *or lead to* the contravention of any of the data protection principles.[3] To assess this, the Registrar must evaluate if the contravention would be a breach of the principles in relation to personal data held in the United Kingdom. That the Registrar is entitled to assess whether the transfer may *lead to* the breach of one of the principles increases the possibility of a prohibition.

Internet transfer: all or none

If the Registrar becomes concerned over the data protection rules, or lack of them, in a non-Convention country, data users may be stopped from transferring data there. At this point Internet data users will face a complete cessation of all Internet publishing if the Registrar exposes even one country as being unsafe for data. Internet data users, especially those publishing on the World Wide Web, will generally be unable to limit their transfers: they publish to all or none of the connected countries. It is for this reason that the Registrar, and this author, strongly suggest that data users consider very carefully whether unlimited Internet publishing is necessary.

Transfer to a Convention state

Where transfer is to a Convention state the Registrar may only limit that transfer for one of two reasons. First, the data user intends to give instructions for the subsequent transfer of the personal data into a non-Convention state *and* this transfer is likely to contravene or lead to a contravention of any of the data protection principles. The most obvious example of this would be a chain e-mail message containing personal data which instructs to, 'forward this message to all your friends across the world'. It is submitted that the Registrar will have substantial difficulty in proving this first reason to prevent a transfer.

---

3   See 'Principles of data protection' at page 274.

The second reason is not yet applicable and relates to the sensitive data to which the Secretary of State may alter or add guiding principles.[4] The Secretary of State has not yet altered or added to these principles.

The limited powers of the Registrar in relation to intra-Convention transfers clearly indicates the advantages of limiting publication to Convention states only.

EXCEPTIONS TO TPN

If the above tests are satisfied there remain possibly two reasons why the Registrar may not serve a TPN. The Registrar cannot prohibit a transfer if required or authorised by statute or required by a Convention which imposes obligations on the United Kingdom.[5] The second reason is more relevant to the Internet.

The Registrar's guidelines state that it may not serve a TPN about personal data which are already outside the United Kingdom.[6] Via the Internet, especially the World Wide Web, data may be published simultaneously around the world. This would have the result that personal data are already outside the United Kingdom, preventing the Registrar's service on the offending Internet data user. Two points must be made about this statement.

The guidelines are purely that, guides. This statement by the Registrar has no basis in statute and so may not be binding. Assuming the guideline to be correct, there is a semantic argument which may be used to serve a TPN despite the data having been published over the Internet. The guideline states that '[t]he Registrar cannot serve a transfer prohibition notice about personal data which are already outside the United Kingdom'. It does not state that these data must have been *transferred* or *disclosed* outside the United Kingdom. So, the guideline's exemption will apply only where the data have actually been downloaded outside the United Kingdom, not merely viewed outside the jurisdiction. Nevertheless, by the Registrar's guidelines, the Registrar will have to act quickly to prevent an international transfer preventing the service of a TPN.

DISCRETION OVER TPN

The Registrar has limited discretion over serving a notice, where it is appropriate. The Registrar must consider whether the notice should be served to prevent damage or distress to any person. Balanced with this, the Registrar must consider the general desirability of free transfer of data between the United Kingdom and elsewhere.[7]

It is crucial that data users appreciate the initial informality before service. The Registrar is unlikely not have some contact with the data user before service. In fact, the Registrar will usually write to the data user to indicate that service is being considered and that representations should be made by the data user. Data users should take this opportunity, whether in writing or orally; this is the last hurdle before the Registrar may serve a TPN.

---

4   Data Protection Act 1984, s 2(3).
5   Data Protection Act 1984, s 12(9).
6   Registrar's Guideline No 7, para 4.11.
7   Data Protection Act 1984, s 12(4).

FORMAT OF TPN

The notice itself specifies the transfers which it prohibits and contains detailed statements as to:

1. the data protection principle or principles which are threatened;
2. the Registrar's reasons for believing those principles to be breached by the proposed transfer;
3. whether the prohibition is absolute, or what steps the data user should take before making the transfer;
4. the time after which the notice has effect;
5. the data user's right to appeal to the Data Protection Tribunal.

Notices will usually not take effect for at least 28 days, but where the Registrar is concerned over international transfers which would pre-empt the notice, or under special circumstances, the notice make take effect urgently. Internet data users are more likely to receive urgent notices than standard, as explained above.

Example of TPN

A transfer prohibition notice was served on Winsor International Limited in respect of personal data: names and addresses of individuals.[8] The notice was to take effect on 3 December 1990. Winsor were to send these personal data to Mr Ben Buxton and his corporations in America, but Mr Buxton was already defending a New Jersey court order to prevent his misleading and illegal mailings.

The mailings, if sent from within the United Kingdom, would have breached the data protection principles. In the main, the mailings were unlawful under consumer protection regulations. The transfer of the personal data would therefore have led to the holding and processing of personal data for an unlawful purpose.

The notice was served on the grounds that the transfer of personal data to Mr Buxton and his corporations would be likely to contravene or lead to the contravention of the first, second and seventh data protection principles.

This example indicates the wide jurisdiction that the Registrar possesses where there is possibility of a breach.

BREACH OF TPN

A breach of a TPN is an offence under section 12(10). The sole defence open to the data user is that the data user exercised all due diligence to avoid the contravention of the notice.

8   See the Data Protection Registrar's Seventh Report.

Chapter seven
Taxation

Conrad McDonnell, Barrister, Gray's Inn Chambers

The Internet is increasingly used for commercial activities. These activities and transactions are taking place at every stratum of the Internet. New 'online' businesses are being created to exploit the opportunities on the web. Some are even able to float on the stock market for millions of pounds. These companies' revenues are often in the form of licence fees for digital material. As security on the Internet improves the majority of these payments will be made using digital cash. Other businesses subsist only on payments from advertisers who are eager to rent space on popular web sites.

This flurry of new activities poses taxation questions. This chapter addresses the following.

1. What are the tax considerations of starting an Internet business?
2. What is the tax treatment of digital cash?
3. Because the Internet is transnational, what are the issues of international taxation and tax planning?
4. How does VAT apply to supplies made over the Internet?
5. How does VAT specifically apply to the following Internet businesses: mail order companies; providers of downloaded material; providers of online material; Internet Service Providers; and sites selling advertising space?

UK TAX SYSTEM – THE BASICS

Liability to tax in the UK is, in the main, imposed by a series of Finance Acts following the Budget each year (in recent years there have sometimes been two). Periodically the Finance Acts and other taxing statutes are consolidated: the most recent consolidating legislation is the Income and Corporation Taxes Act 1988, commonly called the Taxes Act 1988 ('ICTA 1988'); also the Taxation of Chargeable Gains Act 1992 ('TCGA 1992') and the Capital Allowances Act 1990 ('CAA 1990'). All of this legislation is amended frequently.[1]

---

1   For the legislation currently in force, see Butterworths' *Yellow Tax Handbook* published annually.

Other than VAT, tax is administered by the Inland Revenue under the Taxes Management Act 1970. The basic system is that a taxpayer, or his accountant, completes a tax return and the Inland Revenue then produces an assessment. Tax is payable in accordance with the assessment unless the taxpayer appeals against it. Note that from 1996 onwards an optional system of self-assessment has been introduced, whereby the taxpayer is permitted to calculate his own tax liability. Similarly companies are now subject to a self-assessment system known as 'pay and file'.

For most taxpayers the guidance issued by the Inland Revenue is sufficient to enable the correct amount of tax to be paid, and so there is no need to resort to the underlying law. But it is possible that the novelty of the Internet may give rise to fresh questions of tax law; accordingly it is perhaps worth discussing the appeal procedure in a little detail. An appeal against an assessment or a decision of a tax inspector may be on any grounds. The appeal is heard by one of two tribunals: the General Commissioners; and the Special Commissioners. A hearing before either body of Commissioners is similar to other legal proceedings in the UK, except that the strict rules of evidence do not apply, and usually each side bears its own costs. Decisions of the Commissioners are subject to a right of appeal to the High Court, thence to the Court of Appeal and the House of Lords. It is sometimes possible to leapfrog so as to omit either the High Court stage or the Court of Appeal stage.

Tax appeals tend to be on pure questions of law, usually questions of statutory construction. Due to the general public interest it is not uncommon for tax appeals to proceed all the way to the House of Lords, and thus besides the statutes mentioned above there is a strong body of judge-made law. The well-known *Hansard* case, *Pepper v Hart*,[2] is one such example; another example is *Furniss v Dawson*,[3] a very important case which sometimes enables the courts to disregard artificial transactions done purely for tax avoidance purposes.

The tax year runs from 6 April to 5 April in the following year. Individuals pay income tax on their year's income at the basic rate (in recent years this has been 24% or 25%); above a certain threshold higher rates of income tax apply, and there is also a lower rate of 20% applicable to part of the income.[4] Sole traders are, of course, individuals and so are liable to income tax, although their trading income is computed from profit and loss accounts drawn up in the same manner[5] as those of a company. Partners in a partnership are also taxed as individuals, although a few special rules apply. In addition to income tax, individuals must pay capital gains tax on capital profits.

Where an individual derives income from being an employee, then under the PAYE scheme income tax is deducted from each payment of salary; it is normally mandatory for the employer to operate this scheme, even if there is only a single employee and even if the employer is a private individual.

Companies pay corporation tax on both income and capital profits at a rate which varies between the small companies rate (equal to the basic rate of income tax, for companies with profits of less than £300,000 per annum) and the full rate (between 33% and 35% in recent years). Corporation tax is calculated in respect of each accounting period of a company; accounting periods normally last one year, but do not have to coincide with the tax year. Company distributions are

---

2   [1993] AC 593, [1993] 1 All ER 42, [1992] STC 898, HL.
3   [1984] AC 474, [1984] 1 All ER 530, [1984] STC 153, HL.
4   ICTA 1988, s 1.
5   Trading income is computed under the 'Schedule D' rules, found in ICTA 1988, s 18 and s 53.

taxed in a special way: when a distribution is made there is an immediate liability to advance corporation tax ('ACT') at 20% of the grossed-up value of the distribution but that ACT may then be credited against the corporation tax due at the end of the accounting period (sometimes earlier or later accounting periods); in addition, the ACT paid on a distribution may be credited against the shareholder's liability to income tax. There are special arrangements for groups of companies, of course.

Starting up an Internet business

Persons setting up a new business from scratch (this must be a fairly frequent situation in an Internet context) are well advised to consider before commencing what type of business structure to use. From a tax perspective a limited company is not necessarily the most sensible idea; for a small but successful business sometimes a partnership provides the best solution. The reason is that if a company is used the shareholders and the company together pay tax on distributed income at an effective rate of between 45% and 53% (these figures assume the shareholders are subject to higher rate income tax at 40%), whereas the partners in a partnership pay tax at a maximum of 40%. But the advantage of a company, besides the limited liability protection it confers (not much use if the shareholders or directors are in practice required to guarantee its debts), is that retained profits are subject only to corporation tax at between 24% and 33%, thus encouraging growth. A further factor which advisers should bear in mind is that it is relatively easy to incorporate a business which has previously been conducted by a sole trader or a small partnership;[6] it is harder to do this in reverse.[7]

I. Alex and Bill have just left college and decide to set up a software business to develop and sell their debugging package Nitscope. They decide to form a company, Nitscope Ltd (having persuaded their parents to take out second mortgages in order to secure its bank overdraft).

In its first year, before taking into account the salaries of Alex and Bill, Nitscope makes a profit of £25,000: it makes little difference to the overall tax and national insurance contribution bill whether that is paid as salary or as dividends; nor would it make much difference if Nitscope were a partnership.

In the second year the business does much better since, even though it is essentially a two-man band, Nitscope is able to generate large sales through its web site. Before taking into account Alex and Bill's salaries, the company makes a profit of £1,000,000. In this case approximately £80,000 of tax and national insurance contributions would be saved if Nitscope were a partnership rather than a company. Furthermore on a sale of the business the capital gains tax position would be improved.

---

6   Capital gains are rolled over into the company – see TCGA 1992, s 162.
7   Fuller considerations may be found in the chapter 'Choice of business medium' in *Revenue Law – Principles and Practice* by Chris Whitehouse (Butterworths, republished annually).

Expenditure relating to the Internet – is it deductible?

A taxation question commonly of concern to businesses is whether items of expenditure are deductible in computing the amount of taxable profits. The relevant legislation is simple: section 74(1) of the Taxes Act 1988 provides that in computing the amount of the profits to be charged with tax,

> 'no sum shall be deducted in respect of –
> (a) any disbursements or expenses, not being money wholly and exclusively laid out or expended for the purposes of the trade, profession or vocation ...'

In general, expenditure on achieving an Internet presence *will* be an expense incurred wholly and exclusively for the purposes of the trade, and thus it will be deductible business expenditure. This is so even where the material provided over the Internet is free of charge to users, since even then any expenditure incurred in making the material available has presumably been incurred in order to market products or otherwise to provide publicity for a business.

Capital allowances

Expenditure on capital items used in the business is treated in a different way: capital expenses are not deductible in computing trading profits. However, the system of capital allowances does permit some kinds of capital expenditure to be taken into account over a period of years. The most important kind is expenditure on 'plant and machinery'. These words are not defined in the legislation, but 'plant' has been held[8] to include whatever apparatus is used by a businessman for carrying on his business. An important exclusion is expenditure on the premises from which business is conducted: this does not qualify for allowances as plant and machinery (but note that there is a parallel system[9] of industrial buildings allowances which applies to factories and the like, and also extends to office buildings[10] constructed in Enterprise Zones). Computers, telecommunications equipment and other electronic apparatus will qualify for capital allowances under the heading 'plant' (despite the common usage of the word 'machine' as a synonym for computer, in a capital allowances context 'machinery' means apparatus having moving parts and thus would not normally apply to electronic apparatus). Normal domestic mains electricity services do not qualify as plant, being part of the premises, but special electrical installations 'provided mainly' for computers and other equipment do qualify.[11] Wiring and other links between computers also qualify as plant, even if forming part of the structure of an office building.[12]

8 *Yarmouth v France* (1887) 19 QBD 647, 4 TLR 1.
9 CAA 1990, ss 1–21.
10 CAA 1990, s 21(5).
11 *Cole Bros Ltd v Phillips* [1982] 2 All ER 247, [1982] STC 307, HL; provisions recently enacted confirm the decision in that case – see CAA 1990, Sch AA1, Table 1 Column 2 Item 1.
12 CAA 1990, Sch AA1, Table 1 Column 2 Item 7.

Expenditure on computer software (if it is not revenue expenditure) always qualifies for capital allowances: section 67A of the Capital Allowances Act 1990 (introduced by the Finance (No 2) Act 1992) provides:

'(1) If a person carrying on a trade incurs capital expenditure in acquiring for the purposes of the trade a right to use or otherwise deal with computer software, then, for the purposes of this Part –

    (a) the right and the software to which it relates shall be treated as machinery or plant;

    (b) that machinery or plant shall be treated as provided for the purposes of the trade; and

    (c) so long as he is entitled to the right, that machinery or plant shall be treated as belonging to him.

(2) In any case where –

    (a) a person carrying on a trade incurs capital expenditure on the provision of computer software for the purposes of the trade, and

    (b) in consequence of his incurring that expenditure, the computer software belongs to him, but

    (c) the computer software does not constitute machinery or plant,

then for the purposes of this Part the computer software shall be treated as machinery or plant.'

This applies to all software, whether an off-the-shelf package (even if nothing is purchased but a licence to use the software), or software that is bundled with hardware, or bespoke software. Similarly, capital allowances are available in respect of the cost of developing software in-house, assuming that is a capital expense.[13]

There are also special rules for expenditure on production of films, audio tracks and similar material: see generally CAA 1990, section 68.

Royalty payments

Certain payments in respect of foreign-owned copyright material are subject to deduction of income tax at source, otherwise known as withholding tax. The rule applies if the 'usual place of abode' of the owner of the copyright is not within the UK, and catches any payment of or on account of royalties or sums paid periodically for or in respect of that copyright.[14] Video recordings and films are specifically excluded from the rule, as are their soundtracks if not separately exploited: thus Internet 'video on demand' services are likely not to be caught, so long as it can be established that the copyright exploited is a copyright in a video recording or cinematograph film. Payments for 'audio on demand' and software licences are potentially caught, however. The downloading and subsequent licensing of such material for use by a single user for a one-off payment would not be subject to withholding tax, since the payment in that case would not be a royalty nor would any sum be paid periodically: but the commercial arrangements adopted by large users, for example UK-based content providers, may well be

---

13   See generally Revenue Interpretation RI 56, published in November 1993.
14   ICTA 1988, s 536.

subject to this rule. Note that by virtue of the double taxation treaties between the UK and many countries, the application of this rule may differ depending on the country of residence of the copyright owner.[15]

Digital cash

It is not thought that the use of digital cash will substantially alter the tax treatment of any person in the UK. This is because the taxing legislation is concerned with the bottom line, the profits of a company or the annual income of an individual, and is not concerned with the details of individual transactions nor the form that a company's assets may take from time to time. The precise method used to calculate profits is largely a matter of accountancy practice, given that almost all businesses are subject to tax on an accruals basis. Thus the acquisition of a right to receive payment adds to the taxable profits even though payment has not yet been received, and the incurring of future liabilities may similarly be taken into account to reduce profits; sometimes even contingent liabilities may be taken into account. The details of the system used thus do not matter: it is immaterial whether digital tokens are prepaid, or whether Internet transactions give rise to digital debits after the event. So long as a reasonably reliable system of exchanging digital cash is in use then a person's accrued rights and liabilities in respect of that system should properly have exactly the same effect upon taxable profits as do accrued rights and liabilities in respect of a bank account.

Residence and the source of profits

The use of the Internet will not change the residence of a company, since this depends upon where it is incorporated and where it is managed and controlled.[16]

The use of the Internet may have an effect on the country in which profits are considered to arise. For a UK-incorporated company there will be no practical consequences, since such a company is required to pay tax in the UK on its profits wherever arising;[17] the same applies to an individual resident in the UK. A foreign resident, on the other hand, whether a company or an individual, is only assessable in respect of profits from a trade exercised in the UK.[18] Trading *in* the UK is to be distinguished from trading *with* the UK:[19] is the trade conducted in the UK, or is the only connection with the UK that orders are obtained in this country? A common test is whether the contracts are concluded in the UK, although where the circumstances render other factors more important then these other factors may be taken into account.[20] It does seem likely that many forms of trading involving the Internet will escape taxation in the UK on the basis that the trade is not exercised within the UK; but there is as yet very little authority on this interesting question.

15   See 'International taxation', below.
16   Ibid.
17   Schedule D (a)(ii) – see ICTA 1988, s 18(1).
18   Schedule D (a)(iii) – see ICTA 1988, s 18(1).
19   *Grainger & Son v Gough* [1896] AC 325, 3 TC 462, HL.
20   See *Firestone Tyre and Rubber Co Ltd v Lewellin* [1957] 1 All ER 561, 37 TC 111, HL. See also the chapter on contract for where a contract is formed.

Even if it is trading in the UK and thus taxable in the UK on the profits arising, a foreign resident company only becomes liable to pay corporation tax if it is trading through a branch or agency[1] in the UK. If this is not the case it pays merely income tax at the basic rate.[2] Unless there are special trading arrangements in force it seems very likely that a foreign-resident company trading in the UK via the Internet will not be doing so through a branch or agency, since the various UK routers and Internet Service Providers cannot be considered to be agents of the foreign company: their machinery is simply automatic machinery transmitting packets received verbatim.

Those owning the infrastructure of the Internet may have cables or other links extending into many countries, and may thus make profits in many countries: however, an early Privy Council case[3] concerning the transmission of telegrams would appear to indicate that, in the case of a hub-star network, the source of profits is located in the country where the hub is situated.

Filing tax returns over the Internet

At present the transmission of a tax return over the Internet, by e-mail for example, would not satisfy the taxpayer's liability[4] to deliver a tax return to an officer of the Board of the Inland Revenue. This is because returns under the Taxes Acts are required[5] to be in such form as the Inland Revenue prescribes; although the Revenue will accept photocopies of forms, and facsimiles, and in certain cases forms printed by the taxpayer himself, they have not yet prescribed any Internet-based means of delivering tax returns and other tax forms. However, the Revenue in general do adapt to new technology once a certain level of security has been reached, and thus wider use of the Internet by the Inland Revenue can be expected in the future.

In this regard it is interesting to note that in April 1997 the Inland Revenue began to accept electronic lodgement of tax returns:[6] rather than having to complete a tax return, an individual may enter the same information into his personal computer using a program supplied free by the Inland Revenue, which then transmits it directly to the Inland Revenue via a modem, the public telephone system, and a secure gateway.

INTERNATIONAL TAXATION

We shall begin with a broad overview of the world's tax systems.[7] Most countries tax their residents on their world-wide income, but tax non-residents only on income actually earned in that country. This applies both to individuals and to

1   ICTA 1988, s 11.
2   ICTA 1988, s 1(2)(a).
3   *New Zealand Taxes Comr v Eastern Extension Australasia and China Telegraph Co Ltd* [1906] AC 526, PC.
4   Taxes Management Act 1970, s 8(1) for individuals and s 11(1) for companies.
5   Taxes Management Act 1970, s 113.
6   See Taxes Management Act 1970, Sch 3A.
7   A very good guide to taxation in all countries of the world may be found at *http://www.eyi.com/itax*.

businesses. It is thus possible for income to be taxable in two countries simultaneously but this situation is mitigated by Double Taxation Treaties which have the effect that tax is only charged in one or other of the two countries, or sometimes that a part of the tax is chargeable in each country. Not every pair of countries has a Double Taxation Treaty, by a long shot: in fact the UK, which has treaties with approximately one hundred countries, has the most extensive network.

Treaties are almost always bilateral and are often based upon a model treaty created by the Organisation for Economic Co-operation and Development. Treaties on the OECD model tax a business on the basis of the location of its 'permanent establishment'; if there are permanent establishments in both countries, then such of the income as can be attributed to each establishment is taxed in each respective country. Note that there is also a UN model treaty which is often used by developing countries; this tends to tax business income in the territory in which it has its source, irrespective of whether there is a permanent establishment there or not. The USA and the Netherlands have their own model tax treaties. In certain cases treaties depart from the models substantially; in particular, in modern treaties the more obvious methods of offshore tax planning are specifically excluded from treaty benefit.

The term 'permanent establishment' means a branch, an office, etc; in general, it covers any fixed place of business. The Internet was, of course, not in contemplation when the model treaties were drawn up, as a result of which any presence which a business may have in another country by virtue of the Internet will almost certainly not be caught by the definition of a permanent establishment. Therefore by virtue of the Internet it is possible for a business to be conducted in one country but to be taxable exclusively in another country.

---

2. A UK-incorporated and resident company owns a web site providing an information service to subscribers from all over the world, but in particular from the USA. The company has just one office, in the UK, and all information is collated there; and the web pages are stored on the company's own server in the UK. Even though in 1996 the company's accounts show profits of £1,000,000 from its subscribers in the USA, these profits are not subject to tax in the USA but are only taxed in the UK. This is because it does not have a permanent establishment in the USA.[8]

In the above scenario both the company and its web server are in the UK: interesting questions may arise where the company (the author of the web pages) and the web server are in different taxing jurisdictions. Most third party web servers are simply passive repositories for information, but the situation can be imagined where the server carries out a certain amount of processing: it could, for example, be the server which authorises credit card transactions. It could be that the web server will be treated as a branch of the company.

---

8   Article 7, US–UK Double Taxation Agreement of 1975.

Withholding taxes

Some foreign countries impose a tax on licence fees paid abroad: payments made to download Internet material may well constitute licence fees. This is similar to the UK's deduction of tax at source on royalty payments paid abroad.[9]

Under double taxation treaties which the UK is party to, this type of tax (a 'withholding tax') is generally reduced to 10% or 15%. The UK is thus a sensible base from which to conduct a world-wide operation deriving its revenues from licence fees. The procedure for claiming withholding tax reductions varies from country to country; but it would seem sensible for operations of this nature to maintain records of the countries from which payments are received. It is anticipated that where software sales are Internet-based and automated there may be practical problems in maintaining such records: this topic is discussed further below in the VAT section.

Corporate residence and taxation

The UK and most Commonwealth countries tend to treat a company as resident in the territory where it is 'managed and controlled'; the UK additionally regards all UK incorporated companies as being UK-resident[10] no matter where they are managed and controlled. In *De Beers Consolidated Mines Ltd v Howe,*[11] the leading English case on the residence of companies, it was held that a South African-incorporated company was resident in the UK because a majority of the directors lived in London and the board meetings, by which the operations of the company worldwide were controlled and managed, were held in London – even though shareholders' meetings were held in South Africa, and the registered office and head office were in South Africa.[12]

The civil law countries, on the other hand, usually regard a company as taxable in the country of its domicile, that is where it is incorporated. Thus the territory from which it is managed and controlled becomes irrelevant. The USA adopts a similar approach.

Certain countries, notably Hong Kong and various countries in South-East Asia, tax on a purely territorial basis: that is, while all businesses pay tax on income which has its source in the country in question, no business pays tax there on income sourced outside the country in question.

And then of course there are the offshore tax havens, amongst which the best known are perhaps the Bahamas, Bermuda, Panama, and the Channel Islands;[13] in some of these jurisdictions there is simply no tax at all; in others, if certain conditions are fulfilled (these usually being that the company must be 100% foreign-owned and must not do business with residents of the jurisdiction) then a company may be both incorporated and resident in one of these territories without having to pay any tax there other than an annual licence fee.

---

9   ICTA 1988, s 536.
10   Finance Act 1988, s 66.
11   [1906] AC 455, 5 TC 198, HL.
12   For a more extensive discussion see Butterworths' *Simon's Direct Tax Service*, D4.102.
13   An authoritative guide to the facilities available in the world's tax havens is Milton Grundy's *Offshore Business Centres – A World Survey* (7th edn, Sweet & Maxwell, 1997).

Type of jurisdiction	Is a company's foreign income taxable?
UK/Commonwealth	Yes, if company managed and controlled in the jurisdiction
Civil law and USA	Yes, if company incorporated/domiciled in the jurisdiction
Territorial basis	No – only taxable on income arising in the jurisdiction
Offshore haven	No – may require company to be foreign-owned, etc.

Tax planning

It is beyond the scope of this chapter to do more than provide an outline of the type of tax planning techniques that may be considered. In general, tax planning is not recommended except for the very determined: it is expensive and always carries a degree of uncertainty due both to the prospect of future legislative change and to the risk of the Revenue authorities successfully arguing that it does not work.

The use of offshore structures cannot usually assist companies which are both owned and doing business in the UK to escape taxation in the UK. The same is also true of the other 'strong' taxing jurisdictions, notably the USA, the Netherlands, France, Germany, Canada, Australia and New Zealand. The reason is that these jurisdictions have extensive anti-avoidance legislation designed to prevent the use of offshore structures. For example, the UK's 'controlled foreign companies' provisions[14] apply where a company is non-resident and, by virtue of that, subject to a lower level of taxation, but nevertheless is controlled by UK-resident persons.

For a company with business of a traditional type, then, at best the use of an offshore structure does nothing to improve the UK tax situation, and at worst there are large registration fees and taxes to pay in the offshore jurisdiction or, worse still, the company loses business or demoralises its employees because it is perceived as being shady.

Companies trading over the Internet, in contrast to traditional kinds of companies, may find that an offshore structure does have its advantages. This is partly because an Internet-based business is considerably more mobile than a traditional business, and so centres of activity can easily be relocated to any convenient jurisdiction; and partly because the customers in relation to business done over the Internet may be from any country in the world, whereas a traditional business would normally require a branch in each country in which it has customers.

For a company resident in a tax haven jurisdiction to escape taxation in the UK, not only must it be managed and controlled outside the UK, but because of the controlled foreign company rules referred to above[15] it must not be controlled by persons resident in the UK. Control is defined in section 416 of ICTA 1988 and

14   ICTA 1988, s 747.
15   Ibid.

the test for control is a wide test, applicable to shareholders, directors or others.[16] In practice, it is necessary for a majority of the persons actually able to exercise control over the company to be non-UK residents.

Besides avoiding UK tax liability on its non-UK source income, an advantage of non-resident status for a company doing business over the Internet is that even profits arising in respect of trading in the UK are only taxed at the basic rate, 24% in 1996. This is because a company whose only presence in the UK is through the Internet does not carry on a trade through a UK branch or agency;[17] accordingly the company falls outside the corporation tax net and instead pays income tax[18] like an individual, but not being an individual it never becomes liable to pay tax at the higher rate.

An alternative approach, where a company is essentially owned and controlled by UK residents, is not to seek to pay no tax, but simply to site the company in a jurisdiction where there is tax but at a lower rate than in the UK. If the amount of tax paid in that other territory is at least 75% of the amount of tax that would be paid in the UK then the controlled foreign company provisions do not bite.[19] Various territories, for example the Isle of Man, have taxation structures specifically designed to allow companies to take advantage of this rule.[20]

Whether it is best to site a business in a tax haven or to site it in the UK or another taxing jurisdiction with a good tax treaty network very much depends on the nature of the business. Note also that, for reasons connected with VAT, it may be helpful for businesses with customers in the European Union to make sales from a base outside the EU – see the next section.

Finally, it is worth noting that various jurisdictions offer special tax incentives to those setting up in high technology industries; these can amount to complete tax exemptions for five years or more. The following countries offer some form of incentive for high-technology start-ups, although incentives may only be available to businesses employing a minimum number of persons or setting up in particular areas of the country: Canada; China; Denmark; Malaysia; Saudi Arabia; Singapore; Spain (Canary Islands); Taiwan; and Vietnam. And those contemplating setting up their own communications links should bear in mind that many of the smaller island jurisdictions are prepared to negotiate very generous terms to attract businesses which will provide them with a modern communications infrastructure.

VAT

Value added tax is an indirect tax on consumers, sometimes called a turnover tax. It is a European tax: all members of the European Union are required to impose VAT and to do so in broadly the same way. The primary EU legislation is EC Council Directive 77/388 of 17 May 1977, universally referred to by practitioners as the Sixth Directive. Member states are required to enact domestic legislation giving effect to the Sixth Directive. In a few areas member states have some

---

16 For further details, see *Simon's Direct Tax Service*, D4.131 onwards.
17 Defined in ICTA 1988, s 834(1), to mean 'any factorship, agency, receivership, branch or management'.
18 ICTA 1988, s 11.
19 ICTA 1988, s 750.
20 For a list of such territories see *Offshore Red*, Vol 1 no 6, p 110 (Campden Publishing Ltd, 1996).

freedom in the precise rules they adopt: an example is the standard rate of VAT itself, which is at the discretion of each member so long as it is at least 15%.

In the UK, VAT is imposed by statute; as is the case with the direct taxes, major changes are made annually by the Finance Act following the Budget, and the VAT legislation is amended frequently.[1] The most recent consolidating statute was the Value Added Tax Act 1994 ('VATA 1994'). Secondary legislation often contains important provisions; for example, the Value Added Tax Regulations 1995[2] contain much of the law relating to administration and collection of VAT in the UK.

Collection of VAT is the responsibility of HM Customs & Excise. All persons making taxable supplies (basically, all businesses) whose turnover exceeds a certain threshold must register for VAT. In respect of each period (usually three months, but exceptionally one month or twelve months) the taxable person is obliged[3] to complete a VAT return and to pay any VAT due. In general, the VAT regulations impose fairly strict requirements on businesses to maintain proper records[4] and to supply customers with invoices in the correct form.[5]

There is a right of appeal from any decision of HM Customs & Excise to a judicial body known as the VAT Tribunal, thence to the High Court and higher courts. Since VAT is a European tax, points of European law often arise: it is not uncommon for the UK legislation, or the way in which Customs & Excise seek to implement it, to exceed what is permitted under the European legislation and thus be ultra vires. Both the VAT Tribunal and the higher courts hearing VAT appeals are able to refer questions for decision by the European Court of Justice in Luxembourg.

The VAT system in the UK

The rate of VAT in the UK is currently 17½%, although prior to 1991 it was 15%. The VAT system in the UK, as in the rest of Europe, basically taxes the end consumers of goods and services, but is in theory transparent to the producers of those goods and services. A business, although it is obliged to pay VAT on the supplies of goods and services that it makes ('output tax'), is able to pass the whole of that cost on to the consumer in a way readers will be familiar with. On the other hand, a business is able to reclaim the sums with which it has itself been charged in respect of VAT on its purchases ('input tax').

It is a common misconception that the consumer pays the VAT: it is in fact the supplier of goods or services who is liable to pay the VAT. Thus if a trader omits to charge his customers the extra 17.5% in respect of VAT he is none the less liable himself to pay VAT to Customs & Excise. Here may be found the rationale behind the system of VAT invoices: because a business does not itself pay the VAT on its inputs, it requires an invoice from its supplier to show that VAT has been paid before it is able to reclaim that sum as input tax. In the UK it is by law mandatory[6] for a person who is VAT registered[7] to furnish a business customer (a

---

1   Up-to-date versions may be found in Butterworths' *Orange Tax Handbook*, published annually.
2   SI 1995/2518.
3   Value Added Tax Regulations 1995 (SI 1995/2518), reg 25(1).
4   Value Added Tax Regulations 1995, reg 31.
5   Value Added Tax Regulations 1995, regs 13–20.
6   Value Added Tax Regulations 1995, reg 13(1).
7   Other than a retailer – Value Added Tax Regulations 1995, reg 16.

customer who is a 'taxable person' within the meaning of VATA 1994) with a VAT invoice in respect of every taxable supply.

A few types of transaction are outside the scope of VAT altogether: the most important example is any supply which is not made for consideration (note that consideration has a slightly different meaning in a VAT context from its meaning in the law of contract). Then there are supplies which are exempt supplies, for example the provision of education, medical services, insurance and most banking services;[8] pretty much the same rules apply across the whole of Europe as to which supplies are exempt supplies.[9] In contrast, zero-rated supplies are supplies of goods or services which are in theory subject to VAT, but at a reduced rate; in fact the reduced rate is 0% in the UK. Reduced rates of VAT are applied differently in different member states,[10] but in the UK the most important categories for zero-rating are foodstuffs, passenger transport services, and books and newspapers.[11] The practical difference between making an exempt supply and making a zero-rated supply is that a zero-rated supply is within the VAT system and accordingly the supplier is able to deduct input tax incurred in respect of it. For example a publisher will often have no output tax to pay, due to all his supplies being zero-rated, but will nevertheless have incurred input tax due to purchases of paper, inks, binding materials, office equipment, etc; accordingly, every VAT period the publisher will actually receive money from Customs & Excise. The economic effect is that the Treasury receives no VAT in respect of any of the materials which go to make up a zero-rated supply; in contrast, materials consumed in order to make an exempt supply are subject to VAT as if supplied to a consumer.

International supplies and VAT

It is only supplies which are made, or treated as made, in the UK which are subject to VAT in the UK.[12] Goods exported are zero-rated,[13] and there are special schemes for goods supplied to foreign residents in the UK which are subsequently exported. Most services supplied to foreign residents are outside the scope of VAT. However, certain services are subject to VAT in the UK if the supplier is in the UK.

Since the implementation of the European Single Market on 1 January 1993, supplies of goods and services to other EU member states have been treated slightly differently from exports to countries outside the EU. The general rule is that an intra-EU supply of goods is taxable not in the supplier's member state, but in the customer's: accordingly the supply of goods moving from a supplier in the UK to a taxable person (a business customer) in another member state is zero-rated.[14] Similarly, the making of supplies to non-taxable persons (private customers) in another member state may mean that the supplier is required to register for VAT in that other member state, and to pay VAT there (known as 'distance selling') – the corresponding rule in the UK is that EU suppliers must register and pay VAT if the annual value of supplies made to the UK exceeds

8   VATA 1994, Sch 9.
9   Sixth Directive, art 13.
10 The reduced rate is not normally less than 5% – Sixth Directive, art 12.3a.
11 VATA 1994, Sch 8.
12 VATA 1994, s 4(1).
13 VATA 1994, s 30(6).
14 VATA 1994, s 30(8).

£70,000.[15] If a UK supplier is not registered in another member state in this way then, in contrast to the general rule, his supplies to private customers in that other member state are in fact subject to VAT in the UK.

Imports of goods from outside the EU are taxable[16] on entry into the UK (at least, upon leaving the fiscal warehouse), whether imported privately or by a business. For example, where goods are sent from overseas by mail order the Post Office will require[17] payment of the VAT due before delivery will be made. Acquisitions of goods from other EU member states are also subject to VAT in the UK if the customer is VAT-registered here;[18] private customers, on the other hand, do not have to pay VAT on acquisitions from other member states since either the supplier will pay VAT in the UK under the distance-selling rules referred to above, or the supplier will have paid VAT in the member state of origin.

For most common types of services (known as 'Schedule 5 services'[19]) the position is quite similar to that for the supply of goods: the supply is subject to VAT in the country where the customer belongs. The consequence is that supplies of such services are not subject to VAT in the UK if (i) the customer is outside the EU,[20] or (ii) the customer is a business customer in another EU member state;[1] on the other hand, supplies of services to private customers in other member states are always[2] subject to VAT in the UK. However, the position is different for services which are not Schedule 5 services: in this case the supply takes place in the country where the supplier belongs,[3] so that supplies of such services are subject to VAT in the UK if the supplier belongs here,[4] no matter to whom the supply is made.

In contrast with the position for imported goods, private customers receiving supplies of services from outside the EU do not have to pay any VAT. But VAT-registered persons receiving services from abroad must account for VAT in the UK on all Schedule 5 services, additionally on various categories of services for which there is special provision, such as performance arts, conferences and exhibitions, and valuation services.[5] In general VAT registered persons paying VAT under this rule may then deduct such VAT again as input tax.

Internet transactions: supply of goods or services?

Where the use of the Internet is free then, in most cases, VAT issues will not be relevant because VAT is not imposed where there is no consideration given for a supply.[6] But where payment or other kinds of consideration are received for a supply made over the Internet then this will fall within the VAT regime. In almost

15   VATA 1994, Sch 2, para 1.
16   By VATA 1994, s 1(4) VAT is due on imports as if it were a customs duty.
17   See the Postal Packets (Customs and Excise) Regulations 1986, SI 1986/260.
18   VATA 1994, s 10(1).
19   Those listed in VATA 1994, Sch 5, paras 1–8.
20   In this case, an export of services, the supply is outside the scope of VAT altogether.
1   Value Added Tax (Place of Supply of Services) Order 1992 (SI 1992/3121), art 16.
2   Ie, there is no equivalent for supplies of services of the 'distance-selling' rules.
3   VATA 1994, s 7(10).
4   See VATA 1994, s 9 for the place where a supplier of services belongs.
5   VATA 1994, s 8 and Sch 5, paras 1–9; also Value Added Tax (Place of Supply of Services) Order 1992, SI 1992/3121.
6   Sixth Directive, art 2 and see VATA 1994, s 5(2)(a).

all circumstances where a transaction involving the Internet is subject to VAT this will be as a supply of services rather than as a supply of goods.

Both the domestic legislation and the EU legislation go to some lengths to define which supplies are supplies of goods and which are supplies of services. But for almost all purposes there is no distinction between the two. One situation in which there is a difference between the VAT treatment of a supply of goods and of a supply of services is in the context of supplies made from outside the EU: imported goods are subject to VAT upon entry into EU territory, whereas services supplied from outside the EU to a non-registered person are not subject to VAT (services supplied from abroad to a person who is VAT registered, on the other hand, are usually treated in a similar way to imported goods).

In a VAT context, the word 'goods' means tangible, physical goods: the Sixth Directive, article 5, provides:

'1. 'Supply of goods' shall mean the transfer of the right to dispose of tangible property as owner.
2. Electric current, gas, heat, refrigeration and the like shall be considered tangible property.'

The transmission of data and the granting of licences to use copyright material do not fall within the above definitions and therefore cannot be considered to be supplies of goods. Even if data is transmitted by electric means this cannot be characterised as the supply of electric current: article 5.2 is concerned with the supply of energy, and the transmission of data is something different entirely.

Any supply which is not a supply of goods is a supply of services (if effected for consideration).[7] Thus, the following types of transaction are supplies of services (or would be if done for consideration):

- the provision of dial-up Internet access and e-mail facilities;
- the transmission of data packets to a customer;
- the provision of data packet routing services;
- the provision of space on a server for a customer's web pages;
- the registration of a customer's domain name;
- the translation of a domain name into an IP address;
- online data processing in general;
- the provision of advertising space on a web site;
- designing a web page;
- granting licences in relation to copyright material.

No doubt there are other examples. On the other hand, it almost goes without saying that tangible goods are incapable of transmission over the Internet; accordingly Internet-related supplies are never supplies of goods, unless the Internet is merely used as a mechanism for ordering goods which are to be supplied by conventional means.

It is interesting to note in this context that the provision of copyright material over the Internet (that is, the transmission of a digital representation of a copyright work coupled with a licence to store and to use the copyright work so transmitted) is always a supply of services. In other words, the supply of a program, a literary work, an image, a video package or an audio package etc is a supply of services. This is in contrast with the supply of such material otherwise than via the Internet:

7   Sixth Directive, art 6.1 and see VATA 1994, Sch 4, para 1.

in such a case a medium is required to carry the copyright material, and there is a supply of goods at least in relation to the physical medium. Thus the supply of a video, audio or software package *on disk or tape* necessarily involves a supply of goods. In the case of 'normalised' software, that is off-the-shelf software packages, the whole supply may in practice be characterised as a supply of goods:[8] similar treatment extends to consumer video and audio. On the other hand, the supply of what Customs & Excise calls 'specific' software, that is bespoke software or indeed upgrades for software already purchased, is characterised as a pure supply of services, the incidental supply of goods being disregarded for VAT purposes.

There has not yet been any litigation on the point, but the cost of the carrier medium is now so cheap in relation to the overall cost of a software package, or indeed a video or audio package, that in the author's view the true legal position is that *any* supply of copyright material on disk, tape or CD ROM should properly be characterised as a supply of services, the supply of goods being purely incidental. Be that as it may, it can be seen that for as long as in practice the supply of consumer audio, video and software on disk or tape is treated as a pure supply of goods then there will be a difference in the treatment of the same material supplied over the Internet, and this difference does introduce distortions as will be seen below.

Who is the supplier in relation to Internet material?

If there is a taxable supply over the Internet, for example the downloading of software in return for payment charged to a credit card, then it is important to establish who is, in law, the person making that supply for VAT purposes. The possible options are:

A. the owner of the web site;
B. the author of the material (if different from A – what is contemplated here is a site owner who makes available on the site programs in which other people hold the copyright);
C. the owner of the computer hosting the web site (if different from A);
D. the end-user's Internet access provider;
E. the end-user himself.

The question to be answered is, what is the payment for?

Where the payment is made essentially for the licence that the end-user receives, rather than for the actual transmission of the material, then clearly it is B, the copyright holder, who makes the supply since he is the only person able to grant that licence. Of course normally A and B will be the same person. If they are not the same person, and if the licence is apparently granted by A (who is perhaps acting as B's agent) then it may be that A is the taxable person in relation to the supply: in general, the VAT treatment of agency is that there is a supply of services from the agent to the customer, and a second supply of services from the principal to the agent (but sometimes the agent may be looked straight through so that the principal is still the taxable person).[9]

---

8   See, for example, Customs & Excise Notice 702/4/94, which recognises that technically there is both a supply of goods and an associated supply of services, but permits taxable persons to treat the whole as a supply of goods.
9   See VATA 1994, s 47(3).

Where the payment is actually made for the transmission itself (perhaps because the material is not copyright) then it is likely to be A who is the taxable person: it is A who made the data available on the web site in transmissible form. In this case C, the owner of the actual host machine, is not the taxable person because the host machine has merely a passive role as a store for the data: C's machine could be likened to a library shelf, or perhaps more accurately a vending machine.

In the case of a more interactive web site where the host machine performs some data processing functions, for example a web search engine, or an online game, then it seems likely that C makes the taxable supply: it is C's machine which supplies the service. This is important in the context of secondary servers and mirrors. In practice, of course, almost every person providing a site which performs heavy data processing will own his own server or servers and so the question may never arise.

In no case will D be the taxable person, since all that D's computer does is to take the end-user's transmissions, turn them into packets and route them, and to receive packets destined for the end-user and to transmit them to him in usable form. These services the end-user will already have paid for in the contract between him and the access provider: the access provider does the same thing in relation to every packet, and does nothing extra in relation to packets of particular kinds. This is particularly important where D and E are the only persons in the above list who are resident in the UK. Occasionally it is suggested in the press and elsewhere that a tax should be imposed on certain kinds of Internet material coming into the country: so far as the Service Providers are concerned all material routed through them is of the same kind, that is to say data packets, and so it is hard to envisage a system that would work unless a uniform tax were imposed on every packet routed into the country.

So what about E? Of course E cannot be both supplier and customer.[10] The reason for including E in the above list is that some kinds of transactions take place in E's own computer, that is either when E sees material on his computer screen, or (in the case of contracts accepted by conduct) when he clicks with his mouse or otherwise performs the act of acceptance. It might be thought that in some way this could mean that the supply takes place in the UK when otherwise it would not. But the place of formation of a contract, and other factors in connection with the place services are actually performed, have no relevance in a VAT context: as previously indicated, in connection with a supply of services what is relevant is the place the customer belongs (or the place where the supplier belongs, in the case of non-Schedule 5 services).

Specific types of business over the Internet

In general, VAT issues are only likely to arise if supplies are made over the Internet for payment or some other form of consideration. The payment does not have to be made over the Internet to give rise to a VATable supply: there could be payment in advance, perhaps in the form of a periodic subscription, there could be a fee per use, or there could be some other method for payment after the event. Shareware, for example, involves the gratuitous transmission of software but the imposition on the user of an obligation later to pay a fee in certain circumstances,

---

10   In fact the mechanism for imposing VAT on services supplied to a taxable person in the UK by a supplier overseas does treat the services as supplied by that taxable person to himself – VATA 1994, s 8 – but this is not what we are talking about here.

for example if the software is used commercially or if he wishes to register it. So long as there is a *direct link*[11] between the supply over the Internet and the payment received then such payment will constitute consideration for the supply. Five categories of business will now be considered.

I. Mail order

For example, an Internet-based form is used to take orders; the same information is obtained as on a printed form; delivery is made by post in the usual way, with a paper VAT receipt.

The use of the Internet here makes no difference to the VAT treatment. Goods are still supplied: the Internet is simply a more streamlined way of obtaining customer information. This has been confirmed by the VAT Tribunal in *Emphasis Ltd v HM Customs & Excise*[12] where a business which accepted orders for sandwiches and other food via computer was held to be making a zero-rated supply of foodstuffs, and was not, by virtue of the use of the computer, making a standard-rated supply of services as Customs & Excise contended.

2. General Internet services and the supply of copyright material

The provision of software for downloading is the main business contemplated here, since this is frequently done in return for payment. Information and news services, database and search services such as LEXIS/NEXIS also fall into this category, as do online books and newspapers, also video or audio packages for downloading.

As noted earlier, all such supplies are supplies of services.

Whether these types of services are subject to VAT or not depends on who the customer is. Services supplied to customers belonging outside the EU are not subject to VAT, while services supplied to *business* customers in the EU are not subject to VAT in the UK (but are probably subject to VAT in the business customer's own country – this is the customer's responsibility). The place where the customer belongs is judged according to the location of the relevant 'fixed establishment',[13] which usually means the office or branch actually receiving the service.

Suppliers situated in the UK

A UK-based business providing services or information on the Internet, therefore, should pay VAT only on its supplies to UK customers and its supplies to *private* customers based in the other EU member states. All *business* customers must be provided with VAT invoices. It may be possible for the supplier to meet its requirement to do this by sending the VAT invoice by e-mail, since the regulations[14] do not expressly require an invoice to be on paper: but care should

---

11   This is a very important concept in VAT law: the leading case is *Apple and Pear Development Council v HM Customs & Excise* [1988] STC 221, ECJ.
12   LON/95/2355A.
13   VATA 1994, s 9.
14   Value Added Tax Regulations 1995 (SI 1995/2518), regs 13 and 14.

be taken to include all the particulars normally contained in a VAT invoice, and to inform the customer that the invoice is being sent in this manner in order that he may take appropriate steps to keep a copy of the invoice; the supplier should also ensure a copy of the invoice is kept for his own records.[15]

To enable its own VAT accounts to be prepared, a UK business supplying these kinds of services, besides the usual information regarding the date and value of the supply, must gather the following information in relation to each supply made: the country in which the customer is situated, and whether the service is supplied for business or private purposes. These two latter pieces of information can only come from the customer himself, and it will not necessarily be easy to gather this information where the service is supplied automatically, since Internet customers may not see the relevance of the questions.

Heavy reliance is placed on the honesty of the customer. This is particularly so if a different price is charged depending on whether the customer is a UK customer or an EU private customer on the one hand, in which case the supply is subject to VAT, or an EU business customer or a non-EU customer on the other hand, in which case the supply is not subject to VAT. In order to satisfy its obligation to maintain accurate records[16] the supplier must find a way to prevent dishonesty. If the customer realises the implications of saying that he is an EU business customer, or that he is located outside the EU, then he might be tempted to provide incorrect information in order to be charged a lower price. Even where the supplier's machine has been tricked into charging a UK-based customer a VAT-free price the supplier is still in theory liable to HM Customs & Excise for the VAT due, as there has in fact been a supply in the UK; if there is consequently a misdeclaration in the supplier's VAT return then additionally the supplier might be liable to pay a penalty unless there is a reasonable excuse for the inaccuracy.[17]

We will repeat here a principle mentioned earlier, that the VAT is paid by the supplier and not the customer. Thus the dishonest conduct involved in supplying false information to the supplier's machine does not constitute VAT evasion (as defined in VATA 1994, section 60) since the customer has no liability to account for VAT under the VAT Act: that is the supplier's responsibility. The VAT Act 1994, section 72 sets out various criminal offences in connection with VAT, in particular section 72(3) provides that a person who, with intent to deceive, produces, furnishes, sends or otherwise uses for the purposes of the VAT Act a document which is false in a material particular is guilty of an offence; and section 72(6) extends that section to include furnishing, sending or otherwise making use of a document with intent to secure that a machine will respond to it as if it were a true document. But again the customer can have committed no offence within the meaning of the section since any information he sends to the supplier's machine is not sent for the purposes of VATA 1994, it is sent for the supplier's own purposes: this is because VATA 1994 makes no specific provision in the case of services supplied to foreign customers for any document to be furnished by a customer to his supplier. This is to be contrasted with certain situations where the Act does provide for the customer to furnish his supplier with a certificate in order to obtain zero-rating.[18]

One way for suppliers to overcome problems in this area would be simply to charge a uniform price whether the supply is within the scope of VAT or not: it

---

15 Value Added Tax Regulations 1995 (SI 1995/2518), reg 31(1)(c).
16 Value Added Tax Regulations 1995 (SI 1995/2518), reg 31.
17 VATA 1994, s 64(5)(a).
18 See VATA 1994, s 62 for examples.

should be remembered that it is always open to the supplier to charge whatever price he likes, VAT being collected from him at the rate of 17.5/117.5 of the price actually charged[19] in the case of supplies which are within the VAT regime. Another solution which might go part of the way towards meeting the problem would be to require customers to supply a telephone number with full international dialling code: the code could then be checked against the country information supplied. In any event, it is clearly impracticable to determine a customer's location from his IP address which is the one certain piece of information which the supplier has.

Suppliers situated abroad

The supply of services to private consumers (UK or EU) is subject to UK VAT only if the supplier is based in the UK: this is judged by the location of the 'permanent business establishment', ie the head office, or sometimes, if there are offices in more than one country, the office most directly concerned with the supply. Therefore a supplier may avoid VAT on all supplies to private customers in the EU if it is itself located outside the EU. As indicated earlier, the Internet introduces a distortion because the importation of products on disk by private customers in the UK would be subject to VAT, but the supply of the same products over the Internet may not be subject to VAT.

---

3. A computer game is created by a corporation whose office is in California and which has no offices in the EU. The game is made available for downloading on this corporation's web site, in return for credit card payments. Four UK residents purchase a copy of the game.

Penelope, who wishes to play the game, downloads it from the web site, and as she is not a VAT-registered person there is no VAT to pay.

Quentin, a journalist who wishes to write a review of the game, also downloads it from the web site, but because he is a VAT-registered person and the service is supplied to him for the purposes of a business carried on by him, there is VAT to pay: under the self-supply rules he must account for VAT on the supply of the game to him as if it were his own output tax, but in the same VAT period he is able to deduct an equivalent amount as input tax.

Roger uses the web site to order a copy of the game on a disk, and this is subsequently sent to him by post. When the disk comes into the UK there is a charge to VAT, and the Post Office on delivery of the postal packet will require Roger to pay the VAT due.

Samantha imports 100 copies of the game on disk in order to sell them in her shop. She too has to pay VAT on these imports, but at this stage VAT is only chargeable on the wholesale price that she pays. If she is VAT-registered then she may obtain an input tax credit for the VAT paid on importation, but on the other hand she has to pay VAT on any sales she makes. Accordingly her customers will have to pay a VAT-inclusive price.

---

19   VATA 1994, s 19(2).

There is clearly considerable scope for VAT planning here: if the supplier is based outside EU territory then it is possible to avoid VAT on private sales within the EU so long as these are conducted over the Internet. This would give the supplier a competitive advantage over products imported by conventional means.

Books, newspapers and magazines

As a final note, it is generally thought that books, newspapers and magazines published on the Internet do not qualify for zero-rating,[20] however, it may be arguable that they do qualify for zero-rating, particularly in the case of newspapers, journals and periodicals which are identical in form to the printed version. In a recent case, *Customs & Excise Comrs v Colour Offset Ltd*,[1] it was decided that blank diaries were not books for these purposes: but the case contains judicial dicta to the effect that it is not the physical nature of an object that dictates whether it qualifies for zero-rating or not, but its information content. Neither the UK legislation (VATA 1994, section 30(2)) nor the EC legislation (Sixth Directive, Annex H) requires that a supply of a book, newspaper or periodical should be a supply of goods in order to be zero-rated, as opposed to a supply of services. Developments are awaited with interest.

3. Internet material without grant of intellectual property rights

Here we are perhaps looking at a video, audio or games package which is not downloaded but is simply played on the customer's computer using the web viewer: the customer is not licensed to store and use the material in the same way as if the software had been purchased: he simply views the transmission once, in the same way as a television broadcast is viewed, although of course in a more interactive way. Or certain material which may be supplied over the Internet may not be copyright and thus no licence to use it may be required.

The reason for the distinction between this category and heading 2 is that whilst the list of Schedule 5 services includes:

'Transfers and assignments of copyright, patents, licences, trademarks and similar rights

Data processing and provision of information'

it does not include the bare transmission of images, games and the like. The discussion above under heading 2 was, of course, referring to Schedule 5 services, but if the services supplied are not Schedule 5 services then it is possible that a business which is based in the UK and making these kinds of supplies will be subject to VAT on *all* supplies made, including supplies to customers outside the EU. The reason is that such a supply is considered to take place in the UK if the supplier belongs in the UK.[2]

---

20   VATA 1994, Sch 8, Group 3.
 1   [1995] STC 85, QBD.
 2   VATA 1994, s 7(10)(a).

It remains to be seen whether HM Customs & Excise will in practice take this point in relation to supplies over the Internet, since it will almost always be possible to categorise such supplies as 'data processing' or 'provision of information' which fall under paragraph 3 of Schedule 5. Further developments are awaited.

Where a non-Schedule 5 service is supplied by a person belonging outside the UK then such a supply is outside the scope of VAT since the supply is not considered to take place in the UK (unless it falls into one of the special categories such as performance arts,[3] but entertainment services not performed before a live audience are not considered to fall into this category). So in the case of supplies by persons belonging outside the EU, no VAT is imposed on supplies to either business customers or private customers in the UK.

4. Internet Service Providers

Those providing connection to the Internet are, in most cases, providing telecommunications services to their customers, and telecommunications services are not Schedule 5 services. Thus such supplies are subject to VAT in the UK if the supplier belongs in the UK, but they are not subject to VAT otherwise. This will be of particular interest to business customers making exempt supplies, for example banks, since such businesses are unable to recover any VAT paid in respect of inputs used to make exempt supplies.

To counter VAT avoidance in relation to both the supply of telephone services and the provision of Internet connections from offshore, the UK government is seeking changes to the European law so that all telecommunications services (including Internet-related services) will be categorised as Schedule 5 services. Such changes are not likely to be introduced before 1998. If such changes are introduced, supplies made by Internet Service Providers based in the UK will become exempt from VAT if made to subscribers based outside the EU; on the other hand, overseas Service Providers will not be able to avoid VAT on supplies to UK-based business customers, since such supplies will become subject to VAT in the UK under the self-supply rules.

5. Advertising on the World Wide Web

A site owner deriving advertising revenue from advertisements held on its web pages is supplying a service. 'Advertising services' are Schedule 5 services.[4]

In this case, of course, the service is supplied not to readers of the web site, but to the advertiser. Thus the supply by a UK-based supplier is subject to VAT if the *advertiser* is based in the UK (or if the advertiser is a private individual in another EU member state); in the case of a foreign supplier, supplies to UK residents are subject to VAT under the reverse charge rule if the advertiser is VAT registered and placing the advertisement for business purposes, but are not subject to VAT otherwise. Generally the VAT treatment is as under heading 2 above.

---

3   Value Added Tax (Place of Supply of Services) Order 1992 (SI 1992/3121), para 15.
4   VATA 1994, Sch 5, para 2.

4. Whoopee, a US corporation, has a popular web site stored on a US-owned server. It reserves spaces on its home page for other people's advertisements. One such advertising space is made available for a substantial charge to XYZ Ltd, a UK company which is VAT registered.

This is, for VAT purposes, a supply of advertising services by Whoopee to the UK company. Because XYZ Ltd has its only business establishment in the UK, and because the supply is made for business purposes, the supply of services is treated as made by the recipient in the UK and accordingly XYZ Ltd must account for VAT on that supply under the reverse charge rules (VATA 1994, section 8). But unless its own supplies are exempt supplies XYZ Ltd will be entitled to a full credit for this VAT as input tax.

Chapter eight
Securities and financial services

Christopher Luck, Partner, Nabarro Nathanson

More and more financial information, products and services are becoming available on the Internet. In the United Kingdom, share price information and dealing services are available through Electronic Share Information Limited's ESIQuote Service[1] and Infotrade.[2] These provide access to computer screen share dealing through execution-only brokers (ShareLink and City Deal Services).

The Internet is not only used by Service Providers. It is also used by regulators and the markets themselves. For example, the Securities Investments Board (SIB)[3] and Investment Management Regulatory Organisation Limited (IMRO)[4] each have web sites. Their sites include guidance and information for investors.

The provision of financial information and investment services through the Internet is an area which needs to be carefully monitored and regulated so that investors and users are properly protected. This chapter considers the following issues.

1. Who are the regulators and what activities do they regulate?
2. What are the legal rules for those who wish to provide investment business over the Internet?
3. How do these investment business rules apply to those from overseas who may come into contact with the United Kingdom through the global nature of the Internet?
4. What are the rules on using the World Wide Web and e-mail to advertise offering investments or investment services?
5. How can shares be legally offered over the Internet?
6. How is the dissemination of information about securities and investments over the Internet subject to regulation?
7. What are the issues involved with using the World Wide Web to release information about mergers and takeovers?

FINANCIAL SERVICES IN THE UK

A person wishing to publish financial information or offer financial and investment services in the United Kingdom will need to consider, amongst other

1   http://www.esi.co.uk
2   http://www.infotrade.co.uk
3   http://www.sib.co.uk
4   http://www.imro.co.uk

requirements, the provisions of the Financial Services Act 1986 ('FSA') and the Investment Services Directive referred to below.

The FSA created the current framework for the regulation of 'investment business' in the United Kingdom and the protection of the public in respect of the advertising and promotion of 'investments'.

The FSA applies, in principle, to a variety of persons involved with the Internet, especially those acting as providers of financial services and even to access and site providers.

Regulation

A person who carries on 'investment business'[5] in the United Kingdom within the meaning of the FSA must either be an 'authorised person' or an 'exempted person'.[6]

An 'authorised person'[7] is one who has obtained or is deemed to have authorisation to carry on investment business for the purposes of the FSA. This authorisation is usually from a self-regulating organisation (SRO), a recognised professional body (RPB) or, in certain cases, from the Securities and Investment Board (SIB). Certain insurers, friendly societies and operators and trustees of recognised collective investment schemes are also treated as authorised persons under the FSA.

'Exempted persons'[8] include the Bank of England, recognised investment exchanges, recognised clearing houses, listed money market institutions, The Society of Lloyds and persons permitted by the Council of Lloyds to act as underwriting agents at Lloyds, appointed representatives of authorised persons within section 44 of the FSA and various other persons listed in section 45 of the FSA.[9]

The Investment Services Directive

In addition, certain European investment firms which are authorised to carry on investment business in other member states of the European Economic Area may also rely on that authorisation to provide certain investment services in the United Kingdom. This follows the implementation of the Council Directive on investment services in the securities field (No 93/22/EEC) ('the Investment Services Directive') by the Investment Services Regulations 1995 (SI 1995/3275) ('the Investment Services Regulations 1995').

A European investment firm entitled to carry on particular types of investment business in the United Kingdom under the Investment Services Regulations is generally treated as an 'authorised person' under the FSA. As a result a number of provisions of the FSA which refer to 'authorised persons' have been amended to have effect as if they also referred to European investment firms carrying on regulated business in the United Kingdom.

5   See 'What is investment business', below.
6   Financial Services Act 1986, s 3.
7   Financial Services Act 1986, Ch III.
8   Financial Services Act 1986, Ch IV. Exempted persons are generally only treated as such to the extent that they act in their capacity as a person providing or performing a particular service or role.
9   Section 207 of the Financial Services Act 1986 defines various expressions used in that Act including 'appointed representative', 'collective investment scheme', 'exempted person', 'friendly society', an 'operator' in relation to a collective investment scheme, 'recognised clearing house' and 'recognised investment exchange'.

The Investment Services Regulations also include provisions for a 'common passport' for 'UK authorised investment firms' (eg authorised or exempted persons under the FSA) providing listed investment services in other member states.

The 'common passport' offered by the Investment Services Directive is, therefore, likely to be of importance to investment businesses which wish to provide investment services throughout the European Economic Area through the Internet or more conventional means.

THE UNITED KINGDOM REGULATORS

The Secretary of State for Trade and Industry

The responsibility for the regulation of financial services under the FSA was conferred upon the Secretary of State for Trade and Industry. Most of the functions of the Secretary of State for Trade and Industry relating to the regulation of investment business have been delegated to the Treasury and to the SIB as 'the designated agency'[10] under the FSA.

The Securities and Investments Board ('SIB')

The SIB is not a government department but it has the power under the FSA to recognise and de-recognise self-regulating organisations ('SROs') and recognised professional bodies (RPBs) and to prosecute and take proceedings in respect of unauthorised investment business and unauthorised investment advertisements. It has delegated its power to authorise persons carrying on investment business to the SROs and RPBs although the SIB may, in certain limited circumstances, grant authorisation itself.

The SIB's main objective, in relation to the Internet, is to deliver effective and high standards of protection for the investor, such protection to equate with what an investor would receive had he been dealing in a more conventional manner.[11]

Self-regulating organisations (SROs)

An SRO is a body which regulates the carrying on of 'investment business' of any kind by enforcing rules which are binding on those carrying on business of that kind either because they are members of that body or because they are otherwise subject to its control.[12]

The present SROs are:

1. the Investment Management Regulatory Organisation (IMRO);
2. the Personal Investment Authority (PIA); and
3. the Securities and Futures Authority (SFA).

Stockbrokers, securities houses, merchant banks and brokers and dealers in futures are usually members of the SFA; investment managers are generally members of IMRO; and those providing personal investment products and

---

10   Pursuant to s 114 of the Financial Services Act 1986.
11   Martin Hollobone on Financial Services Act 1986 and the Internet, 23 November 1995.
12   Financial Services Act 1986, s 8.

services such as life assurance will seek membership of the PIA. Members of the PIA will in many cases have previously been members of the Life Assurance and Unit Trust Regulatory Organisation (LAUTRO) or the Financial Intermediaries, Managers and Brokers Regulatory Association (FIMBRA) which merged to form the PIA.

Members of an SRO are able to do all types of investment business within the scope of their membership. They must comply with the relevant rules of the particular SRO to which they belong. Failure to do so can result in fines by their SRO and claims for compensation under section 62 of the FSA.

Recognised professional bodies (RPBs)

A person is also an 'authorised person' if he holds a certificate issued for this purpose by a recognised professional body, being a body which regulates the practice of a profession.[13] Therefore, members of a profession will be authorised by their Recognised Professional Body (eg solicitors by The Law Society and Chartered Accountants by the Institute of Chartered Accountants in England and Wales or as may otherwise be applicable for the particular profession). The term 'practice of a profession' does not include references to carrying on a business consisting wholly or mainly of investment business. Members of a profession may, therefore, also seek authorisation by an SRO such as PIA or IMRO.

IS IT A CRIMINAL OFFENCE NOT TO BE AUTHORISED?

It is an offence for a person to carry on, or purport to carry on, 'investment business' in the United Kingdom unless he is an authorised person or an exempted person. If a person commits such an offence he is liable on conviction to a term of imprisonment of up to two years or a fine of up to £5,000 or both.[14]

The offence can extend to the officers of a body corporate or its controller (broadly speaking a person entitled to exercise more than 15% of its votes), to the partners of a partnership or to the officers of an unincorporated association where the offence is committed by the body corporate, partnership or unincorporated association.[15]

There is a defence under section 4(2) of the FSA if a person can prove that he took all reasonable precautions and exercised all due diligence to avoid the commission of the offence. The burden of proof is with the defendant and is to a high standard.

CIVIL CONSEQUENCES

In addition, investment business agreements made by unauthorised persons which breach the FSA are, unless otherwise allowed by the court, unenforceable against the other party. That party is also entitled to recover any money or other property paid or transferred to him under the agreement together with compensation for any loss sustained by him as a result of having parted with it.[16]

13   Financial Services Act 1986, s 15.
14   Financial Services Act 1986, ss 3 and 4.
15   Financial Services Act 1986, s 202.
16   Financial Services Act 1986, s 5.

INVESTMENT BUSINESS ON THE INTERNET

A person using the Internet to provide financial services or to advertise or promote them should ascertain whether or not he is carrying on 'investment business'. If he is, he should ensure that he is an authorised person (ie is a member of and subject to the rules of an SRO or a certified member of an RPB) or an exempted person or is permitted to carry on such activities by the Investment Services Regulations. If he is promoting or advertising investments or financial services he should only do so in compliance with the FSA and any other relevant UK legislation.

A number of persons may be carrying on investment business under the FSA by using the Internet. There are, amongst others, the users who access the Internet to retrieve information, those who set up a web site for themselves or others, those who send information by e-mail or to a bulletin board and site and access providers. Persons advertising or sending information about investments and related services are the most likely to be affected by the FSA although access and site providers may also be caught.

In order to determine whether particular persons and activities are regulated it is necessary to examine what constitutes 'investment business' for the purpose of the FSA.

What is investment business?

The FSA defines 'investment business'[17] as 'the business of engaging in one or more of the activities which fall within the paragraphs in Part II of Schedule 1 to the FSA and which are not excluded by Part III of that Schedule'. The use of the word 'business' in the definition indicates that recreational or educational use, rather than business use, of the Internet should not require authorisation under the FSA.

REGULATED ACTIVITIES

The relevant activities are set out in detail in Part II of Schedule 1 to the FSA and briefly include the following.

Dealing in investments Buying, selling, subscribing for or underwriting investments or offering or agreeing to do so either as principal or as an agent.

Arranging deals in investments Making or offering or agreeing to make arrangements with a view to another person buying, selling, subscribing for or underwriting a particular investment or arrangements with a view to a person who participates in the arrangements buying, selling, subscribing for or underwriting investments.

Managing investments Managing, or offering or agreeing to manage, assets belonging to another person which include investments or which can include investments at the manager's discretion.

Investment advice Giving, or offering or agreeing to give, to persons in their capacity as investors or potential investors advice on the merits of their

17　Financial Services Act 1986, s 1(2).

purchasing, selling, subscribing for or underwriting an investment, or exercising any right conferred by an investment to acquire, dispose of, underwrite or convert an investment.

Collective investment schemes Establishing, operating or winding up a collective investment scheme (this includes investments such as unit trusts, open-ended investment companies and pooled ownership of assets).

The relevant paragraphs of Part II of Schedule 1 to the FSA also include notes and additional sub-paragraphs which elaborate upon and exclude certain activities otherwise falling within the scope of regulated activity.

What are 'investments'?

'Investments' are listed in detail in Part I of Schedule 1 to the FSA and include, amongst others, shares, loan stocks, bonds, warrants, options, futures, long-term insurance contracts, interests in collective investment schemes and rights and interests in any such investments.

EXCLUDED ACTIVITIES

Various exclusions from the activities which would otherwise be investment business activities are set out in Part III of Schedule 1 to the FSA. The exclusions state the relevant paragraphs in Part II of Schedule 1 to the FSA to which they apply and include, for example, the following.

Dealing as principal Certain dealings in shares, debentures, bonds, warrants and certain other investments by a person acting as principal are excluded unless the person is a market maker or dealer in the investments or regularly solicits members of the public to deal in those investments.

Sale of goods and supply of services Certain transactions connected with the sales of goods and supply of services to customers who are not individuals are excluded where the main business of the supplier is not to engage in activities in Part II of Schedule 1 to the FSA.

Advice given or arrangements made in course of profession or non-investment business Certain advice given or arrangements made in the course of carrying on a profession or non-investment business and which is or are a necessary part of such advice or services are excluded.

Newspapers Advice given in a newspaper, journal, magazine or other periodical publication, if the principal purpose of the publication, taken as a whole and including advertisements contained in it, is not to lead persons to invest in any particular investment is excluded.

Advice given in television, sound or teletext services Advice given in any programme included, or made for inclusion in any television broadcasting service (within the meaning of Part I of the Broadcasting Act 1990) or other television programme service, any sound broadcasting service or licensable sound programme service, or any teletext service is excluded. A programme is treated as including an advertisement and any other item in the service.

Application to the Internet

DEALERS

A person offering to buy or sell investments or offering other regulated financial services in the United Kingdom through the Internet will be directly affected by the FSA unless he can fall within one of the exclusions. Financial services providers setting up a home page which allows investment business agreements to be facilitated should be especially aware. For example, a person who deals as principal in investments may be unable to make use of the relevant exemption for dealing in investments if he uses the Internet to hold himself out as engaging in the business of buying investments with a view to selling them and those investments include investments of the kind to which the dealing as principal relates.

INFORMATION PROVIDERS

Information providers should consider whether they are arranging deals in investments by introducing persons to another person who deals in investments. The notes to para 13 of Pt II of Sch 1 to the FSA include certain arrangements which do not constitute 'arranging deals' such as certain introductions to authorised or exempted persons with a view to the provision of independent advice. Information providers should also avoid offering advice on 'investments'. In this context, advice generally includes some form of recommendation, opinion or comparison of investments but should not otherwise cover purely factual information.

ACCESS AND SITE PROVIDERS

An Access or Service Provider is normally providing a communications service and does not carry on investment business. However, where Service Providers provide access or a site to persons carrying on 'investment business' there is a possibility that they may be 'arranging deals in investments' for another person. This activity can constitute 'investment business'.[18] In December 1995 the SIB wrote to access and site providers informing them of the possibility that their activities could fall within the FSA and that they could be committing a criminal offence. The letter states that:[19]

> 'In practice, it is unlikely that an Access and/or Site Provider will be conducting investment business if it merely acts as a conduit through which persons or companies gain access to or a presence on the Net and where it has no knowledge of, or control over, the information or service being provided.'

If the Access or Site Provider only supplies a 'technical' service without knowledge or control or marketing of the service, then the SIB considers that the Access or Site Provider will not be liable. However, the regulatory position is complex and a person who is in doubt of his position is urged by the SIB to seek advice.

The SIB explains that an Access or Site Provider's position becomes less clear if it is involved commercially with an investment firm (ie a stockbroker or financial adviser) to which it is providing access by becoming materially involved in making

18   Financial Services Act 1986, Sch 1, Pt III, para 17(1).
19   Letter published by The Securities and Investments Board in December 1995.

it possible for an investor to invest rather than simply providing the communication service. This level of involvement would bring it within 'arranging'.

The SIB has cited[20] four examples when Access and/or Site Providers should consider their position under the FSA carefully. These are if, for example, they were to:

'(i) provide access and/or an off-the-shelf Net site over which they had control as regards what was placed on the Net or over the nature of information about investments or investment services provided on the site;
(ii) have a joint venture arrangement with someone carrying on investment business (such as a firm providing share dealing services) for whom they had provided access and/or a site;
(iii) promote an investment service under their own name; or
(iv) promote another person's investment service or put investment material on the Net.'

The key is to identify the relationship between the Service Provider and the initial information provider in order to evaluate whether by express or implied agreement the Access/Site Provider is gaining commercially from his position.

ARE THERE ANY EXEMPTIONS FOR THE INTERNET?

There are no exemptions at present which are specific to the Internet. It is, therefore, necessary to see if any of the exemptions set out in Part III of Schedule 1 to the FSA apply to an otherwise regulated activity. In some cases, it may be arguable that a web site or other Internet information might fall within paragraph 25 of Part III of Schedule 1 to the FSA as advice given in a newspaper, journal, magazine or other periodical publication if the principal purpose of the publication, taken as a whole and including any advertisements contained in it, is not to lead persons to invest in any particular investment. The position is not clear but a certificate can be sought under paragraph 25 from the Secretary of State that the paragraph 25 exemption applies. The exemption from giving investment advice contained in paragraph 25A of Part III of Schedule 1 to the FSA for advice given in television, sound or teletext services was not drafted with the Internet in mind and is unlikely to help. In any event, neither of the exemptions in paragraphs 25 and 25A extend to arranging deals.

Given the global nature of the Internet it is also necessary to consider the territorial implications of the FSA and whether material generated or activities carried on overseas can constitute the carrying on of 'investment business'. There are additional exclusions in Part IV of Schedule 1 to the FSA for overseas persons which might be relevant and which are discussed further below.

THE OVERSEAS DIMENSION

Is there UK-regulated 'investment business'?

As mentioned above, the Financial Services Act 1986 regulates the carrying on of business rather than personal or recreational use of the Internet. If business is

---

20 Letter published by The Securities and Investment Board in December 1995.

being carried on it will amount to 'investment business' under the FSA in two situations.[1]

PERMANENT PLACE OF BUSINESS IN THE UNITED KINGDOM?

The first is where the person carries on investment business from a permanent place of business maintained by him in the United Kingdom. A place of business clearly includes a physical location such as an office but might also include a server or a web site provided that it is permanent and maintained by the person carrying on investment business.

INVESTMENT BUSINESS CARRIED ON IN THE UNITED KINGDOM?

The second situation is where a person does not have a permanent place of business in the United Kingdom but carries on investment business here. This will be the case if the person engages in the United Kingdom in one or more of the activities which fall within Part II of Schedule 1 to the FSA (which are not excluded by Parts III or IV of that Schedule) and his so doing constitutes the carrying on by him of a business in the United Kingdom. Investment services offered through the Internet to persons in the United Kingdom are, therefore, likely to amount to the carrying on of a business in the United Kingdom.

As with any other method of communication, such as telephone or mail, an overseas person can, therefore, still fall foul of the FSA, even if he has no place of business in the UK, by using the Internet to obtain investment business in the UK.

INVESTMENT SERVICES DIRECTIVE

An investment firm which is authorised to carry on investment business in another member state of the European Economic Area may be treated as an authorised person or exempted person in the United Kingdom in respect of particular services listed in the Investment Services Regulations. These are discussed further under 'Financial services in the UK', above.

Exclusions for overseas persons

The FSA includes two additional exclusions for persons without a permanent place of business in the United Kingdom which may be of help in the second situation discussed above.

TRANSACTIONS WITH OR THROUGH AUTHORISED OR EXEMPTED PERSONS

The first exclusion[2] is from the activities of 'dealing in investments' and 'arranging deals in investment' where the transaction is with or through an authorised (including a European investment firm carrying on home-regulated investment business

---

1   Section 1(2) and (3) of the Financial Services Act 1986 defines 'investment business' and when a person carries on investment business.
2   Financial Services Act 1986, Sch 1, Pt IV, para 26.

in the United Kingdom under the Investment Services Regulations) or exempted person acting in the course of business in respect of which he is exempt. For example, if an overseas person without a permanent place of business in the United Kingdom uses the Internet to deal or arrange deals in investments with or through an authorised person (eg a stockbroker) then that activity should be excluded.

UNSOLICITED OR LEGITIMATELY SOLICITED TRANSACTIONS

The second exclusion[3] is for transactions which are unsolicited by an overseas person or which have been solicited without a contravention of the cold calling and investment advertisement requirements of the FSA.[4] These requirements are considered further below.

Legal implications

The use of the web by overseas persons to carry on investment business in the UK in breach of section 3 of the FSA has criminal and civil law implications as discussed under 'Financial services in the UK', above.

ACCESS OR SERVICE PROVIDERS

If the Access or Service Provider is more than a conduit for information he may become liable in criminal law as an accomplice if he is aware of the circumstances of the crime being committed by the overseas person.[5] Turning a blind eye or recklessness may be sufficient in this regard.[6]

In addition, section 62 of the FSA gives the court the power to order against a person who has contravened section 3 of the Act and any person who appears to the court to have been 'knowingly concerned' with the contravention to take such steps as the court may direct for restoring the parties to the contravening transaction to the position in which they were before the transaction was entered into. If an Access/Service Provider is aware that unauthorised investment activities are being offered through a server then the Access/Service Provider is exposing itself to the risk that it has become 'knowingly concerned' in those activities.[7]

INVESTMENT ADVERTISEMENTS ON THE INTERNET

Advertisements offering investments or investment services and other promotional material on the Internet targeted at persons in the United Kingdom may also infringe the FSA.

3 Financial Services Act 1986, Sch 1, Pt IV, para 27.
4 Financial Services Act 1986, ss 56 and 57.
5 Financial Services Act 1986, Sch 1, Pt IV, para 26.
6 Daniel Tunkel, 'Financial Services on the Internet: Can the present regulatory system cope?' April 1996.
7 See *SIB v Pantell (No 2)* [1992] 1 All ER 134. It is not essential to be a beneficiary of the particular transaction.

It is a criminal offence punishable on conviction by up to two years' imprisonment or by a fine of up to £5,000, or both, for an unauthorised person to issue or cause to be issued an 'investment advertisement' in the United Kingdom unless its contents have been approved by an authorised person[8] or it falls within a specific exception or exclusion.

SIB can also take civil proceedings for contravention of section 57 which includes obtaining an injunction and restitution order under section 61 of the FSA.

Investment advertisements

An investment advertisement is defined as:[9]

> 'any advertisement inviting persons to enter or offer to enter into an investment agreement or to exercise any rights conferred by an investment to acquire, dispose of, underwrite or convert an investment or containing information calculated to lead directly or indirectly to persons doing so.'

An investment advertisement does not have to invite persons to offer to do any of the things mentioned in the definition. It is sufficient if the material contains information calculated to lead directly or indirectly to persons doing so. The definition is wide and is expanded upon further in the FSA.

WHAT IS AN INVESTMENT AGREEMENT?

The term 'investment agreement' is also widely defined[10] and includes any agreement for the provision of investment services, such as investment advice and also for the purchase or sale of an investment.

WHAT IS AN ADVERTISEMENT?

An advertisement includes for these purposes every form of advertising.[11]

WHAT INTERNET ADVERTISING IS REGULATED?

Subject to certain exemptions, section 57 of the FSA provides that 'no person other than an authorised person shall issue or cause to be issued an investment advertisement in the United Kingdom unless its contents have been approved by an authorised person'.

---

8   Financial Services Act 1986, s 57.
9   Financial Services Act 1986, s 57(2).
10 Financial Services Act 1986, s 44(9). The definition is by reference to the activities in Pt II of Sch 1 to that Act and ignores the exclusions in Pts III and IV of that Schedule.
11 Financial Services Act 1986, s 207(2). The definition is: 'In this Act "advertisement" includes every form of advertising, whether in a publication, by the display of notices, signs, labels or showcards, by means of circulars, catalogues, price lists or other documents, by an exhibition of pictures or photographic or cinematographic films, by way of sound broadcasting or television [or by inclusion in any programme service (within the meaning of the Broadcasting Act 1990) other than a sound or television broadcasting service], by the distribution of recordings, or in any other manner; and references to the issue of an advertisement shall be construed accordingly.'

It is the SIB's general view that, for the purposes of the FSA, where an advertisement held anywhere on the Internet is made available to or can be obtained by someone in the United Kingdom (eg it can be pulled up on a computer screen in the United Kingdom) that advertisement may be viewed as having been issued in the United Kingdom once it is accessed here.

It is not necessary for the advertisement actually to be issued or held in the United Kingdom. An advertisement or other information issued outside the United Kingdom will also be treated as being issued in the United Kingdom if it is directed to persons in the United Kingdom or is made available to them otherwise than in a newspaper, journal, magazine or other periodical publication published outside the United Kingdom, or in a sound or television broadcast transmitted principally for reception outside the United Kingdom.[12]

In considering whether section 57 of the FSA applies to material published overseas it is possible that material on the Internet may constitute a 'magazine or other periodical publication published and circulating, principally outside the United Kingdom but in the SIB's view it does not constitute a sound or television broadcast'. This will depend on the exact circumstances.

In summary, Internet material relating to investments and investment services and made available to or obtainable by a person in the United Kingdom or which is directed at them may constitute an investment advertisement (for example, a person sending e-mails, posting adverts on bulletin boards or information through hypertext links may be affected). Also directory services such as the Internet's yellow pages and the Yahoo! service contain a long list of areas where investment services and classified advertisements can be found. These may lead to or encourage a recipient of that information to enter into an investment agreement.

The position of information providers

Section 57 of the FSA only applies to a person other than an authorised person who 'issues' or 'causes to be issued' an investment advertisement in the United Kingdom. Financial services businesses setting up web sites should exercise caution and ensure that they comply with the FSA as the material on their web site may constitute an 'investment advertisement'.

The position of Access or Site Providers

Section 57 of the FSA applies not only to a person who issues an investment advertisement but also to a person who 'causes' it to be issued. This could include a web page containing investment material by, for example, an investment firm's third-party access provider; an access provider serving PC users in the United Kingdom or possibly a person managing a search engine. At present, none of these parties are able to rely on any of the exemptions under the FSA and the SIB's interpretation is such that it is arguable that a review of the existing regulations is required in order that innocent Service Providers are given protection from prosecution.

SIB's current view is that in certain circumstances an Access and/or Site Provider may be 'issuing' or at least 'causing to be issued' an investment advertisement by virtue of providing access and/or a site on the Internet. It is the SIB's view that if an Access and/or Site Provider has:[13]

1. no knowledge or control over the information/service being put on the Internet; and
2. no commercial interest, financial or otherwise in the information/service being provided;

it is unlikely that it will be viewed as issuing or causing to be issued investment material on the Internet by those for whom it provides access and/or a presence.

Steps to issue an investment advertisement

A person, including an Access and/or Site Provider, issuing or causing the issue of an investment advertisement to the order of another should take appropriate steps to ensure compliance with section 57(1) or the FSA.[14] For example, the advertisement should be issued or approved by an authorised person (which may include a European investment firm carrying on 'home regulated business' in the United Kingdom under the Investment Services Regulations). That authorised person will be responsible to its SRO to ensure that the rules of that SRO are complied with when it issues or approves the relevant advertisement. These require, for example, care and the inclusion of suitable risk warnings in the advertisement. The advertisement will also usually make reference to the fact that it has been approved by an authorised person and the name of the relevant SRO which regulates that person.

DEFENCE

There is a defence[15] available to a person who in the ordinary course of business, other than investment business, issues an advertisement to the order of another person. It must be shown that the person had reasonable grounds to believe that:

1. the person who gave the order was an authorised person (under the FSA); or
2. the content had been approved by an authorised person (under the FSA); or
3. the advertisement was otherwise permitted by certain specific exceptions by or under section 58 of the FSA.

An Access or Site Provider may, therefore, wish to take comfort that particular information which may be sensitive has been and will continue to be approved by an authorised person.

---

13 Speech by Martin Hollobone of the SIB on the use of the Internet in retail financial services delivered in November 1995.
14 Financial Services Act 1986, s 57(1).
15 Financial Services Act 1986, s 57(4).

ARE THERE ANY EXCEPTIONS?

In addition to the specific exceptions set out in section 58(1) of the FSA,[16] the Secretary of State has made various exemption orders[17] which may be relevant to communications through the Internet. These exemptions involve particular categories of individuals or particular types of information and will be of limited application to the Internet given the difficulties of controlling access.

They include, in summary, the following exemptions which are also subject to various conditions if they are to be relied upon.

The Financial Services Act 1986 (Investment Advertisements) (Exemptions) Order 1996

Article 3 Investment advertisements issued by bodies corporate (other than an open-ended investment company) to persons who are reasonably believed to be creditors or members or persons who are entitled to certain other shares, bonds or investments issued by that body corporate or another body corporate within its group provided that the advertisement is not an investment advertisement for any other body corporate.

A body corporate company should, therefore, be able to use the Internet to send an e-mail to its shareholders or even possibly to allow access to a site for the purposes of downloading permitted information by such persons. Care must be taken to ensure that no other person can gain access which would cause loss of the exemption.

Article 4 Investment advertisements containing certain permitted information issued by a body corporate (other than an open-ended investment company) if it or its holding company has issued relevant securities (ie shares which are traded or dealt in on certain EEA markets or other approved securities markets) and advertisements containing or accompanied by the whole or part of a body corporate's accounts or director's report prepared in accordance with the accounting requirements of the United Kingdom or the equivalent requirements of an EEA state are exempted.

Companies can, subject to satisfying the conditions of the exemption, place certain information about themselves on a web site. It will be necessary to check whether this is restricted in relation to any other jurisdiction outside the UK.

Article 5 Investment advertisements relating to bearer securities issued by a body corporate (other than an open-ended investment company).

This exempts certain communications addressed to holders of bearer securities such as bearer bonds. Given their anonymous nature the Internet might present an

---

16   Section 58(1) of the Financial Services Act 1986 exempts particular issuers of advertisements (the Government, a United Kingdom local authority, the Bank of England or a central bank outside the United Kingdom and an international organisation which includes the United Kingdom or another EC member state as a member) and particular types of advertisements (eg listing particulars or a prospectus relating to listed securities).

17   Section 58(3) of the Financial Services Act 1986 also allows the Secretary of State to make orders exempting advertisements with certain characteristics from s 57. In particular, the Financial Services Act 1986 (Investment Advertisements) (Exemptions) Order 1996, SI 1996/1556 and the Financial Services Act 1986 (Investment Advertisements) (Exemptions) (No 2) Order 1995, SI 1995/1586 have consolidated a number of exemptions. SI 1996/1556 revoked SI 1995/1266 and replaced its provisions with amendments relating to the sending of dematerialised instructions for securities in the CREST system and other minor amendments.

effective method of communication but it is important that the material is addressed to the relevant holder.

Article 6   Investment advertisements issued in connection with employees' share schemes. This is more likely to be relevant to a communication by e-mail through a network or on an intranet.

Articles 7 and 8   Investment advertisements issued within groups of bodies corporate and advertisements between participants or potential participants in a joint enterprise. This is also more likely to be relevant to e-mail over a network or on an intranet.

Article 9   Investment advertisements in connection with the sale of goods and supply of services.

Therefore, certain transactions may be promoted and effected through the Internet if they are outside the financial services sector by suppliers whose main business is to supply goods or services and not to engage in activities regulated by the FSA even if they include an investment business element.

Article 10   Certain investment advertisements by persons without a permanent place of business in the United Kingdom with certain persons with which it has previously dealt or has advised abroad. This may be more relevant to e-mail and may be of use to overseas persons.

Article 11   Advertisements issued to persons sufficiently expert to understand the risk involved.

This important exemption allows a person who is not authorised under the FSA to issue an advertisement to certain categories of recipient including larger bodies corporate, unincorporated associations and trusts. The exemption does not extend to private individuals. Broadly speaking a body corporate must have at least 20 members and called-up share capital of net assets of not less than £500,000; or be part of a group which includes a body corporate with called-up share capital or net assets of not less than £5 million, an unincorporated association must have net assets of not less than £5 million and a trust must have assets (before deducting liabilities) of not less than £10 million. This may be relevant to certain e-mail communications and sites which have strict pre-registration requirements prior to access.

Article 12   Advertisements with respect to shares or debentures in a 'private company' relating to persons who might reasonably be regarded as having an existing and common interest with each other and with the company in the affairs of the company and what is to be done with the proceeds of the offer.

Article 13   Certain advertisements by trustees or personal representatives.

Article 14   Certain advertisements by operators of FSA-recognised collective investment schemes.

Article 15   Certain advertisements relating to publications and programmes which contain advice to which paragraph 15 of Schedule 1 to the FSA does not apply by virtue of paragraph 25 or 25A of that Schedule.

Article 16   Advertisements issued by certain securities markets.

Article 17   Advertisements issued by certain property management companies.

Article 18   Advertisements issued in respect of the Parliamentary Commissioner for Administration.

Financial Services Act 1986 (Investment Advertisements) (Exemptions) (No 2) Order 1995

Article 3   Certain advertisements for the purpose of raising share or debenture capital in a company for the purpose of promoting or encouraging industrial or commercial activity or enterprise in the United Kingdom.

Article 4   Advertisements for takeovers of private companies. There are detailed requirements before this exemption can apply and detailed document requirements. The Internet probably does not satisfy them.

Article 5   Advertisements for the sale of body corporate. This is limited to certain defined groups of persons.

Article 6   Dealings in the course of non-investment business. This exemption can apply if a person holds a permission under paragraph 25 of Schedule 1 to the FSA exempting him from 'investment business'.

Article 7   Certain advertisements issued by a person who is not an authorised person and who is not unlawfully carrying on investment business in the United Kingdom if that advertisement is issued to particular kinds of person such as those whose business is to arrange the placing of advertisements.

Articles 8–10   Certain advertisements directed at informing or influencing persons of a particular kind such as a government, local authority or public authority and certain persons involved in investment business.

Article 11   Certain advertisements required or permitted to be published by exchange or market rules. This allows a body corporate which has securities traded or dealt in on the markets listed in the Exemption Order to publish information which is required or permitted by the rules relevant to that market. For example, certain announcements of results or acquisitions could be placed on that company's web site.

Article 12   Certain advertisements by certain exchanges or markets. This exemption is relevant to financial markets themselves.

Article 13   Advertisements by industrial and provident societies relating to investments issued or to be issued by it.

Article 14   Certain advertisements relating to public offers of securities. This allows the publication of prospectuses for unlisted securities in accordance with the Public Offer of Securities Regulations 1995 and certain information relating to such a prospectus or equivalent information for prescribed EEA markets.

Article 15   Advertisements required or authorised under enactments. This allows a communication if required or authorised by any enactment. It is unlikely that it has any particular application to the Internet.

The above exemptions allow certain uses of the Internet without the need for approval by an authorised person. They are not, however, specific to the Internet and will need to be checked carefully to ensure that compliance is possible, especially given the generally unrestricted access afforded by the Internet to information.

Overseas persons

As mentioned above, overseas persons who target UK investors with investment advertisements and offers are still required to comply with the FSA advertising requirements. If such advertisements are not issued or approved by an authorised person, they must fall within the exclusions under section 58 of the Act or the exemptions referred to above.

Where overseas advertisements of a financial nature are principally for circulation outside the United Kingdom and are not directed at, nor intended to be available for, the United Kingdom then it will depend upon the particular circumstances of the case as to whether or not prosecution is appropriate.

The SIB, however, are clearly aware that even though an overseas person may run a 'passive site' abroad, any person with access to the Internet is capable of gaining access to a specific investment advertisement and such access can be viewed as being 'issued' in the United Kingdom. The SIB's viewpoint is that each case must be assessed individually on its precise facts. An overseas person, having advertised generally on the web, who then deals with a UK user, may also be viewed as carrying on unauthorised investment business in the United Kingdom unless he is authorised or treated as being authorised under the FSA or can fall within one of the exemptions in respect of investment activity. In particular, a person may be permitted to carry on such activity under the Investment Services Regulations because it is regulated to carry on investment business in another member state of the European Economic Area. It may also be able to benefit from the exclusions for overseas persons discussed above in respect of investment business where such a person enters into a transaction with or through an authorised or exempted person or does so in circumstances where it is unsolicited (this may be difficult to establish) or legitimately solicited. The essence of the problem is that one cannot limit the access of information on the Internet to exclude individuals or specific jurisdictions.

In deciding to enforce section 57 of the FSA, the SIB may take into account a number of factors including, on a non-exhaustive basis:

1. whether any risks to investors are such that SIB action is needed to protect their interests;
2. whether there are any additional potential infringements of the FSA (such as breach of section 3);
3. whether as a matter of fact any offer was directed at potential UK investors;
4. the degree to which, given the nature of the Internet, someone had taken positive steps to avoid the material being made available to or receivable by persons in the United Kingdom.

In the latter case, it has been suggested that pre-registration to ensure that only those to whom the material was aimed had access might be relevant although it would not in itself prevent the material from having been 'issued in the United Kingdom' for the purposes of the FSA. It may be possible to circumvent pre-registration or it may be superficial.

SIB has also stated that disclaimers to put off enquiries by persons in the United Kingdom and refusing to deal with or on behalf of United Kingdom residents who nevertheless access the site do not seem sufficient to avoid the relevant advertisements being issued in the United Kingdom if as a matter of fact they are received there. This is an area which may require further amendment or clarification by legislation.

UNSOLICITED CALLS

Section 56 of the FSA prevents any person seeking to enter into an investment agreement in the course of or in consequence of an 'unsolicited call' (meaning a personal visit or oral communication without express invitation) made on persons in the United Kingdom or made from the United Kingdom on a person elsewhere except so far as is permitted by regulations made by the SIB.

There is no criminal sanction for a contravention of section 56 but compensation can be ordered by the court.

Section 56 should not be directly relevant to the Internet or at least should not be relevant until such time as it is used for 'oral communication' rather than e-mail.

It could, however, be relevant if a person without a permanent place of business in the United Kingdom enters into an investment agreement with a person in the United Kingdom using the Internet following an unsolicited cold call. In such an event, the exclusion from the need for authorisation for overseas persons without a permanent place of business in the United Kingdom in paragraph 27 of Part IV of Schedule 1 to the FSA will be prejudiced.

OFFERS OF SECURITIES

United Kingdom

The regulation of offers of securities in the United Kingdom depends upon whether the securities being offered are listed or unlisted unsecurities. Any offer of shares on the Internet must comply with these requirements.

LISTED SECURITIES

Listed securities include shares and various debts securities which are traded on the Official List of the London Stock Exchange. Issues of such securities are regulated by Part IV of the FSA and the Listing Rules of the London Stock Exchange ('the Yellow Book'). Such issues usually require the publication and filing of a prospectus or listing particulars. This will be in written form.

UNLISTED SECURITIES

Unlisted securities (securities which are not listed) are subject to the UK Public Offer of Securities Regulations 1995 ('POS Regulations'). Shares traded on the Alternative Investment Market are unlisted securities. The Internet Bookshop became the first UK company to offer its shares on the Internet in March 1996. It was arranging a placing of its shares which were to be traded on Ofex.

The POS Regulations provide that where securities are offered to the public (including any section of the public) in the United Kingdom the offer must be accompanied by a complying prospectus and must be registered, unless certain exemptions apply.

INVESTMENT ADVERTISEMENTS

It should be noted that a prospectus or listing particulars complying with the relevant UK requirements are excluded from the investment advertisement requirements of section 57 of the FSA by section 58(1)(d) of the Financial Services Act 1986 and paragraph 14 of the Financial Services Act 1986 (Investment Advertisements) (Exemptions) Order (No 2) 1995 (SI 1995/1536). If such documents are placed on the Internet it is necessary to ensure, however, that the securities laws of other jurisdictions are not infringed because such information can be accessed overseas. Whilst disclaimers and access restrictions might help in overseas jurisdictions, statements that a document which otherwise amounts to an investment advertisement in the United Kingdom is limited to restricted categories of investors here is unlikely to be sufficient to avoid the requirements for that advertisement to be issued in accordance with section 57 of the FSA.

Overseas

An offer of securities on the Internet may be made in a number of jurisdictions. It is necessary to ensure that the offer complies with the relevant regulations or prohibitions in each jurisdiction.

For example, offers of securities in the United States or to United States persons are subject to the provisions of the Securities Act 1933, the Securities Exchange Act 1934 and the Investment Company Act of 1940. Under United States securities law, securities may not be offered or sold, save for certain limited exceptions, without registration under the Securities Act.

US regulations do not allow offers to be made in the United States without the prior filing of a registered statement with the US Securities and Exchange Commission (the 'SEC'), or written offers to be made in the US other than by means of the filing of a preliminary prospectus and a declaration by SEC that the registration statement is effective. The SEC has already brought successful convictions against persons through which securities were fraudulently offered through the Internet.

Extreme caution is required where securities are being offered in the USA. This is an area outside the scope of this work.

DISSEMINATION OF INFORMATION

The use of the Internet to disseminate information about securities and investments is also subject to specific regulation under the FSA and by the London Stock Exchange.

Misleading statements

Section 47(1) of the FSA makes it a criminal offence for a person to make a statement, promise or forecast which he knows to be misleading, false or deceptive or which dishonestly conceals any material facts. The section also makes it an offence if a person recklessly makes (dishonestly or otherwise) a statement, promise or forecast which is misleading, false or deceptive. In each case the person must have the purpose of inducing, or is reckless as to whether it may induce, another person to enter into or offer to enter into, or to refrain from entering or offering to enter into, an investment agreement or to exercise, or refrain from exercising, any rights conferred by an investment (eg shares).

Therefore, statements on the Internet relating to investments should be prepared with care. For an offence to be committed, section 47(4) requires there to be a connection with the United Kingdom. In particular, the relevant statement must be made in or from, or the facts must be concealed in or from the United Kingdom, or the person on whom the inducement is intended to or may have effect must be in the United Kingdom or the relevant agreement must be one which is or would be entered into or the relevant rights are or would be exercised in the United Kingdom. SIB's view on investment advertisements suggests that a person accessing the information here from a computer might cause the relevant statement to be made here. For example an offence may conceivably be committed by an overseas person making a statement on a web page intended for PC users in a foreign jurisdiction, but seen and acted upon by a UK PC user (for whom it is misleading).

False markets

Section 47(2) of the FSA also makes it a criminal offence to create a false or misleading impression as to the market in or price or value of any investments. There must be a connection with the United Kingdom and the person creating the false or misleading impression must do so to induce another to acquire, dispose of, subscribe for or underwrite investments or to refrain from exercising rights conferred by them.

There is a defence in section 47(3) of the FSA, if a person can prove that he reasonably believed that his act or conduct would not create the false or misleading impression created.

London Stock Exchange regulations

The London Stock Exchange has its own additional requirements which are applicable to Internet information. Quoted companies wishing to use the Internet as a means of communication must follow strict requirements under its listing rules ('the Yellow Book') and its guidance notes on the dissemination of price sensitive information. Companies must generally first provide price-sensitive information to the Company Announcements Office of the London Stock Exchange before it is disclosed on the Internet or elsewhere. If this is not done there is a danger of a false market being created in that company's securities and insider dealing.

SEC requirements

US domestic issues are required to file documents electronically with the SEC through its Electronic Data Gathering, Analysis and Retrieval System

('EDGAR'). This information is then made available on the Internet through information resellers. The SEC is aware of the increasing use of electronic communications and has published releases giving guidance on the use of electronic media for the delivery of prospectuses, tender offer materials and proxy or information or information statements under US securities regulations.[18] The release offers useful guidance and helpful examples of when, if and how delivery is effected. The SEC has also published a further release on the use of the Internet by broker dealers.[19]

Further regulation

The general fear is that the anonymity of the Internet, and of the users worldwide, makes the UK insider dealing laws much more difficult to enforce both against the publisher and those who use information to make a profit. Furthermore, as the Internet grows it may become impracticable for regulations to monitor the vast amount of share and security deals.

TAKEOVERS AND MERGERS

The Internet is potentially capable of use in connection with a takeover. For example, in the USA, IBM announced its US$3.5 billion uninvited takeover bid for Lotus Developments on its home page on the web.

In the United Kingdom, takeovers of public limited companies are subject, in addition to various company and security law requirements, to the City Code on Takeovers and Mergers ('the City Code').

The City Code does not have, and does not seek to have, the force of law but is acknowledged in the City and by institutions in the United Kingdom as setting out the required conduct for a public takeover. It contains principles and rules to ensure fair and equal treatment of shareholders and an orderly framework for the conduct of takeovers. Rulings on its application are made by the Panel on Takeovers and Mergers ('Panel').

The Panel is understood to have stated that takeover information for United Kingdom takeovers be treated in the same way as any other publication on any other medium although there is no guidance specific to the Internet. Accordingly, any announcement or message relating to a UK takeover made through the Internet or accessible through it should comply with the City Code. This means that the content must satisfy high standards of accuracy, there must be adequate and fair presentation of the information in question (Rule 19) and the directors of the offeror or target company will need to accept responsibility for the accuracy of the information and include an appropriate responsibility statement with it.

If the Internet is to be used in connection with a particular takeover the Panel should be consulted at an early stage.

The use of the Internet for a takeover offer in the United Kingdom or involving investors in the United Kingdom will also give rise to issues concerning the authorisation of investment advertisements issued in the United Kingdom and other securities law mentioned above.

18   Release No 33-7233; 34-3644; K-21399. The release is available on the SEC's web site.
19   The release is also available on the SEC's web site.

Chapter nine

Competition

Peter Willis, Solicitor, Nabarro Nathanson

Inevitably in such a rapidly moving industry, the EC regulators, from the Commission's Competition Directorate General IV (DGIV), move more slowly than the technological developments stimulating the markets which they regulate. However, the time-lag in the case of DGIV is relatively small compared with that of other competition authorities, and officials of DGIV have issued a number of policy statements about the application of the EC competition rules to issues arising from the Internet. In addition, the Commission has launched investigations into the activities of a number of players on the market, and the press releases announcing those investigations give an indication of the Commission's concerns. Furthermore, published decisions in cases in neighbouring industries, such as Pay-TV, provide useful guidance.

It is perhaps an indication of the Commission's willingness to tackle new technology that the latest versions of its procedural rules provide for the transmission of documents to and from the Commission by e-mail.[1] The Commission also has its own home page giving a description of its activities, recent press releases, the full text of important documents issued, legislation, decisions, judgments and schedules of the European Courts and speeches and publication of DGIV officials.[2]

The EC competition rules are found in Articles 85 and 86 of the EC Treaty (the Treaty of Rome), in the EC Merger Regulation, Council Regulation (EEC) No 4064/89 (the ECMR) and in substantive and procedural regulations made under the EC Treaty. This chapter does not examine the procedural rules, but summarises the substantive rules as they apply to the Internet and highlights the main concerns identified so far by the Commission.

ARTICLE 85

Article 85 prohibits anti-competitive agreements between businesses, sets out the consequences of infringement and provides a mechanism for the exemption of agreements whose benefits outweigh their anti-competitive effects.

1   Article 19(1)(e) and (2), Commission Regulation 3384/94.
2   http://europa.eu.int/eu/comm/dg04/dg4home.htm

It provides as follows:

'1. The following shall be prohibited as incompatible with the common market: all agreements between undertakings, decisions by associations of undertakings and concerted practices which may affect trade between Member States and which have as their object or effect the prevention, restriction or distortion of competition within the common market, and in particular those which:
(a) directly or indirectly fix purchase or selling prices or any other trading conditions;
(b) limit or control production, markets, technical development, or investment;
(c) share markets or sources of supply;
(d) apply dissimilar conditions to equivalent transactions with other trading parties, thereby placing them at a competitive disadvantage;
(e) make the conclusion of contracts subject to acceptance by the other parties of supplementary obligations which, by their nature or according to commercial usage, have no connection with the subject of such contracts.
2. Any agreements or decisions prohibited pursuant to this Article shall be automatically void.
3. The provisions of paragraph 1 may, however, be declared inapplicable in the case of:
– any agreement or category of agreements between undertakings;
– any decision or category of decisions by associations of undertakings;
– any concerted practice or category of concerted practices;
which contributes to improving the production or distribution of goods or to promoting technical or economic progress, while allowing consumers a fair share of the resulting benefit, and which does not:
(a) impose on the undertakings concerned restrictions which are not indispensable to the attainment of these objectives;
(b) afford such undertakings the possibility of eliminating competition in respect of a substantial part of the products in question.'

The various elements of the prohibition are considered in turn.

Agreement

The word 'agreement' is interpreted widely, covering, in addition to formal written agreements, oral agreements and informal understandings or 'gentlemen's agreements'. The Commission has on occasion inferred the existence of an agreement from the circumstances and the conduct of the parties.[3]

Article 85 applies to both horizontal agreements (between parties at the same level of trade, such as price fixing or co-operation agreements between two content providers or Service Providers) and vertical agreements (between parties at

---

3   *Newitt/Dunlop-Slazenger* (1992) OJ L131/32; *Zera/Montedison* and *Hinkens/Stähler* (1993) OJ L272/28.

different levels, such as an agreement between a content provider and a Service Provider or telecommunications network operator).

Article 85 will also apply where there is no specific agreement between the parties, for example, where one undertaking supplies to another on standard terms and conditions of business.[4]

Decisions of trade associations

Decisions of a trade association, its rules and non-binding recommendations to its members are treated in the same way as agreements between the members of the association.

Concerted practices

Article 85 applies equally to concerted practices which are 'a form of co-ordination between undertakings which, without having reached the stage where an agreement properly so-called has been concluded, knowingly substitutes practical co-operation between them for the risks of competition'.[5]

So, where a number of Service Providers do not actually agree between them the subscription charges which they will impose between them, but act on the basis that they will follow each others' prices, they may be in breach of Article 85.

Between undertakings

To fall within Article 85, an agreement must be between undertakings. The term 'undertaking' covers almost all legal and natural persons carrying on a commercial or economic activity. Individual private subscribers to the Internet are unlikely to be undertakings and agreements to which an individual and only one undertaking are parties may therefore fall outside Article 85. It is likely that the Commission would not allow an anti-competitive agreement to slip through its net for that reason alone and, if necessary, would probably consider that there was a network of agreements between all the players involved, including the subscriber, the telecommunications carrier, the Service Provider and the content provider. Furthermore, there will be no agreement where an anti-competitive practice results from the unilateral acts of an undertaking. Unilateral practices of a non-dominant undertaking will therefore fall outside Article 85. However, as indicated above, the Commission can infer the existence of an agreement from the conduct of the parties.

---

4   *Bayer Dental* (1990) OJ L351/46; Case C-277/87 *Sandoz v Commission* [1990] ECR I-45.
5   Case 48/69 *ICI v Commission* [1972] ECR 619 (*Dyestuffs*).

Restriction of competition

Article 85 prohibits agreements which have the object or effect of preventing, restricting or distorting competition within the Common Market. It does not matter whether the restriction or distortion of competition is the object of the agreement or merely its effect. This follows from the wording of Article 85 which is equally capable of applying in both cases, although agreements with a blatantly anti-competitive object tend to be treated rather more severely. In addition, the European Court of Justice, in particular, has tended to take a more lenient view of restrictions in vertical agreements, such as distribution or licensing agreements, than of those in horizontal agreements.[6] The Commission is currently rethinking its attitude toward restrictions in vertical agreements and a relaxation of its current rigour towards certain restraints in distribution and licensing agreements is possible.

EXAMPLES OF RESTRICTIONS

The examples of anti-competitive provisions given in Article 85 cover a wide range of practices.

Pricing

'Directly or indirectly fix purchase or selling prices . . .'[7]

This prohibition applies equally to horizontal price fixing agreements or cartels and to vertical resale price maintenance. It would cover both an agreement between two content providers to charge a certain rate for each hit and an agreement between content and Service Providers relating to the charge to be passed on to the subscriber by the Service Provider. In both cases, the rationale for the prohibition is that price-fixing prevents an efficient business from passing on the economic benefits which it would otherwise be able to offer, harming customers in the short term and shielding inefficient businesses from market forces in the long term.

Other trading conditions

'Or any other trading conditions'[8]

An agreement on other trading conditions often restricts non-price competition on points such as the level or quality of service and may therefore infringe Article 85.

---

6   Case 56/65 *Société Technique Minière v Maschinenbau Ulm GmbH* [1966] ECR 235; Case 258/78 *Nungesser v Commission* [1982] ECR 2015; Case 161/84 *Pronuptia de Paris v Schillgalis* [1986] ECR 353.
7   Article 85(1)(a).
8   Ibid.

Limiting markets

'Limit or control production, markets, technical development or investment'[9]

Article 85 also prohibits agreements which, for example, seek to impose quotas (for example by limiting subscriber numbers or limiting access to particular services). The rationale is that such limitations may operate to keep demand, and therefore prices, high.

Market sharing

'Share markets or sources of supply'[10]

One of the main objectives of the EC Treaty was to create a common market, within which goods and services could move freely. Agreements which attempt to partition markets therefore constitute some of the most serious infringements of Article 85. Prohibited market sharing agreements include agreements allocating particular geographic markets, services or customers between the parties, whether expressly or by implication. The grant of an exclusive licence of intellectual property or the appointment of an exclusive distributor in a particular territory may also contravene Article 85 because of the market sharing inherent in such arrangements (but may be eligible for exemption).

Discrimination

'Apply dissimilar conditions to equivalent contractions with other trading parties, thereby placing them at a competitive disadvantage'[11]

Discrimination usually takes the form of the operation of differential pricing or discount policies, favouring customers in one country over those in another, or offering more favourable terms to customers who take their entire requirements of a product from the supplier concerned.

Tying

'Make the conclusion of contracts subject to acceptance by the other parties of supplementary obligations which, by their nature or according to commercial usage, have no connection with the subject of such contracts'[12]

Forcing a customer to purchase particular hardware or software as a condition of subscribing for a particular service is a form of tie. It clearly restricts the ability of

9   Article 85(1)(b).
10 Article 85(1)(c).
11 Article 85(1)(d).
12 Article 85(1)(e).

the subscriber to choose alternative hardware or software, which may be more suitable or cheaper.

Effect on trade between member states

The EC competition rules apply only to agreements affecting trade between member states. Agreements and practices which have no such effect may fall within national competition laws. The effect on trade between member states must be appreciable for there to be an infringement of Article 85. This question is considered below.

In order for an agreement to affect trade between member states 'it must be possible to foresee with a sufficient degree of probability on the basis of a set of objective factors of law or fact that the agreement in question may have an influence, direct or indirect, actual or potential, on the pattern of trade between member states'.[13]

In practice, this test is relatively easily satisfied. It is sufficient that the agreement alters the normal flow or pattern of trade or causes trade to develop differently from the way in which it would have developed in the absence of the agreement.[14] If the products or services concerned are traded or are likely to be traded between member states, an effect is likely to be presumed. However, the Commission may also consider the likely future development of patterns of inter-state trade and also the impact of the agreement on upstream and downstream markets.[15] Agreements between undertakings in the same member state, relating exclusively to the national market, may have the effect of foreclosing that national market to products or services from outside and may therefore have the requisite effect on trade between member states.[16]

It should be assumed that most agreements relating to the Internet are capable of having an effect on trade between member states. Where a subscriber in one member state can communicate with other subscribers, Service Providers and content providers in any other member state, there is the possibility of an effect on trade between member states each time the Internet is accessed. However, the effect on trade between member states will be a question of fact in each case and it is possible to envisage certain combinations of services which are most likely to give rise to an effect on trade between member states. For example, the provision of information in Finnish, relating to the opening times and contents of a museum in Helsinki, is unlikely to attract much attention from outside Finland. It is then likely that an agreement between the content provider and a Finnish Service Provider to give access to this information will have little or no effect on trade between member states. However, most other cases will be less clear cut and, particularly in the light of the Commission's attitude towards networks of agreements,[17] it is advisable not to rely on the absence of effect on trade between member states as a way of avoiding Article 85.

13   Case 56/65 *Société Technique Minière v Maschinenbau Ulm GmbH* [1966] ECR 235 at 249.
14   Case 71/74 *FRUBO v Commission* [1975] ECR 563.
15   *Vacuum Interrupters* (1977) OJ L48, p 32; Case 123/83 *BNIC v Clair* [1985] ECR 391; Cases C-89, 104, 114, 116-117, 125-129/85 *A Ahlström Oy v EC Commission* [1988] ECR 5193.
16   Case 8/72 *Vereeniging van Cementhandelaren v EC Commission* [1972] ECR 977.
17   See *Notice on Agreements of Minor Importance* (1986) OJ C 231/2, updated (1994) OJ C 368/20. See also Commission Notice inviting comments on revision of the 1986 Notice: (1997) OJ C 29/3.

APPRECIABILITY

For an agreement to infringe Article 85 at all, both the restriction of competition and the effect on trade between member states must be appreciable. EC competition law disregards minor agreements. The ECJ has ruled that 'an agreement falls outside the prohibition in Article 85(1) where it has only an insignificant effect on the market, taking into account the weak position which the persons concerned have on the market of the product in question'.[18] In that case, an agreement between parties enjoying a share of no more than 0.5% of the German market for a particular product was held to fall outside Article 85 because its effect was so small. A share of around 5%, however, was not too small to fall outside Article 85 altogether.[19] It will also be relevant to consider the market share of competitors and the turnover of the parties.

COMMISSION NOTICE ON MINOR AGREEMENTS

To provide some guidance, the Commission has issued notices setting out its views on appreciability. In the latest notice, dating from 1986, and updated in 1994, the Commission states that an agreement will not have an appreciable effect on trade between member states or on competition:[20]

1. where the goods or services which are the subject of an agreement, together with the parties' and their respective corporate groups' equivalent products or services, account for no more than 5% of the market for such goods or services in the area of the EC affected by the agreement; and
2. the aggregate annual turnover of the parties' corporate groups (excluding tax) does not exceed ECUs 300 million.

The question of whether goods and services are equivalent is a function of their characteristics, their price and intended use. In other words, equivalence depends on the correct definition of the relevant market, which is considered in more detail below. The notice provides further guidance on the calculation of market share and turnover.

The area of the EC affected by the agreement will be the whole EC, where the goods or services are regularly provided in all member states, or a smaller area if not.

The Commission's notice is merely intended to provide guidance on the question of appreciability: even agreements between parties whose turnover or market share falls well in excess of the figures will not fall within Article 85 where in fact there is no appreciable effect on trade between member states.

The Commission and the European Court of Justice take the view that where an individual agreement falls outside Article 85 because it does not have an appreciable effect on trade between EC member states and does not appreciably restrict competition, it may nevertheless infringe Article 85 if it forms part of a network of similar agreements which together seal off the market to other competitors and the individual agreement in question makes a significant

---

18 Case 5/69 *Völk v Vervaecke* [1969] ECR 295.
19 Case 19/77 *Miller v Commission* [1978] ECR 131.
20 *Notice on Agreements of Minor Importance* (1986) OJ C 231/2, (1994) OJ C 368/20 (1997) OJ C 29/3. The Commission is currently inviting comment on revision of the Notice.

contribution to the sealing off effect.[1] The Commission has taken this a step further, stating that if a particular agreement, all agreements of that kind entered into by one of the parties or all agreements of that kind in the relevant market have an appreciable effect on competition or trade between member states, Article 85 will apply. The application of this test could result in a finding of infringement where individual agreements between players on the Internet do not have an appreciable effect on trade between member states or cause an appreciable restriction on competition, but where a network of such agreements has that effect. If subscribers are tied into particular Service Providers, whether by pricing or by a provision of particular methods of access, and the effect is to lock out other potential Service Providers, the appreciability test may be satisfied in relation to the individual elements of the network.

Consequences of infringement

The consequences of infringing Article 85(1) are as follows.

1. A prohibited agreement is void and unenforceable.[2] This means that Article 85 can be used as a defence to, for example, an action for breach of contract seeking to enforce an anti-competitive clause. If the anti-competitive provisions of an agreement can be severed, the remainder of the agreement will continue to be valid and enforceable.
2. The Commission may bring proceedings and may order the parties to bring the infringement to an end. Alternatively, the Commission sometimes seeks an undertaking (sometimes referred to by the Commission as a 'commitment' in order to avoid confusion), in lieu of a formal decision. The Commission also has the power to impose fines of up to 10% of their previous year's world-wide group turnover on undertakings or associations of undertakings which intentionally or negligently infringe Article 85.[3] The highest individual fine to date was 75 million ECUs imposed on the packaging company TetraPak.
3. Article 85 gives rise to rights which individuals and businesses can enforce in the national courts.[4] This means that those who suffer loss or damage as a result of an infringement (for example as a result of paying excessive prices or being excluded from a market by an anti-competitive agreement) are entitled to bring proceedings in the national courts for injunction and damages. The European Commission is increasingly encouraging victims of anti-competitive practices to enforce their rights directly before the courts and national competition authorities rather than bring infringements to the attention of the Commission.[5]

---

1   Case 234/89 *Delimitis v Henninger Bräu AG* [1991] ECR I-935.
2   Article 85(2).
3   Article 15(2), Regulation 17/62.
4   Case 127/73 *Belgische Radio en Televisie (BRT) v SABAM* [1974] ECR 51.
5   *Notice on Co-operation between National Courts and the Commission in Applying Articles 85 and 86 of the EEC Treaty* 1993 OJ C 39/6; *Draft Notice on Co-operation between National Competition Authorities and the Commission in Handling Cases Falling within the Scope of Articles 85 or 86 of the EC Treaty* (1996) OJ C 262/5.

Exemption

As explained above, Article 85(1) sets out an automatic prohibition on agreements which satisfy the relevant conditions. In considering the application of Article 85(1), relatively little analysis of the economic impact of an agreement is undertaken (other than for the purposes of assessing appreciability). Instead, the anti-competitive effects of an agreement are weighed against its economic benefits when the Commission decides whether or not the agreement is eligible for exemption. Exemption is a declaration by the Commission that, although an agreement infringes Article 85(1), the prohibition should not apply because of the merits of the agreement.

Article 85(3) provides as follows:

'The provisions of paragraph 1 may, however, be declared inapplicable in the case of:
- any agreement or category of agreements between undertakings;
- any decision or category of decisions by associations of undertakings;
- any concerted practice or category of concerted practices;

which contributes to improving the production or distribution of goods or to promoting technical or economic progress, while allowing consumers a fair share of the resulting benefit, and which does not:
(a) impose on the undertakings concerned restrictions which are not indispensable to the attainment of these objectives;
(b) afford such undertakings the possibility of eliminating competition in respect of a substantial part of the products in question.'

Article 85(3) therefore imposes both positive and negative conditions: the agreement must provide certain benefits in order to be eligible, but even where those benefits are present, there will be no exemption if the restrictions go further than is required or if the agreement has a significant foreclosing effect on the market.

Exemptions may be individual following notification to the Commission, or automatic, if an agreement is drafted so as to fall precisely within the terms of one of a series of 'block exemption' regulations.

Block exemptions exist for various forms of intellectual property licences and for certain exclusive distribution agreements. However, the exclusive distribution block exemption is of very limited use for businesses operating on the Internet, because it applies only to agreements relating to goods for resale, not to services.[6] The block exemption provides a useful indication of the Commission's attitude towards analogous agreements relating to the distribution of services, but the fact remains that even where an exclusive services agreement is drafted so as to conform as far as possible to the principles set out in the block exemption, it will not be eligible to benefit from the block exemption and will require individual notification if it infringes the basic prohibition.

The Commission's practice is not to issue a block exemption until it has had the opportunity to issue one or more individual exemptions and to gain experience of the legal and economic issues involved. It has not yet done so in relation to the Internet. Meanwhile, businesses active on the Internet, entering into exclusivity

---

6   Regulation 1983/83, Article 1. See Contract on Goods or Services.

agreements or other relationships which may infringe Article 85, must decide whether to notify their agreements to the Commission for individual exemption, with the knowledge that a final decision may take a couple of years and in any event they may receive only an administrative 'comfort letter' closing the file, or whether to do nothing and to take the risk of Commission enforcement action, unenforceability of any anti-competitive provisions and action by third parties before the courts.

Application to the Internet

The Commission has not yet published any decisions relating to agreements in the Internet sector. However, it is possible to apply existing principles to Internet practices by analogy, particularly in relation to vertical restraints. It is also possible to discern, from the Commission's announcements of investigations into a number of business alliances, its wider concerns about market access.

SOFTWARE DISTRIBUTION BY THE INTERNET

A major preoccupation of the Commission in enforcing the EC competition rules has been to ensure that manufacturers and distributors do not attempt to partition national markets in order to preserve pre-existing price differentials. In its exclusive distribution block exemption, therefore, the Commission, while allowing manufacturers to grant their national distributors a certain degree of territorial protection, insisted that distributors should be free to respond to approaches made to them by potential customers outside their territories. Although the manufacturer is entitled to prohibit a distributor from active solicitation of sales outside his territory, the intention is that the possibility of passive sales should act as a deterrent to price differentials between national markets.

Likewise, some of the Commission's heaviest fines have been imposed on manufacturers which sought to impose export bans on their distributors or otherwise attempted to reinforce national boundaries.[7]

The Internet introduces different opportunities for distribution. Where a manufacturer of software can distribute its products down the line directly to each customer, there is no need for distributors. In theory, this should mean that the manufacturer can no longer justify charging different prices to customers in different territories. In practice, however, direct distribution is likely to reduce intra-brand competition, the possibility of parallel imports from other distributors in the network, which acts as a restraint on excessive differential pricing.

Some national markets within the EC have traditionally been higher priced than others. A manufacturer distributing its software, or updates to its software, directly to customers via the Internet may feel that it can retain higher prices because there is no longer any possibility of parallel imports. It may seek to provide differential access in order to preserve the price differentials. However, the Commission is likely to take an equally serious view of market division and price differentiation in 'virtual' distribution networks as it does in the case of the

---

7   *Dunlop-Slazenger*, supra fn 3, p 346; *Zera/Montedison*, supra fn 3, p 346.

physical distribution of products. As an illustration, the exclusive distribution block exemption provides that there will be no exemption, or that exemption may be withdrawn, where there is insufficient intra-brand competition.

In practice, however, it may be difficult for manufacturers to police and enforce price differentials, because it may be difficult for them to verify where a connection has been made.

The Commission also takes a serious view of less overt attempts to partition markets. In 1993, the Commission took action against a manufacturer which produced different varieties of a herbicide for different national markets within the EC, where each variety was approved by the authorities only within the member state in which the manufacturer intended to distribute it and where there was no justification for the variations other than the desire to partition national markets.[8]

STRATEGIC ALLIANCES

The Commission has issued a notice setting out the basis on which it will assess joint ventures and other forms of strategic alliance.[9] Essentially, the Commission will consider the impact of the joint venture on competition between the parents and the joint venture and between the parents themselves, and the impact on third parties. Joint ventures between non-competitors are unlikely to cause problems for competition, but joint ventures between competitors may have significant effects on the relationship between the parents and on the market position of third parties. If the joint venture is active on the same market as its parents, or upstream or downstream of one or more of the parents, there is a risk that it will eliminate or at least weaken competition between the parents and exclude third parties from the market. Whether or not the parties are actual or potential competitors is a question of fact in each case. The Commission will consider whether the parties might at some future point become competitors. Where a carrier and a content provider link up, the Commission may therefore take the view that not only are the parties on related markets (the carrier being downstream from the content provider) but also that the carrier is capable of moving into the content market itself and is therefore at least a potential competitor of the content provider.

Even where there is no indication that the carrier will move on to the content market, the Commission is likely to have concerns about such linkages. In July 1996, the Competition Commissioner, Karel Van Miert, said at the IIC Telecommunications Forum:

> 'let me just say at this point that where ventures draw together the content provision and transmission systems we will be keeping a very close eye on the competition implications.'

The concern expressed by Commissioner Van Miert lies at the heart of the Commission's inquiry into the alliance between America Online (the US market leader), Bertelsmann (the largest publishing group in Germany and in Europe as a whole) and Deutsche Telekom (the dominant telecommunications operator in Germany and the largest in Europe). The Commission announced the opening of

---

8   *Zera/Montedison*, supra fn 3, p 346.
9   Commission notice concerning the assessment of cooperative joint ventures pursuant to Article 85 of the EEC Treaty (1993) OJ C 43, p 2.

its inquiry in December 1995.[10] The agreement envisaged specialisation in the services offered by the parties, with DT's subsidiary Telekom Online specialising in services to businesses and AOL in services to private customers.

The joint venture was important because of the size of the parties. In particular, DT held a dominant position on the German market for online services through Telekom Online, providing the BTX and Datex-J Services, and also controlled networks essential for the development of competing online services.

The particular concerns expressed by the Commission in its press release were to prevent the alliance from retarding the development of online services.

The Commission asked the parties to provide information on the conditions under which:

– Service Providers would be able to provide access to the content of publications controlled by the partners, or to purchase advertising space to promote new services;
– publications not belonging to the parties would be able to offer their content online;
– other Service Providers would be able to use the networks and services of DT; and
– agreements with other Service Providers might exist.

The Commission's concerns in this case mirror concerns expressed at the creation of the Europe Online alliance and the Microsoft Network.[11] There is clearly a risk that large ventures between market leaders will have a significant foreclosing effect on the market. The Commission is particularly concerned that a business which enjoys a position of market power in one market should not be able to extend this power into other markets. This theme is also dealt with in the following section, in relation to dominant undertakings.

ARTICLE 86

Whereas Article 85 is concerned with the control of anti-competitive agreements, Article 86 prohibits undertakings which enjoy a dominant position on a particular market within the EC from abusing that position. As in the case of Article 85, the abuse must appreciably affect trade between member states for an infringement to occur. The consequences of infringing Article 86 are the same as those of infringing Article 85, with the obvious exception that there is no agreement to be unenforceable.

'86. Any abuse by one or more undertakings of a dominant position within the common market or in a substantial part of it shall be prohibited as incompatible with the common market in so far as it may affect trade between Member States. Such abuse may, in particular, consist in:
(a) directly or indirectly imposing unfair purchase or selling prices or unfair trading conditions;

10 Commission Press Release December 6 1995 1p/95/1354.
11 Commission Press Release 1p/95/1001.

(b) limiting production, markets or technical development to the prejudice of consumers;

(c) applying dissimilar conditions to equivalent transactions with other trading parties, thereby placing them at a competitive disadvantage;

(d) making the conclusion of contracts subject to acceptance by the other parties of supplementary obligations which, by their nature or according to commercial usage, have no connection with the subject of such contracts.'

Relevant market

Dominance does not occur in a vacuum: it must be defined by reference to product and geographic markets.

PRODUCT MARKET

The relevant product market is the market for the product in question and all other products which are substantially substitutable in terms of their use, price and characteristics. There is no clear guidance as to when one product is considered substitutable for another, but the ECJ has commented that for the purposes of defining the market, the Commission should investigate: 'the characteristics of the products in question by virtue of which those products are particularly apt to satisfy an inelastic need and are only to a limited extent interchangeable with other products'.[12]

It is necessary to consider not only demand substitutability, or the extent to which substitutes are available to purchasers of the product, but also supply substitutability, or the extent to which suppliers of products which are not demand substitutable can switch sources to produce or market demand substitutable products.[13] For example, a browser software package to run on a particular operating system may be demand substitutable for a number of competing browsers capable of running on the same operating system. It may also be supply substitutable with other browsers running on different operating systems, but which could readily be adapted by their manufacturers to run on the first system. In this case, the relevant market would include both groups of software in addition to the first package.

Both the Commission and the ECJ have defined the product market very narrowly on occasion.[14] The Commission has defined the market for the spare parts for the equipment of a particular manufacturer as a distinct relevant product market, even if the primary product itself is part of a wider market for products of a similar type.[15] Likewise, the Commission has defined the relevant market in transport cases as the market for transport services between two particular

---

12 *Europemballage & Continental Can v Commission* Case 6/72 [1973] ECR 215.

13 *Continental Can*, see fn 12 supra; *Nederlandsche Banden-Industrie Michelin NV v Commission* Case 322/81 [1983] ECR 3461.

14 Cf *BBI/Boosey and Hawkes*: Interim Measures (1987) OJ L286, p 36, where the Commission defined the relevant market as the market for brass band instruments for British-style brass bands (rather than the market for brass instruments as a whole).

15 Case 22/78 *Hugin v Commission* [1979] ECR 1869.

points.[16] It is therefore probably inappropriate to consider the Internet as one single product market. It should properly be assessed as a number of distinct product markets. It may, for example, be appropriate to consider the market for the provision of a particular item of content as a market in its own right. The provision of a link to a particular Service Provider may also be a distinct product market. Some product markets may be very competitive, others occupied by a dominant undertaking. Each case will require an analysis of the function of the market.

GEOGRAPHIC MARKET

The geographic market is the area in which the goods or services concerned are subject to the same conditions of competition. The extent of the area will depend upon factors such as transport costs, language barriers, regulatory and legal differences and customer preferences. There are strong arguments for suggesting that many of the product markets in the Internet will be worldwide in extent. Conditions of competition and transport are much the same throughout the world, in particular because the net can be accessed from any point for the cost of a local call. However, in some cases a narrower geographic market definition is more appropriate, particularly where the practices of national telecommunications operators, which enjoy a dominant position within their home territories but not outside, are concerned.

It should perhaps be noted that the Commission has considerable discretion in defining the relevant market. If it is keen to investigate a particular practice, it would be more likely to find a market on which the business concerned is dominant.

Dominance

Dominance has been defined as the ability to an appreciable extent to act independently of customers, suppliers and competitors.[17]

It depends on a number of factors:

- the market shares of the undertaking and of its competitors;
- access to raw materials and capital;
- the technical knowledge and expertise of the undertaking and of its competitors;
- the exclusionary effect of any sales or distribution networks; and
- barriers to entry, such as the cost of setting up manufacture.

One of the most important factors is the existence of a large market share.[18] The ECJ has indicated that a market share of around 75% is indicative of dominance[19] and a share of 85% or 90% is conclusive proof of dominance.[20] At the other end of the scale, a market share of 10% is too small to give rise to dominance.[1]

---

16   Access to the port of Rødby (1994) OJ L55, p 52; *Sea Containers/Stena Sealink*: Interim measures (1994) OJ L15, p 8.
17   *Michelin*: see fn 13, page 357; Case 27/76 *United Brands v Commission* [1978] ECR 207.
18   Case 85/76 *Hoffman-La Roche v Commission* [1979] ECR 461.
19   *Hoffman-La Roche*, see fn 18, supra.
20   *Hoffman-La Roche*, see fn 19, supra.
 1   Case 75/84 *Metro v Commission (No 2)* [1986] ECR 3021.

In between the two extremes, the position is less clear. The Commission has left open the possibility of dominance with a market share of as low as 20%,[2] but a rule of thumb is that dominance is likely to be found only with a market share of more than about 40%. At this level, however, other factors, such as the market shares of competitors and the durability of the market share, are relevant.

The dominant position must exist in the Common Market or a substantial part of it. In other words, an entirely localised position of dominance will not be caught by Article 86. What is a substantial part will be a question of fact in each case.

Abuse

The enjoyment of a dominant position is not in itself contrary to the EC competition rules. It is the abuse of this position which is prohibited. Abuse may consist of a dominant company exploiting its customers, for example by charging excessively high prices. Alternatively, it is abusive for a dominant undertaking to seek to reinforce its position by excluding competition still further. The abuse need not occur on the market on which the culprit is dominant in order to fall within Article 86. It may occur on a related market.[3]

Article 86 gives a number of examples of abuse.

UNFAIR PRICING PRACTICES

Both unfairly high prices[4] and unfairly low prices can be abusive. One of the most difficult abuses to assess is the practice of predatory pricing, or pricing below cost in order to eliminate a competitor.

Pricing below the average or variable costs (those which change according to output, such as labour, raw materials and energy) will be regarded as abusive, as there can be little or no justification for selling at such a low price except as part of a strategy to exclude a competitor from the market.

Prices below average total cost (the sum of variable costs and fixed costs, such as premises and equipment costs which remain constant), but above average variable cost, will only be regarded as abusive where there is also an exclusionary intent.[5]

A dominant Service Provider offering subscription charges which did not reflect the cost of providing the service, subsidising the losses from other areas of business and intending to eliminate competitors, would therefore be in breach of Article 86.

Microsoft investigation

The US Department of Justice commenced an investigation into Microsoft's Internet Browser software, following complaints by Netscape Communications. It is likely, although it has not been confirmed, that the Commission is also investigating similar complaints in view of the close co-operation between the Commission and the US Department of Justice, and both authorities' parallel investigations in 1994 into Microsoft's activities in the market for operating software.

2   Commission's 9th and 10th Competition Policy Reports, 1980 and 1981.
3   Case 311/84 *Centre Belge d'Etudes de Marché Télé-marketing v CLT* [1985] ECR 3261.
4   *British Leyland* (1984) OJ L 207, p 11; upheld on appeal Case 226/84 [1986] ECR 3263.
5   *ECS/Akzo* (1985) OJ L 374, p 1; upheld on appeal Case C-62/86 *Akzo Chemie BV v Commission* [1991] ECR I-3359; *Tetra Pak* (1992) OJ L 72, p 1; upheld by CFI: Case T-83/91 *Tetra Pak International SA v Commission* [1994] ECR II-755 and by ECJ: Case C-333/94P.

In the most recent case, Netscape alleged that Microsoft has induced PC manufacturers to prefer Microsoft's Explorer over Netscape's Navigator, by means of discounting practices.

The allegations are very similar to those made in 1993 by Novell,[6] to the effect that Microsoft had abused its dominant position in the markets for DOS and Windows by:

- entering into 'per processor' licences under which royalties were calculated by reference to the number of processors supplied by the manufacturer whether or not it actually installed MS DOS;
- tying the supply of Windows to the supply of MS DOS;
- ensuring that PC manufacturers pre-loaded Microsoft products prior to shipment.

The Commission's investigation ended by the offer of undertakings by Microsoft. Although Microsoft subsequently challenged the US consent decree with temporary success, the EC findings were not challenged. The undertakings required Microsoft not to enter into licence agreements with a duration of more than one year, not to impose minimum quantity requirements on licensees, not to employ per processor licences and not to employ per system licences unless licensees are clearly given the right to purchase competing products.

If substantiated, the latest allegations against Microsoft bear a striking resemblance to those in the earlier case.

INEFFICIENCY AND LIMITING TECHNICAL DEVELOPMENT

Although there have been very few cases on the subject,[7] it appears that inefficiency or limiting technical development, for example by failing to market new technology, can constitute an abuse.

DISCRIMINATION

Discriminatory treatment of customers, particularly in the application of prices, may infringe Article 86. Price discrimination consists of charging different prices to customers in the same circumstances without justification, or charging uniform prices to customers whose circumstances are different. Price discrimination is often seen in the form of a differential discount policy. Discounts which are not related to cost savings to the supplier may be abusive. Discounts intended to secure loyalty on the part of customers, for example, may also infringe Article 86.[8]

TYING

The practice of tying the purchase of one product or service to the purchase of another,[9] where the tie is not objectively justified (for example on technical

6   Commission Press Release IP(94) 653; Commission Press Release BI0/95/42.
7   Case 41/90 *Höfner and Elser v Macrotron* [1991] ECR 1-1979; Case C-179/90 *Merci Convenziondli Porto di Genova v Siderurgica Gabrielli ('Port of Genoa')* [1991] ECR 1-5889.
8   *BPB Industries* 1989 OJ L 10, p 50; upheld by CFI: Case T-65/89 *BPB Industries and British Gypsum v Commission* [1993] ECR II-389; upheld by ECJ: Case C-310/93P [1995] ECR I-865.
9   *Eurofix-Bauco/Hilti* (1988) OJ L 65, p 19; upheld by CFI: Case T-30/89 *Hilti v Commission* [1991] ECR II-1439; upheld by ECJ: Case C-53/92 [1994] ECR I-667.

grounds) is abusive. As in the case of Article 85, a requirement that customers purchase particular software in conjunction with a subscription to a Service Provider may be abusive.

REFUSAL TO SUPPLY

Although not expressly mentioned in Article 86, the refusal to supply goods and services without objective justification may be abusive.[10] The object of such a refusal is often to exclude a competitor from the market or from a related market. The refusal is more likely to be abusive where it is applied to an existing customer, but the Commission has also found an abuse where the effect of the refusal was to prevent a new market entry.[11]

Refusal to license copyright may be abusive depending on the circumstances. The extent to which the refusal to license is abusive is critical to the application of Article 86 to the Internet, given the importance of information ownership and licensing to the industry as a whole. Because a copyright licence is vital for accessing, transmitting and reproducing electronic information on the Internet, the denial of a licence prevents access to the information.

EC competition law attempts to balance the need for competition, for which the free availability of licensed information is necessary, against the need to give proper protection to creative effort, investment and research and development.

The Commission and European Courts have considered this question in considerable detail over the last few years in the *Magill* case.[12] Although it involved the refusal to license copyright in weekly television listings, it has significant implications for operations on the Internet.

In the *Magill* case, Irish and English broadcasters refused to grant copyright licences for their weekly television schedules to the Irish publisher, Magill, who wished to launch a TV programme listings guide showing all the broadcasters' programmes and competing with all of the 'TV Times', 'Radio Times' and the 'RTE Guide'. Following the refusal, Magill complained to the Commission. The Commission held that the TV companies' refusal amounted to an abuse of their dominant position on the market for the production of the listings information and required the broadcasters to license the information. The broadcasters appealed, initially to the Court of First Instance, and subsequently to the full European Court of Justice.

The European Court of Justice upheld the judgment of the Court of First Instance, thereby approving the decision of the Commission.

The conclusion from the *Magill* case is that a mere refusal to license copyright (and other intellectual property rights) is not in itself an abuse under Article 86: it must be linked to other anti-competitive conduct. The European Court of Justice approved various factors identified by the Court of First Instance as constituting an exceptional case and therefore qualifying the refusal as abusive. However, it was not clear from the judgment of the ECJ that all those factors must always be present. Each case must be considered individually, but the presence of the following factors is likely to indicate an abuse:

10 Case 6/73 *Commercial Solvents v Commission* [1974] ECR 223, upholding Commission decision at (1972) OJ L 299, p 51.
11 *Sea Containers/Stena Sealink: Interim Measures* (1994) OJ L 15, p 18.
12 *Magill TV Guide/ITP, BBC & RTE* (1989) OJ L 78, p 43; upheld by CFI: Cases T-69 & 76/89 *RTE and ITP v Commission* [1991] ECR II-485; upheld by ECJ: Cases C-241 and 242/91P.

1. where the refusal has the effect of reserving to the copyright owner a monopoly in a secondary market (a market ancillary to or downstream from the primary market in which it is dominant and in which the refusal takes place);
2. where the refusal prevents the party seeking the licence from introducing a new product or service; and
3. where there is no technical or other justification for the refusal.

Applying these principles to the Internet, it appears that in certain cases it may be abusive for a provider of content in paper form, for example, to refuse to license copyright in the content to a person wishing to distribute the information over the Internet, where its sole objective in doing so is to reserve to itself the market for disseminating the information electronically, perhaps through its own related Service Provider. The content provider here might argue that it already offers the service which the competing Service Provider wishes to offer, in other words, electronic access to the information concerned. However, if the competing Service Provider can show that it would provide some new or additional service (by analogy with *Magill*, for example, a service providing access to information from several different sources, such as timetables of several airlines or access to all the daily newspapers simultaneously), the refusal of a licence might be abusive. However, EC competition law recognises that a copyright owner is entitled to a reasonable return and so it allows copyright owners to charge a reasonable royalty if they are required to license their rights under this principle. So far, the principle has not been tested in other cases and there are suggestions that *Magill* should be regarded as something of an exception. However, the decision in *Magill* is consistent with other more recent decisions of the Commission relating to refusals to supply and point towards the formulation of a general principle that it may be abusive to use dominance in one market to reserve to oneself dominance in a related market. This principle also appears in the essential facilities doctrine discussed below.

Where the copyright owner has in the past granted licences to some applicants, any subsequent referral (other than on objectively justifiable grounds) may be discriminatory. Discrimination is equally abusive for Article 86 (as indicated above) but the advantage of being able to base a claim on a discriminatory licensing policy is that there is no need to show that the strict *Magill* criteria are satisfied.

THE ESSENTIAL FACILITIES PRINCIPLE

The essential facilities principle first appeared within the EC (it had been applied in the United States for many years) in 1992.

Sealink at Holyhead

In the first essential facilities case, in June 1992, Sealink was the port authority for Holyhead in Anglesey, and also operated ferries from there to Ireland.[13] When its ferries passed the berth of another operator, B&I, the water movement forced B&I

---

13   *Sealink/B&I – Holyhead*: Interim Measures [1992] 5 CMLR 255.

to disconnect its loading ramp. Sealink changed its timetable so that this happened twice a day instead of once. B&I complained to the European Commission, which ordered Sealink to change to a timetable which did not result in two sailings per day past a moored B&I vessel. The Commission stated that a company which both owns and operates an essential facility, in this case a port, should not grant its competitors access on terms less favourable than those which it gives its own services.

In the following year, the Commission again considered Sealink's dual role at Holyhead.[14] This time, the port operator had refused to grant suitable slots to allow Sea Containers to launch a new fast SeaCat service, while granting its own ferry operating subsidiary slots to launch a similar service. The Commission said:

> 'the owner of an essential facility which uses its power in one market in order to protect or strengthen its position in another related market, in particular, by refusing to grant access to a competitor, or by granting access on less favourable terms than those of its own services, and thus imposing a competitive disadvantage on its competitor, infringes Article 86.'

Significantly, *Sea Containers* expressly refers to the need to protect new market entrants as well as existing players. This had not been clear from previous refusal to supply cases. It also confirms that it may be abusive to use dominance on one market to secure a position on a downstream market.

The essence of an essential facility

So what amounts to an essential facility? In *Sea Containers*, the Commission defined it as 'a facility or infrastructure, without access to which competitors cannot provide services to their customers'.

US decisions shed a little more light on the subject, suggesting the following factors:

1. a facility is essential only if no practical alternatives are available and the complainant cannot compete effectively without it;
2. the complainant is itself necessary in order to provide competition on the market;
3. compulsory access to the facility should be an exceptional remedy and should be ordered only if it improves competition (which is unlikely if it ultimately deters investment and innovation); and
4. the owner of the facility should be entitled to rely on its legitimate business interests in order to deny access.

It seems that the owner of an essential facility has a positive duty to co-operate with users, even to the extent of limiting its own use, although it is not required to support parasitic competitors indefinitely.

14   *Sea Containers/Sealink* – see fn 11, supra.

Non-discriminatory facilities management

The Commission provided useful guidance in its 1993 Competition Report. It said that where a company both owns and uses an essential facility, it cannot normally expect to fulfil satisfactorily its duty to provide non-discriminatory access and to resolve its conflicts of interest unless it takes steps to separate its management of the essential facility from its use of it. This could include:

1.   different employees responsible for management and use of the facility;
2.   the establishment of a non-discriminatory code of practice;
3.   a consultation procedure involving other users of the facility; and
4.   arrangements for independent arbitration in the event of a dispute.

Application in other sectors

The Commission has now heard a number of cases involving access to ports (most recently the Breton port of Morlaix).[15] However, the essential facilities doctrine has not yet made much of an appearance outside this relatively narrow field, although there is plenty of scope for it. Any 'bottleneck' in the supply chain is a potential candidate for the application of the principle. In the telecommunications sector the former monopolist will frequently own the infrastructure required by its new competitors on the service provision markets. Likewise in the development of the new commercial mobile satellite communication networks such as ICO and Globalstar, natural, contractual or intellectual property constraints on uplink facilities and orbital and frequency resources may give rise to requests for access.[16]

Where a telecommunications network constitutes an essential facility, Service Providers may be able to gain access through specific interconnection and access rights granted under telecommunications liberalisation directives. However, where these directives do not apply, or where the essential facility to which access is required is not a telecommunications network but, for example, particular content or a particular contractual network of Service Providers and content providers, the principle may be of some assistance. A content provider wishing to break out onto the Internet may require a link with a particular Service Provider in order to permit access to its site. Refusal by the Service Provider to host the content provider may amount to denial of an essential facility if the content provider has no viable alternative. This potential application reflects the Commission's concerns in relation to the creation of strategic alliances, discussed above.

EC MERGER REGULATION

The EC Merger Regulation[17] requires the prior notification to the European Commission of 'concentrations having a Community dimension', where:

1.   the aggregate world-wide group turnover of all the undertakings concerned amounts to more than 5 million ECUs (approximately £4 million);

---

15   *ICG/CCI Morlaix* [1995] 5 CMLR 177.
16   Inmarsat-P(ICO). Commission notice (1995) OJ C 304, p 6; Commission launches investigations into global mobile satellite systems: Press Release IP/95/549.
17   Regulation 4064/89 (1989) OJ L395 p; reprinted with corrections (1990) OJ L257, p 14.

2. the overall EC turnover of each of at least two of the undertakings is more than 250 million ECUs (approximately £200 million); and
3. not more than two-thirds of the turnover of each undertaking concerned is in the same member state. (So mergers which primarily concern one member state fall outside the Regulation.)

For the purposes of calculating turnover, the entire group of each undertaking is included. However, if the merger involves the acquisition of only part of a business, then the turnover of only that part is taken as the vendor's turnover.[18]

The key question in deciding whether an acquisition amounts to a concentration is whether there has been a change in the structure of control. Essentially, if one party gains control (either alone or jointly with existing shareholders) of another party, then there is a concentration. A change of control will be apparent where one party acquires all the shares of the other, or acquires a majority of voting rights. However, the acquisition of a minority interest may also give rise to joint control, if the minority shareholder has the right to determine the management of the business, or has significant veto rights. Particularly important veto rights include those relating to the business plan and the budget. In contrast, other rights, such as the right to object to any enlargement of share capital, are seen as simple minority protection rights, which do not give control.[19]

The creation of a joint venture will fall within the EC Merger Regulation if the joint venture (a 'concentrative joint venture') is an autonomous economic entity and does not lead to co-ordination of the parents' competitive behaviour.[20] The creation of a joint venture which does co-ordinate the parents' competitive behaviour (a 'co-operative joint venture') falls outside the Merger Regulation altogether and is considered under Article 85.[1]

The Commission has issued a useful guidance note on the concentrative/co-operative distinction.[2] Essentially, the joint venture is likely to be co-operative if the parents retain any activity on the market on which the joint venture is active, or on related markets. However, the question is complex, and where there is any doubt at all, early contact with the Commission for informal discussions is recommended.

A concentration with a Community dimension, on the basis of the turnover thresholds set out above, must be notified to the Commission on an extremely detailed questionnaire, within one week after signature of the agreement. Following notification to the Commission, the merger must be suspended for three weeks. Failure to notify or to suspend a merger may lead to a fine.[3]

The Commission assesses a concentration with a Community dimension to determine whether or not it is compatible with the Common Market. A concentration which creates or strengthens a dominant position, significantly impeding effective competition in the Common Market or in a substantial part of it, will be declared incompatible with the Common Market.[4]

---

18 Article 5(2), Reg 4064/89.
19 Article 3(3), Reg 4064/89 and Commission Notice on the notion of a concentration (1994) OJ C 385, p 5.
20 Article 3(2), Reg 4064/89.
1   Article 3(2), Reg 4064/89 and Article 6, Commission Notice on the distinction between concentrative and cooperative joint ventures (1994) OJ C 385, p 1.
2   Commission Notice, see fn 1, supra.
3   Article 4 (prior notification); Article 7 (suspension); Article 14 (fines) Regulation 4064/89.
4   Article 2, Reg 4064/89.

Most concentrations are cleared after a one-month preliminary investigation. A few mergers which raise serious doubts move to a second stage investigation, which can last for up to a further four months.

A concentration with a Community dimension, falling within the ECMR, is not covered by Article 85 or Article 86. Neither do these Articles apply to any ancillary restrictions (such as non-competition covenants or exclusive licence or supply arrangements) which are essential to the concentration.[5]

As stated above, grounds on which a notified concentration may be blocked under the ECMR are that it creates or reinforces a dominant position on the market. It is significant therefore, that two of the relatively small number of prohibition decisions taken by the European Commission under the ECMR revolve around attempts by network operators, enjoying essentially gatekeeper functions, to extend dominance into related broadcasting and content markets.

In the *MSG* case in 1994,[6] Berlesmann, the leading German publisher, Kirsch, the leading supplier of feature films and television programming and a Pay-TV operator outside Germany, and Deutsch Telekom, the German public telecommunications operator and owner and operator of nearly all the German cable television networks, proposed to set up a joint venture, MSG, for the technical, commercial and administrative handling of Pay-TV and other communication services, including conditional access and subscriber management.

The Commission found that MSG would probably be the only supplier of those services on the German market in the near future and would therefore have a monopoly. The creation of a future monopoly, according to the Commission, should not necessarily be considered as the creation of a dominant position for the purposes of the Merger Regulation, provided that the future market remained open to future competition. In the *MSG* case, however, the Commission considered that the market for the services offered by the joint venture would be sealed off from the outset, given that the most likely potential competitors, who might otherwise be expected to create an infrastructure for Pay-TV and provide the necessary services, were the parties to the joint venture. It was scarcely conceivable that competing operators could enter the market once MSG had been established. Undertakings offered by MSG, in particular to offer non-discriminatory access to competitors, were insufficient to outweigh the creation of the dominant position. The undertakings offered were largely behavioural, and did not address the fundamental structural problem of the creation of a dominant position.

Similarly, in July 1995, the Commission blocked a proposed joint venture, Nordic Satellite Distribution (NSD), between Norsk Telekom A/S (NT), TeleDanmark A/S (TD) and Industriforvaltnings AB Kinnevik (Kinnevik).[7]

The parties to NSD were three leading players in the Nordic TV and media industries. NT was Norway's largest cable TV operator, controlled one of the two Nordic satellite positions and was an important Pay-TV distributor in Norway. TeleDanmark was the largest Danish cable TV operator and also controlled, together with Kinnevik, most of the other Nordic satellite capacity. Kinnevik was the most important provider of Nordic satellite TV programmes and the largest Nordic Pay-TV distributor and also had interests in cable TV operators.

The object of NSD was to transmit satellite TV programmes to cable TV operators and directly to households with satellite dishes. NSD would effectively

---

5   Article 22, Reg 4064/89; Commission notice on ancillary restrictions (1990) OJ C 203, p 5.
6   (1994) OJ L364, p 1.
7   Commission Press Release IP(95) 801.

lead to a concentration of the activities of NT, TD and Kinnevik, resulting in the creation of a highly vertically integrated operation extending from production of TV programmes through operation of satellites and cable TV networks to retail distribution services for Pay-TV and other encrypted channels. The Commission found that NSD would create or strengthen a dominant position on three markets: on the market for provision of satellite TV transponder capacity to the Nordic region, NSD would create a dominant position; it would strengthen its dominant position on the Danish market for cable TV; and on the market for distribution of satellite Pay-TV and other encrypted TV channels direct to home, NSD would create a dominant position.

The Commission found that the vertically integrated nature of the operation meant that the market positions downstream (cable TV operations and Pay-TV) would reinforce the market positions upstream (satellite transponders and programme provision) and vice versa. Overall, the parties would achieve such strong positions that they would be able to foreclose the Nordic market for satellite TV.

The principle underlying both these decisions is the theme underlying this entire chapter: that any attempt to create or reinforce vertical integration between content and transmission, or to foreclose an entire market, will attract unfavourable attention from the Commission.

Until the Commission issues its expected decisions relating to the Internet, it is difficult to speculate what other issues, if any, will cause concern in Brussels.

UK COMPETITION LAW

Unlike EC competition law, UK competition law does not set out any automatic prohibition of certain forms of anti-competitive conduct. Instead, the legislation provides for a case-by-case assessment of agreements and practices, in which they can be tested against the public interest.

The institution with the primary responsibility for administering UK competition law is the Office of Fair Trading ('OFT'). Following initial investigation, the OFT may bring proceedings before the Restrictive Practices Court or may recommend reference to the Monopolies and Mergers Commission.

The UK competition rules are found in the following legislation:

- the Restrictive Trade Practices Act 1976, which regulates restrictive agreements;
- the Resale Prices Act 1976, which regulates resale price maintenance;
- the Competition Act 1980, which regulates unilateral anti-competitive practices; and
- the Fair Trading Act 1973, which regulates monopolies and mergers.

The Restrictive Trade Practices Act 1976

The Restrictive Trade Practices Act 1976 ('RTPA') requires the registration at the OFT of agreements between two or more parties carrying on business in the UK in the supply of goods, or between two or more parties carrying on business in the

UK in the supply of services, in which two or more parties accept relevant restrictions relating to goods or services respectively.[8]

The RTPA also applies to certain agreements for the exchange of information about prices or terms and conditions of sale of goods (but not services).[9] A recommendation containing relevant restrictions, made by a trade association to its members, is treated as an agreement between the members.[10]

The term 'agreement' under the RTPA is very widely defined. It can mean any form of agreement or arrangement between two or more persons, whether or not it is legally enforceable. This includes informal, oral arrangements and so called 'gentleman's agreements'. A series of separate agreements will be treated as a single agreement for the purposes of the RTPA where execution of those agreements is mutually interdependent.[11]

The definition of a restriction includes 'a negative obligation, whether express or implied and whether absolute or not'.[12]

In relation to goods, relevant restrictions are those which relate to the following:

- prices to be charged, quoted or paid, recommended or suggested retail prices;
- terms or conditions of sale or purchase;
- quantities or descriptions of goods to be produced, supplied or acquired;
- processes of manufacture to be applied to any goods or quantities or descriptions of goods to which such processes are to be applied; or
- the persons or classes of persons to whom goods are to be supplied, from whom goods are to be acquired or the areas or places in which goods are to be supplied or from which goods are to be acquired.

A list of similar restrictions exists for services.[13]

As an illustration, an agreement between two UK Service Providers about the prices which they will charge to subscribers or the areas in which they will supply services would be registrable.

There are a number of exemptions from the RTPA, including exemptions for certain exclusivity agreements and intellectual property licences.

Orders adopted under the Deregulation and Contracting Out Act 1994 create categories of 'non-notifiable' agreements.[14] There is no need to notify an agreement to which the parties and the groups to which they belong have an aggregate turnover in the UK of no more than £20 million, or if the agreement falls within the terms of an EC block exemption, or if although not infringing Article 85 (for example, because it has no appreciable effect on trade between member states) it would fall within the terms of an EC block exemption.

Agreements which are registrable under the RTPA must be registered with the OFT within three months after the date of the agreement. Once registered, an agreement is open for public inspection, although it is possible to apply for

8   Restrictive Trade Practices Act 1976 (RTPA), s 1; s 9 – registration requirement; s 6 – goods; s 11 – services.
9   Restrictive Trade Practices (Information Agreements) Order 1969 (SI 1969/1842).
10   RTPA, s 8 – goods; RTPA, s 12 – services.
11   RTPA, s 43(1); *British Basic Slag Ltd's Application* [1963]1 WLR 727, CA; *Schweppes (No 2)* [1971] 1 WLR 1148.
12   RTPA 1976, s 43(1).
13   RTPA, s 6 – goods; RTPA, s 11; Restrictive Trade Practices (Services) Order 1976 (SI 1976/98) – services.
14   Restrictive Trade Practices (Non-notifiable Agreements) (EC Block Exemptions) Order 1996 (SI 1996/349); Restrictive Trade Practices (Non-Notifiable Agreements) (Turnover Threshold) Order 1996 (SI 1996/348).

commercially sensitive information to be deleted from the public register and placed on a special confidential section of the register.[15]

Once an agreement has been registered, the OFT must bring the agreement before the Restrictive Practices Court ('RPC') which decides whether the restrictions operate against the public interest. However, where the restrictions are of minor significance, or are exempt under the EC competition rules, the OFT is relieved of this obligation and in fact most agreements escape a reference in this way.[16]

Once a reference has been made, the RPC will declare that the restrictions are contrary to the public interest unless the agreement satisfies one or more of the narrowly defined public interest tests set out in the RTPA. Although the OFT usually prefers to seek undertakings, the RPC has the power to impose orders and may also accept undertakings, breach of which is a contempt of court.

Non-registration of a registrable agreement renders the restrictions in it void and unenforceable. In addition, any person who suffers loss or damage as a result of the restriction may bring proceedings for breach of statutory duty and may claim damages and/or an injunction.

The Resale Prices Act 1976

The Resale Prices Act 1976 ('RPA') applies to both collective and individual resale price maintenance, ie two or more persons agreeing to impose resale price maintenance on their dealers, or a supplier attempting to enforce resale price maintenance against its dealers. The RPA applies only to goods.

As in the case of the RTPA, unlawful price maintenance clauses are void and unenforceable and any person suffering loss as a result may bring proceedings for damages and/or an injunction. The OFT may also bring proceedings before the RPC.

The Competition Act 1980

The Competition Act 1980 applies to anti-competitive practices, an anti-competitive practice being any course of conduct which has or is intended to have or is likely to have the effect of restricting, distorting or preventing competition.

The Competition Act 1980 covers practices similar in scope to those prohibited by Article 86 of the EC Treaty.

The Competition Act provides for an initial investigation by the OFT, followed by a possible reference to the Monopolies and Mergers Commission ('MMC'), although the OFT may accept undertakings in lieu of a reference. If referred, the MMC will consider whether the practice is in the public interest.

The disadvantage of the Competition Act is that it provides little incentive for a business not to indulge in anti-competitive practices because there is no outright prohibition, but only a possibility of an order or an undertaking following a lengthy investigation.

15 RTPA, s 23(3).
16 RTPA, s 21(2).

There are currently various exemptions from the Competition Act, in particular for practices carried out by businesses with an annual turnover of less than £10 million and with less than a 25% share of a relevant market and which are not members of a group with an annual turnover or market share over this threshold.[17]

Monopoly control

Sections 47–56 of the Fair Trading Act 1973 ('FTA') gives the UK authorities the power to correct the adverse consequences of a monopoly. For the purposes of the FTA, a monopoly exists where:

1. 25% or more of all goods or services of a particular description are supplied in the UK, or in a specific part of it, by or to one person or group of companies; or
2. 25% or more of all such goods or services are supplied by or to a number of persons (who are not members of the same group of companies) who so conduct their respective affairs as to prevent, restrict or distort competition in connection with goods or services. This is referred to as a complex monopoly situation.

As in the case of the Competition Act, initial investigations under the FTA are carried out by the OFT, which decides whether there are grounds to make a reference to the MMC, or if possible to seek undertakings in lieu of a reference.

The FTA covers a wide range of practices and it is important to note that it is not necessary that there should be any abuse of market power; the Act applies equally to 'market failure' and the consequences of oligopolistic market structures. Examples of practices falling within the monopoly provisions of the FTA include content providers collectively (but not by agreement between them) granting access on discriminatory terms and conditions (complex monopoly) or a Service Provider with a large market share seeking to exclude competitors by means of predatory pricing.

Merger control under the Fair Trading Act 1973

The FTA allows the Secretary of State to refer to the MMC 'mergers qualifying for investigation'. These occur where:

1. two or more enterprises cease to be distinct; and
2. at least one of the enterprises is carried on in the UK or by or under the control of a company incorporated in the UK; and[18]
3. the merger has taken place within the last four months (unless it has taken place in secret); and[19]

---

17   Anti-Competitive Practices (Exclusion) Order 1980 (SI 1980/979).
18   Fair Trading Act 1993 (FTA), s 64(1).
19   FTA, s 64(4) (reduced from six months by the Deregulation (Fair Trading Act 1973) (Amendment) (Merger Reference Time Limits) Order 1996 (SI 1996/345)).

4. either the market share test or the assets test set out below is satisfied.

MARKET SHARE TEST

A merger qualifies for investigation where the parties are both engaged in the supply or consumption of goods or services of the same description and have between them at least 25% of the market for those goods or services in the UK or a substantial part of it. The OFT has a wide discretion as to how it defines the relevant market and so may draw it very narrowly if it wishes to do so.[20]

THE ASSETS TEST

A merger also qualifies for investigation if the gross value of the assets taken over exceeds £70 million, having deducted any allowances for depreciation, renewals or diminution in value, but without deducting liabilities.[1]

Enterprises cease to be distinct when they are brought under common control and ownership and this includes situations where one party is able to exercise material influence over the policy of another. The OFT has applied this to acquisitions of stakes of as small as 10% in a company.[2]

It is usual to seek clearance from the OFT of mergers qualifying for investigation and as in the case of the other UK competition legislation, the OFT has the power to seek undertakings in lieu of a reference.

20　FTA, s 64(1)(a), (2) and (3).
1　FTA, s 64(1)(b).
2　FTA, s 65.

Chapter ten
Banking

Susan Knüfer, Solicitor, Nabarro Nathanson

The move of suppliers and consumers onto the Internet has been closely followed, not surprisingly, by banks. Some, primarily in the United States of America, allow investors to deal directly with the bank over the World Wide Web. Their sites are a metaphor for their branches. Electronic cheques and digital money can be deposited; balances can be checked and bills can be paid.

The experience so far in England has been more conservative. The web sites, or online presences of English banks, have been simply used to send payment instructions to the bank where a customer's account is held, receive bank statements electronically, and transfer funds electronically. Banking institutions both sides of the Atlantic, however, are preparing themselves for the influx of digital cash; if the predictions of the growth in Internet commerce are accurate, banks will need to accept e-cash to serve their customers.

This chapter considers the following issues.

1. When is a financial institution operating over the Internet acting as a bank?
2. What are the different models of Internet banking which have already been adopted?
3. What is the legal nature of electronic money, or digital cash?
4. What are the money laundering considerations over the Internet?

WHAT IS A BANK?

There appears to be a nonchalant acceptance that the institutions which are offering financial services on the Internet are indeed banks. It is time to dispel the myth.

In the UK, under section 3 of the Banking Act 1987 (the 'Banking Act'):

> 'no person shall ... accept a deposit in the course of carrying on (whether there or elsewhere) a business which for the purposes of [the Banking Act] is a deposit-taking business unless that person is an institution for the time being authorised by the Bank [of England] under the following provisions of ... [the Banking Act].'

A 'deposit' is defined under section 5 of the Banking Act as:

> 'a sum of money [(whether denominated in a currency or in ECUs)] paid on terms –
> (a) under which it will be repaid, with or without interest or a premium, and either on demand or at a time or in circumstances agreed by or on behalf of the person making the payment and the person receiving it; and
> (b) which are not referable to the provision of property or services for the giving of security.'

Finally, for the purposes of the Banking Act, a business is a deposit-taking business if:

> '(a) in the course of the business money received by way of deposit is lent to others; or
> (b) any other activity of the business is financed, wholly or to any material extent, out of the capital of or the interest on money received by way of deposit.'

There are a number of exemptions and qualifications to these fundamental provisions but, in essence, any person who is accepting deposits in the UK needs to be an authorised institution. On the face of it, therefore, a lender or an institution providing payment or other money-related services (subject to complying with any other laws and regulations which may be relevant), would not be in breach of the Banking Act.

Whilst there are various levels at which banking services are effected on the Internet in the UK, for example, by sending payment instructions to the bank where a customer's account is held, receiving bank statements over the Internet, transferring funds electronically and providing electronic cash, there is no clear evidence that banks in the UK are currently operating as such. They are not accepting deposits on the Internet.

Indeed, the banks' regulators, the Bank of England, and other associations such as the British Bankers' Association and the Association of Payment Clearing Services ('APACS') have not issued any guidelines regarding banking and the Internet, not having formulated any views on this topic to date. Similarly, the Financial Law Panel have had no cause to consider the legal implications of Internet banking.

BANKING MODELS

In America Internet banking has developed to a greater degree and, whilst the regulators have adopted a 'wait and see' approach, they recognise the need to implement formal guidelines and, to this end, have established working groups to determine the scope of such guidelines. In the United States, the requirement for a banking licence to be held varies from state to state. However, in essence, accepting deposits is an activity which gives rise to the need for a banking licence on a federal basis.

The following examples of Internet 'banks' are worthy of analysis.

Electronic cash bank

Mark Twain Bank is a public company regulated by multiple US governmental entities. It is an institution authorised under the US Federal Reserve System (the 'Fed') (as to which, see below) and has been established for over 30 years with over US$3 billion in assets. Accounts may be opened by non-US citizens and residents.

Mark Twain Bank offers electronic cash ('e-cash') facilities for its customers. Any individual who would like to take advantage of the e-cash system is required to open an account with Mark Twain Bank – a 'world currency access' account. Money is deposited in this account and whilst there may earn interest and enjoy being insured by the Federal Deposit Insurance Corporation ('FDIC'). Whenever a customer requires e-cash he will contact the bank to instruct it to transfer money out of his account into the 'e-cash mint'. This mint is owned and controlled by Mark Twain Bank but has no authorisation in itself and there are currently no regulations regarding it. (Mark Twain Bank employees are, however, in contact with the Fed who are expected to approve the e-cash mint formally and provide regulations for it shortly.) Currently, as soon as the money leaves the world currency access account it is no longer insured by the FDIC. The customer will be able to interact with the mint via his computer and will be able to instruct the mint as to how many electronic 'coins' he requires. The mint will then validate, certify and issue the electronic coins which will then be transmitted to the customer's computer.

The electronic coins can then be used in various transactions and may be passed on to the computers of shops operating on the Internet. These shops then transmit the coins back to the issuing bank who will reconvert the coins into hard currency. Naturally, this envisages that the merchants concerned will also have an account with Mark Twain Bank or some other equivalent and compatible institution.

Any unused electronic coins may be returned to the e-cash mint and then transferred back to the customer's world currency access account.

The e-cash system together with all software and updates will be provided by Digicash BV in Holland (as to which, see below) for the foreseeable future.

The virtual bank

This type of bank is quite distinct from the system that Mark Twain Bank are in the process of establishing. There is no attempt here to use any type of electronic cash. Rather it is comparable to telephone banking. All that is required is a location on the Internet to which customers can connect. Normal banking transactions can then be carried out via the computer link.

The most publicised example of this type of virtual bank is Security First Network Bank ('SFNB') in the US. SFNB provides customers with current/cheque accounts and also sends out ATM cards and Visa cards. SFNB work out of their headquarters in Atlanta with a single branch in Pineville, Kentucky. They aim to offer better rates due to lower overheads and have stressed the importance of security (hence the name) utilising pages on advertising how secure the system is from outside penetration.

First Virtual, USA offers the customer, amongst other things, a payment service by virtue of which it transfers payments from buyers to sellers and keeps track of accounts, which it achieves by operating accounts for customers and sellers and settling payments itself without permitting sensitive information to travel over the Internet. The payments are made up to a pre-agreed limit and credit card numbers are obtained separately by telephone transactions being verified by e-mail callbacks initiated by the customer (this is achieved by a series of prompts, ie 'yes', 'no', 'fraud'). Customers confirm transactions by selecting the appropriate response.

First Virtual provides electronic forms of transfers without holding a banking licence.

Digital cash

Digicash BV was set up by David Chaum, an American professor who now runs the company from Amsterdam. The digital cash system is unlike traditional electronic transfer systems in that it is more closely related to the transfer of physical cash payments. There is no direct contractual relationship between the payee and a third party. Instead there is a contingent contractual liability. A digital token is transferred from the debtor to the creditor and a contractual liability of the third party (an issuing bank such as Mark Twain Bank) is contingent because it arises only if a token is presented to the bank for payment. Tokens may be transferred an infinite number of times before that liability arises.

The way the Digicash system operates is as follows.

1. A customer opens an account with a bank.
2. The customer deposits paper currency into that account.
3. Whenever the customer wishes to withdraw digital money he uses his computer to generate a 100-digit serial number that will be used for his 'electronic bank note' and gives it a currency denomination.
4. The customer then uses his private encryption key on the serial number and sends it to the bank.
5. The bank uses its public encryption key on the message.
6. The bank then deducts the money from the customer's account.
7. The bank's digital signature is then added to the serial number with the message and sent back to the customer.
8. The customer now has digital money.
9. The customer can spend the money by sending the coded message to a merchant.
10. The merchant simply checks the bank's digital signature by using the bank's public decryption key. A successful decryption means the note must have been authorised by the bank (similar to a watermark on a bank note).
11. A merchant can then send this message to the bank who will deposit paper currency in the merchant's account at the bank in exchange for the electronic message.

This process is almost identical to the system operated by Mark Twain Bank. The legal issues concerning Digicash therefore remain the same. These include:

1. authorisation to hold deposits;
2. requirement for an authorised institution to conduct its business in a prudent manner including ensuring the maintenance of sufficient capital adequacy and liquidity, having adequate provisions for diminution in the value of the bank's

assets and for future liabilities and maintaining adequate records and systems of control;
3.   data protection and confidentiality;
4.   money laundering.

Internet banks in the United Kingdom

We have seen how, in the US, it is possible for funds to remain on deposit in the banking system at all times except when transferred over the Internet (for example, to a trusted third party) or for e-cash to be derived from a bank account but to be stored on an individual's personal computer. The Americans have identified certain regulatory implications of banking on the Internet, including:

– encryption export controls;
– money laundering and criminal enforcement;
– economic sanctions;
– 'core' bank regulatory issues;
– monetary policy;
– consumer protection;
– taxation; and
– dispute resolution.

The fundamental question in relation to core bank regulatory issues is whether e-cash systems constitute the business of 'banking' so as to be subject to the full range of US bank regulatory requirements including chartering, capitalisation, deposit insurance, reserve, examination and other requirements. The statutory, regulatory and case law definitions of banking vary from state to state and there are also varying definitions at federal level.

By contrast, in the UK, the cornerstone of the banking regulatory regime is enshrined in section 3 of the Banking Act and it is in the light of this provision that the state of play in the UK is analysed below. Over 154 European banks now have sites on the World Wide Web and this is fast becoming a cost-effective way of providers of 'banking' services to issue glorified brochures offering marketing information and ultimately for banks and non-banks alike to offer a 'fully fledged banking service'.

In England, banks such as Lloyds TSB have also launched themselves onto the Internet. TSB's excursion onto the Internet follows on from the fairly recent launch of its telephone banking system. Again, the intention is to allow those with a computer and a modem to connect with their bank and send instructions through. In legal terms this is no more than an extension of the bank's mode of communication and does not impact upon any of the legislation concerning deposit-taking, authorisation or regulations.

There are also moves afoot to expand on the current scope of PC banking (where a customer's personal computer interfaces a closed network provided by, for example, Compuserve along a telephone line rather than on the global bulletin board) so that video images can be transmitted along fast telecommunication lines. In this way, your friendly local bank manager may appear beside your electronic copy of your bank statement in substitution for a visit to the local branch.

As indicated, the above services can be provided by a non-bank and it is therefore not surprising that banks are deeply involved in the evolution of virtual services.

ELECTRONIC MINTS

There is an unspoken fear rippling through western governments that the advent of electronic cash could destroy the preserve of governments in issuing currency. Unlike traditional money, e-cash has the likelihood of being able to retain its value and to be regarded as acceptable global currency. Not only ought electronic purses to be more convenient and safer than physical cash but also may be treated as a status symbol. The electronic purse stores cash digitally, as OS and IS in computer chips and has been launched around the world by Proton, Danmønt, Mondex (supported by Midland and NatWest), Europay (issuer of Mastercard in Europe which has developed an electronic purse called Clip) and Visa, who have launched an Olympics card. None of the above are at present aimed at the Internet whereas Digicash is exclusively effected over the Internet (discussed above in the section entitled 'Digicash BV'). As we have seen, Digicash involves the use of tokens which may be spent only once and utilises 'blinding' techniques to ensure that verifications do not reveal the identity of the consumer. But, is it money?

The meaning of 'money'

The Oxford Dictionary definition of 'money' is:

> 'current coin as medium of exchange, measure of value ... hence, anything serving the same purpose as a coin';

and

> 'money in reference to its purchasing power ... hence, possessions or property viewed as convertible into money.'

The *Dictionary of Finance* defines 'money' as:

> 'a means of facilitating exchange of goods and accumulation of financial wealth, commonly recognisable as banknotes, coins, bank deposits; and
> (i) a medium of exchange;
> (ii) a unit of value (the basic, economistic definition);
> (iii) a store of wealth.'

The legal definition of 'money' contained in *Halsbury's Words & Phrases* is:

> 'the term "money" is commonly regarded as one which does not bear precise meaning in the eyes of the law. It depends on the *context* in which it is used (*Perrin v Morgan* [1943] AC 399). It can be a testator's personal property, and/or real property.'

On balance, the creation of e-cash is analogous to the minting of money and the e-cash itself is treated like physical cash but to date has not been characterised as the equivalent of money for the purposes of the definition of 'deposit' under the Banking Act. On this basis, non-banks such as Digicash BV could play an integral role in the minting of money without being an authorised institution, provided they are linked to deposit accounts with authorised banks.

Whilst central banks remain silent on the implementation of specific regulations to govern the use of electronic purses and e-cash, the European Monetary Institute ('EMI') has recommended that, except in restricted circumstances, only credit institutions be allowed to use electronic purses.[1] The rationale for this recommendation is that in the opinion of the EMI, it is clear that money received by the issuer of an electronic purse is, in economic terms, a bank deposit and, accordingly, the protection of the consumer and the money transmission system is paramount. This working party has been set up by Europe's monetary authorities to look into the implications of such transactions and has concluded that EU central banks should scrutinise the security features of the cards concerned and make sure statistics on their use are collated. The European Union has its own electronic money trial, the Cafe project.

Bank regulators such as the Bank of England may regard themselves as not having jurisdiction where an offshore bank advertises for (and possibly accepts) deposits on the Internet. This concern was highlighted by the Bank of England's sharp warning to potential UK investors in an Antigua-based institution which is advertising for deposits on the Internet. The Bank of England views the deposits as offshore deposits which fall outside their regulatory scope but they clearly appear to be deeply concerned and rather powerless to take action at this stage.

MONEY LAUNDERING AND TAX AVOIDANCE

The ability of encryption to preserve confidentiality whilst confirming the integrity of information transmitted and authenticating the underlying transaction would appear to be at odds with, if not at the expense of, the laws underpinning enforcement of such crimes as money laundering and tax evasion. Given that in a typical Digicash transaction the bank concerned would have no means of matching withdrawals from an account by one of its customers with moneys deposited at an account held by another customer, this anomaly could give rise to opportunities being created for moneys entering the e-cash system to exit as freshly-laundered cash. Alternatively, moneys remitted to the e-cash mint in the Mark Twain Bank scenario could be interpreted as clean cash on their return to the world currency access account.

In conclusion, institutions that provide financial services on the Internet such as effecting payment over the Internet or creating e-cash (for example Digicash BV) are not automatically converted into banks by virtue of their activities. Conversely, if the institutions concerned are in fact accepting deposits, merely providing the deposit in digital form will not necessarily circumvent the need for authorisation as a bank.

1   See Report to the Council of the European Monetary Institute on Prepaid Cards by the Working Group on EU Payment Systems, May 1994.

Glossary

Definitions without asterisks are reproduced with kind permission from The Economist Pocket Information Technology *by John Browning (published by Profile Books).*

Active X*
A family of EXECUTABLE CODE developed by Microsoft.

Agent
A much-ballyhooed piece of software that will do its master's bidding without direct supervision, even remotely, over a network. For example, an agent will find travel information without requiring its owner to know anything about electronic airline reservation systems.

Anonymous ftp site*
An interactive service provided by many hosts allowing anyone to transfer documents, FILES, programs, and other archived data using FTP. The user LOGS ON with a general identity, often anonymous and an E-MAIL address as PASSWORD. The site then permits access to its publicly accessible files. No one is barred entry.

Anti-viral
A program that can detect, and sometimes eliminate, computer viruses.

Application
Describes a word processor, spreadsheet, accounting program or other piece of software which does useful work directly for the end user. Systems Software, by contrast, includes programming languages, operating systems and other things needed to build and to run applications software.

Backup
To save a copy of data stored on a DISK on to another medium, usually tape or optical disk. Backup is meant to provide a reserve copy of data lest something terrible should happen to the disk.

Bit
Abbreviation of binary digit, thus zero or one (see BINARY).

Binary
Loosely used to describe anything without shades of grey; that is, which can be either black or white, true or false, on or off. Strictly, it refers to a number system based on the number two. Instead of powers of ten, as in the decimal system, numbers are expressed in terms of powers of two. The only allowable digits are zero and one. Thus 27 in decimal ($2 \times 10^1 + 7 \times 10^0$) is 11011 in binary ($1 \times 2^4 + 1 \times 2^3 + 0 \times 2^2 + 1 \times 2^1 + 1 \times 2^0$). This number system is convenient for describing electronic circuits, which are either on (with current) or off (without).

Bit map
A grid of dots which contains the information needed to display a picture on a computer screen or printer. Typically each dot corresponds to the colour of a particular point, or pixel, on the screen. Display the dots in the appropriate rows and columns and, lo and behold, a picture appears (the colour of dots, in turn, is coded as BITS, hence the name).

This correspondence between dots in the bit map and points on the screen makes bit maps extremely easy to use on any given screen. But it also makes them extremely hard to move from one screen to another, because different screens lay out rows and columns in different proportions (see also VECTOR GRAPHICS, of which the converse is true).

Bridge
Equipment used to connect two local area networks. Bridges can connect networks using different communication protocols (for example, TCP/IP and AppleTalk), as well as different transmission mechanisms (for example Ethernet and token ring). A ROUTER, by contrast, is used to connect networks with the same PROTOCOL.

Browser*
A program which allows a person to read documents on the world wide web and to move between their links. Companies can sell their browser, but often they give away prototype, or beta, versions.

Bug
An error or problem with computer hardware or software. It is named after a moth, discovered by a computing pioneer, Grace Hopper, which immolated itself in the circuitry of an early computer. The computer was repaired by replacing a damaged vacuum tube. The moth is now preserved in the Computer Museum in Cambridge, Massachusetts.

Bulletin board
A computer system used for posting electronic messages. Messages are organised into files on the bulletin board's HARD DISK, usually by topic. People can dial up the bulletin board and read what has been said on a given topic and, if they like, add their own comments. Little more is required to run a bulletin board than a personal computer and MODEM. By the early 1990s the USA alone had over 50,000 public bulletin boards, ranging from big commercial operations (like Prodigy, backed by IBM) to systems set up by teenagers in their bedrooms to share information with their friends.

Byte
Eight BITS, the most commonly used measure of data-storage capacity. Large HARD DISK drives, for example, store gigabytes (that is, billions of bytes) of information. A nibble is half a byte, or four bits.

Cache*
Caching is when a SERVER with vast storage capacity holds copies of the most popular pages on the WORLD WIDE WEB. If this web cache is located on the LOCAL AREA NETWORK users can be saved the delay of gaining access to overburdened sites.

CD-ROM
Short for Compact Disk, Read-Only Memory, the medium of choice for the first generation of MULTIMEDIA publishers. Compact disks, the same kind as are used for sound recording, can store a lot of data – about 640 megabytes, 600 or so times more than a FLOPPY DISK. That is enough to store the text from several hundred books, two hours of high quality sound, an hour of television quality video, or some combination of the above.

Checksum
A way of detecting errors in computer data. The BINARY values of the data are added together to form a checksum. The checksum is transmitted with the data. If the sum of the binary values of the received data differs from the received checksum, then something has gone wrong.

Click*
What people do with a mouse button to instruct the pointer on screen to activate something. VIEWERS click on LINKS to follow them and double-click on programs to run them.

Client*
The generic name for a computer which accesses a server on the Internet, INTRA-NET, and WORLD WIDE WEB.

Compression
Techniques for reducing the amount of data needed to convey some amount of information.

CPU

Short for central processing unit. The brains of a computer; the chip or chips that execute programs.

Crash

A verb or noun describing what happens when a computer or program ceases to function. It originally derived from DISK crash, which described what happens when the magnetic heads designed to read information from a disk drive instead bury themselves into it.

Cyberspace

The virtual geography created by computers and networks; the world behind the screen. Perhaps the most vivid vision of cyberspace comes from William Gibson. In his science fiction novel, *Neuromancer* – which for many is the defining vision of the techno-future – he describes, quoting from an imaginary children's show being transmitted across the network of the future, a virtual world in which data is made visible, and the network becomes geography.

De-encrypt*

The process of unscrambling encrypted text or data. With the secret key this should take seconds; without, it should take millions of years.

Database

A computerised filing system which forms the core of most corporate computer systems. Databases store and retrieve information, and as the number of different kinds of information kept on computers increases, databases are evolving to cope.

Digital

Data stored as a sequence of discrete BINARY digits, as opposed to analogue, which is data stored as a continuously varying signal.

Digital signature

A cryptographic technique which ensures that an electronic document really does come from the person whose name is at the top. It usually relies on PUBLIC-KEY CRYPTOGRAPHY.

Disk

A medium for the storage of data. Most disks now in use are magnetically coated, and store the 1s and 0s of DIGITAL data by imprinting (or not imprinting) a tiny magnetic field on the disk. Optical disks work on a similar basis with a laser and a reflective (or non-reflective) coating (see also FLOPPY DISK and HARD DISK).

Domain

A named part of a network. It is most often used to refer to one of the independent networks which make up the Internet. Under Internet addressing conventions, any computer with an address ending in, say, dog.com is said to be in the dog domain. This means that it shares the same administrator with other computers in the same domain. Given the global scope of computer networks, sharing the same domain obviously has nothing to do with physical proximity.

Domain name*

The name given to a DOMAIN on the Internet. A domain name is a URL.

Download

To transfer data from a remote (usually large) computer to a local (usually small) one (contrast to UPLOAD).

Encrypt*

The complex mathematical process of disguising text or data. PUBLIC-KEY ENCRYPTION allows a message to remain intelligible to all but its intended recipient.

E-mail

Short for electronic mail. Just as the name implies, a message sent electronically from one computer to another. E-mail is typically text, but emerging standards for MULTIMEDIA mail enable anything that can be put in DIGITAL form to be e-mailed. Roughly one-fifth of the traffic on the Internet consists of e-mail.

Executable code*

A program which is run on a client computer from over the Internet and WORLD WIDE WEB. The most common example is a JAVA APPLET which is a program which runs automatically when a

WEB SITE is viewed. Executable code livens up static web sites.

Fibre-optic
A fine glass fibre which transmits light, much the same as a copper wire transmits electricity. Because it can be switched on or off extremely rapidly – much faster than an electric current – fibre optic can carry far more data than conventional copper wire.

File
The organising unit of a computer DISK. Computer files are by intention roughly analogous to the sort found in a filing cabinet; a collection of (presumably logically related) information stored together under a single name.

Finger
The name of a program used to get information about a computer user over a network. On the Internet, for example, typing finger bloggs@somewhere.com will usually produce a list of the full names and E-MAIL addresses of everyone named bloggs on the somewhere.com network.

Firewall
Hardware, but more usually software, designed to protect networked systems from damage by outsiders, while maintaining connectivity. The firewall sits between a local network and the big, wide world (usually the Internet). To protect the local network from evil-intentioned intruders, the firewall may admit only designated users, or allow only designated commands to be issued from outside. Balancing flexibility with security is, needless to say, a perennial headache in designing firewalls.

Floppy disk
A portable form of computer DISK used to record relatively small quantities of electronic data. Floppy disks originally consisted of a round piece of cardboard, coated with a magnetic recording material similar to that used in recording tape. They were soft and floppy, hence the name. More modern, higher capacity floppy disks are made of magnetically coated plastic, and they are in fact quite stiff.

Forum*
A collection of THREADS accessible through an ONLINE SERVICE PROVIDER. Users can submit new postings for everyone to read, or, reply to other's rantings.

Frame*
A portion of a web page which can treated as a space all of its own: it can be scrolled while the remainder of the page stays static; it can remain rock-solid while the rest of the page breezes past.

Ftp
Short for File Transfer Protocol. This refers to both the program which transfers FILES from one computer to another across the Internet, and the technical standards which it uses. Bulk transfers of data with ftp make up about one-third of Internet traffic.

Gateway
A device that connects two different computer systems or networks, particularly those using different technical standards or communications PROTOCOLS.

Gopher
A collection of programs that make it easier to find information on the Internet. While TELNET and FTP require knowledge of specific file names and computers, Gopher can find material by subject category. Gopher was named after the school mascot of the University of Minnesota, where it was developed. Although still widely used, it has been overshadowed by the growth of the WORLD WIDE WEB.

Hard disk
Or Winchester drive, after one of the inventors of the technology. This is a fixed, rigid disk, typically permanently installed within a computer. Like a FLOPPY DISK, it is made by coating magnetic material onto a disk. But the rigid construction of hard disks means that they can be rotated more rapidly, and that data can be packed more precisely into smaller magnetic markings on the disk. Faster rotation means that data can be read and written more rapidly; more precise markings mean that more data can be packed onto the disk. By 1997 hard disks of 1 gigabyte were common; while

most floppies held only about 1 megabyte, a difference of three orders of magnitude.

Header
Data about data. Typically included at the beginning of a FILE, a document or a data PACKET sent over a communications network, the header typically contains information to identify the attached data, to state how much data is attached, what sort of data it is, how long it is and to help detect and/or correct errors.

Home page*
Strictly speaking the first page of a WEB SITE, although now used to mean a presence on the WORLD WIDE WEB. All other pages on a WEB SITE are usually accessible by following a LINK from the home page. The terms WEB SITE and home page are used interchangeably.

HTML
Hypertext mark-up language, the programming language which creates the documents and LINKS used by the WORLD WIDE WEB. The language contains both commands for laying out text and graphics on a page and also commands to link one document to another, or to link a document to an interactive computer program.

Hypertext
Text that need not be read from beginning to end, but can instead by browsed in any number of different orders, at the reader's whim, by following internal route-marks called links. A typical application of hypertext is in reference works, like this one. In an electronic version of this book, cross-references would not only be distinguished by special type, but they could also be 'live'. Click on them with a mouse and – whoosh – the computer brings up the appropriate entry on the screen.

http://www*
This is the opening sequence of characters usually used as the URL for a page on the WORLD WIDE WEB. For more secure access the sequence may begin, 'https://'.

Inbox*
The storage area on a CLIENT computer or a SERVER where E-MAILS are received and stored.

Internet Service Provider*
A company which allows its customers to gain access to or a presence on the Internet and WORLD WIDE WEB by making a local telephone call with a modem. Most provide E-MAIL accounts.

Internet Service Providers are also referred to as ISPs, Service Providers and even plain Providers. The term Internet Access Providers is sometimes used and refers to those companies who do not have their own database services and administration services; they purely provide a link to the Internet.

Internet protocol
The IP in TCP/IP, these are the technical standards which specify how packets on the internet are routed from one machine to another. Each PACKET travels independently, and packets may follow very different routes.

Internetworking
A generic term used to describe the process of linking together different networks – as is done, for example, in the Internet (and from which the Internet took its name).

Intranet*
An internal network which uses the same technology as the WORLD WIDE WEB to show and link documents. It is not necessarily linked to the internet itself, but when it is, it can allow in VIRUSES and hackers from outside.

Java applet*
This EXECUTABLE CODE is written using a special computer language called HotJava, designed by Sun Microsystems Inc. At its simplest an applet may produce an animation on a WEB SITE and there are predictions that applets will soon become applications used by NETWORK COMPUTERS. This would allow a WEB SITE to include a word processor, or a game, which could be used simply by accessing the site.

Link
A connection between two items of HYPERTEXT. In some HYPERTEXT systems links can be labelled to make explicit the relationship they denote. So one link

might be labelled 'supporting argument' and another 'contrary argument'. In theory, labels make it easier to solve the perennial problem of hypertext links, which is maintaining a sense of direction in the sea of information. In practice, adding more information (on the labels) to all that is already there can easily be mishandled to create more confusion.

Local area network
A data network that links nearby computers, typically in the same room, or at least in the same building. Today's most common local area networks are Ethernet and Token ring. On the horizon, however, are faster networks based on fibre optics.

Log on
To begin using a computer, a process which usually requires entering your name and password at the keyboard. Hence 'log-on prompt', which is what appears on the computer display after you have successfully logged on. Login is of course the same thing with different words.

Logic bomb*
A nasty section of code which is covertly inserted into a program or operating system. It triggers some activity whenever a specified condition is met. The activity is generally destructive.

Mailing list
Mailing lists take advantage of the ease with which E-MAIL can be duplicated to create privately organised discussion groups. E-MAIL sent to a central mailbox is automatically duplicated and sent to everyone on the list, which may contain thousands of names. Not surprisingly, mailing lists have sprung up across the Internet like mushrooms on an autumn morning – both private and open to all – to discuss just about anything and everything.

Mall*
A WEB SITE acting as a digital shopping mall. One WEB SITE is used by many different site owners who each have their own portion of the main site. Often the owner of a mall will provide secure payment mechanisms for each of the tenants.

Malicious code*
Any program or computer code which is designed to cause damage. Includes VIRUSES, WORMS, LOGIC BOMBS and TROJAN HORSES.

Memory
Where data and programs are stored on a computer. Computer memory comes in two basic forms. Main memory sits inside the machine, and holds that data on semiconductor memory chips. Computers that run a variety of different programs use RAM. Appliances and computer games which simply repeat the same programs over and over again, use ROM. Retrieval from main memory is quick, in the order of a few billionths of a second. But main memory is relatively expensive and often impermanent. Any information stored in RAM disappears when the power is turned off.

Modem
Acronym for Modulator-Demodulator, a device that translates a stream of digital data into a staccato series of bleeps and bloops that can be sent over a telephone line, or some other analogue communications channel. More specifically, it is a device that does, and undoes, modulation.

Multimedia
Just what the word says: multimedia is the combination of different media – text, video, audio, graphics, and so on – with a bit of computing power to hold them all together. To deliver multimedia requires a high-capacity communications channel, either network or CD-Rom. The hope, and hype, is that by combining different media, authors (or however multimediators are described) will be able to create things new and more wonderfully informative and educational than any yet dreamed of. The risk, of course, is that they will instead create a noisy, flashy mess. While the promise is bright, actual performance is so far finely balanced.

Newsgroup
An electronic forum for the discussion of a given topic. About 12,000 newsgroups now make up the USENET, a part of the Internet devoted to debate on topics ranging from sex to high-energy physics.

Newsgroups are open to all, and are organised as an exchange of E-MAIL messages.

News reader

A program used to read USENET news. News readers help to organise E-MAIL into a discussion of a specific subject. Mail is sorted by subject and time, so that someone entering the group discussion can follow the thread of electronic argument between many participants. Responses, in turn, are automatically sent to the proper address, with the proper subject.

Network computer*

Using high-speed connections these stripped-down computers rely wholly on the Internet or an INTRANET for their intelligence, storage and utility. As a result the promise is that they will be cheaper than personal computers.

Online

The opposite of offline; that is, enjoying a network connection to another computer.

Online Service Provider*

A company which allows online access to its computers and networks. It stores useful information such as weather reports and newspaper articles, as well as hosting FORUMS. Most supply E-MAIL accounts. Competing with INTERNET ACCESS PROVIDERS, these companies generally provide their customers with access to the Internet via their network.

Packet

A way of organising data for communication. Instead of a steady stream of BITS and BYTES, most computer communications split data into discrete packets. As well as data, each packet typically contains the address to which the packet is being sent, a number which denotes that packet's place in the sequence and information which helps to detect and correct errors. Some packets also contain information about what type of data is being sent. Others serve administrative functions in setting up routes and managing the flow of data.

The advantage of packets is their flexibility and efficiency. Packets from different communications can easily be intermixed to maximise use of a line. Packets from the same communication can travel by different routes to speed passage over a crowded network. Given the speed of today's computers, packets can easily carry time-sensitive data, like interactive video, or voice conversations. But the drawback to packet data is, none the less, the extra overhead of splitting data into packets at one end and recombining them at the other.

Packet-switched

Describes a network that sends data one PACKET at a time and so does not keep open a connection between two machines when no data is flowing between them. For many applications, particularly with computer data, the extra overheads of addressing each packet separately are well worth the savings in efficiency gained from not holding open temporarily unused connections.

Password

A sequence of characters which serves as a kind of text key in gaining access to computers. To maintain security, passwords should be known only to their owners and be hard to guess. The perennial dilemma in managing passwords – that is, words which are not in the dictionary and which contain numbers and/or punctuation marks – is that they are also hard to remember.

PGP

Short for Pretty Good Privacy, a freely distributed implementation of the RSA ALGORITHM for PUBLIC-KEY ENCRYPTION, created by Phil Zimmerman. PGP is controversial for several reasons. It has been distributed internationally in defiance of a US export ban on software containing technology for public-key cryptography. It was also distributed without the permission of the holders of the patent on the RSA ALGORITHM. Yet it works and, for those concerned with privacy, PGP is the most secure way of keeping computer data from prying eyes.

Pixel

Acronym for picture element, or the dots which make up an image on the typical computer screen.

PPP
Point to Point Protocol, technical standards that enable the use of the Internet's communication protocols, TCP/IP, over a dial-up telephone line (an alternative to SLIP).

Protocol
A kind of canned dialogue that enables two computers to negotiate, even when they have no idea of the meaning of the symbols that they are sending back and forth. For example, a protocol might specify the sequence of commands which one computer uses to send E-MAIL to another: what to say when a message is coming, how to reply after it has been received, and so on. While humans can make up dialogues as they go along, computers can only stick to the scripts laid down for them in the protocol.

Public-key encryption
A technology for encrypting messages which overcomes the major weaknesses of earlier codes and ciphers: the difficulty of exchanging a key between coder and decoder. Each code has a key which specifies how the message was encoded, and, in turn, how it can be decoded. Should that key fall into prying hands, the code is useless, hence the plot of many spy novels.

Public-key encryption solves the problem of communicating the key by splitting it into two parts. One part is public, listed in something like a telephone directory. The second is private, and told to nobody. To send a secret message, encrypt the text with the public key of the intended recipient. Then only someone with that person's private key will be able to decode it. Equally, a message can be given a digital signature, to ensure that it does indeed come from the person whose name is at the top, by encrypting it with that person's private key, and then decrypting it with the corresponding public key.

The mathematics underlying public-key cryptography is complex, and involves large prime numbers. But so far these are some of the very few encryption techniques that cannot reliably be broken by code-breakers using supercomputers.

RAM
Short for Random Access Memory, the MEMORY chips used in most computers. RAM stores data on an array of transistors. Each element of the array is accessed by location. If the transistor at a given location holds a charge it is interpreted as a BINARY 1, if not then 0.

RAM is quick. Its data can be accessed in billionths of a second, and data can be accessed equally quickly anywhere in the array. RAM is rapidly growing more capacious. By the mid-1990s chips storing over 16 million bits of information were relatively commonplace, and the semiconductor laboratories were at work on chips storing over 64 million bits. (Simple geometry insists that memory-chip capacity will always grow by multiples of four; if you double the number of circuits that can fit on each side of a rectangle.)

Router
A device which connects two distinct LOCAL AREA NETWORKS which use the same technical PROTOCOLS. (Contrast to BRIDGE, which connects LOCAL AREA NETWORKS using different PROTOCOLS.)

RSA algorithm
The most widely used technique for PUBLIC-KEY ENCRYPTION, named after the initials of its creators, three academics at the Massachusetts Institute of Technology, Rivest, Shamir and Adelman.

Script
A kind of program. Typically a script is a program that co-ordinates the work of other programs. So, for example, a communications script might automate the dialing, LOG-ON and other exchanges necessary to connect to an on-line database. Because they customise existing programs, or automate small tasks, scripts are typically small and relatively simple.

Search engine*
A WEB SITE housing a program that can search for information on the Internet. The programs are very quick: in a matter of seconds they can pick out the occurrence of one word from 16 billion web pages. Few companies who own search engines charge their users; generally they

make their profit by selling advertising space on the site.

Server

Describes computer systems which divide labour among machines linked by networks. Rather like Adam Smith's pin factory, each machine does what it is suited for. So a file server is equipped with lots of DISK space to store data; a name server holds the information necessary to serve as the network's telephone directory. Not only does specialisation avoid duplication of effort, but it also makes server systems easier to improve. If, say, all heavy-duty number-crunching is done by a calculation server, then simply replacing that one machine with a more powerful one can improve the performance of the whole network. Servers serve CLIENTS.

SLIP

Serial Line Interface Protocol, a version of the Internet protocol adapted for the slow speeds and low reliability of dial-up telephone lines.

TCP/IP

The network PROTOCOLS used on the Internet. It stands for TRANSMISSION CONTROL PROTOCOL and INTERNET PROTOCOL.

Telnet

The process which enables someone to login to a remote computer and use its services via the Internet. Contrast to FTP, which enables a person to get data from a remote computer, or remote procedure call, which enables a program to access the services of a remote computer.

Thread*

A collection of related postings to a BULLETIN BOARD or FORUM. Users post replies to previous postings creating a thread of discussion on a common subject. USENET has the greatest collection of threads.

Transmission Control Protocol

The TCP/IP, these technical standards determine how messages are broken up into PACKETS for transmission over the Internet – using the INTERNET PROTOCOL – and reassembled again at the other end.

Trojan horse

A program used to capture unsuspecting people's LOG-ONS and PASSWORDS. Typically a Trojan horse looks like the screen ordinarily presented when first logging on to a computer. But, unlike the usual screen, it records the LOG-ON and PASSWORD – where the creator of the Trojan horse can later retrieve them – before allowing the user to go about his or her business.

Upload

To send data 'up' from a small computer to a larger one. (Contrast to DOWNLOAD.)

URL*

This acronym for Uniform Resource Locator refers to the standard for specifying an object on the Internet, such as a page of the WORLD WIDE WEB or a file on an ftp site. URLs for the WORLD WIDE WEB have the prefix 'HTTP://'; ftp sites use 'ftp://'. Like real addresses, a URL can become outdated resulting in the unhelpful error message, 'Document not found at ...'.

USENet

USENet is the world's largest conversation. It consists of over 10,000 NEWSGROUPS, each using E-MAIL to discuss a specific topic, from alt.sex, unsurprisingly the most popular news group, to comp.unix.wizards, which provides technical advice on the more arcane features of the Unix operating system.

Viewer*

A person who uses a BROWSER to look at pages on the WORLD WIDE WEB.

Vector graphics

Refers to graphics in which the computer remembers the shapes by a description of their geometry – the line segments that make up the figures – rather than simply a BIT MAP of its representation on a particular screen.

Web site*

A collection of colourful documents on the WORLD WIDE WEB. They can be used as an electronic brochure or be more active performing tasks for their VIEWERS such as searching databases or taking orders. Web sites are often joined to others by a LINK.

World Wide Web

The technology that makes the Internet usable by mere humans, the WORLD WIDE WEB (WWW) is a system of linking text, graphics, sound and video on computers spread across the globe.

The basic technology of the web was originally created by Tim Berners-Lee at CERN, Europe's atom-smasher sited near Geneva, to help physicists keep track of all the data generated by their experiments. At the heart of the technology is a programming language, HTML, which allows a phrase or graphic in one document to be linked to another document anywhere on the global Internet. When a person CLICKS a mouse on that highlighted phrase, the linked document is fetched and brought to the screen automatically.

Refinements to the technology of the web have in fact expanded the use of links beyond simply fetching pre-existing documents. A LINK can also trigger a computer program which creates a document, say by querying a database. Or it can bring to the screen a form, to be filled in interactively. Or it can launch E-MAIL. In this way, the web is rapidly becoming an easy-to-use, general-purpose interface for the Internet and the computers on it.

Many companies are putting up web sites to provide information about their products. Others are using the technology to sell goods directly over the network, in a kind of electronic mail-order. The World Wide Web is proving to be the software that brings the Internet to the masses, and vice versa.

WORM

Write Once, Read Many, a form of storage that writes data irreversibly to a disk, typically an optical DISK. It is useful for archival storage, but not much else.

Worm

A program that propagates itself across a network, automatically transferring itself to distant machines and running itself there (from whence it transfers itself to more machines). In contrast to a VIRUS which secretes itself inside another program – and thus is only spread when the program carrying it is spread – worms take charge of their own reproduction.

Zone

A group of computers on a network. In a company each department might have its own zone, which is administered more or less independently from the rest. The obvious advantage of zones is that breaking up administrative problems into small pieces lessens their complexity, if only by making it harder for an administrator in one zone inadvertently to mess up another's computers.

Index